# SPOKEN MARSHALLESE

# PALI LANGUAGE TEXTS: MICRONESIA

Social Science Research Institute
University of Hawaii

Donald M. Topping
Editor

# SPOKEN MARSHALLESE
AN INTENSIVE LANGUAGE COURSE WITH GRAMMATICAL NOTES
AND GLOSSARY

BYRON W. BENDER

The University Press of Hawaii
Honolulu

*First printing 1969*
*Second printing 1978*

Copyright© 1969 by University of Hawaii Press
(since 1971, The University Press of Hawaii)
All rights reserved

Library of Congress Catalog Card Number 68-65039
ISBN 0-87022-070-5
Manufactured in the United States of America

with deep and grateful acknowledgment
of the painstaking and insightful help
of Takaji Abo and Tony de Brum, but with
final responsibility mine alone

Preface

Spoken Marshallese is a course of 30 lessons designed to give the student a basic fluency in the Marshallese language, and a feeling for its structure that will enable him to converse freely with islanders on a broad range of subjects without additional formal instruction. The course is designed for teaching by modern drill methods, and is based on a scientific analysis of the language. Tapes averaging between 30 and 60 minutes duration are available* for each lesson to supplement class work, or to enable students to work on the language independently.

Individual lessons consist of one or more short but authentic dialogues, from 15 to 20 structural drills of a variety of designs, grammatical notes, and a listing of new vocabulary. Earlier lessons include drills on difficult sound contrasts, and later lessons include short prose passages, proverbs, and miscellaneous other selections designed to display important syntactic structures in context and give practice in reading the language as well. Lessons introducing key paradigms display them in reference sections. Illustrations are included where they are germane.

The total number of vocabulary items introduced is about 1500, but because of the nature of the structure of the language, the student completing the course is able to form many times this number of new words by recombining parts of words. The morphology of the language is treated exhaustively; all major syntactic patterns and a number of important idioms are included. The course provides material for at least 300 hours of classroom drill and should take the capable student to a Foreign Service Institute rating of at least 2 in both speaking and reading.

The Marshall Islands have an indigenous population of only 20,000, but by virtue of their strategic location have acquired a disproportionate weight on the international scene since World War II. Kwajalein, Eniwetok,

*From the National Center for Audio Tapes, Bureau of Audiovisual Instruction, University of Colorado, Boulder, Colorado 80302.

and Bikini will not soon pass from memory. With new Trust Territory government programs and the advent of the Peace Corps to the islands, there are today an estimated 250 non-indigenous civil employees working out of the District Center at Majuro, and a much larger group--exact number unknown, but estimated to approach 2000--of Stateside personnel who work at the Kwajalein missile base of the Pacific Test Range. The former work closely with the Marshallese populace and have a deep interest in the language; this group turns over about once every two years. The latter group--at Kwajalein--has sufficient contact with Marshallese speakers to stimulate interest in the language on the part of many, and a much higher turnover rate. (The interest in the language on the part of these Kwajalein residents was sufficient to cause the publication on local presses of a small English-Marshallese dictionary in 1962, and the printing of another edition of an earlier 'Navy' dictionary in 1968.)

The amount of scientific information contained in the course--in the introduction, grammatical notes, reference sections, and vocabulary listings--is sufficiently exhaustive to make this volume the most comprehensive treatment of the language to date. As such, it should be in considerable (and continuing) demand in the scholarly community.

Byron W. Bender

## CONTENTS

MAP OF THE MARSHALL ISLANDS........................ x

INTRODUCTION....................................... xi

LESSON

| | | | | |
|---|---|---|---|---|
| ONE.............. | 3 | SIXTEEN.......... | 162 |
| TWO.............. | 10 | SEVENTEEN........ | 170 |
| THREE............ | 15 | EIGHTEEN......... | 178 |
| FOUR............. | 23 | NINETEEN......... | 188 |
| FIVE............. | 33 | TWENTY........... | 199 |
| SIX.............. | 43 | TWENTY-ONE....... | 209 |
| SEVEN............ | 55 | TWENTY-TWO....... | 218 |
| EIGHT............ | 67 | TWENTY-THREE..... | 230 |
| NINE............. | 77 | TWENTY-FOUR...... | 238 |
| TEN.............. | 90 | TWENTY-FIVE...... | 248 |
| ELEVEN........... | 103 | TWENTY-SIX....... | 256 |
| TWELVE........... | 118 | TWENTY-SEVEN..... | 264 |
| THIRTEEN......... | 129 | TWENTY-EIGHT..... | 274 |
| FOURTEEN......... | 141 | TWENTY-NINE...... | 290 |
| FIFTEEN.......... | 152 | THIRTY........... | 302 |

GLOSSARY........................................... 315

FINDER LIST........................................ 367

INDEX.............................................. 435

## MARSHALL ISLANDS

```
                    165 E                    170 E

                                          ◐ Pokak*

                                          Ratak
                                          Chain
                                                    ◐ Bikar*
                                                          Taka* ◐◑ Utirik
   ◯
   Eniwetok(*)    Bikini(*) Rongelap                Jemo* ◐ Ailuk
                           ◐                        Likiep ◯ Wotje
                    Ailinginae* Rongerik*               ◐ Erikub*
                                                             ◐ Maloelap
                                                               ◐ Aur
   ● Ujelang                    Kwajalein
                       Ujae ◐
                          ◐◐ Lib                         Majuro ◯
                                   Namu● Jabwot●                  Arno ◯
                                        Ailinglaplap                     ◐ Mili
                                                         Jaluit ◯           Narik*
                                              Namorik●  Kili●
                                              Ebon ◐      (*)=temporarily uninhabited
   (Kusaie--easternmost of                                  *=uninhabited
    the Caroline Is.)
```

10 N

5 N

INTRODUCTION

## The Sounds of Marshallese

### General advice on mastering the sounds

The Marshallese sound system is quite different from that of English, and has a number of sounds for which there are no close equivalents in English. The best general advice we can give is to imitate your teacher closely. And, as one linguist has pointed out, if you sound good to yourself at first, this is probably a bad sign, and means that you are substituting English sounds in a language where they do not belong. If, on the other hand, your first attempts at close mimicry of your teacher make you sound odd to yourself, this probably means that you are getting out of the mold of your English sound habits and nearer to the Marshallese mark.

What you want to do is to establish an entirely new set of sound habits. Strive for perfection from the beginning. Avoid practicing wrong habits, for, as with all habits, the longer they are practiced, the harder they are to break. All physiologically normal Marshallese children learn perfectly good pronunciation, as you could have had you been born there. Your job now is somewhat complicated by the fact that you have settled into English sound habits, but it is far from impossible. Many adults do learn foreign languages with near-native pronunciation, and the chances are that you can achieve this in Marshallese, if you strive from the beginning.

The task is twofold: 1) you will need to learn to hear new sound signals that your English ears had learned to ignore, and 2) you will need to learn articulations abandoned with the babbling stage. Put yourself in a babbling frame of mind again, and you will have the flexibility to begin sounding good to Marshallese ears.

### Sounds and Spellings

No spelling system can represent on paper everything that you will need to listen for. In fact, looking at a spelling on paper too soon can give you a false sense of security and close your ears to the many important parts of the sounds that are not shown on paper. This is why all new material in these lessons should be drilled extensively orally before it is ever seen in print.

But print has its value as a memory device, especially for adult minds that have become dependent on it. With this in mind, we have provided written materials for each lesson. Two different spellings are used. The first is a phonetic spelling based on a scientific analysis of the language. Although it does not indicate all the nuances of sound you will need to learn in order to avoid a foreign accent, it does show all the differences that are significant for distinguishing one word from another in Marshallese. Then, for reference and use after you have become tuned in to the sound to the point where discrepancies on paper will not trip you up, you are given a sample of one of the spellings used by Marshallese writers. Marshallese spelling is like English in that the letters do not fit the sounds too well, and the situation is further complicated by the fact that Marshallese literary tradition is not long enough for one standardized spelling to have developed.

Thus our reasons for giving you a scientific phonetic spelling in addition to a typical Marshallese spelling are two: 1) the latter would lead you astray in many ways as to the sounds, and 2) there is no one agreed-upon Marshallese spelling. Most Marshallese spellers have many practices in common, as you will note when you come to read some of their products, but mixed in with these are a number of idiosyncracies. Our phonetic spelling is sufficiently different from usual Marshallese spelling that you will probably have little trouble with confusing the two; usually it appears on the right hand side of the page.

Marshallese Dialects

Considering the vast area covered by the Marshalls, the language is amazingly homogeneous, but there are two major dialects which differ sometimes (but not often) in the choice or the pronunciation of a word. These two dialects coincide with the two chains of islands: the eastern or Ratak chain, and the western or Rälik chain. However, at focal centers like Majuro, or Ebeye on Kwajalein, one finds speakers of both dialects. The western (Rälik) dialect has slightly higher prestige today, since the early missions were located in that chain, and that dialect was used in translations of the Bible, but in some ways the eastern (Ratak) dialect is more conservative and interesting to the linguist. Do not be overly concerned if your teacher uses different words or expressions, or pronounces words differently from what is indicated in your printed lesson materials. When this happens, do not challenge him in any way, but simply make a note of the divergence for your own later reference. Eventually you will want to become conversant with both dialects, and if your study of the language goes deep enough, you will find that there are minor dialects within the major dialects: Mejit, for example is divergent in the east, as in Ujelang in the west. The differences you note will be of the same order as some of the following within English: *pail* vs. *bucket*, *polecat* vs. *skunk*, *faucet* vs. *spigot* vs. *tap*, *either*, *advertisement*, *garage*, *Caribbean*, and *Hawaii*.

## Developing a scientific outlook on language and culture

All these lessons can hope to do is to introduce you to the sounds, grammar, and vocabulary of Marshallese, in that order of priority. For without the signals, you can learn neither the grammar nor the vocabulary, and without the grammar, you cannot learn vocabulary in any depth. At the end of this course you should be tuned in to the sound signals and have a feel for grammar or sentence construction within a limited vocabulary. The big task of building vocabulary and getting a feeling for denotations and connotations will be yours to do within a Marshall Islands context. You will then find much these lessons did not contain or only hinted at. You will find Marshallese linguistic taboos quite different from ours, with double-entendres the national pastime, off-color (from an American point of view) joking in certain mixed groups, but the strict avoidance of the same in other groups (even all-male) where taboo relatives are present. Through the language you will get much closer to Marshallese life and culture.

## The vowel sounds

Basically there are four vowels in Marshallese. The plain values of the three familiar letters used in the phonetic spelling--a̱, e̱, i̱--are close to their short values in English, as in s̱at, s̱et, s̱it. The fourth vowel symbol used, an ampersand (&), should be considered a cross between e̱ and i̱, with a plain value somewhere between that of the vowels in s̱e̱t and s̱i̱t.

| Vowel sound | | Examples |
|---|---|---|
| & | m&j | dead |
| | n&n | a tree: *Morinda citrifolia* |
| | p&n | hard |
| | l&p | egg |
| | y&l | nest |
| | -j&y&l | three (with pl. pronouns) |
| | y&j | up; east |
| | j&yj&y | writing |
| a | dan | water, liquid |
| | maj | eye |
| | pad | stay |
| | yal | shave |
| | mayal | axe; metal |
| | may | breadfruit |
| | jayan | cent(s) |
| | jan | from |
| e | men | thing |
| | yen | let him |
| | leyen | fruit |
| | yej | he is (doing something) |
| | meyej | mate on a ship |
| | mey | which |
| | jeyen | chain |
| | jen | let's |
| i | dim | tight |
| | nin | to pound |
| | lij | to mash |
| | jil | dark colored |
| | jinjin | to curse |
| | pil | drop of liquid |
| | yin | I am to; of |
| | niy | coconut |

The above can be considered the basic or plain values for the vowels. As we shall see, these become modified in two different ways when the vowels stand next to certain other consonants. But in order to explain this, we shall first have to introduce the consonant sounds.

The consonant sounds

The consonant sounds are best viewed in three groups, according to their effect on neighboring vowels: the PLAIN or LIGHT consonants, the HEAVY consonants, and the ROUNDED consonants. All the consonants in the above examples for the vowel sounds have been light consonants; these keep neighboring vowels at the plain values illustrated in the examples. Some consonants are passed over quickly in pronunciation, while others are held and dwelt on a bit before passing on. Those that are held longer are written doubly in the phonetic spelling.

<u>Light consonants</u>

| | | | |
|---|---|---|---|
| d | a trilled *r*-sound, but with the tongue trilled against the upper teeth instead of against the roof of the mouth, as for *r* | diy<br>y&d<br>m&d&y<br>yeddap | bone<br>baby mat<br>soft coconut meat<br>it sticks |
| j | like a Russian palatalized *t*-sound; sometimes similar to English *s*, *sh*, *ch*, *j*, *z*, for all of which it substitutes in loan words | jep<br>laj<br>mij&l<br>m&jj&y | cheek<br>wild<br>thick<br>opening between islets |
| l | no equivalent in English; an *l*-sound made with the tongue tip touching the upper teeth | liy<br>yil<br>malim<br>palley | the letter 'l'<br>taro sprout<br>permitted<br>foreigner |
| m | like the *m* in English *music* or the *me* in *meow*; when long, like the *mb m* in *dumb mute* | m&y<br>yim<br>jeman<br>yemmed | fortress<br>and<br>his father<br>it is overripe (breadfruit) |
| n | close to the English *n* in *need*, but with the tongue against the upper teeth; when long, like the *n*'s in *ten nests* | ney<br>yen<br>yan&y<br>yennan | leg, foot<br>let him<br>islet<br>it is moldy |
| p | like the *b* in English *beauty*; when long, like | pap<br>yip | coconut frond (midrib)<br>crooked |

xvi

|   | the p's in keep<br>pure | jap&y<br>yippan | wooden bowl<br>with him |
|---|---|---|---|
| y | sometimes sounds like English y, but more often heard only in its effect on neighboring vowels | yiy<br>yay&y<br>p&yin<br>kiyyeh | at<br>the letter 'e'<br>his arm, hand<br>now |

Heavy consonants

The heavy consonants shift neighboring vowels from their plain values illustrated above roughly as follows: a̲ becomes *ah*, e̲ becomes *uh*, and &̲ and i̲ come to resemble varieties of the comic strip *ugh!* without lip rounding. A b̲ can be considered a heavy p̲; h̲ a heavy y̲; ḻ, m̄, and n̄ can be considered heavy l, m, n, respectively; r̲ a heavy d, and t̲ a heavy j. Both k̲ and g̲ belong to the same group in that they also have a heavy effect on neighboring vowels, although they have no light counterparts. (The letter g̲ is used in shorthand fashion for a value close to the *ng* in *singer*.)

| b | similar to the *bw* in *bwana*; more like the *p*'s of *top pueblo* when long (double) | bah<br>kab<br>kebah<br>kebbat | say<br>and; just; cup<br>copper<br>get ahead of |
|---|---|---|---|
| h | softer than the English *h*; often heard mainly in its effect on neighboring vowels | hak<br>tah<br>hah&h<br>haheh | frigate bird<br>what?<br>mine, my<br>swim |
| g | like the *ng* in *sing* or *singer* (but without the extra 'hard' *g*-sound in *longer* and *finger*) | gah<br>hag<br>kagir<br>kagget | I<br>wind, breeze<br>belt<br>struggle, persevere |
| k | like the *c* of *cut*, but without the puff of breath of the English consonant; like the *ck* *c* of *wreck cars* when double | kaḻ<br>ḻak<br>hakeh<br>hakkik | loincloth, diaper<br>to lock<br>but (how about...)<br>fingernail (Ratak) |

| | | | |
|---|---|---|---|
| ḷ | something like the *l* of *lost* or *ball*, with the tongue touching the roof of the mouth; not like the *l* of *least* | ḷag<br>haḷ<br>haḷap<br>haḷḷag | storm<br>sun<br>lineage head<br>stare |
| ṁ | like the *meo* of *someone* | ṁ&k<br>haṁ<br>teṁah<br>keṁṁan | tired<br>your (sg.)<br>light bulb<br>make, do |
| ṅ | an *n*-sound made with the tongue tip curled back to touch the roof of the mouth (no close equivalent in English); has a 'dark' *r*-color | ṅaṁ<br>kaṅ,<br>raṅ<br>ṁeṅehṅeh<br>k&ṅṅat | mosquito<br>those<br>happy<br>a tree: *Scaveola frutescens* |
| r | a trilled *r*--tongue tip trilled against front part of roof of mouth, behind gum ridge | rah<br>bar<br>berah<br>berray | branch<br>head; rock<br>my head<br>to split |
| t | tongue touches the upper teeth instead of the gum ridge behind them; no puff of breath; more like English *d* singly between vowels, but like *d t* of *had to* when double | tab<br>bat<br>betah<br>bettah | fog, haze<br>hill; slow<br>butter<br>batter (baseball) |

Rounded consonants
------------------

The rounding referred to in this name is the rounding of the lips when these consonants *and* neighboring vowels are pronounced. These consonants are more closely related to the heavy consonants than they are to the plain ones. Thus g̱ can be considered a g pronounced with concomitant lip rounding; similarly, ḻ is a rounded ḷ, ṇ̱ a rounded ṅ, q a rounded k, ṟ a rounded r, and w a rounded h. This rounding carries over to contiguous vowels, and converts the value of i̱ to a value close to the *oo* of *food*, &̱ to the *oo* of *good*, *e* to the long *o* of *go*, and *a* to the *aw* of *law*.

| | | | |
|---|---|---|---|
| g̈ | something like the *ng o* of *wrong one* | G̈eg̈ | Jaluit islet (N̈oḦ) |
| | | jeg̈ | mangrove tree |
| | | jeg̈ak | to measure |
| | | g̈ertak | to snore |
| | | yeg̈g̈ertaktak | habitually snores |
| | | hayeg̈ayg̈ay | clamor |
| l̈ | something like the *lo* of *lore* | l̈&y | pond |
| | | tel̈ | mountain |
| | | l̈et | canoe mast top |
| | | l̈iyit | drink noisily |
| | | lel̈yatyat | mind, consciousness |
| | | qil̈il̈ | cockroach |
| n̈ | something like the *rno* of *inferno* | n̈ab | popping sound |
| | | n̈ej | snapping sound |
| | | kajn̈en̈ | talk through the nose |
| | | ṁen̈ | deceive |
| | | ṁen̈ey | deceive him |
| | | n̈&mp&y | alcoholism |
| q | something like the *qu* of *aqua* | qey | you (sg., abs.) |
| | | y&q | you (sg., obj.) |
| | | j&q&y | to dwell |
| | | ṁ&yiq | goods |
| | | qqaɫ | coconut sennit |
| | | (yeqqaɫ) | (Rälik pronunciation) |
| | | (qeqaɫ) | (Ratak pronunciation) |
| ɾ | something like the *rro* in the Spanish pronunciation of *burro* | ɾeybejaw | hands in pockets |
| | | ɾij | wake up |
| | | ɾet | kind, type |
| | | yaɾ | to carve |
| | | ṁiɾ | hip |
| | | ɾeɾɾeɾ | to bark |
| w | sometimes like English *w*, but often heard mainly in its effect | wah | canoe |
| | | wab | wharf, pier |
| | | taw | sugar cane |
| | | ɫaw | hibiscus |

|                    |          |       |           |
|--------------------|----------|-------|-----------|
| on neighboring vowels | waw&w | the letter 'o' |
|                    | jewwan   | lazy  |           |

The following minimally contrasting pairs of words serve to isolate and highlight the rounding effect of the rounded consonants:

| bek   | bring, take        | mag   | coconut about to fall |
| beq   | sand               |       |                       |
|       |                    | maǥ   | pate                  |
| key   | question particle  | jehet | shirt                 |
| qey   | you (sg., abs.)    | jewet | bullet                |
| bekey | take it            | łag   | storm                 |
| beqey | sandy              | łaǥ   | house fly             |

Summary of consonant sounds

|              |           |         | light | heavy | rounded |
|--------------|-----------|---------|-------|-------|---------|
| Semiconsonants |         |         | y     | h     | w       |
| Stops . . . . | Velar    | - oral  | -     | k     | q       |
|              |           | - nasal | -     | g     | ǥ       |
|              | Labial    | - oral  | p     | b     | -       |
|              |           | nasal   | m     | ṁ     | -       |
|              | Dental    | - oral  | j     | t     | -       |
|              |           | - nasal | n     | ṅ     | n̈      |
| Liquids . . . | Lateral  |         | l     | ł     | l̈      |
|              | Trill     |         | d     | r     | r̈      |

Note that symbols with a single mark (ṁ, ṅ, ł) all represent heavy sounds, while those with a double mark (ǥ̈, n̈, l̈, r̈) all represent rounded sounds.

Their effects on the vowels

In choosing examples to illustrate the light and heavy consonants above, an attempt was made to find words whose consonants were all of one type or the other, so that the effect of each type on vowels would be most clear. (This was not possible for the rounded consonants because words containing them are relatively rare.)

Now it may prove helpful to consider what happens when the consonants in a word are of more than one type--when a vowel is caught between the competing influences of consonants of differing types. This can probably be illustrated best by observing words of one syllable, of the pattern: consonant-vowel-consonant. These are grouped below according to the various combinations, with the three semiconsonants (y, h, w) serving as cover labels for the consonants of their respective types:

| y - h | | h - y | |
|---|---|---|---|
| liṁ | murky water | ṁil | behavior |
| jik | bower | kij | louse |
| l&b | grave | b&l | taro pit |
| p&t | pillow | t&p | wood shavings |
| yeb | dance | bey | enough; because |
| yeṅ | that over there | ṅey | that by you |
| daṁ | forehead | ṁad | loiter |
| jar | pray | raj | whale |

| h - w | | w - h | |
|---|---|---|---|
| biw | gun | wib | soft, tender |
| tiw | gizzard | wit | flower |
| b&q | book; blister; bladder | q&b | bent |
| t&w | get off; down | w&t | rain |
| teḷ | mountain | ḷet | canoe mast top |
| tew | rope; channel | wet | only |
| teł | kind, type | łet | kind, type |
| rew | those (humans) | wer | fish gills |
| taw | sugar cane | wat | puffer fish |

| y - w | | w - y | |
|---|---|---|---|
| diw | to boil | wid | piece |
| jiw | perpendicular | wij | drown; cork; uproot |
| p&w | ripe pandanus key | w&p | a tree: *Barringtonia asiatica* |
| j&w | float loose--ship | w&j | toward you (Rälik) |
| jeq | alight | qej | congeal |
| mew | to heal | wem | pull something out |
| yaw | tattoo | way | injection |
| jaw | run (engine) | waj | watch |

Note that the two columns above are mirror images of each other. This feature can be used in a pronunciation drill, combining counterparts from the two columns as nonsense words--for example: liṁṁil, ṁilliṁ; jikkij, kijjik; l&bb&l, b&ll&b, etc.

<u>Words beginning in yiy... and wiw...</u>

Most words beginning in <u>yiy</u> differ in pronunciation between the two dialects in a way very similar to that of words beginning in double consonants such as <u>lliw</u> 'angry', <u>tt&r</u> 'run', <u>qqał</u> 'coconut sennit', <u>ṁṁan</u> 'good', etc. (discussed in the second grammatical note of Lesson Four). The Rālik dialect adds an extra yi, while the Ratak dialect shortens the existing yiy so that it sounds little longer than the y of English *yes*:

| Word | Rālik pronunciation | Ratak pronunciation | Meaning |
|---|---|---|---|
| yiyał | [yiyiyał] | [$^{yi}$yał] | road |
| yiyep | [yiyiyep] | [$^{yi}$yep] | basket |
| yiy&y | [yiyiy&y] | [$^{yi}$y&y] | centipede |

There has been a great deal of dialect mixture with respect to these words in yiy, and a few are now usually given the Rālik pronunciation in both dialects. Such words are marked in the phonetic spelling by an apostrophe before the word:

| 'yiyewen | [yiyiyewen] | → | [yiyiyewen] | to meet |
|---|---|---|---|---|
| 'yiy&k | [yiyiy&k] | → | [yiyiy&k] | to mix |
| 'yiyeh | [yiyiyeh] | → | [yiyiyeh] | year |

A few others are usually given the Ratak pronunciation in both dialects. This is indicated by putting the apostrophe further to the right ('towards the east'), before the second y, to indicate that the first part of the word is passed over very rapidly (Ratak fashion) in both dialects:

| yi'yah | [$^{yi}$yah] | ← | [$^{yi}$yah] | where? |
|---|---|---|---|---|
| yi'yaqey | [$^{yi}$yaqey] | ← | [$^{yi}$yaqey] | aloha |
| yi'y&y | [$^{yi}$y&y] | ← | [$^{yi}$y&y] | there |

Remember: words beginning in yiy with no apostrophe are pronounced differently in the two dialects. The Rālik pronunciation dwells on the yiy; the Ratak pronunciation passes over it rapidly. Words with an initial apostrophe ('yiy...) are given the western 'dwelling on' pronunciation in both dialects, while those with a later apostrophe (yi'y...) are given the eastern 'passing over lightly' pronunciation in both.

Words in initial wiw also receive special treatment in each dialect. The Rālik dialect again preposes yi, while the Ratak dialect adds an additional wi instead:

| wiw&y | [yiwiw&y] | [wiwiw&y] | ride, get on |
|---|---|---|---|
| wiwañ | [yiwiwañ] | [wiwiwañ] | gray haired |
| wiweyew | [yiwiweyew] | [wiwiweyew] | that way over there |

Rhythm and Intonation

The matters of pitch, loudness, and timing of the voice have not been analyzed and marked in the spelling system beyond the indication of double (long) vs. single consonants. This latter distinction--whether a sound is held or passed over quickly--is the key to both loudness (or relative prominence) and rhythm in the language, and the doubling of symbols in the phonetic spelling should help the student remember and recreate the utterances he has heard with proper loudness and timing values. The other matter the student should pay attention to and mimic his instructor closely on is the rise and fall of the voice, especially at the end of sentences. This has not been marked in the spelling, although the punctuation sometimes gives clues. In later lessons there are some drills on meaningful contrasts in intonation in which the distinctions are analyzed and discussed.

Words to the Instructor

These lessons are written in a form that assumes that the instructor has had training in modern foreign language teaching--they contain a minimum of instructions to the teacher. However, here are a few general rules of thumb that any language teacher would do well to keep in mind. It is suggested that they be reread at least once a week.

1. <u>Students must memorize the material</u>. With the exception of reference sections, all the language material in each lesson from dialogue through drill must be over-learned with accurate pronunciation from the beginning. Most drill lines will have to be modeled in their entirety at first; later the amount of cue material for each can be successively reduced until a minimal cue is reached. English cues can be used as a culminating activity.

2. <u>Students must know what they are saying at all times</u>. From the moment an utterance is first modeled the instructor must communicate to the student its meaning, and each time it is practiced the instructor must continue to ask himself and take measures to find out whether each student knows what he is saying. This does not mean that he should know some English equivalent for each Marshallese word (in fact, this is not good practice), but that he should have a general idea of the meaning of the entire utterance.

3. <u>Students must be challenged at every moment</u>. Corollary: The instructor must develop a good sense of when to move on--to move from one student to another, from one drill to another, from choral to individual work, from review to new material, etc.

4. <u>Students must be given a maximum of practice in speaking the language, never in talking about the language</u>. Each class hour should be evaluated in terms of the number of minutes each student was actually practicing speaking the language. Obviously, from this point of view, the more choral drill the better. Individual drill should only be used for spot checks on control of pronunciation or structure, and for variety in connection with Point 3 above. Grammar should never be discussed in class. Grammatical notes have been included for those students who feel a need to view the language analytically in addition to learning it, but the reading and discussion of them should be kept outside the class hour.

5. <u>Students must be helped to go beyond each lesson</u>, to apply the patterns learned in each lesson to real life situations, under the guidance of the teacher. The DDT formula which calls for dialogue and drill to be followed by 'talk' is a good one to keep in mind. As a culminating activity for each lesson, the teacher should help the students to substitute other words in the dialogues and drills--words that have more relevance to the students' own lives than could have been anticipated by the writer. As more and more lessons have been learned, such activity can begin to approach free and unstructured conversation.

6. <u>Students must be given constant review</u>. Although patterns and words keep recurring from lesson to lesson, no review lessons as such are provided. The teacher should make it a practice to intersperse review material from preceding lessons alongside new material from the current lessons throughout each class hour. Never overestimate the students' ability to retain. Make sure they do through constant review.

Finally, the teacher must plan each class hour thoroughly in advance. Walking into class with this book under his arm is not enough, no matter how well he knows the language. The plan must be a flexible one that can be easily modified as the class hour develops. But there must be a plan.

7. <u>Learn the phonetic spelling</u>. Although the traditional spelling will seem more familiar to you at first, you will not find the phonetic spelling difficult to master. It will give you new insights into the sound system of your language and the problems your students face in acquiring a good pronunciation.

## Getting Started--Useful Expressions

*Hello. Goodbye.*  
Yokwe.  
(to one or more)  
Yi'yaqey.

*Hello. Goodbye.*  
Yokwe yok.  
(to one person)  
Yi'yaqey y&q.

*Hello. Goodbye*  
Yokwe kom.  
(to more than one person)  
Yi'yaqey q&ṁ.

*Thank you.*  
Kommol.  
(to one person)  
Qeṁṁewel.

*Thank you.*  
Kom emmol.  
(to more than one person)  
Q&ṁ ṁṁewel.

*You're welcome.*  
Kin joij.  
('with kindness')  
K&n j&wij.

*'the Marshallese language'*  
kajin Majŏl  
kajin Ṁahjeł

*I don't know.*  
Ijaje.  
Yijahj&y.

*I don't know Marshallese.*  
Ij'aje kajin Majŏl.  
Yijahj&y kajin Ṁahjeł.

*I'm studying.*  
Ij ekkatak.  
Yij kkahtak.

*I'm studying Marshallese.*  
Ij ekkatak kajin Majŏl.  
Yij kkahtak kajin Ṁahjeł.

*How do you say 'study' in Marshallese?*  
Etan *'study'* ilo kajin Majŏl?  
Yetan *'study'* yilew kajin Ṁahjeł?

*I didn't hear.*  
Ijjab roñ.  
Yijjab reg̣.

*Please say that again.*  
Bar ba mŏk.  
Bar bah ṁek.

*It isn't clear yet.*  
Ejaḧin alikkar.  
Yejjahgin halikkar.

*What time is it?*
Jete awa kiđ?             Jetey hawah kiyyeh?

*We'll see each other again tomorrow.*
Jenaj bar lo dron         Jenahaj bar lew dewen
 ilju.                     yiljiw.

SPOKEN MARSHALLESE

## LESSON ONE

### Pronouns; Going Places; Where?

**DIALOGUE**

A: Yokwe yok.　　　　　　　Yi'yaqey y&q.

B: Yokwe. Kwɥj etal Ħan　　Yi'yaqey. Qej yetal gan
　 ia?　　　　　　　　　　　 yi'yah?

A: Ij etal Ħan Rita. Ak　 Yij yetal gan Riytah.
　 kwe?　　　　　　　　　　 Hak qey?

B: Ij etal Ħan Laura.　　　Yij yetal gan Łewrah.

A: Hello.
B: Hello. Where are you going?
A: I'm going to Rita. And you?
B: I'm going to Laura.

**DRILLS**

1. Yokwe yok.　　　　　　　Yi'yaqey y&q.
　　　komro　　　　　　　　　　q&ṁrew
　　　komjil　　　　　　　　　q&ṁj&y&l
　　　komeaħ　　　　　　　　　q&ṁyag
　　　komuij　　　　　　　　　q&ṁw&j
　　　kom　　　　　　　　　　　q&ṁ

2. Kwɥj etal Ħan ia?　　　 Qej yetal gan yi'yah?
　　　komro ej　　　　　　　　q&ṁrew yej
　　　komjil ej　　　　　　　 q&ṁj&y&l yej
　　　komeaħ ej　　　　　　　 q&ṁyag yej
　　　komuij ej　　　　　　　 q&ṁw&j yej
　　　komij　　　　　　　　　　q&ṁij

3. Ij etal Ħan Rita.　　　 Yij yetal gan Riytah.
　　　　　　　　Laura　　　　　　　　　　Łewrah
　　　　　　　　Namodrik　　　　　　　　 Naṁdik
　　　　　　　　Ebon　　　　　　　　　　　Yepwen
　　　　　　　　Jaluit　　　　　　　　　 Jalw&j
　　　　　　　　Ailinglaplap　　　　　　 Hay&l&g-
　　　　　　　　　　　　　　　　　　　　　 łapłap

4. Ij etal Ḧan Rita.          Yij yetal gan Riytah.
   kimro ej                   k&mrew yej
   kimjil ej                  k&mj&y&l yej
   kimeaḦ ej                  k&myag yej
   kimuij ej                  k&mw&j yej
   kimij                      k&mij
   kijro ej                   k&jrew yej
   kijjil ej                  k&jj&y&l yej
   kijeaḦ ej                  k&jyag yej
   kijuij ej                  k&jw&j yej
   jej                        jej

5. Ej etal Ḧan Kwajalein.     Yej yetal gan Kiwajleyen.
   irro ej                    y&rrew yej
   irjil ej                   y&rj&y&l yej
   ireaḦ ej                   y&ryag yej
   iruij ej                   y&rw&j yej
   rej                        rej

6. Kwȫj etal Ḧan Ailuk.       Qej yetal gan Hay&l&q.
   komro ej                   q&ṁrew yej
   komjil ej                  q&ṁj&y&l yej
   komeaḦ ej                  q&ṁyag yej
   komuij ej                  q&ṁw&j yej
   komij                      q&ṁij

Note: You may have noted in your teacher's pronunciation some short vowel sounds between words or between consonants within words that are not indicated in the writing systems above. In a sense, these are the reverse of English contractions in that they appear in rapid speech, but disappear in slow, deliberate speech. This is an automatic matter that you will develop a feeling for. Native speakers are generally no more aware of these 'excrescent' vowels than you are of the *p* in *something*.

GRAMMATICAL NOTES

1. The drills in this lesson give practice in using the personal pronouns. The system is summarized here for ready reference. Like English, there are three persons, and both singular and plural forms. In addition, the first person plural must be specified as to whether the person spoken to is included or excluded. There are three forms for each pronoun: absolute, subject, and object. The absolute form would be equivalent to *me* in the English (sub-standard)

expression: 'Me, I like potatoes,' and the subject form equivalent to *I* in the same expression. The object form would be equivalent to *me* in 'He hit me,' and the possessive equivalent of *my* or *mine* is not handled by separate pronouns in Marshallese, but by suffixed endings in special constructions which will be introduced later. Thus, the basic system of the Ralik dialect is as follows:

| Person | Absolute | | Subject | | Object | |
|---|---|---|---|---|---|---|
| singular | | | | | | |
| 1 | ña | gah | i | yi- | iɵ | y&h |
| 2 | kwe | qey | kwɵ- | qe- | yok | y&q |
| 3 | e | y&y | e- | ye- | e | y&y |
| plural | | | | | | |
| 1 incl. | kij | k&j | je- | je- | kij | k&j |
| excl. | kim | k&m | kimi- | k&mi- | kim | k&m |
| 2 | kom | q&ṁ | komi- | q&ṁi- | kom | q&ṁ |
| 3 | ir | y&r | re- | re- | ir | y&r |

Many Ratak (eastern chain) people use *kɵmi* <u>kemiy</u> instead of *kom* for the 2nd person plural, and *kɵmmen* k&mm&m instead of *kim* for the 1st person plural exclusive form.

2. The plural absolute (and object) pronouns can optionally be further specified as to numbers between two and five by a set of suffixes.

| Number | Suffix | | Ratak Variants | |
|---|---|---|---|---|
| 2 | -ro | -rew | | |
| 3 | -jil | -j&y&l | -jil | -j&l |
| 4 | -eaн | -yag | -men | -man |
| 5 or more | -uij | -w&j | | |

Note that when the pronouns thus specified as to number are used as the subject of a sentence, they are treated syntactically as if they were singular and followed immediately by the 3rd person singular subject form: *e(j)* <u>yej</u>. The full set of pronouns is given in the reference section at the end of this lesson.

3. The *-j* that is added to the subject forms of the pronouns in the dialogue and drills indicates action in progress (something like the *-ing* ending in English) and will be referred to as the 'progressive' suffix.

## SOUND DRILLS

1. The ñ-sound (g̱) of Marshallese is equivalent to the *ng* in English *sing*, but the problem for you is that in English it never occurs at the beginning of words, while in Marshallese it often does. To learn to pronounce it at the beginning of words, start with the word *singer* and try removing the first part *(si...)* so that you will be saying *nger, nger, nger*. When you can do this with ease, practice saying the following Marshallese words, imitating your teacher's pronunciation.

| Ña  | gah | I        | Ñan  | gan   | to       |
|-----|-----|----------|------|-------|----------|
| Ñe  | gey | if, when | Ñäät | gayat | when?    |
| Ñi  | giy | tooth    | Ñaj  | gaj   | fragrant |

2. The pronouns *kim* and *kom* both contain m-sounds, but these are not identical, and for some pairs of words may serve as the only distinguishing signals. Following are a few pairs of this type:

|   | 1 ṁ |   |   | 2 m |   |
|---|---|---|---|---|---|
| mwe | ṁ&y | rat-a-tat-tat | me | m&y | fortress |
| mwaj | ṁaj | eel, worm | mej | maj | eye |
| mṻñü | ṁegay | food | Mṻñü | megay | islet in Jaluit Atoll |
| jemam | jeṁaṁ | your (sg.) father | jemam | jemam | our (excl.) father |
| kijem | kijeṁ | your (sg.) food | kijem | kijem | our (excl.) food |
| am | haṁ | your (s) | am | ham | our (s) (excl.) |

## VOCABULARY

| Ailinglaplap | Hay&l&g̱łapłap | Rälik Atoll |
| Ailuk | Hay&l&q | Ratak Atoll |
| ak | hak | but, or |
| Ebon | Yepwen | Rälik Atoll |
| etal | yetal | go |
| ia | yi'yah | where? |
| Jaluit | Jalw&j | Rälik Atoll |
| Kwajalein | Kiwajleyen | Rälik Atoll |
| kwöj= kwö + j | qej | 2nd person sg. subj. pronoun + progressive |

| | | |
|---|---|---|
| Laura | Ḷewrah | village at west end of Majuro Atoll; name inherited from Navy code name; also called Majuro **Majr&w** |
| Namodrik | Naṁdik | Ralik Atoll |
| n̄an | gan | to |
| Rita | Riytah | village at east end of Majuro Atoll; name inherited from Navy code name |
| yok | y&q | you (sg., obj.) |
| yokwe | yi'yaqey | aloha, to love, greet, bid farewell, sympathize |

REFERENCE--Pronouns

SINGULAR

| Person | Absolute | Object | Subject | Possessive Suffix |
|---|---|---|---|---|
| 1st | gah | y&h | yi- | -hi |
| 2nd | qey | y&q | qe- | -ṁ |
| 3rd | y&y | y&y | ye- | -n |

PLURAL

Rālik Dialect/*Ratak Dialect

| Person (and specified number) | Absolute/Object | Subject** | Possessive Suffix |
|---|---|---|---|
| 1st incl. | k&j | je- | -d |
| (2) | k&jrew | jerew | -rrew |
| (3) | k&jj&y&l /k&jj&l | j&y&l /j&l | -dj&y&l /-dj&l |
| (4) | k&jyag /k&jman | j&yyag /j&yman | -dyag /-dman |
| (4+) | k&jw&j | j&w&j | -dw&j |
| 1st excl. | k&m /k&mm&m | k&mi- | -m |
| (2) | k&mrew /kemrew | | -mrew |
| (3) | k&mj&y&l /k&mj&l | | -mj&y&l /-mj&l |
| (4) | k&m(j&y)yag /k&m(j&y)man | | -m(j&y)yag /-m(j&y)man |
| (4+) | k&mw&j | | -mw&j |
| 2nd | q&ṁ /kemiy | q&ṁi- | -miy |
| (2) | q&ṁrew /kemiyrew | | -miyrew |
| (3) | q&ṁj&y&l /kemiyj&l | | -miyj&y&l /-miyj&l |
| (4) | q&ṁ(j&y)yag /kemiy(j&y)man | | -miy(j&y)yag /-miy(j&y)man |
| (5) | q&ṁw&j /kemiyw&j | | -miyw&j |

*Ratak dialect pronouns are given (only when they differ from the Rālik forms) on the second line, preceded by a slash.
**Subject forms are given only when they differ from the object forms.

```
3rd              y&r              re-         -y&r
     (2)         yerrew           rejerew     -y&rrew
     (3)         y&rj&y&l         r&j&y&l     -y&rj&y&l
                 /y&rj&l                      /-y&rj&l
     (4)         y&r(j&y)yag      reyag       -y&r(j&y)yag
                 /y&r(j&y)man                 /-y&r(j&y)man
     (4+)        y&rw&j           r&w&j       -y&rw&j
```

## LESSON TWO

Someone is going; when?
yes-no questions; negative;
future; conditional

### DIALOGUE

A: Timūj ej etal ḥan ia?         Tiyṁej yej yetal gan
                                  yi'yah?
B: Ej etal ḥan Rita.             Yej yetal gan Riytah.
A: Ak ejjab etal ḥan             Hak yejjab yetal gan
   Laura ke?                      Łewrah key?
B: Aet enaj etal ḥan             Hay&t yenahaj yetal gan
   Laura.                         Łewrah.
A: N̈äät?                         Gayat?
B: N̈e eroltok jen Rita.          Gey yerawalteq jan
                                  Riytah.

A: Where is Timos going?
B: He's going to Rita.
A: But isn't he going to Laura?
B: Yes, he's going to Laura.
A: When?
B: When he gets back from Rita.

### DRILLS

1. **Negative--with jab**

   Timūj ej etal ḥan Rita.        Tiyṁej yej yetal gan
                                   Riytah.
   Timūj ejjab etal ḥan           Tiyṁej yejjab yetal
     Rita.                         gan Riytah.
   Rej etal ḥan Laura.            Rej yetal gan Łewrah.
   Rejjab etal ḥan Laura.         Rejjab yetal gan Łewrah.
   Kwūj etal ḥan Kili.            Qej yetal gan K&l&y.
   Komij etal ḥan Namu.           Q&mij yetal gan Naṁ&w.
   Ij etal ḥan Ailuk.             Yij yetal gan Hay&l&q.

10

2. Yes-no questions--with key

| | |
|---|---|
| Ij etal. | Yij yetal. |
| Ij etal ke? | Yij yetal key? |
| Kwöj etal. | Qej yetal. |
| Kwöj etal ke? | Qej yetal key? |
| Ej etal. | Yej yetal. |
| Erro ej etal. | Yerrew yej yetal. |
| Rej etal. | Rej yetal. |
| Komij etal. | Q&ṁij yetal. |
| Komro ej etal. | Q&ṁr&w yej yetal. |
| Jej etal. | Jej yetal. |
| Timöj ej etal. | Tiyṁej yej yetal. |
| Kimij etal. | K&mij yetal. |

3. Yes and no answers--with jahab and hay&t

| | |
|---|---|
| Kwöj etal ke Ħan Rita? | Qej yetal key gan Riytah? |
| Aet, ij etal Ħan Rita. | Hay&t, yij yetal gan Riytah. |
| Jab, ijjab etal Ħan Rita. | Jahab, yijjab yetal gan Riytah. |
| Ej etal ke Ħan Rita? | Yej yetal key gan Riytah? |
| Aet, ej etal Ħan Rita. | Hay&t, yej yetal gan Riytah. |
| Jab, ejjab etal Ħan Rita. | Jahab, yejjab yetal gan Riytah. |
| Komij etal ke Ħan Rita? | Q&ṁij yetal key gan Riytah? |
| Timöj ej etal ke Ħan Rita? | Tiyṁej yej yetal key gan Riytah? |
| Rej etal ke Ħan Rita? | Rej yetal key gan Riytah? |

4. Negative questions--with jab and key

| | |
|---|---|
| Timöj ejjab etal Ħan Rita. | Tiyṁej yejjab yetal gan Riytah. |
| Timöj ejjab etal Ħan Rita ke? | Tiyṁej yejjab yetal gan Riytah key? |
| Rejjab etal Ħan Laura. | Rejjab yetal gan Ŀewrah. |
| Kwöjjab etal Ħan Kili. | Qejjab yetal gan K&l&y. |

Komij jab etal Ḣan        Q&ṁij jab yetal gan
Namu.                      Naṁ&w.

Ijjab etal Ḣan Ailuk.     Yijjab yetal gan Hay&l&q.

5. Answers to negative questions

   *(Answer the questions in Drill 4 with the answers
   your teacher models for you (see Grammatical Note,
   3): either* <u>hay&t</u>, <u>yejjab yetal</u> *and* <u>jahab</u>, <u>yej
   yetal</u>, *or* <u>hay&t, yej yetal</u> *and* <u>jahab, yejjab
   yetal</u>.*)*

6. Future--with nahaj

   Ej etal Ḣan Namu.            Yej yetal gan Naṁ&w.
   Enaj etal Ḣan Namu.          Yenahaj yetal gan Naṁ&w.

   Ej etal Ḣan Ailuk.           Yej yetal gan Hay&l&q.
   Enaj etal Ḣan Ailuk.         Yenahaj yetal gan
                                 Hay&l&q.

   Kwöj etal Ḣan Mille.         Qej yetal gan Mil&y.

   Rej etal Ḣan Laura.          Rej yetal gan Ŀewrah.

   Komij etal Ḣan Ujelaḣ.       Q&ṁij yetal gan Wijlag.

   Jej etal Ḣan Likiep.         Jej yetal gan Likiyep.

   Kimij etal Ḣan Aur.          K&mij yetal gan Hawir.

   Ij etal Ḣan Uliga.           Yij yetal gan Wilkah.

   Erro ej etal Ḣan Laura.      Yerrew yej yetal gan
                                 Ŀewrah.

   Timöj ej etal Ḣan            Tiyṁej yej yetal gan
   Laura.                       Ŀewrah.

7. Conditional--independent clause in future with
   nahaj and dependent clause introduced by gey.

   *(Change the following to future and add the clause*
   gey yerawalteq jan Riytah.*)*

   Ej etal Ḣan Namu.            Yej yetal gan Naṁ&w.
   Enaj etal Ḣan Namu Ḣe        Yenahaj yetal gan Naṁ&w
   eroltok jen Rita.            gey yerawalteq jan
                                 Riytah.

   Ej etal Ḣan Ailuk.           Yej yetal gan Hay&l&q.
   Enaj etal Ḣan Ailuk          Yenahaj yetal gan
   Ḣe eroltok jen Rita.         Hay&l&q gey yerawal-
                                 teq jan Riytah.

Kwōj etal ñan Mille.          Qej yetal gan Milɛy.
Rej etal ñan Laura.           Rej yetal gan Ɫewrah.
Komij etal ñan Ujelañ.        Qɛmij yetal gan Wijlag.
Jej etal ñan Likiep.          Jej yetal gan Likiyep.
Kimij etal ñan Aur.           Kɛmij yetal gan Hawir.
Ij etal ñan Uliga.            Yij yetal gan Wilkah.
Erro ej etal ñan Laura.       Yerrew yej yetal gan Ɫewrah.
Timōj ej etal ñan Laura.      Tiymej yej yetal gan Ɫewrah.

## VOCABULARY

| | | |
|---|---|---|
| aet | hayɛt | yes |
| Ailuk | Hayelɛq | Ratak Atoll |
| Aur | Hawir | Ratak Atoll |
| ejjab | yejjab | is not (he, she, it) |
| enaj | yenahaj | will be (3rd person) |
| jen | jan | from, since |
| ke | key | question particle |
| Kili | Kɛlɛy | Ralik Island |
| Likiep | Likiyep | Ratak Atoll |
| Mille | Milɛy | Ratak Atoll |
| ñāāt | gayat | when |
| Namu | Namɛw | Ralik Atoll |
| ñe | gey | when, if |
| roltok | rawalteq | return, turn around |
| Ujelañ | Wijlag | westernmost atoll in the Marshalls |
| Uliga | Wilkah | islet of the administrative center at Majuro |

## GRAMMATICAL NOTES

A number of patterns are introduced in this lesson to give you some early flexibility in what you can say.

1. Note that in making sentences negative, <u>jab</u> is inserted before the main verb, but follows the progressive -<u>j</u>. In later lessons we will meet even more complex verb phrases with more elements than these three (progressive, negative, and main verb), but we will always find that the subject prefixes like <u>ye-</u>, <u>re-</u>, <u>qe-</u>, are prefixed to the first element of the verb phrase. They are only prefixed to the main verb

itself when it is the only element in the verb phrase, as in gey YErawalteq jan Riytah. Note that in the future sentences practiced in this lesson, the subject prefixes are attached to nahaj, which precedes the main verb. And as we have seen, in simple progressive statements they are prefixed to -j: YEj yetal gan yi'yah.

2. Note the contrast in vowel length between jab *not* and jahab *no*.

3. Answers to affirmative questions in Marshallese like those in Drill 3 present no complication from an English point of view, but with negative questions like those in Drill 4 there are some complications. It seems that the old Marshallese pattern was to use hay&t in assenting to the negation--Yes, he's not--and jahab in negating the negation of the question--No, he is. But today--probably under the influence of English--both patterns are used, and your teacher will probably have his own ideas about which is the best Marshallese. Be guided by him in this matter, remembering that usage is divided. It is probably a good idea to spell out exactly what you mean in your answers to negative questions by answering more than just hay&t or jahab, as in Drill 5.

SOUND DRILL

The distinction in sound between the Marshallese vowels & and e is extremely difficult for English speakers to learn to hear and produce. Here are some pairs to practice on, which have the vowels before y where they both sound close to the vowel sound in English *may*, for example.

|  | 1 &  |  | 2 e |
|---|---|---|---|
| m&y | fortress, weir | mey | which |
| l&y | albatross | ley | ma'am |
| k&y | porpoise | key | question particle |
| hah&y | gather | hahey | current |
| b&yb&y | silly | beybey | tuna |

## LESSON THREE

Do you have a/some...?; possessive;
Where is your/my...?; Here/there it
is; I don't know.

### DIALOGUE

A: Ewŏr ke am binjel?      Yewer key haṁ pinjeł?
B: Ejelok aŭ binjel.        Yejjelaq hah&h pinjeł.
A: Ak ewŏr ke am ben?      Hak yewer key haṁ peyen?
B: Aet. Ieo.                Hay&t. Yi'yeyew.

A: Do you have a pencil?
B: No, I don't.
A: Then do you have a pen?
B: Yes. Here it is.

### DRILLS

1. Ewŏr ke am <u>binjel</u>?      Yewer key ham <u>pinjeł</u>?
   ben                              peyen
   waj                              waj
   majet                            majet
   beba                             p&ybah

2. Aet, ewŏr aŭ binjel.      Hay&t, yewer hah&h pinjeł.
   *(Give similar affirmative answers to the questions in Drill 1.)*

3. Jab, ejelok aŭ binjel.    Jahab, yejjelaq hah&h pinjeł.
   *(Give similar negative answers to the questions in Drill 1.)*

4. Ewŏr ke kijŏm <u>jikka</u>?    Yewer key kijeṁ <u>jikkah</u>?
   raij                            rahyij
   bilawŭ                          pilahway
   bwil                            bil
   lole                            ław ł&y

15

5. Aet, ewŭr kijŭ jikka.          Hay&t, yewer kij&h jikkah.
   Jab, ejelok kijŭ jikka.        Jahab, yejjelaq kij&h
                                  jikkah.
   *(Give similar affirmative and negative answers to
   the questions in Drill 4.)*

6. Ewŭr ke limŭm kobe.            Yewer key liṁeṁ kawp&y?
              ti                               tiy
              kola                             k&wɫah
              bia                              piyah
              dren                             dan

7. Aet, ewŭr limŭ kobe.           Hay&t, yewer lim&h kawp&y.
   *(Give similar affirmative and negative answers to
   the questions in Drill 6.)*
   Jab, ejelok limŭ kobe.         Jahab, yejjelaq lim&h
                                  kawp&y.

8. Ewŭr ke nejim toli?            Yewer key najiṁ tawɫ&y?
              bol                              bawaɫ
              kŭjaḣjaḣ                         kejagjag
              likaebeb                         ɫikayebyeb
              kita                             kitah
              ajri                             hajiriy
              bao                              bahwew
              kuuj                             kiwij
              piik                             piyik
              kidru                            kidiw

9. Aet, ewŭr nejŭ toli.           Hay&t, yewer najih tawɫ&y.
   Jab, ejelok nejŭ toli.         Jahab, yejjelaq najih
                                  tawɫ&y.
   *(Give similar affirmative and negative answers to
   the questions in Drill 8.)*

10. Ewŭr ke wam kŭrkŭr?           Yewer key waham kerker?
               tibḣil                          tipg&l
               kaar                            kahar
               tirak                           tirak
               otobai                          wetewbah-
                                               yiy
               wa                              wah
               tima                            tiyṁah
               booj                            bewej
               limakaak                        liṁahak-
                                               hak

11. Aet, ewŏr waŭ kŏrkŏr.  Hay&t, yewer wah&h kerker.
    Jab, ejelok waŭ kŏrkŏr.  Jahab, yejjelaq wah&h kerker.
    *(Give similar affirmative and negative answers to the questions in Drill 10.)*

12. Ewŏr ke ḧim <u>kab</u>?  Yewer key giyiṁ <u>kab</u>?

    | | |
    |---|---|
    | pilej | <u>pīlyej</u> |
    | jibun | jibwin |
    | ainbat | hayinbat |
    | tibat | tiybat |
    | jibun bok | jibwin bawak |
    | tŭre | t&r&y |
    | kab kilaj | kab kilhaj |
    | kab drekŭ | kab dekay |
    | kikŏr | kik&r |

13. Aet, ewŏr ḧiŭ kab.  Hay&t, yewer giyih kab.
    Jab, ejelok ḧiŭ kab.  Jahab, yejjelaq giyih kab.
    *(Give similar affirmative and negative answers to questions in Drill 12.)*

14. 'Where is your...?'
    Ewi binjel eo am?  Yewiy pinjeł yew ham?
    Ewi jikka eo kijŏm?  Yewiy jikkah yew kijeṁ?
    Ewi kobe eo limŏm?  Yewiy kawp&y yew liṁeṁ?
    Ewi toli eo nejim?  Yewiy tawl&y yew najiṁ?
    Ewi kŏrkŏr eo wam?  Yewiy kerker yew wahaṁ?
    Ewi kab eo ḧim?  Yewiy kab yew giyiṁ?
    *(Ask similar questions about other vocabulary items introduced in this lesson.)*

15. Another way to ask 'Where is your...?'
    Eber ia binjel eo am?  Yepad yi'yah pinjeł yew ham?
    Eber ia jikka eo kijŏm?  Yepad yi'yah jikkah yew kijeṁ?
    *(These questions mean essentially the same thing as those in Drill 14: 'Where is your...?' Ask similar questions about other vocabulary items introduced in this lesson.)*

16. 'Where is my...?'
    Ewi binjel eo aŭ?  Yewiy pinjeł yew hah&h?
    Ewi jikka eo kijŭ?  Yewiy jikkah yew kij&h?
    *(Ask similar questions about other items.)*

17. Another way to ask 'Where is my...?'
Eber ia binjel eo aṍ?    Yepad yi'yah pinjeł yew hah&h?
Yepad yi'yah jikkah yew kij&h?
*(Ask similar questions about other items.)*

18. Some answers.
Eḿe.    Here it is (close to me).    Y&g&y.
Eḿene.   There it is (close to you).   Yegney.
Ijaje.   I don't know.                 Yijahj&y.
*(Answers to the questions in Drills 14 and 15 can get quite complicated and most will have to be postponed until later lessons, but here for the moment are some simple ones. Practice using these in response to the various questions you construct above.)*

GRAMMATICAL NOTES

1. We note in this lesson a classification of objects which determines the possessive word to be used. In general we can say that kij&h and kijeṁ are used for food (and cigarettes); līm&h and līṁeṁ for drinks; najih and najiṁ for children, pets, toys, and musical instruments; wah&h and wahaṁ for vehicles; giyih and giyiṁ for eating utensils; and hah&h and haṁ for other alienable objects.

Later you will learn still other similar possessive words. For example, ketkah and ketkaṁ are used for plants, and mawarih and mawariṁ are used for baits.

Sometimes different possessives may be used with one and the same word depending on the sense in which it is used. For example, jibiṁ bahwew means 'your pet bird (other than a chicken)' [literally, 'your grandmother bird'], kijeṁ bahwew means 'your chicken for eating', najiṁ bahwew means 'your pet rooster or hen' [literally, 'your child bird'], and geṅaṁ bahwew means 'your catch of birds'.

2. The possessive classifying words that are introduced in this lesson can be analyzed as consisting of a stem and one of the possessive suffixes from the pronoun reference list at the end of Lesson One. Following are the stems, which can be considered as falling into four groups according to their final vowels:

|          | i-stems              |         | e-stems |
|----------|----------------------|---------|---------|
| naji-    | child                | kije-   | food    |
| giyi-    | tooth                | lime-   | drink   |
| jibi-    | grandmother, grandchild |      |         |
| mawari-  | bait                 |         |         |

|          | short a-stems |         | long a-stems       |
|----------|---------------|---------|--------------------|
| qeña-    | catch         | haha-   | general possessive |
| ketka-   | plant         | waha-   | canoe              |

To these are added the suffixes:

| -hi  | my           | -d    | our (incl. you) |
|------|--------------|-------|-----------------|
| -ṁ   | your (sg.)   | -m    | our (excl. you) |
| -n   | his, her, its| -miy  | your (pl.)      |
|      |              | -yy&r | their           |

In most cases, simply combining the stems and suffixes gives us the correct forms. There are, however, a few exceptions that need to be covered by special rules.

(a) The most general rule concerns the fact that historically Marshallese has lost the last vowel of all words. Whereas formerly there were only words ending in vowels (as is still the case in some Polynesian languages), the loss of final vowels has created in Marshallese many words that end in consonants, and has 'clipped short' words ending in long vowels. One such example that concerns us here is the word for *canoe*, the stem of which is waha- (which is what we find when the stem has suffixes with consonants attached to it), but which is shortened to wah when it stands alone, bare of suffixes.

(b) This same 'erosion from the right' has affected our one possessive suffix which has a final vowel with no following consonant--the first person singular suffix for *my*. Although we list this suffix as -hi (which it was historically), its vowel, like other original final vowels, has been dropped, but leaves its effect on *e-stems* and *long a-stems*. Thus, *my food* was kijehi but has become kij&h, *my canoe* was wahahi but has become wah&h. *My child* and *my catch*, on the other hand, show no such vowel change, and in effect simply add -h, giving najih and qeñah, respectively.

This can all be summarized in the following rules for each of the four stem types:

(1) <u>i-stems</u>       ...i + -hi > ...ih      najih
(2) <u>e-stems</u>       ...e + -hi > ...&h      kij&h
(3) <u>short a-stems</u> ...a + -hi > ...ah      qenah
(4) <u>long a-stems</u>  ...aha + -hi > ...ah&h  wah&h

(c) Stems containing a light *m* (m) have it changed to a heavy *m* (ṁ) before the heavy *m* of the second person singular suffix:

    lime-  lim&h my drink
    *but*  liṁeṁ your drink
    jema- jemah my father
    *but*  jeṁaṁ your father

3. The term <u>kab kilhaj</u> 'drinking glass' and <u>jibwin bawak</u> 'fork' illustrate two important points to remember:

 (a) In Marshallese, adjective-like modifiers--such as <u>kilhaj</u> 'glass' and <u>bawak</u> 'forked'--follow the words they modify--rather than precede, as in English.

 (b) Although a word may obviously have been borrowed from English--like <u>kab</u> or <u>jibwin</u>--its meaning may have been shifted or extended, as is the case with these two words: <u>kab</u> has become a general term for all drinking utensils, and forks are one kind of <u>jibwin</u>.

4. The vocabulary that follows is quite long but contains a large number of words that have been borrowed from English. These should not be so difficult to remember. There is, however, one caution that applies. Just as *boeuf* and *mouton* have been borrowed from French into English but anglicized--given compatible English pronunciations--so also the Marshallese words of English origin have undergone 'Marshallization.' Do not be tempted to take the easy way out and give them English (foreign) pronunciations. If you do, you will be less easily understood by those who do not know English, *and* you will be missing a most valuable opportunity for getting an early feel for the essence of Marshallese pronunciation habits. The scientific spelling should furnish you clues to some of the puzzling changes that have taken place in the process of 'Marshallization.'

## VOCABULARY

| | | |
|---|---|---|
| aet | hay&t | yes |
| ainbat | hayinbat | iron pot, pot |
| ajri | hajiriy | child |
| ak | hak | in that case, but |
| am | haṁ | your, yours |
| aʊ | hah&h | my, mine |
| bao | bahwew | hen, chicken, fowl |
| beba | p&ybah | paper |
| ben | peyen | pen |
| ber | pad | stay, remain, be somewhere |
| bia | piyah | beer |
| bilawḁ | pilahway | flour, bread |
| binjel | pinjeł | pencil |
| bok | bawak | forked, box |
| bol | bawał | ball |
| booj | bewej | boat |
| bwil | bil | gum |
| drekḁ | dekay | stone |
| dren | dan | water |
| ejelok | yejjełaq | there is none |
| eḥe | y&g&y | here it is (close to me) |
| eḥene | yegney | there it is (close to you) |
| eo | yew | the |
| ewi | yewiy | where? (singular) |
| ewʊr | yewer | there is, are |
| ieo | yi'yeyew | here it is, take it |
| jab | jahab | no |
| jaje | jahj&y | not know |
| jibun | jibwin | spoon |
| jikka | jikkah | cigarettes |
| kaar | kahar | car |
| kab | kab | cup, glass: general term for drinking utensil |
| ke | key | question particle |
| kidru | kidiw | dog |
| kijʊ | kij&h | my food |
| kijʊm | kijeṁ | your food |
| kikʊr | kik&r | small bivalve shell found in sand--used to scrape copra meat from nut and to eat with |
| kilaj | kilhaj | glass |
| kita | kitah | guitar |
| kobe | kawp&y | coffee |
| kojaḥjaḥ | kejagjag | musical instrument |
| kola | k&włah | cola |

| | | |
|---|---|---|
| kɔrkɔr | kerker | paddling canoe |
| kuuj | kiwij | cat |
| likaebeb | likayebyeb | top |
| limakaak | liṁahakhak | kite |
| limʉ | lim&h | my drink |
| limʉm | liṁeṁ | your drink |
| lole | ɬawɬ&y | candy |
| majet | majet | matches |
| otobai | wetewbahyiy | motor bike, scooter |
| piik | piyik | pig |
| pilej | pilyej | plate |
| raij | rahyij | rice |
| ti | tiy | tea |
| tibat | tiybat | teapot, tea kettle, coffee pot |
| tibḦil | tipg&l | sailing canoe |
| tima | tiyṁah | ship (from English *steamer*) |
| tirak | tirak | truck |
| toli | tawl&y | doll |
| tʉre | t&r&y | tray |
| wa | wah | canoe; general term for vehicle |
| waj | waj | watch |

REFERENCE--Some possessive paradigms

| | | general | food | drink | child |
|---|---|---|---|---|---|
| Sg. | 1 | hah&h | kij&h | lim&h | *najih |
| | 2 | haṁ | kijeṁ | liṁeṁ | najiṁ |
| | 3 | han | kijen | limen | najin |
| Pl. | 1(incl.) | had | kijed | limed | najid |
| | 1(excl.) | ham | kijem | limem | najim |
| | 2 | hamiy | kijemiy | limemiy | najimiy |
| | 3 | hay&r | kij&yy&r | lim&yy&r | najiyy&r |

| | | canoe | tooth | plant | catch |
|---|---|---|---|---|---|
| Sg. | 1 | wah&h | giyih | ketkah | qeñah |
| | 2 | wahaṁ | giyiṁ | ketkaṁ | qeñaṁ |
| | 3 | wahan | giyin | ketken | qeñan |
| Pl. | 1(incl.) | wahad | giyid | ketkad | qeñad |
| | 1(excl.) | waham | giyim | ketkam | qeñam |
| | 2 | wahamiy | giyimiy | ketkamiy | qeñamiy |
| | 3 | wahay&r | giyiyy&r | ketkayy&r | qeñayy&r |

*naji- is the Ratak dialect stem; for the Ralik dialect it is n&ji-.

## LESSON FOUR

More comings and goings--hither, thither, and yon: directionals; future negative; the construct particle; the locative particle

### DIALOGUE

A: Komro ej itok ke?   Q&ṁrew yej yiteq key?
B: Jab. Kimro ej ber wōt.   Jahab. K&mrew yej pad wet.
A: Ak John ej itok ke?   Hak Jawan yej yiteq key?
B: Bwōlen enaj iwōj.   B&l&n yenahaj yiw&j.
A: Etke komjil ejjab itok ibben dron?   Yetkey q&ṁj&y&l yejjab yiteq yippan dewen?
B: Ekwe emman. Kejeañ etal.   Yeqey yeṁṁan. K&jyag yetal.

A: Are you two coming?
B: No, we're staying here.
A: How about John--is he coming?
B: Maybe he'll join you.
A: Why don't the three of you come together?
B: Well, O.K. Let's (the four of us) go.

### DRILLS

1. Future (Positive and Negative)

Examples:
John <u>ej</u> itok in ber.   Jawan <u>yej</u> yiteq yin pad.
  John's coming to stay.

John <u>enaj</u> itok in ber.   Jawan <u>yenahaj</u> yiteq yin pad.
  John will come to stay.

John <u>eban</u> itok in ber.   Jawan <u>yeban</u> yiteq yin pad.
  John won't come to stay.

23

Ej itok in ber.
Enaj
Eban

Yej yiteq yin pad.
Yenahaj
Yeban

Rej etal in jerbal.
Renaj
Reban

Rej yetal yin jerbal.
Renahaj
Reban

Ij etal ḧan Namu.
Inaj
Iban

Yij yetal gan Naṁ&w.
Yinahaj
Yiban

Komuij etal in ikkure.
Kom naj
Kom ban

Q&ṁw&j yetal yin qqir&y.
Q&ṁ nahaj
Q&ṁ ban

KwÖj itok in tutu.
KwÖnaj
Koban

Qej yiteq yin tiwtiw.
Qenahaj
Qeban

2. Kijeaḧ etal in tutu.
   jerbal
   ikkure
   katak
   jikul

K&jyag yetal yin
   tiwtiw.
   jerbal
   qqir&y
   kahtak
   jikiwiɫ

3. BwÖlen enaj iwÖj in
   tutu.
   jerbal
   ikkure
   katak
   jikul

B&l&n yenahaj yiw&j
   yin tiwtiw.
   jerbal
   qqir&y
   kahtak
   jikiwiɫ

4. Etke komjil ejjab itok
   in tutu?
   jerbal
   ikkure
   katak
   jikul

Yetkey q&ṁj&l yejjab
   yiteq yin tiwtiw?
   jerbal
   qqir&y
   kahtak
   jikiwiɫ

5. Ej ber wÖt i Ailuk.
   Mille
   Likiep
   Namodrik
   Jaluit

Yej pad wet yiy
   Hay&l&q.
   Mil&y
   Likiyep
   Naṁdik
   Jalw&j

6. Ej ber wɵt in <u>jerbal</u>.          Yej pad wet yin
                                          <u>jerbal</u>.
       jikul                              jikiwi⅄
       ikkure                             qqir&y
       katak                              kahtak
       tutu                               tiwtiw

7. Ej ber wɵt in (i)                     Yej pad wet yin (yiy)
   <u>jerbal</u>.                         <u>jerbal</u>.
   jikul                                  jikiwi⅄
   Mille                                  Mil&y
   katak                                  kahtak
   Likiep                                 Likiyep
   Namodrik                               Naṁdik
   tutu                                   tiwtiw
   ikkure                                 qqir&y
   Jaluit                                 Jalw&j
   Ailuk                                  Hay&l&q

8. Practice with both *etal in* <u>yetal yin</u> and *ilen*
   <u>yilan</u>: See Grammatical Note 1.
   Kijeaḧ etal in <u>tutu</u>.            K&jyag yetal yin <u>tiwtiw</u>.
   Kijeaḧ ilen <u>tutu</u>.               K&jyag yilan <u>tiwtiw</u>.
       jerbal                             jerbal
       ikkure                             qqir&y
       katak                              kahtak
       jikul                              jikiwi⅄

9. Practice with both *itok in* <u>yiteq yin</u> and *iten*
   <u>yiten</u>:
   Etke komjil ejjab itok                 Yetkey q&ṁj&y&l yejjab
      in tutu?                               yiteq yin tiwtiw?
   Etke komjil ejjab iten                 Yetkey q&ṁj&y&l yejjab
      tutu?                                  yiten tiwtiw?
       jerbal                             jerbal
       ikkure                             qqir&y
       jikul                              jikiwi⅄
       katak                              kahtak

10. Ej <u>itok</u> ḧɵɵt wa eo?            Yej <u>yiteq</u> gayat wah yew?
        <u>ilok</u>                          yilaq
        tartok                               tarteq
        tarlok                               tar⅄aq
        roltok                               rawalteq
        rollok                               rawal⅄aq
        botok                                pewteq
        bolok                                pew⅄aq

```
    tokeaktok                tekyakteq
    tokeaklok                tekyakłaq
    jeraktok                 jerakteq
    jeraklok                 jerakłaq
```

11. *(Practice answering the questions in Drill 10 with the following pattern.)*

```
    Enaj itok ilju.          Yenahaj yiteq yiljiw.
         ilok                        yilaq
         tartok                      tarteq
         (etc.)                      (etc.)
```

12. Ej iwōj ḨḨḨt wa eo?      Yej yiw&j gayat wah yew?
    Enaj itok ilju.          Yenahaj yiteq yiljiw.
    Ej itok ḨḨḨt wa eo?      Yej yiteq gayat wah yew?
    Enaj iwōj ilju.          Yenahaj yiw&j yiljiw.

    *(Continue this drill using the verbs introduced in Drill 10, being careful to choose -teq or -w&j from the speaker's viewpoint--see Grammatical Note 3.)*

13. 'Is he coming to stay with me?'
```
    Ej itok ke iba?          Yej yiteq key yippah?
    Aet, ej iwōj.            Hay&t, yej yiw&j.
    Jab, ejjab iwōj.         Jahab, yejjab yiw&j.
    Aet, enaj iwōj.          Hay&t, yenahaj yiw&j.
    Jab, eban iwōj.          Jahab, yeban yiw&j.
```

*(Continue by supplying parallel answers to the following questions, being careful to choose correctly among yiteq, yiw&j, and yilaq and to give appropriate subjects to your answers.)*

```
    Ej iwōj ke ibam?         Yej yiw&j key yippaṁ?
    Aet, ej itok.            Hay&t, yej yiteq.
    (etc.)                   (etc.)
    Ej ilok ke iben?         Yej yilaq key yippan?
    Kwōj itok ke iba?        Qej yiteq key yippah?
    Kwōj ilok ke iben?       Qej yilaq key yippan?
    Rej itok ke iba?         Rej yiteq key yippah?
    Rej iwōj ke ibam?        Rej yiw&j key yippaṁ?
    Rej ilok ke iben?        Rej yilaq key yippan?
```

14. 'Is he going with me?'
```
    Ej itok ke iba tok?          Yej yiteq key yippah teq?
    Aet, ej iwōj ibam wōj.       Hay&t, yej yiw&j yippaṁ
                                 w&j.
```

Jab, ejjab iwōj ibam wōj.
Aet, enaj iwōj ibam wōj.
Jab, eban iwōj ibam wōj.

Jahab, yejjab yiw&j yippaṁ w&j.
Hay&t, yenahaj yiw&j yippaṁ w&j.
Jahab, yeban yiw&j yippaṁ w&j.

*(Continue by supplying parallel answers to the following questions, being careful to use appropriate subjects, directionals, and forms of* yippa-.*)*

Ej iwōj ke ibam wōj?
Aet, ej itok iba tok.

*(etc.)*
Ej ilok ke iben lok?

Yej yiw&j key yippaṁ w&j?
Hay&t, yej yiteq yippah teq.

*(etc.)*
Yej yilaq key yippan laq?

*(Repeat, substituting* rej *(and where possible* yij *and* qej*) for* yej *in the questions, and give appropriate answers.)*

## GRAMMATICAL NOTES

1. In this lesson the 'construct particle' is introduced. It is called this because it functions to join the word that precedes it and the one that follows it into a construction. The results thus obtained may be translated into English in a variety of ways. Here are a few examples:

yetal yin jerbal         go to work
ṁṁahan yin Jepahan       Japanese man
dan yin yidahak          drinking water
Qekahn&w&j yin ṁṁewel.   You are extremely
                         generous. (Thank
                         you very much.)

In rapid speech it may be fused more closely with the preceding word, like a suffix. When this happens, the y is dropped, and there may be other changes, as for example with yiten (from yiteq yin) and yilan (from yilaq yin) in Drills 8 and 9.

2. The word qqir&y 'play' introduced in Drill 1 is typical of a large group of Marshallese words which are referred to as 'double consonant stems.' As this name implies, all such stems begin with a doubled consonant. The actual sounding out of such words requires that a vowel be added, but the two dialects differ in where the vowel is added. The Ratak (eastern) dialect inserts the extra vowel between the consonants, while

the Rḁlik (western) dialect puts it before the double consonants and also puts a y before the added vowel, at the front of the word.

|  Rḁlik  |  Ratak  |
|---|---|
| (y_)qqir&y | q(_)qir&y |

The vowel to be added is the same as the one that follows the doubled consonants, except that when the following one is a, e is added:

| Stem | Rḁlik | Ratak | Meaning |
|---|---|---|---|
| qqir&y | (yi)qqir&y<br>ikkure | q(i)qir&y<br>kukure | 'play' |
| tt&r | (y&)tt&r<br>ettðr | t(&)t&r<br>tðtðr | 'run' |
| bbej | (ye)bbej<br>ebbðj | b(e)bej<br>bðbðj | 'swollen' |
| ṁṁan | (ye)ṁṁan<br>emðn | ṁ(e)ṁan<br>mðmðn | 'good' |

When such stems have subject prefixes added, no vowel other than that of the prefix is added. This makes words like 'I play' yi + qqir&y and 'he is good' ye + ṁṁan identical to the Rḁlik pronunciation of the bare stems without the prefixes.

When you have mastered this rule, you will have control of one of the major differences between the two dialects. To help remind you of the words to which the rule applies, this and future lessons omit the extra vowels *in the phonetic spelling* when such words occur without subject prefixes; you can soon learn in either Rḁlik or Ratak fashion, depending at first on the pronunciation of your teacher and later--when you are using the language--on the dictates of the situation.

However, *in the Marshallese spelling*, these words will be spelled with the extra vowel added according to the Rḁlik pronunciation.

3. Whereas English has essentially a two-way frame of reference built into many of its words involving location and direction:

|  close to or<br>toward speaker | further or away<br>from speaker |
|---|---|
| come | go |
| bring | take |
| here, hither | there, thither |
| this, these | that, those |
| here | away |

the basic set of Marshallese directionals introduced in this lesson involves a three-way division of the same semantic area, which correlates closely with the three persons of the pronoun system:

| 1<br>toward me | 2<br>toward you | 3<br>toward a third location,<br>away from both of us |
|---|---|---|
| teq | w&j (Rɨlik)<br>waj (Ratak) | łaq |

These directionals may occur alone as words, as in Drill 14, or suffixed to certain verb formatives, as in <u>yiteq</u>, <u>yiw&j</u>, <u>yilaq</u>, <u>tarteq</u>, etc.

In moving from an English to a Marshallese mode of thought in this matter, your biggest task will be to separate 2 from 3 -- 'toward addressee' as distinct from the more general 'away from speaker' of English.

4. In the Rɨlik dialect one can say:

<u>Yej yiteq gayat wah yew</u>?   When is the canoe coming?
and
<u>Yej yiteq gayat Tiymej</u>?   When is Timos coming?

But <u>yiteq</u> is not used in the Ratak dialect. There the equivalents to the above sentences would be:

Yej <u>tarteq</u> gayat wah yew?
    pewteq
    tekyakteq

and

Yej wayteq gayat Tiymej?

This last sentence introduces a Ratak equivalent for <u>yiteq</u> when referring to the moving of humans only: <u>wayteq</u>. The Ratak counterpart of <u>yilaq</u> is <u>waylaq</u>, and of <u>yiw&j</u>, <u>wahw&j</u> (again, for humans only). For vessels or vehicles, the Ratak dialect uses words like <u>pewteq</u>, <u>tarteq</u>, <u>tekyakteq</u> instead of <u>yiteq</u>.

Thus, in the Ratak dialect, the first two lines of Drill 14 would be:

    Yej wayteq key yippah teq?
    Hay&t, yej wahw&j yippaṁ waj.

All the drills in this lesson have been written in the
Rṳlik dialect. After you have mastered them in this
form, you may want to go through them using Ratak
forms if your teacher is sufficiently familiar with
that dialect to guide you.

5. Note that while ḻaq generally has a heavy ḻ, there
are two exceptions in this lesson in which this ḻ is
changed to a light one:
    yilaq
    waylaq

In later lessons you will find a third exception:
    keylaq ('jump, fly')

6. The words yippa<u>h</u>, yippa<u>ṁ</u> and yippa<u>n</u> in Drills 13
and 14 are the stem yippa- plus the possessive suffixes
-h(i), -ṁ, -n and are translated respectively 'with
me', 'with you (sg.)', and 'with him (her, it)'.

SOUND DRILL

Continuing with the <u>&</u> - <u>e</u> distinction, which we practiced in a 'y' environment in Lesson 2, let us now
practice the same sound types in other environments.
When y does not precede or follow these two vowels and
when w does not follow, both these vowel sounds resemble the English hesitation form 'uh', but they must
be distinguished from each other since they often constitute the only and therefore crucial difference between words. Here are some key examples to practice
with your teacher.

|  | & |  |  | e |  |
|---|---|---|---|---|---|
| aü | hah&h | 'my, mine' | aü | haheh | 'to swim' |
| wit | w&t | 'rain' | wüt | wet | 'only' |
| mük | ṁ&k | 'tired'(Rṳl.) | mük | ṁek | 'please' |
| wür | w&r | 'lobster' | wür | wer | 'have, there is (are)' |
| wün | w&n | 'turtle' | wün | wen | 'who?' |

(Note that the traditional spelling often does not
distinguish these pairs of words.)

Some other words you have already learned that contain
these sounds include:

```
            yiw&j              qej
            b&l&n              wet
            k&m                teprak
            K&l&y
```

PROVERB -- Jabǿn kennan -- Jaben kennahan

    'Mǿkajkaji, jaljali,    'Mekajkajiy, jaɫjaɫiy,
    batbat.'    batbat.'

Roughly: 'Speed it up, unsnarl it, slow it down.'

    Equivalent: 'Haste makes waste.'

## VOCABULARY

| | | |
|---|---|---|
| ban | ban | unable, weak, tired, cannot |
| bat | bat | slow |
| bo | pew | arrive, lower sail--canoes and ships only |
| bwǿlen | b&l&n | perhaps, maybe |
| ekwe | yeqey | well |
| emman | ṁṁan | good |
| etke | yetkey | why |
| ikkure | qqir&y | play |
| iba | yippah | with me |
| ibam | yippaṁ | with you (sg.) |
| iben | yippan | with him (her, it) (3rd per. sg.) |
| ilju | yiljiw | tomorrow |
| in | yin | to, in order to, of, etc. (construct particle) |
| ilok | yilaq | go (away from both of us) |
| itok | yiteq | come (to me) |
| iwǿj | yiw&j | come, go (to you) |
| jab | jahab | no |
| jab | jab | not |
| jaljal | jaɫjaɫ | loosen, unwind, unsnarl |
| jerak | jerak | leave, hoist sail--canoes and ships only |
| jerbal | jerbal | work |
| jikul | jikiwiɫ | school |
| katak | kahtak | study |
| Kili | K&l&y | island in Rǟlik chain |
| lok | ɫaq | there |
| mǿkaj | ṁekaj | fast |
| naj | nahaj | will |
| Namu | Naṁ&w | atoll in Rǟlik chain |
| tar | tar | come, go, ride--of or on vessels or vehicles only |

31

| | | |
|---|---|---|
| tokeak | tekyak | arrive at, reach |
| tok | teq | here, to me--to the speaker |
| tutu | tiwtiw | bathe, wet |
| Utirik | Witr&k | Ratak Atoll |
| wöj | w&j | to you--to the addressee |
| wöt | wet | only, still, just, continue |

## LESSON FIVE

To and from; going with a
purpose; wearing clothes
and other things; arrivals
and departures

### DIALOGUE

A: KwȢj itok jen ia?   Qej yiteq jan yi'yah?

B: Ij itok jen Rita--   Yij yiteq jan Riytah--
   ak kwe, kwȢj etal    hak qey, qej yetal gan
   Han ia?              yi'yah?

A: Ij etal Han MIECO    Yij yetal gan Miyeykew
   in wia.              yin wiyah.

B: Ij iwȢj ibbam. KwȢj  Yij yiw&j yippaṁ. Qej
   kabbok ta?           kapp&q tah?

A: Ij kabbok jodri;     Yij kapp&q jewdiy; yelap
   elab an bwil Han     han bil gan jiwijwij.
   jujuj.

A: Where are you coming from?
B: I'm coming from Rita. And you, where are you
   going?
A: I'm going to MIECO to buy (something).
B: I'm coming with you. What are you looking for?
A: I'm looking for zories; it's too hot for shoes.

### DRILLS

1. Ij itok jen Rita.       Yij yiteq jan Riytah.
   <u>Kili</u>                     <u>K&l&y</u>
   Arno                    Harñew
   Jemo                    Jeymaw
   Mieco                   Miyeykew

2. Ij etal Han Mieco in    Yij yetal gan Miyeykew
   <u>wia</u>.                     yin <u>wiyah</u>.
   jerbal                  jerbal
   ikkure                  qqir&y
   mubi                    miwpiy
   mȢHȜ                    ṁegay

3. Ij etal Ħan Mieco in      Yij yetal gan Miyeykew
   wia jodri.                 yin wiyah jewdiy.
       binjel                     pinjel
       beba                       p&ybah
       nuknuk                     niqniq
       juj                        jiwij
       at                         hat
       jŭt                        jehet
       waj                        waj
       riĦ                        riyig
       mej                        maj
       kaĦir                      kagir

4. Inaj roltok in wia.       Yinahaj rawalteq yin
                                 wiyah.
   Inaj rolten wia.          Yinahaj rawalten
                                 wiyah.
       jerbal                    jerbal
       ikkure                    qqir&y
       mubi                      ḿiwpiy
       mŭĦŭ                      ḿegay

5. Elab an bwil Ħan          Yełap han bil gan
   jujuj.                        jiwijwij.
       atat                      hathat
       jŭtŭt                     jehethet
       kojoj                     kawajw&j
       takinkin                  takinkin
       mejmej                    majmaj
       riĦiĦ                     riyigyig
       wajwaj                    wajwaj
       nuknuk                    niqniq
       kaĦirĦir                  kagirgir

6. Ńe iroltok jen Hawaii,    Gey yirawalteq jan Hawah-
   inaj jujuj.                   yiy, yinahaj jiwijwij.
       atat                      hathat
       jŭtŭt                     jehethet
       wajwaj                    wajwaj
       riĦiĦ                     riyigyig
       mejmej                    majmaj
       kojoj                     kawajw&j
       takinkin                  takinkin
       jodri                     jewdiy
       jintŭb                    jint&b

   (Continue, substituting ye-, qe-, re-, etc. for
   yi- above.)

7. 'She is wearing...'

    Ej marmar lien.           Yej ṁarṁar liyeṅ.
       <u>beṅkůl</u>                  payagkeł
       driedre               diy&d&y
       jokankan             jewkankan
       jemij                 j&ym&j
       likko                 liqq&w
       nien-ittit           niyen-yittit
       kabirůrů             kabirehreh
       jakůlkůl             jakk&lk&l
       bujůk                 biwj&k
       kaḧajḧij             kagajg&j
       wutwut                witwit

8. 'She is going to buy...'

    Ej ilen wia <u>marmar</u>.      Yej yilan wiyah
                                       ṁarṁar.
       beṅkůl               payagkeł
       driedre               diy&d&y
       jokankan             jewkankan
       jemij                 j&ym&j
       likko                 liqq&w
       nien-ittit           niyen-yittit
       kabirůrů             kabirehreh
       jakůlkůl             jakk&lk&l

9. 'She is putting on her...'

    Lien ej konak(e)        Liyeṅ yej keṅak(ey)
    <u>jokankan</u> eo an.        <u>jewkankan</u> yew han.
    jemij                     j&ym&j
    likko                     liqq&w
    nien-ittit              niyen-yittit
    jakůlkůl                jakk&lk&l
    beṅkůl                  payagkeł

10. 'She is putting on (her)...' (Continued for exceptional items.) *(Teacher should use the underlined words as cues.)*

    Lien ej marůk(e) <u>marmar</u>    Liyeṅ yej ṁarek(ey)
    <u>eo</u> můran.                   ṁarṁar <u>yew</u> ṁeran.

    Lien ej diůk(e) <u>driedre</u>    Liyeṅ yej diyek(ey)
    <u>eo</u> dien.                    <u>diy&d&y</u> <u>yew</u> diyen.

    Lien ej <u>kabirůrůik</u>(i)     Liyeṅ yej <u>kabirehrehyik</u>-
    tien.                        (iy) tiyen.

Lien ej bujǫke boran.     Liyeñ yej biwjękęy beran.
Lien ej kañaj(e) bǫran.   Liyeñ yej kagaj(ey) beran.
Lien ej wutwut.           Liyeñ yej witwit.

11. 'He is wearing...'
    Ej jormǫta leen.        Yej jeṛṁetah ḷeyeñ.
       jiñlij                  jiyiglij
       jedoujij                jedawijij
       kadru-nen               kadiw-neyen
       tabtab                  tabtab
       ñi-ñat                  giy-gat
       nuknuk                  niqniq

12. 'He is going to buy...'
    Ej ilen wia jormǫta.    Yej yilan wiyah
                              jeṛṁetah.

*(Continue, substituting all the words from Drill 11.)*

13. 'He is putting on his...'
    Leen ej diǫk(e) binjel     Ḷeyeñ yej diyek(ey)
    eo an.                     pinjeḷ yew han.
    
    Leen ej marǫk(e) emmar     Ḷeyeñ yej ṁarek(ey)
    eo mǫran.                  ṁuṁar yew ṁeran.
    
    Leen ej kǫnak(e) mej       Ḷeyeñ yej keñak(ey)
    eo mejan.                  maj yew mejan.
    
    Leen ej kǫnak(e) ñi-       Ḷeyeñ yej keñak(ey)
    ñat eo ñin.                giy-gat yew giyin.
    
    Leen ej kǫnak(e) riñ       Ḷeyeñ yej keñak(ey)
    eo an.                     riyig yew han.
    at eo                      hat yew
    waj eo                     waj yew
    juj ko                     jiwij kew
    nuknuk ko                  niqniq kew
    jodri ko                   jewdiy kew
    jormǫta eo                 jeṛṁetah yew
    jiñlij eo                  jiyiglij yew
    jedoujij eo                jedawijij yew
    kadru-nen eo               kadiw-neyen yew
    tabtab eo                  tabtab yew

14. *(The underlined portions of the following sentences are cues for the teacher to give. The entire sentence is the desired response on the part of the student.)*

<u>Ej joktok ñāāt balun eo?</u>    <u>Yej jeqteq gayat baḷwin yew?</u>

Balun eo ej joktok <u>ñāāt?</u>    <u>Baḷwin yew</u> yej jeqteq gayat?

<u>Ñāāt eo</u> balun eo ej joktok?    <u>Gayat yew</u> baḷwin yew yej jeqteq?

<u>Enaj joktok</u> ñāāt balun eo?    <u>Yenahaj jeqteq</u> gayat baḷwin yew?

Balun eo <u>enaj joktok</u> ñāāt?    Baḷwin yew <u>yenahaj jeqteq</u> gayat?

<u>Ñāāt eo</u> balun eo <u>enaj joktok?</u>    <u>Gayat yew</u> baḷwin yew <u>yenahaj jeqteq?</u>

*(Run through parallel cues and responses, substituting the following verbs for* **joktok** *in the above sentences:)*

    ketok                             kayteq
    tŭkeaktok                     tekyakteq
    kelok                             kaylaq
    bellok                          peḷḷaq
    tŭbraktok                  teprakteq

15. *(Follow the procedure of Drill 14.)*

    Ej <u>botok</u> ñāāt wa eo?    Yej <u>pewteq</u> gayat wah yew?
        tartok                       tarteq
        itaktok                    yitahakteq
        tŭkeaktok               tekyakteq
        roltok                      rawalteq
        jeblaktok                jebḷahakteq
        tŭbraktok                teprakteq
        jeblak                      jeplahak
        jerak                        jerak

16. *(Follow the procedure of Drills 14 and 15.)*

    Ej <u>joklok</u> Kwajalein ñāāt balun eo?    Yej <u>jeqḷaq</u> Kiwajleyen gayat balwin yew?
        tŭkeaklok                tekyakḷaq
        itaklok                   yitahakḷaq
        tŭbraklok               teprakteq

|  |  |
|---|---|
| jeblaklok Ḣan | jebłahakłaq gan |
| rollok Ḣan | rawałłaq gan |

17. Ej <u>bolok</u> Laura ḢüḢt wa eo?   Yej <u>pewłaq</u> Łewrah gayat wah yew?
    tokeaklok        tekyakłaq
    itaklok          yitahakłaq
    tübraklok        teprakłaq

18. *(Practice answering the questions in Drills 14 through 17, using* <u>yiljiw</u> *'tomorrow'. For example:)*

    Yej jeqteq yiljiw.
    Yenahaj jeqłaq yiljiw.

19. Bonus drill--another use for <u>kenak</u>: 'I love you.' (You are all around me.)

    Ikünak yuk.            Yikeñak y&q.

## GRAMMATICAL NOTES

1. The vocabulary of this lesson again is large, but as in Lesson Three contains a number of loans which should reduce your memory burden. Most of these loans are articles of apparel. Some are both the name of the article and a verb meaning to wear the article. For others to form the verb for wearing we must repeat all or a portion of the word. This process, which linguists call 'reduplication', is a very important one in Marshallese, and you will meet it again serving other purposes in later lessons. Examples from this lesson include:

| wit | flower | witwit | wear a flower |
| hat | hat | hathat | wear a hat |
| riyig | ring | riyigyig | wear a ring |
| jiwij | shoe | jiwijwij | wear shoes |
| jehet | shirt | jehethet | wear a shirt |
| takin | socks | takinkin | wear socks |
| kagir | belt | kagirgir | wear a belt |
| waj | watch | wajwaj | wear a watch |

From these examples it is clear that only the final syllable is involved in this type of reduplication. To distinguish it from several other types, we will refer to it as FINAL-SYLLABLE REDUPLICATION. The words <u>kagajg&j</u> and <u>kawajw&j</u> are also formed by reduplication but are complicated by vowel changes too

complex to be discussed here. What you should take
from this discussion is a general feeling for how
final-syllable reduplication works in Marshallese;
it will afford you many insights into the grammar of
the language as you proceed.

2. Drills 10 and 13 introduce a number of new grammatical patterns, and you may wish to skip them until the more general patterns of the lesson have been learned. Some of the grammatical complications include:

(a) Special transitive forms like keṅak(ey), ṁarek(ey), diyek(ey), kagaj(ey), kabirehrehyik(iy), and biwjæk&y. In later lessons you will see that many verbs have special transitive forms like these, and you will learn more about where they can or must be used.

(b) Some more possessive words like those introduced in Lesson Three: ṁeran, diyen, tiyen, beran, and mejan. Whereas tiye- refers only to lips and bera- to head, the others can refer to several different objects (for example, mera- to both necklaces and fish baskets) and thereby take on a classifying function as did the possessives introduced earlier.

(c) In Drill 13, the kew occurring after niqniq, jiwij and jewdiy is the plural form of yew for non-humans, and comes from a large set of demonstrative or locational words which will be discussed at length in Lesson Eight. For the moment you should memorize the sentences of Drills 10 and 13 as wholes. These will then provide an internalized basis for grammatical insights that will come to you gradually.

3. Drills 14 through 17 provide more practice on the use of directionals with the movement of planes and surface vessels. They are also designed to give a feel for optional variations in word order. Be careful to distinguish the two words spelled *jeblak*. The phonetic spelling shows the two points at which they differ.

## SOUND DRILL

We have practiced the æ - e distinction in environments before light and before heavy consonants. Let us now practice the same distinction in the environment before rounded consonants where these two vowels have two different [o]-like sounds.

|     | æ      |                      |     | e      |                                    |
| --- | ------ | -------------------- | --- | ------ | ---------------------------------- |
| to  | tæw    | 'down; to get off'   | to  | tew    | 'channel, pass'                    |
| no  | ñæw    | 'stone fish'         | no  | ñew    | 'wave'                             |
| ko  | kæw    | 'escape'             | ko  | kew    | 'plural particle; inanimate'       |
| jojo| jæwjæw | 'little chicken'     | jojo| jewjew | 'flying fish'                      |
| buk | bæq    | 'book; blister'      | bok | beq    | 'sand; sandspit'                   |

Other examples of these two sounds you have already met include:

      yæq                        yiteq
      jamḃæw                   Harñew
      Nam̃æw                   jewdiy
      kappæq                   Miyeykew
      Jalwæj                   Ɫewrah
      Hayæłæq                 Yepwen

<u>PROVERB</u>

    Kwojab ḑlkoj pein ak.     Qejab yalqej pæyin hak.

Literally: Don't bend the wing of the frigate bird.

Equivalent: Don't bite the hand that feeds you.

<u>VOCABULARY</u>

| ak     | hak          | frigate bird--*iroij in bao*--king of the birds |
| ------ | ------------ | ----------------------------------------------- |
| an     | han          | his, her, its (general possessive)              |
| Arno   | Harñew       | Ratak Atoll                                     |
| at     | hat          | hat (from *hat*)                                |
| atat   | hathat       | wear a hat                                      |
| ḑlkoj  | yalqej       | bend                                            |
| balun  | bałwin       | airplane (from *balloon* (dirigible))           |
| bel-   | pal-         | (with directionals) fly, glide, jump, wave (of flags) |
| beñkḑl | payaǵkeł     | (wear a) bracelet (from *bangle*)               |
| bḑran  | beran, bera- | his (her, its) head                             |
| bujḑk  | biwjæk       | wear hair in a knot                             |
| bujḑke | biwjækæy     | tie hair (transitive)                           |

| | | |
|---|---|---|
| bwil | bil | hot, burning |
| diɵk(e) | diyek(ey) | (wear) something on ear (transitive) |
| driedre | diy&d&y | (wear) something on ear, earring |
| elab | yełap | be big, great (3rd per. sg.) |
| emmar | m̄ar, m̄era- | fish basket |
| itak | yitahak | bump, touch |
| jakɵlkɵl | jakk&lk&l | (wear) panties |
| jeblak | jebłahak | return |
| jeblak | jeplahak | sail away |
| jedoujij | jedawijij | (wear) trousers--short or long (from *trousers*) |
| jemij | j&ym&j | (wear a) slip (from *chemise*) |
| Jemo | Jeymaw | uninhabited atoll near Likiep --sanctuary for birds and turtles |
| jen | jan | from, than |
| jintɵb | jint&b | go barefoot; eat only one thing |
| jiHlij | jiyiglij | (wear an) undershirt |
| jodri | jewdiy | zories--Japanese 'go-ahead' slippers with thongs between toes |
| jok | jeq | alight, land, settle down on surface |
| jokankan | jewkankan | (wear a) dress |
| jormɵta | jełm̄etah | (wear) undershorts |
| jɵt | jehet | shirt (from *shirt*) |
| jɵtɵt | jehethet | wear a shirt |
| juj | jiwij | shoes (from *shoes*; note however that <u>jiwij</u> is not a plural in Marshallese) |
| jujuj | jiwijwij | wear shoes |
| kabbok | kapp&k | look for |
| kabirɵrɵ | kabirehreh | (wear) lipstick (from <u>birehreh</u> red) |
| kadru-nen | kadiw-neyen | (wear) short trousers ('short-its legs') |
| kaHaj(e) | kagaj(ey) | make it fragrant (transitive) |
| kaHajHij | kagajg&j | have perfume on (from <u>gaj</u> fragrant) |
| kaHir | kagir | belt |
| kaHirHir | kagirgir | wear a belt |
| ke- | key- | (plus directionals) jump, fly |
| ko | kew | the (plural of *eo* <u>yew</u>--non-humans) |

| | | |
|---|---|---|
| kŭnak(e) | keñak(ey) | put on, become surrounded by, love |
| koj | kawaj | blanket |
| kojoj | kawajw&j | use a blanket |
| leen | łeyeñ | that man, boy |
| lien | liyeñ | that woman, girl |
| likko | liqq&w | (wear a) half-slip |
| marmar | ṁarṁar | (wear a) necklace |
| marŭk(e) | ṁarek(ey) | wear a necklace or fish basket (transitive) |
| mej | mejan, meja- | eye, face, (sun) glasses |
| mejmej | majmaj | wear glasses |
| mŭran | ṁeran | his fish basket, her necklace |
| MIECO, Mieco | Miyeykew | Marshall Islands Import Export Company |
| mŭṅŭ | ṁegay | food, eat |
| mubi | ṁiwpiy | movie, see a movie |
| nien-ittit | niyen-yittit | bra (container for breasts) (Ratak: niyen-tittit) |
| nuknuk | niqniq | cloth, (wear) clothing |
| ñi-ñat | giy-gat | (wear) false teeth ('teeth-palate') |
| pein | p&yin, p&yi-(pay) | his, (her, its) hand, arm, wing |
| riñ | riyig | ring (from *ring*) |
| riñiñ | riyigyig | wear a ring |
| ta | tah | what? |
| tabtab | tabtab | (wear) long trousers |
| takin | takin | socks (from *stocking*) |
| takinkin | takinkin | wear socks |
| tien | tiyen, tiye- | his, (her, its) lips |
| tŭbrak | teprak | achieve, reach--a goal or destination |
| waj | waj | (a) watch |
| wajwaj | wajwaj | wear a watch (from *watch*) |
| wia | wiyah | buy (or sell) |
| wut | wit | flower, flowering shrub |
| wutwut | witwit | wear flowers |

## LESSON SIX

Names; ages; numbers;
telling time; days of
the week, months of
the year; some demonstratives

### DIALOGUE

A: Etam?  Yetaṁ?
B: Eta in Ali.  Yetah yin Haɫiy.
A: Jete am iiȣ?  Jetey haṁ 'yiyeh?
B: Roḧoul-ruo, ak kwe?  R&g&wil riwew, hak qey?
A: Eta in Timȣj. Joḧoul-ruo aȣ iiȣ.  Yetah yin Tiyṁej. J&g&wil riwew hah&h 'yiyeh.
B: Kwȣj jikul ke?  Qej jikiwiɫ key?
A: Aet, ij jikul ilo jikul en an kien.  Hay&t, yij jikiwiɫ yilew jikiwiɫ yeṅ han kiyen.

A: What is your name?
B: My name is Ali.
A: How old are you?
B: Twenty-two -- and you?
A: My name is Timos. I'm twelve.
B: Do you go to school?
A: Yes. I go to the government school.

### DRILLS

1. Practice counting in chorus, individually, and individuals in succession around the class. *(See the REFERENCE section.)*

2. Practice the days of the week in similar fashion.

3. Practice the months of the year.

4. *(Teacher holds up a certain number of fingers.)*

Jete eo adri?  Jetey yew haddiy?

*(Sample answer:)*
Ruo.  Riwew.

5. *(Teacher writes an arabic numeral on blackboard, indicating desired answer.)*

    Jete beij in buk ne am?      Jetey peyij yin b&q hey haṁ?

    *(Sample answer:)*
    Rubuki.     Ribiqiy.

    Jete alen in buk ne am?     Jetey halenin b&q hey ham?

    Jibuki.     Jibiqiy.
    *(half the number of pages)*

6. *(Teacher draws clock face on blackboard and points to an hour.)*

    Jete awa kiʊ?     Jetey hawah kiyyeh?

    *(Sample answer:)*
    Joħoul awa kiʊ.     J&g&wil hawah kiyyeh.

7. *(Teacher writes a time on the board.)*

    Jete awa kiʊ?     Jetey hawah kiyyeh?

    *(Sample answer:)*
    (10:10) Joħoul minit jen joħoul.     J&g&wil minit jan j&g&wil.

    Joħoul minit elikin joħoul.     J&g&wil minit yalikin j&g&wil.

    Emotlok joħoul minit jen joħoul.     Yemewetłaq j&g&wil minit jan j&g&wil.

    ( 9:50) Joħoul minit ħan joħoul.     J&g&wil minit gan j&g&wil.

    Mʊttan joħoul ħan joħoul.     Mettan j&g&wil gan j&g&wil.

    Limħoul minit jen ruatimjuʊn.     L&mg&wil minit jan riwatim-jiwen.

    ( 9:30) Ruatimjuʊn jimettan.     Riwatim-jiwen jimettan.

    Ruatimjuʊn awa jimettan.     Riwatim-jiwen hawah jimettan.

    (12:00) Joħoul-ruo awa lukon-boħ.     J&g&wil-riwew hawah liqen-b&ǧ.

    JoHoul-ruo awa
     raeleb.

    (12:30) JoHoul-ruo
     awa jimettan elikin
     raeleb.

    JoHoul-ruo awa
     jimettan elikin
     lukon-boH.

    ( 6:00) Jiljino awa
     jibboH.

    Jiljino awa jota.

    ( 5:00) Lalim awa
     jorantak.

    J&g&wil-riwew hawah
     rahyelep.

    J&g&wil-riwew hawah
     jimettan yalikin
     rahyelep.

    J&g&wil-riwew hawah
     jimettan yalikin
     liqen-b&ǧ.

    Jiljinew hawah
     jibb&ǧ.

    Jiljinew hawah j&wtah.

    Ƚal&m hawah jewrahantak.

8. Jete am iiÖ?

    *(Sample answer:)*
    JilHul aÖ iiÖ.

    Jetey haṁ 'yiyeh?

    Jilgiwil hah&h 'yiyeh.

9. Ñäät eo kwar lotak?

    *(Sample answer:)*
    Maj ruHoul-juÖn ran,
     juÖn taujin
     ruatimjuÖn-buki
     eHoul-juÖn.

    Gayat yew qehar letak?

    Mahaj r&g&wil-jiwen
     rahan, jiwen tawijin
     riwahtim-jiwen-biqiy
     y&g&wil-jiwen.

10. Ñäät eo kwar itok
     Han MajÖl?

    *(Sample answer:)*
    Tijemba, juÖn taujin
     ruatimjuÖn-buki
     jiljino-Houl-jiljino.

    Gayat yew qehar yiteq
     gan Mahjel?

    Tiyjeṁbah, jiwen tawijin
     riwahtimjiwen-biqiy
     jiljin&w-g&wil-jiljinew.

11. Ñäät eo kwar driojlok
     jen jikul.

    *(Sample answer:)*
    JuÖn taujin ruatimjuÖn-
     buki jiljino-Houl
     lalim.

    Gayat yew qehar diyw&jɫaq
     jan jikiwil?

    Jiwen tawijin riwahtim-
     jiwen-biqiy jiljin&w-
     g&wil Ƚal&m.

12. Practice simple addition.

    Ruo im ruo, emen.

    JuHoul im juHoul,
     ruHoul.

    Riwew yim riwew, yeman.

    J&g&wil yim j&g&wil,
     r&g&wil.

13. Practice simple subtraction.
    Emen bʉk ruo, ruo.  Yeman bek riwew, riwew.
    Ruḧoul bʉk juḧoul, juḧoul.  R&g&wil bek j&g&wil, j&g&wil.

    Ruo jen emen, ruo.  Riwew jan yeman, riwew.
    Juḧoul jen ruḧoul, juḧoul.  J&g&wil jan r&g&wil, j&g&wil.

14. Practice simple multiplication.
    Ruo alen ruo, emen.  Riwew halen riwew, yeman.
    Juḧoul alen juḧoul, jibuki.  J&g&wil halen j&g&wil, jibiqiy.

15. Practice simple division.
    Emen ajij ruo, ruo.  Yeman hajy&j riwew, riwew.
    Jibuki ajij juḧoul, juḧoul.  Jibiqiy hajy&j j&g&wil, j&g&wil.

16. Practice answering questions like the following.
    Jete drijikul ilo kilaj in?  Jetey rijikiwił yilew kilhaj yin?
    Lalim.  Ɬal&m.

    Jete ladrik ilo kilaj in? (etc.)  Jetey ładdik yilew kilhaj yin? (etc.)

    Jete ledrik ilo kilaj in?  Jetey leddik yilew kilhaj yin?

    Jete jea ilo rum in?  Jetey jeyah yilew riwiḣ yin?

    Jete wintʉ'n rum in?  Jetey wintehen riwiḣ yin?

    Jete kejamin rum in?  Jetey kejamin riwiḣ yin?

    Jete *blackboard* ilo rum in?  Jetey biłyak-bewet yilew riwiḣ yin?

    Jete teḧki jarom ilo rum in? (etc.)  Jetey teyegkiy jaɽem yilew riwiḣ yin? (etc.)

17. Substitution

    Ij jikul ilo <u>jikul en</u>    Yij jikiwił yilew <u>jikiwił</u>
    <u>an kien</u>.    <u>yeñ han kiyen</u>.
    jikul en an katlik    jikiwił yeñ han katlik
    jikul en an birotijen    jikiwił yeñ han birew-
                              tiyjen
    jikul en an bata    jikiwił yeñ han bahtah
    jikul en an *mission*    jikiwił yeñ han miyjen

18. Practice asking and answering questions like the following.

    Etan leen?    Yetan łeyeñ?
        Etan in Tom.        Yetan yin Tawañ.

    Etan lien?    Yetan liyeñ?
        Etan in Meri.        Yetan yin Meydiy.

    Jete an iiö?    Jetey han 'yiyeh?
        Ruħoul-ruo an iiö.        R&g&wil-riwew han 'yiyeh.

    Ej jokwe ia?    Yej j&q&y yi'yah?
        (I) Rita.        (Yiy) Riytah.

    Ej jikul ke?    Yej jikiwił key?
        Aet.        Hay&t.

    Ej jikul ia?    Yej jikiwił yi'yah?
        Ilo jikul en an kien.        Yilew jikiwił yeñ han
                              kiyen.

    Ej jerebal ke?    Yej jerbal key?
        Aet.        Hay&t.

    Ej jerebal ia?    Yej jerbal yi'yah?
        MIECO.        Miyeykew.
        Iben kien.        Yippan kiyen.
        Iben Robert.        Yippan Rewbet.

    Ta jerebal eo an?    Tah jerbal yew han?
        Dri kaki.        Rikakiy.
        Dri wia.        Riwiyah.

    Ej etal ħan ia kiö?    Yej yetal gan yi'yah
                                  kiyyeh?
    Ej etal ħan MIECO.    Yej yetal gan Miyeykew.

    Etam le?    Yetañ łey?
        Eta in Tom.        Yetah yin Tawañ.

    Etam le?    Yetañ ley?
        Eta in Meri.        Yetah yin Meydiy.

48

    Kar etan ḷt eo etarro?    Kar yetan yat yew
                                       yetarrew?
    Tom.                           Tawaṁ.
    Jete am iiṻ?               Jetey haṁ 'yiyeh?
    Ruḧoul aṻ iiṻ.           R&g&wil hah&h 'yiyeh.
    (etc.)                        (etc.)

19. Answer questions like the following with possessive pronouns.

    An wṻn buk e?            Han wen b&q y&y?
    Am buk ne.                 Haṁ b&q ṅey.
    Aṻ buk ne.                 Hah&h b&q ṅey.
    An buk ne.                 Han b&q ṅey.
    An wṻn binjel e?         Han wen pinjeḷ y&y?
      An Tom binjel ne.      Han Tawaṁ pinjeḷ ṅey.
    An wṻn beba e?          Han wen p&ybah y&y?
      Ijaje an wṻn beba ne.    Yijahj&y han wen p&ybah
                                      ṅey.
    An wṻn jea e?            Han wen jeyah y&y?
    (etc.)                        (etc.)

20. Practice answering questions like the following, using *mot* and *jako*.

    Eber ia Tom?              Yepad yi'yah Tawaṁ?
      Emotlok.                 Yemewetḷaq.
      Emottok.                 Yemewetteq.
      Emotwṻj.                 Yemewetw&j.
      Ejako.                     Yejak&w.

GRAMMATICAL NOTES

1. Names play a much different role in Marshallese culture than they do in our own. Names are not usually mentioned in greetings, and are rarely used in the presence of the individual. They may be used by parents in calling children, and by teachers or church elders in calling roll. First names are often inherited from deceased grandparents, and surnames are normally the first name of one's father. One never asks a surname directly, and even first names are usually asked obliquely, as in Drill 18 'What was the name of us two?'. Thus the dialogue of this lesson actually starts off in very un-Marshallese fashion with *Etam?*, but this does occur today as the two

cultures meet--for example when a patient visits the Public Health Clinic at the District Center.

2. The numbers from six through nine by virtue of their length alone seem to be fossilized compounds, and there is enough formal resemblance to tempt one to try an analysis. Seven can be thought of as 'three-three and one', eight as 'two (fours?)...' and nine as "two fours and one'. Be sure to note the similarities and differences among respective units, decades, and hundreds; for example: 1, 10, and 100.

3. In this and the preceding lesson you have met several words which when unsuffixed have one syllable with the vowel a, but which change this a to e when a suffix is added after the a that appears in the second syllable:

| Without suffix | Meaning | With Suffix | Stem |
|---|---|---|---|
| bar | head | beran | bara- |
| (ṁ)ṁar | necklace, fishbasket | ṁeran | ṁara- |
| maj | eye | mejan | maja- |
| yat | name | yetan | yata- |

There seems to be a general rule in Marshallese that prohibits certain sequences of a...a and changes the first to e. Thus words like the above can be considered as having stems as given in the fourth column. When they remain unsuffixed, the stem-final a is dropped, there are no longer two a's in sequence, and the first vowel remains a. But when they are suffixed and the stem-final vowel is retained, the first a is forced to change by the rule that prohibits a...a sequences.

4. The words y&y, yin, ṅey, yeṅ, yew are part of a complex demonstrative-locational system which will be learned and discussed fully in Lesson Eight. As with the directionals discussed in Grammatical Note 3 of Lesson Four, your biggest task for the moment will be to distinguish the environs of the addressee (ṅey) from those further out (yeṅ). Note that the yin of this set (as in yetah yin) is a different word from yin the construct particle. The portion of the system you have met thus far can be viewed as follows:

| | | |
|---|---|---|
| y&y | | this here (close to me) |
| yin | | this here (close to both of us) |
| ɦey | | that there (close to you) |
| yeɦ | | that there (close to neither of us) |
| yew | | the (out of sight, in the past) |

## SOUND DRILLS

Make sure you can hear the difference between i, e, and &.

1. In light environments:

| | | |
|---|---|---|
| ki | kiy | 'key' |
| ke | k&y | 'porpoise' |
| ke | key | 'question particle' |
| mi | miy | 'syllable of the musical scale: ''mi''' |
| me | m&y | 'fortress' |
| me | mey | 'that, which' |
| it | yit | 'to make fire by friction' |
| it | y&t | 'do what?' |
| eta | yetah | 'my name' |

2. In heavy environments:

| | | |
|---|---|---|
| aʉ | hahih | 'to die' |
| aʉ | hah&h | 'my, mine' |
| aʉ | haheh | 'to swim' |
| wit | wit | 'flower' |
| wʉt | w&t | 'rain' |
| wʉt | wet | 'only' |

3. In rounded environments:

| | | |
|---|---|---|
| tu | tiw | 'gizzard' |
| to | t&w | 'down; to get off' |
| to | tew | 'channel, pass' |
| bu | piw | 'stuffed from overeating' |
| bo | p&w | 'falling of ripe pandanus key' |
| bo | pew | 'second story' |

## PROVERB

Juʉn jot, ruo mule.     Jiwen jewet, riwew ṁil&y.

  Literally: 'One missile, two doves.'

  Equivalent: 'Kill two birds with one stone.'

## VOCABULARY

| | | |
|---|---|---|
| adri | haddiy, haddiyi- | finger, toe, digit |
| alen | halen | time(s), rows, stories of building, sheets of paper |
| ajij | hajy&j | divide, divide up, distribute |
| ät | yat, yeta- | name |
| awa | hawah | hour |
| bata | bahtah | priest, Father (from English) |
| beij | peyij | page (from English) |
| bök | bek | take, bring, carry |
| boħ | b&ǵ | night, last night |
| brotijen | birewtiyjen | Protestant (from English) |
| buk | b&q | book (from English) |
| dri | ri- | person of, person from, person who |
| dri kaki | rikakiy | preacher, teacher |
| driojlok | diyw&jlaq | go out, graduate |
| e | y&y | this here (close to me) |
| elikin | yalikin | after, its back, behind it |
| en | yeń | that there (close to neither me nor you) |
| eta (-m; -n) | yetah (-m; -n) | my name (your; his, her) |
| etarro | yetarrew | the name of the two of us |
| in | yin | this here (close to both of us) |
| iiö | 'yiyeh | year (from English) |
| ilo | yilew (Ratak) yil&w (Rälik) | in, at |
| jako | jak&w | missing, gone--destination and location unknown |
| jarom | jałem | lightning, electric(ity) |
| jea | jeyah | chair (from English) |
| jete | jetey | how many? |
| jibboħ | jibb&ǵ | morning |
| jimettan | jimettan | half |
| jokwe | j&q&y | live, dwell |
| jorantak | jewrahantak | dawn |
| jot | jewet | bullet, missile, something for throwing |

| | | |
|---|---|---|
| jota | j&wtah | evening |
| katlik | katlik | Catholic (from English) |
| kejam | kejam | door(way) |
| kejamin | kejamin | its door(s) (<u>kejam</u> fused with construct particle) |
| kien | kiyen, kiye- | government, law, commandment |
| kilaj | kilhaj | class (from English) |
| kiǔ | kiyyeh (Rǚl.) kiyin (Rat.) | now |
| kwar | qehar | you were, you did (2nd per. sg. subject prefix plus <u>har</u> past tense) |
| ladrik | ɬaddik | boy |
| ladik eo | ɬadik yew | the boy |
| le | ɬey | sir |
| le | ley | ma'am |
| ledrik | leddik | girl |
| ledik eo | ledik yew | the girl |
| lotak | ɬetak | be born |
| lukon | liqen, liqe- | middle of |
| lukon-boh | liqen-b&ǰ | midnight |
| Majǔl | Mahjel | Marshall (Islands) (from English) |
| minit | minit | minute(s) (from English) |
| mot | mewet | gone, came--movement completed and location known |
| mǔttan | ṁeṭtan, ṁetta- | piece of, part of |
| mule | ṁilǎy | dove |
| ne | ñey | that there (close to you) |
| raeleb | rahyelep | noon |
| rum | riwiṁ | room (from English) |
| teħki | teyegkiy | flashlight |
| teħki jarom | teyegkiy jaɬem | electric light |
| wintǔ | winteh | window (from English) |
| wintǔ'n | wintehen | window of (<u>winte</u> fused with construct particle) |
| wǔn | wen | who? |

REFERENCE

| | | |
|---|---|---|
| 1 | juɵn | jiwen |
| 2 | ruo | riwew |
| 3 | jilu | jiliw |
| 4 | emen | yeman |
| 5 | lalim | łal&m |
| 6 | jiljino | jiljinew (or jiljin&w) |
| 7 | jiljilimjuɵn | jiljilim-jiwen (or jijilim-jiwen) |
| 8 | rualitɵk | riwahliyt&k |
| 9 | ruatimjuɵn | riwahtim-jiwen |
| 10 | joɦoul | j&g&wil |
| 11 | joɦoul-juɵn | j&g&wil-jiwen |
| 12 | joɦoul-ruo | j&g&wil-riwew |
| 20 | roɦoul | r&g&wil |
| 30 | jilɦul | jilgiwil |
| 40 | eɦoul | y&g&wil |
| 50 | limɦoul | l&mg&wil |
| 60 | jiljino-ɦoul | jiljin&w-g&wil |
| 100 | jibuki | jibiqiy |
| 111 | jibuki-joɦoul-juɵn | jibiqiy-j&g&wil-jiwen |
| 200 | rubuki | ribiqiy |
| 300 | jilubuki | jil(iw)biqiy |
| 400 | ɇbuki | yabiqiy |
| 500 | limabuki | limabiqiy |
| 600 | jiljino-buki | jiljinew-biqiy |
| 1000 | juɵn-taujin | jiwen-tawijin |

## Days of the week

| | |
|---|---|
| Mandre | Mandey |
| Juje | Jiwjey |
| Wɵnje | Wenjey |
| Taije | Tahyijey |
| Bɵlaidre | Bełahyidey |
| Jedredre | Jadeydey |
| Jabɵt | Jabet |

## Months of the year

| | |
|---|---|
| Janodre | Janewdey |
| Bebodre | Papewdey |
| Maj | Mahaj |
| Aperɵl | Yepereł |
| Mɇe | May&y |
| Jun | Jiwin |
| Julae | Jiwłahyey |
| Okoj | Waqej |

Jebötemba     Jebtembah
Okotoba       Wektewbah
Nobemba       Newbembah
Tijemba       Tiyjembah

## LESSON SEVEN

Time expressions--from the year
before the year before last to
the year after next

DIALOGUE

A: Jete awa kiʊ?            Jetey hawah kiyyeh?

B: Ruo awa.                Riwew hawah.

A: Jete awa ien kemem?      Jetey hawah 'yiyen
                                         keyemyem?

B: Rar ba lalim awa          Rehar bah łal&m hawah
     jimettan.                   jimettan.

A: Enaj jemlok ǂǂǂt?         Yenahaj jeṁłaq gayat.

B: Iar roǂ ke enaj jemlok    Yihar reǧ key yenahaj
     lukon buǂnin.             jeṁłaq liqen biǧniyin.

A: What time is it?
B: Two o'clock.
A: What time is the party?
B: They said 5:30.
A: What time will it be over?
B: I heard it will finish at midnight.

DRILLS

1. Jenaj kemem             Jenahaj keyemyem
    <u>lalim awa jimettan.</u>      <u>łal&m hawah jimettan.</u>
    ǂe ejibboǂ                gey yejibb&ǧ
    ǂe eraeleb               gey yerahyeleb
    ǂe ejota                  gey y&j&wtah
    jotenin                   jawt&yniyin
    ǂe eboǂ                   gey y&b&ǧ
    buǂnin                    biǧniyin
    lukon buǂnin            liqen biǧniyin
    ǂe ejorantak           gey yejewrahantak
    ǂe eran                   gey yerahan

*(In Drills 2 and 3, substitute the expressions
from Drill 1.)*

2. Enaj roltok <u>lalim awa</u>    Yenahaj rawalteq <u>łal&m
    <u>jimettan.</u>                 hawah jimettan.</u>

3. Enaj jemlok <u>lalim awa</u>　　Yenahaj jeṁłaq <u>łal&m</u>
　　jimettan.　　　　　　　　　 hawah jimettan.

4. Ij roḧ ke enaj jemlok　　　 Yij reǧ key yenahaj jeṁłaq
　　<u>ilju ej jibboḧ.</u>　　　　　　 <u>yiljiw yej jibb&ǧ.</u>
　　ilju ej jota　　　　　　　　　yiljiw yej j&wtah
　　ilju ej raeleb　　　　　　　　yiljiw yej rahyelep
　　ilju ej jorantak　　　　　　　yiljiw yej jewrahantak

5. Ej iuwe <u>rainin</u> ḧan　　　　Yej wiw&y <u>rahyinyin</u> gan
　　Kwajalein.　　　　　　　　　 Kiwajleyen.
　　　　buḧnin　　　　　　　　　　　 biǧniyin
　　　　jotenin　　　　　　　　　　　jawt&yniyin
　　　　jibboḧnin　　　　　　　　　　jibb&ǧniyin
　　　　tireb in　　　　　　　　　　 tiryep yin
　　　　tima in　　　　　　　　　　　tiṁah yin
　　　　balun in　　　　　　　　　　 bałwin yin
　　　　wik in　　　　　　　　　　　 wiyik yin
　　　　alliḧ　　　　　　　　　　　　hall&g yin
　　　　iiʊ in　　　　　　　　　　　 'yiyeh yin
　　　　jʊmar in　　　　　　　　　　 jaṁar yin
　　　　rak in　　　　　　　　　　　 rak yin
　　　　aḧan-eaḧ in　　　　　　　　　hagan-yag yin
　　　　Kirijmʊj in　　　　　　　　　Kirijṁ&j yin
　　　　Ijitʊ in　　　　　　　　　　 Yijiteh yin
　　　　U. N. Day in　　　　　　　　 Yiwyent&y yin
　　　　New Year in　　　　　　　　　Niwiyyeh yin
　　　　Tijemba in　　　　　　　　　 Ṭiyjeṁbah yin
　　　　Mandre　　　　　　　　　　　 Mandey yin

6. *(Using the correct responses for Drill 5 as cues, change each to refer to the comparable unit of time immediately preceding. Be sure to change the verb phrase to agree.)*

<u>Cue:</u>
　　Ej iuwe rainin ḧan　　　　　　Yej wiw&y rahyinyin gan
　　Kwajalein.　　　　　　　　　　 Kiwajleyen.
<u>Response:</u>
　　Ear iuwe inne ḧan　　　　　　 Yehar wiw&y yinney gan
　　Kwajalein.　　　　　　　　　　 Kiwajleyen.

<u>Cue:</u>
　　Ej iuwe buḧnin ḧan　　　　　　Yej wiw&y biǧniyin gan
　　Kwajalein.　　　　　　　　　　 Kiwajleyen.
<u>Response:</u>
　　Ear iuwe boḧ ḧan　　　　　　　Yehar wiw&y b&ǧ gan
　　Kwajalein.　　　　　　　　　　 Kiwajleyen.
　　*(etc.)*　　　　　　　　　　　  *(etc.)*

7. *(Using the correct responses for Drill 6 as cues, change each to refer to the next earlier unit of time.)*

Cue:
   Ear iuwe inne Ħan          Yehar wiw&y yinney gan
     Kwajalein.                     Kiwajleyen.
Response:
   Ear iuwe inne eo lok          Yehar wiw&y yinney yew
     juőn Ħan Kwajalein.         łaq jiwen gan Kiwajleyen.
     *(etc.)*                            *(etc.)*

8. *(Repeat Drills 6 and 7, this time making the RESPONSES negative and not repeating the place.)*

Cue:
   Ej iuwe rainin Ħan           Yej wiw&y rahyinyin gan
     Kwajalein.                     Kiwajleyen.
Response:
   Ear jab iuwe inne.            Yehar jab wiw&y yinney.
     *(etc.)*                            *(etc.)*

9. *(Using the correct responses for Drill 6 as cues, change each to refer to the comparable unit of time in the present, making the response negative and omitting the place.)*

Cue:
   Ear iuwe inne Ħan          Yehar wiw&y yinney gan
     Kwajalein.                     Kiwajleyen.
Response:
   Ejjab iuwe rainin.            Yejjab wiw&y rahyinyin.

10. *(Substitute Enaj (<u>Yenahaj</u>) for Ej (<u>Yej</u>) in Drill 5.)*

11. *(Substitute Eban (<u>Yeban</u>) for Ej (<u>Yej</u>) in Drill 5.)*

12. *(Using the correct responses for Drill 5 as cues, give a double response, first substituting Eban <u>Yeban</u> for Ej <u>Yej</u> then substituting Enaj (<u>Yenahaj</u>) and changing the time unit to the comparable one NEXT in time (omitting the place).)*

Cue:
   Ej iuwe rainin Ħan           Yej wiw&y rahyinyin gan
     Kwajalein.                     Kiwajleyen.

Response:
    Eban iuwe rainin Ḧan Kwajalein; enaj iuwe ilju.

    Yeban wiw&y rahyinyin gan Kiwajleyen; yenahaj wiw&y yiljiw.

13. *(Make this drill parallel to Drill 12, but advance each time unit in the double response one degree more into the future. Use the responses to Drill 10 as cues.)*

Cue:
    Enaj iuwe rainin Ḧan Kwajalein.

    Yenahaj wiw&y rahyinyin gan Kiwajleyen.

Response:
    Eban iuwe ilju Ḧan Kwajalein; enaj iuwe jŭklaj.

    Yeban wiw&y yiljiw gan Kiwajleyen; yenahaj wiw&y jekłaj.

14. *(Substitute appropriate time expressions into frames such as the following:)*

    Enaj roltok _____.    Yenahaj rawalteq _____.

    Jenaj bar lo dron _____.    Jenahaj bar lew dewen _____.

    Ear tŭkeak tok _____.    Yehar tekyak teq _____.

    Ear mare _____.    Yehar ḿarey _____.

15. *(Go back to Drills 10 through 12 of LESSON FOUR and create new responses using appropriate time expressions you have learned in this lesson.)*

    *(Use as cues the time clauses from Drill 1 that contain Ḧe e- (gey ye-), and change these to past tense by substituting ar (har) for naj (nahaj), and ke ej (key yej) for Ḧe e- (ney ye-). Do the same for Drills 2 and 3.)*

Cue:
    Jenaj kemem Ḧe ejibboḧ.    Jenahaj keyemyem gey yejibb&ǵ.

Response:
    Jar kemem ke ej jibboḧ.    Jehar keyemyem key yej jibb&ǵ.

Cue:
    Enaj roltok ħe eraeleb.    Yenahaj rawalteq gey
                                                    yerahyelep.
Response:
    Ear roltok ke ej            Yehar rawalteq key yej
      raeleb.                                rahyelep.

GRAMMATICAL NOTES

1. Note the use of <u>key</u> to introduce dependent clauses following independent ones with -<u>j</u> or <u>har</u> in the last line of the dialogue and in Drills 4 and 16; note how this contrasts with the use of <u>gey</u> following <u>nahaj</u> in Drill 1, 2, 3 and 16. Note also the contrast between -<u>j</u> following <u>key</u> and its absence following <u>gey</u> in Drill 16. Do not try to formulate rules for matters such as these yet; at this point you have insufficient evidence. The best strategy is simply to memorize or internalize thoroughly each such pattern in order to begin to gain a feeling for how the language works rather than a set of complex conscious rules. The former is common to those who speak a language; the latter to grammarians who do not.

2. Note the complex vowel changes in the word for *evening*:

        j&wtah                evening
        jewtah               last evening
        jawt&yniyin        this evening
        jawtiyin            evening of (with
                                     construct particle)

3. The reference section contains a summary of the time expressions drilled in this lesson and even more complex ones as well. These (with two exceptions for 'dawn') are constructions of a phrase type:

    rahyelepen yiljiw        'noon of tomorrow'

Drill 4 contains a few examples of an alternative clause type:

    yiljiw yej rahyelep      'tomorrow it is noon'

You can construct other clause-type expressions on this same model:

              yinney yej jibb&ğ
              jekłaj yej rahyelep
                  *(etc.)*

The clause types are limited to the less complicated constructions:

yinney yej rahyelep

but seldom if ever:

yinney yew łaq yej rahyelep

4. The pattern given for hall&g in the reference section can also be used for the following: wiyik, 'yiyeh, jaṁar, rak, hagan-yag, tiryep, tiyṁah, bałwin, Kirijṁ&j, Yijiteh, Yiwyent&y, Niwiyyeh and all the names of months and days. Notice the use of various members of the demonstrative set in this pattern, especially the use of yew for past, and yin and yeṅ for present and future. (See Grammatical Note 4 of Lesson Six.)

5. As you may have noted already, consonant clusters go against the grain of Marshallese phonetic habits. This is not a matter of genetics or physical ability, but of (language) custom. It stems from the patterns present in the Malayo-Polynesian parent language. The only clusters permitted without the insertion of a short, excrescent vowel are of identical consonants (jimeTTan, haDDiy, etc.) or closely related ones (wiNTeh, tiyjeMBah, etc.). Thus when English words with clusters of less compatible consonants are borrowed into Marshallese, such clusters are broken up by the insertion of a vowel:

|  |  |
|---|---|
| tiryep | 'trip' |
| jikiwił | 'school' |
| yijiteh | 'Easter' |
| (etc.) |  |

## SOUND DRILL

Learn to distinguish and produce the following pairs of words:

| b | | | p | | |
|---|---|---|---|---|---|
| bwebwe | beybey | tuna | bebe | peypey | decide |
| bwü | bay | fishpole | be | pay | arm, hand |
| bao | bahwew | bird | bao | pahwew | to appear |
| bata | bahtah | priest | bata | pahtah | war |
| ob | w&b | chest | wöb | w&p | name of a tree |
| jab | jahab | no | jab | jahap | red snapper |

Some words you have already learned that contain these
same sounds include:

| jahab | jaṁb&w | bil | pad |
|-------|--------|-----|-----|
| jab | teprak | Likiyep | pinjeł |
| yejjab | ban | yełap | kapp&q |
| p&ybah | bat | Yepwen | peyij |
| jerbal | b&l&n | yippan | yippaṁ |

SHORT PROSE SELECTION

there are           atolls
Ewŏr jilHuul - emen <u>ailiH</u> ilo Majŏl.
Yewer jilgiwil - yeman <u>hay&l&g</u> yilew Mahjeł.

JoHoul - rualitok   ailiH  in Rŭlik im joHoul -
J&gewil - riwahliyt&k hay&l&g yin Raylik yim j&g&wil -

jiljino ailiH in Ratak.  Rŭlik ej etan ailiH
jiljin&w hay&l&g yin Rahtak. Raylik yej yetan hay&l&g

    situated western         ocean
ko rej <u>ekkar</u> <u>iturilik</u>    ilo <u>meto</u> in Majŏl, im
kew rej <u>kkar</u> <u>yitiwriylik</u> yilew <u>metew</u> yin Mahjeł, yim

                            east          people
Ratak ej Han ko rej ekkar <u>iturear</u>.  <u>Armij</u> ro
Rahtak yej gan kew rej kkar <u>yitiwr&yhar</u>. <u>Harm&j</u> rew

                                differ slightly
ilo ailiH in Rŭlik kab Ratak, <u>eoktak</u> jidrik
yilew hay&l&g yin Raylik kab Rahtak, <u>y&w&ktak</u> jidik

    speak        each other
aer <u>ekkonono</u> jen <u>dron</u>.  Majŏl ej district eo
hay&r <u>kkenewnew</u> jan <u>dewen</u>. Mahjeł yej tijtiryik yew

easternmost
<u>rear</u> - tata ilo Trust Territory.  Majuro ej
<u>r&yhar</u> - tahtah yilew Tiraj Teyr&yt&wr&y. Majr&w yej

     seat of the government          many
ijo <u>jeban</u> <u>kien</u> eo an Majŏl im <u>eloH</u> armij
yijew <u>j&yban</u> <u>kiyen</u> yew han Mahjel yim <u>yeleg</u> harm&j

    each           outside   live there
jen <u>kajojo</u> ailiH ko <u>ilikin</u> rej jokwe ie.
jan <u>kajj&wj&w</u> hay&l&g kew <u>yilikin</u> rej j&q&y yi'y&y.

Ebeye
Ebeje, ilo ailiH in Kwajleen ej <u>jikin</u> eo
Yebjay, yilew hay&l&g yin Kiwajleyen yej <u>jikin</u> yew

```
kein     karuo      an    kien    ilo    ailiñ     in   Majōl.
k̄&yin    kariwew    han   kiyen   yilew  hay&l&g   yin  M̄ahjeł.

              these
Armij     rein     ion     Ebeje    rej  jerbal  ilo    Kwajalein,
Harm&j    r&yin    yewen   Yepjay   rej  jerbal  yilew  Kiwajleyen,

          to fly      missiles     soldiers              America
jikin     kōkelok     mijel   an   dritarinae    in      Amedka.
jikin     kekkeyłaq   miyjeł  han  rittariñahyey yin     Hamedkah.

                                   the places
Bikini    im    Enewetak      rej  ijoko      Amedka      ear
Pikinniy  yim   Yan&yweytak   rej  yijekew    Hamedkah    yehar

tested  bombs
teej    bam    ie.
teyej   bahaṁ  yi'y&y.
```

## VOCABULARY

| | | |
|---|---|---|
| ailiñ | hay&l&g | atoll |
| alliñ | hall&g | month, moon |
| alliñ in lal | hall&g yin lał | next month |
| añan-eañ | hagan-yag | winter season--'wind from the north' |
| armij | harm&j | people |
| ba | bah | say |
| bam | bahaṁ | bomb |
| Bikini | Pikinniy | Bikini |
| boñ | b&g̊ | night, last night |
| buñnin | big̊niyin | tonight |
| dri tarinae | rittariñahyey | soldier |
| dron | dewen | each other |
| ear | yehar | past tense, 3rd per. sg. |
| Ebeje | Yepjay | Ebeye |
| ekkar | yekkar | arrange |
| ekonono | kkenewenew | speak |
| eloñ | yeleg | many (there are many) |
| Enewetak | Yan&yweytak | Eniwetok |
| eoktah | yew&ktak | change, differ (3rd per. sg. e-) |
| ewōr | yewer | there is, there are (3rd per. sg. e-) |
| iar | yihar | past tense, 1st per. sg. |
| ie | yi'y&y | there |
| ien | 'yiyen | time |
| Ijito | Yijiteh | Easter (from English) |
| ijo | yijew | the place |
| ijoko | yijekew | the places |

| | | |
|---|---|---|
| ilikin | yilikin | (on the) outside |
| ilju | yiljiw | tomorrow |
| im | yim | and |
| ion | yi'yewen | on |
| iturear | yitiwr&yhar | (in the) eastern part |
| iturilik | yitiwriylik | western part |
| iuwe | wiw&y | ride, get on a vessel or vehicle |
| jeban | j&yban | head of, seat of |
| jemlok | jeṁlaq | end |
| jibboH | jibb&ǧ | morning |
| jirik | jidik | slightly |
| jikin | jikin | place of, his place |
| jimettan | jimettan | half |
| jŭmar | jaṁar | summer vacation--school (from *summer*) |
| jota | jewtah | last evening |
| kab | kab | and |
| kajojo | kajj&wj&w | each |
| kemem | keyemyem | feast--traditional for first birthday |
| kien | k&yin | these |
| Kirijmŭj | Kirijṁ&j | Christmas (from English) |
| kŭkkelok | kekkeylaq | cause to fly |
| mare | ṁarey | get married (from *marry*) |
| meto | metew | ocean, sea, navigation |
| rak | rak | south; summer season |
| mijel | miyjeł | missile (from English) |
| reartata | r&yhartahtah | easternmost |
| ran | rahan | day |
| rein | r&yin | these (human) |
| ro | rew | the (human) |
| roH | reǧ | hear |
| teej | teyej | test (from English) |
| tima | tiyṁah | ship--metal hulled (from *steamer*) |
| tireb | tiryep | (field) trip (from Engl.) |
| U. N. Day | Yiwyent&y | United Nations Day (October 24) |
| wik | wiyik | week (from English) |
| wik yiH lal | wiyik yin lał | next week |

<u>REFERENCE</u>--Past and future times

    ran eo turin inne      rahan yew tiłin yinney
       eo lok juŭn              yew łaq jiwen
         *the day before the day before yesterday*

| | |
|---|---|
| ran eo turin inne | rahan yew tițin yinney |
| *the day before yesterday* | |
| inne eo lok juɵn | yinney yew łaq jiwen |
| *the day before yesterday* | |
| inne | yinney |
| *yesterday* | |
| rainin | rahyinyin |
| *today* | |
| ilju | yiljiw |
| *tomorrow* | |
| jɵklaj | jekłaj |
| *the day after tomorrow* | |
| ran en turin jɵklaj | rahan yeñ tițin jekłaj |
| *the day after the day after tomorrow* | |
| buḧin eo turin inne eo lok juɵn | b&ǰ&n yew tițin yinney yew łaq jiwen |
| *four nights ago* | |
| buḧin inne eo lok juɵn | biǰin yinney yew łaq jiwen |
| *three nights ago* | |
| buḧin inne | biǰin yinney |
| *night before last* | |
| boḧ | b&ǰ |
| *last night* | |
| buḧnin | biǰniyin |
| *tonight* | |
| buḧin ilju | biǰin yiljiw |
| *tomorrow night* | |
| buḧin jɵklaj | biǰin jekłaj |
| *night of the day after tomorrow* | |
| jotin eo turin inne eo lok juɵn | jawtiyin yew tițin yinney yew łaq jiwen |
| *four evenings ago* | |
| jotin inne eo lok juɵn | jawtiyin yinney yew łaq jiwen |
| *three evenings ago* | |
| jotin inne | jawtiyin yinney |
| *evening before last* | |

| | |
|---|---|
| jota | jewtah |
| | *last evening* |
| jotinin | jawt&yinyin |
| | *this evening* |
| jotin ilju | jawtiyin yiljiw |
| | *tomorrow evening* |
| jotin jŭklaj | jawtiyin jekłaj |
| | *evening of the day after tomorrow* |
| jibboHin eo turin inne eo lok juŏn | jibb&ğ&n yew tiłin yinney yew łaq jiwen |
| | *three mornings ago* |
| jibboHin eo turin inne | jibb&ğ&n yew tiłin yinney |
| | *day before yesterday morning* |
| jibboHin inne eo lok juŏn | jibb&ğ&n yew tiłin yinney |
| | *day before yesterday morning* |
| jibboHin inne | jibb&ğ&n yinney |
| | *yesterday morning* |
| jibboHnin | jibb&ğniyin |
| | *this morning* |
| jibboHin ilju | jibb&ğ&n yiljiw |
| | *tomorrow morning* |
| jibboHin jŭklaj | jibb&ğ&n jekłaj |
| | *day after tomorrow morning* |

*For 'noon', substitute*

| (Substitute) | in the above for: | (Substitute) |
|---|---|---|
| raelebenin | jibboHnin | jibb&ğniyin | rahyelepniyin |
| raeleben... | jibboHin | jibb&ğ&n | rahyelepen... |

*For 'afternoon'*

elikin raelebenin     yalikin rahyelepniyin
elikin raeleben...     yalikin rahyelepen...

*For 'dawn'*

{ He ejorantak     gey yejewrahantak }
{ ke ej jorantak     key yej jewrahantak }
    *before dawn, during the night*
    *after dawn, during the day*

jorantakin...          jewrahantakin...
        *for dawns of other days*

        <u>For 'midnight', substitute
        in the 'night' pattern for:</u>
lukon boḧnin      boḧnin       biǧniyin     liqen biǧniyin
lukon buḧin...    buḧin        biǧin        liqen biǧin...
lukon boḧ         boḧ          b&ǧ          liqen b&ǧ

alliḧ eo turin alliḧ        hall&g yew tiťin hall&g
  eo lok juön                yew ɫaq jiwen
    *the month before the month before last*

alliḧ eo lok juön           hall&g yew ɫaq jiwen
        *month before last*

alliḧ eo lok                hall&g yew ɫaq
        *last month*

alliḧ in                    hall&g yin
        *this month*

alliḧ in löl                hall&g yin laɫ
        *next month*

alliḧ in tok juön löl       hall&g yin teq jiwen laɫ
        *month after next*

alliḧ en lok löl            hall&g yeṅ ɫaq laɫ
        *month after next*

alliḧ en turin alliḧ        hall&g yeṅ tiťin hall&g
  in löl                    yin laɫ
        *month after next*

alliḧ uweo lok löl          haɫɫ&g wiweyew ɫaq laɫ
        *month after next*

## PROVERB

Joij eo mour eo, lḧj        J&wij yew m&wir yew, laj
  eo mij eo.                yew m&j yew.
        Roughly: Kindness brings life,
              hate brings death.

## LESSON EIGHT

Demonstratives: 'Be quite specific
about where it is, whether it's
visible or not, plural or not, and
if plural, whether human or not.';
some kin terms.

### DIALOGUE

A: An wön ne binjel?  Han wen ney pinjeł?
B: Ejjab aö. Emmanlok  Yejjab hah&h. Yenhhanłaq
   binjel en aö.  pinjeł yen hah&h.
A: Emmantata e aö.  Yenhhantahtah y&y hah&h.
B: Kwar lo ke binjel  Qehar lew key pinjeł kan
   kan an Meri?  han Meydiy?
A: Aet, ak renana jen  Hay&t, hak renahnah jan
   binjel kane am.  pinjeł kaney han.
B: Elab wönůůn binjel  Yełap wenyan pinjeł kay
   kü aö.  hah&h.
A: Mol ke binjel kein  Mewel key pinjeł k&yin
   arro remmantata.  harr&w renhhantahtah.

A: Whose pencil is that (by you)?
B: Not mine. My pencil (over there) is better.
A: Mine (here) is best.
B: Did you see Mary's pencils (there by her)?
A: Yes, but they're not as good as yours (there by you).
B: My pencils (these here by me) are expensive.
A: These pencils of ours are undoubtedly the best.

### DRILLS

1. An wön ne binjel?  Han wen ney pinjeł?
              buk            b&q
              beba           p&ybah
              ben            peyen
              jea            jeyah
              tebel          teybeł
              jook           jawak
              kein ejjeor    k&yin jjeyeł

*(Substitute the words from No. 1 above for the word pinjɨł in Drills 2 through 11 below.)*

2. Aʉ <u>binjel</u> e.   Hah&h <u>pinjɨł</u> y&y.

3. Aʉ <u>binjel</u> en iloan   Hah&h <u>pinjɨł</u> yeṅ
   rum en.   yilewwahan riwiṁ yeṅ.

*(In addition to the substitutions for the word penjił from Drill 1 above, substitute the words for <u>yin</u> given below to make Drill No. 4 a variable substitution drill.)*

4. Ewʉr <u>binjel</u> iloan   Yewer <u>pinjɨł</u> yilewwahan
   rum <u>in</u>.   riwiṁ <u>yin</u>.
   ne   ṅey
   kʉ   kay
   kan   kaṅ
   ko   kew
   e   y&y
   kane   kaṅey
   kein   k&yin

*(Continue, substituting appropriate words from Drill 1 above for <u>pinjɨł</u>, and appropriate words from Drill 4 above for <u>kaṅ</u>.)*

5. Emman <u>binjel kan</u> ilo   Yeṁuhan <u>pinjɨł kaṅ</u> yilew
   imʉn wia <u>kan</u>.   yiṁen wiyah <u>kaṅ</u>.

*(In addition to substituting in the slots used above, substitute in the slot of <u>hamiy</u> below as appropriate. Use objects in the classroom to make the drills meaningful.)*

6. Enana <u>binjel kan</u> jen   Yenahnah <u>pinjɨł kaṅ</u> jan
   <u>binjel kane ami</u>.   <u>pinjɨł kaṅey hamiy</u>.
   aʉ   hah&h
   am   haṁ
   ad   had
   arro   harrew
   aer   hay&r
   aerro   hay&rrew
   (etc.)   (etc.)

*(Continue in like manner, substituting in frames of Drills 7 through 11.)*

7. Elab wŭnen <u>binjel kŭ aŭ</u>.   Yełap weñyan <u>pinjeł kay hah&h</u>.

*(In Drills 8 and 9, be sure to keep proper agreement between the directional of <u>ley-</u>, the location connected with the demonstrative, and the person of the possessive pronoun.)*

8. Kien ear <u>letok binjel kein ad</u>.   Kiyen yehar <u>leyteq pinjeł k&yin had</u>.

9. Ear <u>letok binjel ko an</u>.   Yehar <u>leyteq pinjeł kew han</u>.

10. Ewi <u>binjel</u> eo <u>am</u>?   Yewiy <u>pinjeł</u> yew <u>hañ</u>?

11. Erki <u>binjel</u> ko <u>aŭ</u>?   Y&rkiy <u>pinjeł</u> kew hah&h?

12. Ewi <u>ladik</u> eo <u>nejim</u>?   Yewiy <u>ładik</u> yew <u>najiñ</u>?
    ledik    jetim          ledik    jatiñ
             jeim                    j&yiñ
             jein Tom              j&yin Tawañ

             jetin                  jatin
              Meri                  Meydiy
             jetŭ                   jatih
             jeiŭ                   j&yih
             jetimi                jatimiy
             jeimi                 j&yimiy
             nejin Jon            najin Jawan

             nejŭ                   najih
             jeram                 jerañ
             jera                   jerah
             jeran Ali            jeran Hałiy

13. *(Substitute the words from Drill 12 in the following frame.)*
    Erri <u>ladik</u> ro <u>nejim</u>?   Y&rriy <u>ładik</u> rew <u>najiñ</u>?

14. *(Be sure to keep agreement in substituting from among the following.)*
    Cue:
    <u>Ewi binjel eo am</u>?   <u>Yewiy pinjeł yew hañ</u>?
    Response:
    <u>Ewi binjel eo am</u>?   <u>Yewiy pinjeł yew hañ</u>?

C: ko                          kew
R: Erki binjel ko am?          Yɛrkiy pinjeł kew haṁ?
C: buk                         bɛq
R: Erki buk ko am?             Yɛrkiy bɛq kew haṁ?
C: eo                          yew
R: Ewi buk eo am?              Yewiy bɛq yew haṁ?
C: mani                        ṁaniy
R: Ewi mani eo am?             Yewiy ṁaniy yew haṁ?
C: ko                          kew
R: Erki mani ko am?            Yɛrkiy ṁaniy kew haṁ?
C: nejim                       najiṁ
R: Erki mani ko nejim?         Yɛrkiy ṁaniy kew najiṁ?
C: ladik                       ładdik
R: Er i ladik ro nejim?        Yɛrriy ładik rew najiṁ?
C: eo                          yew
R: Ewi ladik eo nejim?         Yewiy ładik yew najiṁ?

(Continue with the following cues.)

| Cue | | Response | | | |
|---|---|---|---|---|---|
| ro | rew | Yɛrriy | ładik | rew | najiṁ? |
| jetim | jatiṁ | " | " | " | jatiṁ? |
| jeram | jeraṁ | " | " | " | jeraṁ? |
| eo | yew | Yewiy | " | yew | " ? |
| ledik | leddik | " | ledik | " | " ? |
| nejim | najiṁ | " | " | " | najiṁ? |
| jeen | jayan | " | jayan | " | " ? |
| am | haṁ | " | " | " | ham ? |
| erki | yɛrkiy | Yɛrkiy | " | kew | " ? |
| buk | bɛq | " | bɛq | " | " ? |
| eo | yew | Yewiy | " | yew | " ? |
| beba | pɛybah | " | pɛybah | " | " ? |
| mak | ṁahak | " | mahak | " | " ? |
| nejim | najiṁ | " | " | " | najiṁ? |
| nejü | najih | " | " | " | najih? |
| ladik | ładdik | " | ładik | " | " ? |
| jetim | jatiṁ | " | " | " | jatiṁ? |
| nejim | najiṁ | " | " | " | najiṁ? |
| jeen | jayan | " | jayan | " | " ? |
| am | haṁ | " | " | " | haṁ ? |
| binjel | pinjeł | Yewiy | pinjeł | yew | haṁ ? |

15. *(Repeat Drill 7 in the form of a conversation between pairs of students, as follows:)*

A: Elab wÖnen binjel kÜ aÜ.
B: Mol ke ke elab wÖnen binjel kane am?
A: Aet, mol ke elab wÖnḧir.

Yełap weñyan pinjeł kay hah&h.
Ṁewel key key yełap weñyan pinjeł kañey haṁ?
Hay&t, ṁewel key yełap weñayy&r.

A: Elab wÖnen buk en an.
B: Mol ke ke elab wÖnen buk en an?
A: Aet, mol ke elab wÖnen.

Yełap weñyan b&q yeñ han.
Ṁewel key key yełap weñyan b&q yeñ han?
Hay&t, ṁewel key yełap weñyan.

A: Elab wÖnen jea kane an kien.
B: Mol ke ke elab wÖnen jea kÜ an kien?
A: Aet, mol ke elab wÖnḧir.
   *(etc.)*

Yełap weñyan jeyah kañey han kiyen.
Ṁewel key key yełap weñyan jeyah kay han kiyen?
Hay&t, ṁewel key yełap weñayy&r.
   *(etc.)*

16. *(Repeat Drill 8 in the form of a conversation between pairs of students, as follows:)*

A: Kien ear letok binjel kein ad.
B: Kien ear letok binjel kein ad ke?
A: Aet, kien ear liktok(i).

Kiyen yehar leyteq pinjeł k&yin had.
Kiyen yehar leyteq pinjeł k&yin had key?
Hay&t, kiyen yehar liyteq(iy).

A: Kien ear letok binjel e aÜ.
B: Kien ear lewÖj binjel ne am ke?
A: Aet, kien ear letok(e).

Kiyen yehar leyteq pinjeł y&y hah&h.
Kiyen yehar leyw&j pinjeł ñey haṁ key?
Hay&t, kiyen yehar leyteq(ey).

A: Kien ear lewÖj binjel ne am.
B: Kien ear letok binjel e aÜ ke?
A: Aet, kien ear lewÖj(e).

Kiyen yehar leyw&j pinjeł ñey haṁ.
Kiyen yehar leyteq pinjeł y&y hah&h key?
Hay&t, kiyen yehar leyw&j(ey).

A: Kien ear lelok binjel kan an.

Kiyen yehar leyłaq pinjeł kañ han.

B: Kien ear lelok binjel        Kiyen yehar leyłaq pinjeł
   kan an ke?                   kañ han key?
A: Aet, kien ear lilok(i).      Hay&t, kiyen yehar
                                liyłaq(iy).
   (etc.)                       (etc.)

17. (Practice asking and answering questions like the
    following:)

   Ewŏr ke jeim im jetim?        Yewer key j&yiṁ yim jatiṁ?
   Aet, ewŏr.                    Hay&t, yewer.
   Aet, ewŏr juŏn jeiŭ           Hay&t, yewer jiwen j&yih
     im ruo jetŭ.                  yim riwew jatih.
   Aet, ewŏr juŏn jeiŭ           Hay&t, yewer jiwen j&yih
     kŏrŭ, juŏn jeiŭ               keray, jiwen j&yih
     eman, im juŏn jetŭ            ṁṁahan, yim jiwen jatih
     kŏrŭ.                         keray.
   Aet, ewŏr ruo jeiŭ            Hay&t, yewer riwew j&yih
     eman, im juŏn jetŭ            ṁṁahan, yim jiwen jatih
     ledrik.                       leddik.
   Ejelok (jeiŭ im jetŭ).        Yejjełaq(j&yih yim jatih).
   Ewŏr ke jein im jetin         Yewer key j&yin yim jatin
     Tom?                          Tawaṁ?
   Ewŏr ke jein Meri?            Yewer key j&yin Meydiy?
   Ewŏr ke jetin Ali?            Yewer key jatin Hałiy?
   Ewŏr ke jeim?                 Yewer key j&yiṁ?
   Ejelok, ak ewŏr juŏn          Yejjełaq, hak yewer
     jetŭ.                         jiwen jatih.
   Ewŏr ke jein im jetin         Yewer key j&yin yim jatin
     Meri im Tom?                  Meydiy yim Tawaṁ?

GRAMMATICAL NOTES

1. The demonstratives are crucial to Marshallese grammar, and the rules governing their use and meaning are extremely complex. The full set is presented in the reference section at the end of this lesson. You have met some in earlier lessons, some further uses are drilled in this lesson, and additional uses will be presented in later lessons. Work on all the drills until your responses become automatic; there is no shortcut.

2. Note in Drills 12 through 14 that ładdik and leddik have a single d when followed by demonstratives. Note also that the flexibility of Drill 14 is possible only because words for 'money' can take either the general possessive haha- or the one for pets and toys naji-, the basic meaning of which is 'child'.

3. Note the use of weṅyan in Drill 7 even for plural items such as pinjeł k&yin had. This is not the 3rd person singular 'its cost' but rather an occurrence of the construct particle yin fused with the stem for 'cost', translated instead as 'cost of'. (With some words such as this it can only occur fused, never separate.) The third line of each conversation in Drill 15, where the items are not repeated, contains instead the possessive form 'its cost', the form of which is identical with the fused construct: weṅyan when singular, but different when plural: weṅayy&r 'their cost'.

4. Note the two key's in the questions of Drill 15. The first is the question particle, the second the dependent clause introducer 'that...' practiced in the last lesson.

5. Note the vowel change in the stem of ley- to liy- for plural items in the final lines of the conversations in Drill 16 when the object is plural but not repeated. The liy- form could also be used optionally in all lines of this Drill and in Drills 8 and 9 for plural objects even when they are stated:

  Kiyen yehar leyteq pinjeł k&yin had.
     *or*
  Kiyen yehar liyteq pinjeł k&yin had.
    *but only*
  Kiyen yehar leyteq pinjeł y&y hah&h.

The ey and iy in parentheses in Drill 15 are singular and plural object pronouns, respectively 'it' and 'them', which are used instead of repeating the name of the object (pinjeł k&yin had, etc.) in the last line of each conversation. With verb stems that undergo this vowel change they are optional; with others they are obligatory in lieu of a specific object.

| | |
|---|---|
| Yehar kag y&k yew kijen key? | 'Did he eat his fish?' |
| Hay&t, yehar kagey. | 'Yes he ate it.' |
| Yehar kag y&k kew kijen key? | 'Did he eat his fish (pl.)?' |
| Hay&t, yehar kagiy. | 'Yes, he ate them.' |

Other common verb stems that undergo singular-plural vowel change are jew- 'throw', and bek 'bring, take, carry':

| | |
|---|---|
| Yehar jewłaq b&q yew key? | 'Did he throw the book away?' |
| Hay&t, yehar jewłaq(ey). | 'Yes, he threw it away.' |
| Yehar jewłaq b&q kew key? | 'Did he throw the books away?' |
| Yehar jiwłaq b&q kew key? | 'Did he throw the books away?' |
| Hay&t, yehar jiwłaq(iy). | 'Yes, he threw them away.' |
| Yehar bekteq b&q yin key? | 'Did he bring this book?' |
| Hay&t, yehar bekteq(ey). | 'Yes, he brought it.' |
| Yehar bik(iy) teq b&q k&yin key? | 'Did he bring these books?' |
| Hay&t, yehar bik(iy) teq. | 'Yes, he brought them.' |

6. The suffixes -laq and -tahtah may be used to indicate comparative and superlative degrees, respectively, of certain words like ṙuṁan and nahnah, but note that the word jan is often used for comparative constructions without -łaq, as in the fifth line of the dialogue: ...renahnah JAN pinjeł kañey haṁ.

<u>SOUND DRILL</u>

1. Practice distinguishing:

| | |
|---|---|
| ṙuṁan | 'good' |
| ṙuṁahan | 'man' |
| yeman | 'four' |

using the Rälik pronunciation of the first two: [yeṁuṁan], [yeṁuṁahan]. Practice saying:

     yeman ṙuṁahan reṁuṁan     'four good men'

<u>SONG</u>

```
       remember with nostalgia          the place
Ij   yokwe    lok ailiñ   eo  añ   ijo   iar   lotak
Yij  yi'yaqey łaq hay&l&g yew hah&h yijew yihar łetak

       surroundings           path
ie,      melan ko ie,    im  ial  ko ie,      im
yi'y&y, melan kew yi'y&y, yim yiyał kew yi'y&y, yim

people coming and going, never will  from it
iaieo       ko   ie,    ij  jamin ilok  jane,  bwe ijo
yiyahy&w   kew yi'y&y, yij jamin yilaq jan&y, bey yijew
```

```
my place rightful       heritage      forever
jikŪ  emol,    im  aŬ   lemorŬn in dreo,   emŬn
jikih yeṁewel, yim hah&h ɫayṁeran yin d&yyew, yeṁṁhan
                        die
lok Ħe  inaj    mij ie.
ɫaq gey yinahaj m&j yi'y&y.
```

VOCABULARY

```
an wŬn          han wen                 whose?
arro            harrew (had + rew)      belonging to the two
                                          of us
buk             b&q                     book (from English)
eman            ṁṁhahan                 man
erki            y&rkiy                  where are they
                                          (non-humans)?
erri            y&rriy                  where are they
                                          (humans)?
ijo             yijew                   yij- place + yew the >
                                          the place
iloan           yilewwahan,
                  yilewwaha-            inside (it)
imŬn            yiṁen, yiṁe-            house (of), (its (his,
                                          her)) house
imŬn wia        yiṁen wiyah             store
jeen            jayan                   cent (from English)
jeiŬ, -m,       j&yih, -ṁ, -n           my (your, his, (her))
  -n                                      older sibling
jetŬ, -m,       jatih, -m, -n           my (your, his, (her))
  -n                                      younger sibling
jera, -m,       jerah, -m, -n           my (your, his, (her))
  -n                                      friend
jook            jawak                   chalk (from English)
kein            k&yin jjeyeɫ            eraser, 'tool for
  ejjeor                                  scattering, removing'
kŬɤʮ            keray                   woman
kwar            qehar                   your (sg.) were, did
                                          (2nd per. sg. past
                                          tense)
letok           leyteq                  give: leye- + direc-
                                          tional
lo              lew                     see
mak             ṁahak                   money, dollar (from
                                          German Mark)
mani            ṁaniy                   money (from English)
mol             ṁewel                   true
tebel           teybeɫ                  table (from English)
```

| | | |
|---|---|---|
| wőn | wen | who? |
| wőnen | weñyan, weñya- | (its) cost, cost (of) |
| wőnŭir | weñayyɑr | their cost |

REFERENCE--Demonstratives

| Person | Meaning | Singular | Plural Non-human | Plural Human |
|---|---|---|---|---|
| 1 incl. | this/these (close to us both) | yin | kɑyin | rɑyin |
| 1 excl. | this/these (close to me) | yɑy | kay | ray |
|  | + | 'yiyɑh | kaykay | rayray |
| 2 | that/those (close to you) | ñey | kañey | rañey |
|  | + | ñeyñey | kaykañey | rayrañey |
| 3 | that/those (close to neither of us) | yeñ | kañ | rañ |
|  | + | 'yiyeñ | kaykañ | rayrañ |
| 0 | the (not visible or past in time) | yew | kew | rew |
|  | that/those (distant but visible) + | wiweyew | kewkew | rewrew |
| ? | where is/ are? | -wiy yewiy | -kiy yɑrkiy | -riy yɑrriy* |
|  | (or) | yɑw | yɑrkiy | yerriy† |

*Ratak dialect
†Rŭlik dialect

Note: The forms labeled with '+' in the meaning column are used when singling out specific objects or people from among others. Notice what happens to the meaning when <u>yew</u>, <u>kew</u>, <u>rew</u> are singled out.

## LESSON NINE

Past tense; sentence, personal,
and locative demonstratives

### DIALOGUE

A: Kwo jelā ke ekkal im?           Qejełay key kkal y&ṁ?
B: Aet, iar jikul in               Hay&t, yihar jikiwił yin
   kamtŏ.                             kahaṁteh.
A: Bar Jon ke?                     Bar Jawan key?
B: Jab, Jon ear jikul in           Jahab, Jawan yehar jiki-
   taktŏ.                             wił yin takteh.
A: Kwar katak ia kajin             Qehar kahtak yi'yah kajin
   Marshall?                          Ṁahjeł?
B: I Hawaii.  Ak kwe?              Yiy Hawahyiy.  Hak qey?
A: Iba make.                       Yippah makey.

A: Can you build houses?
B: Yes, I went to a carpenter's school.
A: Did John go too?
B: No, John went to medical school.
A: Where did you learn how to speak Marshallese?
B: In Hawaii.  And you?
A: By myself.

### DRILLS

1.  <u>Iar</u> jikul in kamtŏ.        <u>Yihar</u> jikiwił yin
                                          kahaṁteh.
    kwar                              qehar
    ear                               yehar
    kim ar                            k&m har
    jar                               jehar
    kom ar                            q&ṁ har
    rar                               rehar

2.  *(Change the following to past tense.)*
    Ij etal in jikul.                 Yij yetal yin jikiwił.
      Iar etal in jikul                 Yihar yetal yin jikiwił.
    Ej itok in jerbal.                Yej yiteq yin jerbal.

Rej ikkure.          Rej qqir&y.
Kimij jab iwōj.       K&mij jab yiw&j.
Renaj etal.            Renahaj yetal.
Jej etal in tutu.      Jej yetal yin tiwtiw.
Kwōj jikul ia?        Qej jikiwił yi'yah?
Taro ejjab mōñā ke?   Tarew yejjab ṁegay key?
Ij ekkal im.           Yij kkal y&ṁ.
Kwojeḷā ke ekkal im?   Qejełay key kkał y&ṁ.

3. Jekab ear jikul in     J&ykap yehar jikiwił yin
    taktō.                   takteh.
    kamtō                    kahaṁteh
    dri kaki                 rikakiy
    nōj                       nehej
    injinia                 yinjiniyah

4. Kwojeḷā ke kajin       Qejełay key kajin
    Majōl?                   Mahjeł?
    belle                    palley
    Jeina                    Jeyinah
    Jeban                    Jepahan
    Biranij                 Birahnij
    Niboñ                   Nibbeğ

*(Sample answers:)*

    Aet, ijeḷā kajin       Hay&t, yijełay kajin
    Majōl.                   Mahjeł.
    Jab, ijaje kajin       Jahab, yijahj&y kajin
    Majōl.                   Mahjeł.

5. Conversation drill. *(Practice the following until pairs of students can converse according to this model. Inquire about other languages the student may know.)*

A: Kwar katak ñāāt kajin    Qehar kahtak gayat kajin
    Majōl?                   Mahjeł?

B: Iar katak kajin Majōl    Yihar kahtak kajin Mahjeł
    ke ij jikul i           key yij jikiwił yiy
    Hawaii.                Hawahyiy.
    ber ie                   pad yi'y&y
    jerbal ie               jerbal yi'y&y
    drik                     dik
    dri tarinae            rittariyiṅahyey
    jerbal ippen Peace    jerbal yippan Piyij
      Corps                  Kewer

			ber ilo Nebi
			jerbal Kwajalein
			ber Majuro
A:	Kwokanuij jelŭ kajin
			Marshall.
			kwokadrik
			elap am
B:	Ejjab kanuij, ak ebwe
			jidrik.

			pad yilew Neypiy
			jerbal Kiwajleyen
			pad Majr&w
			Qekahn&w&j jełay kajin
			Mahjeł.
			qekadik
			yełap hańh
			Yejjab kahn&w&j, hak
			yebey jidik.

6. Conversation drill. *(Do this drill in similar fashion. Inquire about other skills.)*

A:	Kwojela ke ekkal im?
			eńwŭr
			entak
			kŭmkŭm
			aŭ
			kowainini
			umum mŭ
			kamtŭ
			inoń
			taktŭ
			bwinbwin
			tiraib
			iakiu
			kattir
			amimŭno

			Qejełay key kkal y&ńh?
			yaǧed
			y&ntak
			keńhkeńh
			haheh
			kewwahyiniyniy
			wińhwińh may
			kahańhteh
			yinaǧ
			takteh
			b&nb&n
			tirahyip
			yi'yakiyiw
			katt&r
			hamiyńheńew

B:	Ijaje. Kwomaroń ke
			katakin iŭ?
A:	Ijjab kanuij jelŭ,
			ak inaj kajioń.

			Yijahj&y. Qemareǧ key
			kahtakin y&h?
			Yijjab kahn&w&j jełay,
			hak yinahaj kajj&y&ǧ.

7. *(Change the following to past tense according to the example.)*

			Inaj ruj ńe ejorantak.

			Iar ruj ke ejorantak.

			Jenaj kemem ńe eien
			kemem.
			Renaj eńwŭr ńe eien
			eńwŭr.
			Renaj aluij pija ńe
			eien aluij.

			Yinahaj łij gey
			yejewrahantak.
			Yihar łij key yej
			jewrahantak.
			Jenahaj keyemyem gey
			yeyiyen keyemyem.
			Renahaj yaǧed gey
			yeyiyen yaǧed.
			Renahaj halw&j pijah
			gey yeyiyen halw&j.

| | |
|---|---|
| Inaj mōn̄n̄ n̄e eien mōn̄n̄. | Yinahaj ṁegay gey yeyiyen ṁegay. |
| Kwonaj mōn̄n̄ n̄e eraeleb ke? | Qenahaj ṁegay gey yerahyelep key? |
| Enaj katak bwinbwin n̄e ejikul. | Yenahaj kahtak b&nb&n gey yejikiwił. |
| Jenaj iakiu n̄e emwij jerbal. | Jenahaj yi'yakiyiw gey y&ṁ&j jerbal. |
| Renaj amimōnō n̄e ewōr ien. | Renahaj hamiyṁen̄ew gey yewer 'yiyen. |
| Enaj inon̄ n̄e ebon̄. | Yenahaj yinaǧ gey y&b&ǧ. |
| Enaj kōmkōm n̄e ewōr an kein kōm. | Yenahaj keṁkeṁ gey yewer han k&yin keṁ. |
| Jenaj aō n̄an wa en n̄e ebo. | Jenahaj haheh gan wah yen̄ gey yepew. |

*(Repeat, using <u>kar</u> instead of <u>har</u>.)*

8. *(Practice answering the questions in Drills 10 through 14 of LESSON EIGHT using sentence demonstratives (see REFERENCE section).)*

| | |
|---|---|
| Ewi binjel eo am? | Yewiy pinjeł yew haṁ? |
| En̄n̄e. | Y&g&y. |
| Erki binjel ko aō? | Y&rkiy pinjeł kew hah&h? |
| Irkane. | Yerkan̄ey. |
| Ewi ladik eo nejim? | Yewiy ładik yew najiṁ? |
| En̄n̄uweo. | Y&gwiweyew. |
| Erri ladrik ro nejū? | Y&rriy ładik rew najih? |
| Irrn̄ran. | Y&rrayran̄. |

*(etc., using other appropriate forms from the Reference section.)*

9. *(Ask and answer questions like the following, using the personal demonstratives in as many different ways as possible.)*

| | |
|---|---|
| Ejeln̄ ke kajin Majōl lein? | Yejełay key kajin Ṁahjeł łeyin? |
| Aet, ejeln̄. | Hay&t, yejełay. |
| Jab, ejaje. | Jahab, yejahj&y. |
| Ejeln̄ ke kajin Majōl lōmaran? | Yejełay key kajin Ṁahjeł leṁahran̄? |
| (Rejeln̄ ke kajin Majōl lōmaran?) | (Rejełay key kajin Ṁahjeł leṁahran̄?) |
| Ejeln̄ ke kajin Majōl leo nejim? | Yejełay key kajin Ṁahjeł leyew najiṁ? |
| leo mōttam | leyew ṁōttaṁ |

lio jeram               liyew jerañ
ladik eo nejim          ɫadik yew najiñ
lio ibam                liyew yippañ
kijake                  kijak&y
kijak ran               kijak rañ
lɵllab en               ɫeɫɫap yeñ
lellab rɵ               ɫeɫɫap ray
likao in                likahwew yin
jiroɧ ro mɵttam         jireǵ rew ɧettañ
lɵllab eo jemam         ɫeɫɫap yew jeɧañ
lellab eo jinen Tom     ɫeɫɫap yew jinen Tawañ

*(Continue, substituting other personal demonstratives, and other languages.)*

10. *(Ask questions like the following.)*

    Lɵt en ej ekkal im?       Ḷet yeñ yej kkal y&ñ?
    Lɵt ran rej eɧwɵr?        Ḷet rañ rej yaǵed?
    Lɵt uweo ej entak?        Ḷet wiweyew yej y&ntak?
    Lɵt ne ej kɵmkɵm?         Ḷet ñey yej keɧkeɧ?
    Let ran rej tutu iar?     Let rañ rej tiwtiw yiyhar?

    *(Continue, using verbs from Drills 6 and 7.)*

11. *(Continue, asking questions with the following pattern, using the same verbs as in Drill 10. Be guided by your teacher in obtaining appropriate combinations of the demonstrative and locative-demonstrative.)*

    Lɵt en ej ekkal im           Ḷet yeñ yej kkal y&ñ
      ijen?                        yijeñ?
    Lɵt ien ej ekkal im          Ḷet 'yiyeñ yej kkal y&ñ
      ijjien?                      yijjiyyeñ?
    Lɵt ran rej eɧwɵr ijen?      Ḷet rañ rej yaǵed yijeñ?
    Lɵt raran rej eɧwɵr          Ḷet rayrañ rej yaǵed
      ijjien?                      yijjiyyeñ?
    Lɵt uweo ej entak            Ḷet wiweyew yej y&ntak
      ijjuweo?                     yijjiwiweyew?
    Lɵt ne ej kɵmkɵm             Ḷet ñey yej keɧkeɧ
      ijɵne?                       yijeñey?
    Let rein rej umum            Let r&yin rej wiɧwiɧ
      ijɵkein?                     yij&k&yin?
    Let ro rej umum              Let rew rej wiɧwiɧ
      ijɵkan?                      yijekañ?
    Let uweo ej umum             Let wiweyew yej wiɧwiɧ
      ijɵkoko?                     yijekewkew?
    Let roro rej umum            Ḷet rewrew rej wiɧwiɧ
      ijɵkoko?                     yijekewkew?

12. *(Practice answering the questions you have made in Drills 10 and 11 with answers like the following:)*

| Tom | Tawaṁ |
|---|---|
| Leo nejin Ali. | Ḷeyew najin Haḷiy. |
| *Chief* kamtŭ eo an Mieco. | Jiyip kahaṁteh yew han Miyeykew. |
| Dri jikul ro. | Rijikiwiḷ rew. |
| Lŭmaro jittaken. | Ḷeṁahrew jittakyeṅ. |
| Ijaje. Ijjab kile lŭt en. | Yijahj&y. Yijjab kiley ḷet yeṅ. |
| Ladrik eo mwin. | Ḷadik yew ṁiyin. |
| Limaro mŭkein. | Liṁahrew m&k&yin. |
| Lŭllab eo. | Ḷeḷḷap yew. |
| Jiroṅ ro mŭkan iar. | Jireğ rew ṁekaṅ yiyhar. |

GRAMMATICAL NOTES

1. The simple past tense is formed by inserting <u>har</u> or <u>kar</u> into the verb phrase after the subject prefixes. The Rălik dialect prefers <u>har</u>, the Ratak <u>kar</u>. Both are practiced in Drill 7, and Drills 1 through 3 may also be done with <u>kar</u>. Later we will find <u>kar</u> used in both dialects in contrary-to-fact statements of condition and desire. Although combinations of the subject prefixes with <u>har</u> are written as in the phonetic spelling for simplicity and ease of analysis, their actual pronunciation is as indicated:

|  |  |
|---|---|
| yihar | [yiyhar] |
| qehar | [qahar] |
| yehar | [yeyhar] |
| jehar | [jahar] |
| rehar | [rahar] |

Thus <u>yihar</u> 'I, past tense' is identical to <u>yiy har</u> 'at the lagoon beach' in rapid pronunciation: [yiyhar].

2. Two of the sentence demonstratives <u>y&g&y</u> and <u>yegney</u> were introduced in Lesson Three. These are so called since they can constitute a full sentence in reply to questions as to location, and may be translated: 'Here/there it/he/she/they is/are.' See Drill 8.

3. The avoidance of personal names referred to in Lesson Six results in a proliferation of what are called 'personal demonstratives'. These are summarized in the reference section, and practiced in Drills 9 through 12.

4. The locative demonstratives in the plural (yij&k&yin etc.) are translated rather indefinitely: 'somewhere around here', etc.

SOUND DRILLS

Learn to distinguish and produce the following pairs of words:

1.     **t**                                  **j**

| | | | | | |
|---|---|---|---|---|---|
| tata | tahtah | 'very' | jaja | jahjah | 'carry child on hip' |
| tok | teq | 'hither' | jok | jeq | 'to land, alight' |
| ʉt | yat | 'name' | ʉj | yaj | 'to weave' |
| at | hat | 'hat; gall bladder' | aj | haj | 'thatch; liver' |
| bat | bat | 'slow, late' | baj | baj | 'bus; pubic area' |
| wit | wit | 'flower' | wij | wij | 'to drown someone; balsa (Rat.)' |
| wʉt | w&t | 'rain' | wʉj | w&j | 'towards you; balsa (Rʉl.)' |
| wat | wat | 'puffer fish' | waj | waj | 'watch' |

2.     **ñ**                                      **n**

| | | | | | |
|---|---|---|---|---|---|
| nam | ñañ | 'mosquito' | nam | nañ | 'secondary lagoon' |
| ne | ñey | 'that close to you' | ne | ney | 'leg, foot' |
| nok | ñeq | 'wet (Rat.); midrib of coconut' | nok | neq | 'huddle because of cold' |
| en | yeñ | 'that over there' | en | yen | 'he should...' |
| kan | kañ | 'those over there' | kan | kan | 'eat (transitive) (Rat.)' |
| kon | qeñ | 'fit tightly' | kwʉn | qen | 'you should...' |

SHORT PROSE SELECTION

        about
Ewʉr tarrin joñoul rualitik taujin armij ilo
Yewer <u>tarrin</u> j&g&wil riwahliyt&k tawijin harm&j yilew

Majṻl today rainin.
Mahjeł rahyinyin.

Elṻn half-caste abkaj in Nibboḧ, Germany Jemene, Jeina, Portugal Boreke,
Yeleg hapkahaj yin Nippeǰ, Jameney, Jeyinah, Bewdekay

im bar elṻḧ lṻl. Ailiḧ kein rar ber under iumin
yim bar yeleg lał. Hay&l&g k&yin rehar pad yiwṁin

bein the hand of Jibein, Jemene, Jebaan, im elkin after bata war eo
p&yin Jip&yin, Jameney, Jepahan, yim yalikin pahtah yew

until lok Ḧan rainin, rej bed iumin bein Amerka.
laq gan rahyinyin, rej pad yiwṁin p&yin Hamedkah.

Kien eo an Amerka ej help jibaḧ armij rein bwe ren
Kiyen yew han Hamedkah yej jipaq harm&j r&yin bey ren

progress wṻnmanlok im bṻk jikier their place ibben lṻl ko other jet.
wenṁahanłaq yim bek jikiyy&r yippan lał kew jet.

**PROVERB**

Eo ellu eluj.  Yew yelliw yeliwij.
He who loses his temper loses.

**VOCABULARY**

| | | |
|---|---|---|
| abkaj | hapkahaj | half-caste (from English) |
| aluij | halw&j | look at |
| amimṻno | hamiyṁeṅew | (make) handicraft |
| aṻ | haheh | swim |
| bar | bar | also, again |
| bata | pahtah | war |
| bṻ | pay, p&yi- | arm, hand, paw, wing |
| bein | p&yin | hand of, his hand |
| belle | palley | foreign, clothes-wearing |
| Biranij | Birahnij | France (from English) |
| bwe | bey | enough, remainder, left over; because, so that |
| bwinbwin | b&nb&n | count, arithmetic |
| drik | dik | small, little, young |
| ekkal | kkal | build |

| | | |
|---|---|---|
| ekkŭm | kkeṁ | break, snap--wood, pencil, comb, etc. |
| entak | y&ntak | climb a coconut tree and pick coconuts |
| eḦwŭr | yaǰed | go fishing, to fish |
| iakiu | yi'yakiyiw | baseball (from Japanese) |
| iar | yiyhar | at the lagoon beach: <u>yiy</u> locative + <u>har</u> lagoon beach |
| | yihar [yiyhar] | 1st sg. past tense: <u>yi</u> + <u>har</u> past |
| ij(j)- | yij(j)- | place (fused with demonstratives; see reference section) |
| illu | lliw | angry |
| im | y&ṁ, yiṁe- | house |
| injinia | yinjiniyah | engineer (of ship), mechanic (from English) |
| inoḦ | yinaǰ | legend, recount legends |
| iumin | yiwṁiṅ, yiwṁi- | under (it) |
| Jepan | Jepahan | Japan (from English) |
| Jeina | Jeyinah | China (from English) |
| jelŭ | jełay | know (how) |
| Jemene | Jameney | Germany (from English) |
| jema, -m, -n | jemah, jeṁaṁ, jeman | my, your, his father |
| jet | jet | several, few, rest of, others |
| jidrik | | a little |
| jinŭ, jinem, jinen | jin&h, jineṁ, jinen | my, your, his mother |
| jikier | jikiyy&r, jiki- | (their) places |
| jiroḦ | jireǰ | girl--adolescent, unmarried |
| jittaken | jittakyeṅ | east end of island |
| kadrik | kadik | greatly; understatement: <u>ka-</u> causative + <u>dik</u> small: make small |
| kajin | kajin | language of |
| kajioḦ | kajj&y&ǰ | try, endeavor |
| kamtŭ | kahaṁteh | carpentry, work as carpenter (from English) |
| kanuij | kahn&w&j | really |
| kar | kar | Ratak variant of <u>har</u> for simple past tense; used by both dialects for contrary to fact conditionals |

| | | |
|---|---|---|
| kattir | katt&r | drive; literally 'cause to run' ka- causative prefix + tt&r run |
| kein | k&yin | tool, equipment, utensil, thing for |
| kein kŭm | k&yin keṁ | stick for picking breadfruit; literally: 'thing for breaking, snapping' |
| kijak... | kijak... | guy, fellow, gal--must be followed by a demonstrative |
| kile | kiley | recognize |
| kŭmkŭm | keṁkeṁ | pick breadfruit with a stick |
| kowainini | kewwahyiniyniy | make copra, ka- causative prefix + wahyiniy copra |
| lab | ɬap | big, large, great, much |
| likao | likahwew | boy--adolescent, unmarried |
| let | let (Rŭl.) litah (Rat.) | which woman, girl? |
| lŭt | ɬet (Rŭl.) ɬetah (Rat.) | which man, boy? |
| lŭl | laɬ, laɬi- | below, down, earth, country |
| lok | ɬaq | more |
| luj | liwij | lose (from English) |
| mŭ | may | breadfruit |
| maroṁ | mareɥ | can, be able, ability, power |
| mŭkan | ṁekaṅ | those houses: ṁe + kaṅ |
| mŭkein | ṁ&k&yin | these houses: ṁe + k&yin |
| mŭtta, -m, -n | mettah, -m, -n | piece, part; partner |
| mwin | ṁiyin | this house: ṁe + yin |
| Nebi | Neypiy | navy (from English) |
| Niboṁ | Nibbeɥ | Japan(ese) (from English) |
| nŭj | nehej | nurse (from English) |
| pija | pijah | picture, movie, draw pictures (from English) |
| ren | ren | (they) will, should, ought to: 3rd pl. subject prefix + n |
| taktŭ | takteh | be a doctor, see a doctor (from English) |
| tarrin | tarrin | approximately |
| tiraib | tirahyip | drive (from English) |
| tutu | tiwtiw | wet, bathe, shower |

| | | |
|---|---|---|
| um | wiṁ | earth oven |
| umum | wiṁwiṁ | bake in earth oven |
| waini | wahyiniy | copra |

REFERENCE--Sentence demonstratives

*(Arranged like demonstratives in reference section of Lesson Eight--which see for meanings.)*

| person/number | sg. | pl. (non-human) | pl. (human) |
|---|---|---|---|
| 1st incl. | y&gyin | y&rk&yin | y&rr&yin |
| 1st excl. | y&g&y | yerkay | y&rray |
| + | y&gyiy&h | yerkaykay | y&rrayray |
| 2nd | yegṅey | yerkaṅey | y&rraṅey |
| + | yegṅeyṅey | yerkaykaṅey | y&rrayraṅey |
| 3rd | yegyeṅ | yerkaṅ | y&rraṅ |
| + | y&gyiyeṅ | yerkaykaṅ | y&rrayraṅ |
| distant | yegyew | y&rkew | y&rrew |
| + | y&gwiweyew | y&rk&wk&w | y&rr&wr&w |

Note: The forms given above are one Ratak pronunciation. Another Ratak pronunciation may be derived by prefixing <u>yi</u>'- to the above and changing any *first vowels* that are & to e. Rᵾlik pronunciations may be derived by effecting the same vowel changes, but *without* prefixing <u>yi</u>'-. Two exceptions to this latter statement are the Rᵾlik 'distant plural' forms, in which *all* vowels are e: <u>yerkewkew</u>, and <u>yerrewrew</u>.

Personal demonstratives

The following are demonstratives used to refer to people, formed by combining either the 'man-1' (ł) or the 'woman-1' (l) and some vowel material with the demonstratives.

| meaning | | masculine | feminine |
|---|---|---|---|
| 1st incl. sg. | | ł&yin | liyin |
| | pl. | łeṁahr&yin | liṁahr&yin |
| 1st excl. sg. | | ł&hy&y | liy&y |
| | sg. + | ł&yiy&h | liyiy&h |
| 1st excl. pl. | | łeṁahray | liṁahray |
| | pl. + | łeṁahrayray | liṁahrayray |
| 2nd sg. | | łeṅey | liyṅey |
| | sg. + | łeṅeyṅey | liyṅeyṅey |
| 2nd pl. | | łeṁahraṅey | liṁahraṅey |
| | pl. + | łeṁahrayraṅey | liṁahrayraṅey |

| | | | |
|---|---|---|---|
| 3rd sg. | | łeyeń | liyeń |
| | sg. + | łeyiyeń | liyiyeń |
| 3rd pl. | | łeṁahrań | liṁahrań |
| | pl. + | łeṁahrayrań | liṁahrayrań |
| distant sg. | | łeyew | liyew |
| | sg. + | łewiweyew | liwiweyew |
| distant pl. | | łeṁahrew | liṁahrew |
| | pl. + | łeṁahrewrew | liṁahrewrew |

The following may be fully expanded like the above by substituting the regular demonstratives from the reference section of Lesson Eight for yin and r&yin.

| | | | |
|---|---|---|---|
| boy/girl | sg. | ładik yin | ledik yin |
| | pl. | ładik r&yin | ledik r&yin |
| old man/ woman | sg. | łełłap yin | lełłap yin |
| | pl. | łełłap r&yin | lełłap r&yin |
| which? | | | |
| (Rəl.) | sg. | łet yin | let yin |
| (Rat.) | sg. | łetah yin | litah yin |
| (Rəl.) | pl. | łet r&yin | let r&yin |
| (Rat.) | pl. | łetah r&yin | litah r&yin |
| personal name prefix | | ła- | li- |
| affectionate name for any young child | | łabbiraw | lijjireģ |

The following only occur after a sentence addressed to someone, and may be translated 'sir', 'ma'am', etc.

| | | | |
|---|---|---|---|
| address | sg. | ... łey | ... ley |
| | pl. | ... łeṁah | ... liṁah |

The following also refer to people and are used with demonstratives but do not have the l-correlation of those above.

| | | | |
|---|---|---|---|
| young man/ woman | sg. | likahwew yin | jireģ yin |
| | pl. | likahwew r&yin | jireģ r&yin |
| guy/gal | sg. | kijak yin | (kijak yin) |
| | pl. | kijak r&yin | (kijak r&yin) |

Locative demonstratives

The following may be analyzed as yij(j)e- fused with the demonstratives.

| person/number | sg. | pl. |
|---|---|---|
| 1st incl. | yijin | yij&k&yin |
| 1st excl. | yij&y | yijekay |
| + | yijjiyiy&h | yijekaykay |
| 2nd | yijeñey | yijekañey |
| + | yijeñeyñey | yijekaykañey |
| 3rd | yijeñ | yijekañ |
| + | yijjiyiyeñ | yijekaykañ |
| distant | yijew | yijekew |
| | yijjiwiweyew | yijekewkew |

## LESSON TEN

-n: mild commands and more futures;
kar and some contrary to fact
questions and answers; bey 'so that'

### DIALOGUE

A: Melaⱨ, al!      Meyłag hal!
B: I jok in al.      Yijewek yin hal.
A: Etke kwojok in al?      Yetkey qejewek yin hal?
B: Ta ewʊr, I jok.      Tah yewer, yijewek.

A: Melaⱨ, sing!
B: I'm too shy to sing.
A: Why are you ashamed to sing?
B: Never mind, I'm embarrassed.

### DRILLS

1. Melaⱨ, al!      Meylag, hal!
   Jolikiep      Jawlikiyep
   Kaibʊke      Kayib&key
   Loliin      Lawliyin
   Jinna      Jinnah

2. In al.      Yin hal.
   kwʊn      qen
   en      yen
   jen      jen
   kimin      k&min
   komin      q&ṁin
   ren      ren

3. I jok in al.      Yijewek yin hal.
          eb      yeb
          mʊⱨⱨ      ṁegay
          jibiij      jipyij
          jutak      jiwtak
          koleiat      qełeyiyahat
          lamʊj      lamⱨ&j
          jinteb      jint&b

4. I <u>jok</u> in al.　　　　Yi<u>jewek</u> yin hal.
    mijak　　　　　　　　mijak
    tabur　　　　　　　　tabiɫ
    baaj　　　　　　　　 bahaj
    bikʉt　　　　　　　　pik&t
    makoko　　　　　　　 ṁak&wk&w

5. *(Mix cues from Drills 3 and 4 to make a variable
    substitution drill. Add various subject pronouns,
    including some plural ones specified as to number,
    to increase the complexity of the drill even more.)*

6. Al kin juʉn al in　　Hal k&n jiwen hal yin
    <u>belle</u>.　　　　　　　　<u>palley</u>.
    Bʉlau　　　　　　　　Beɫahwiw
    Ruk　　　　　　　　　Riq
    Bonebe　　　　　　　 B&w&np&y
    kauboe　　　　　　　 kahwiwbewey
    jar　　　　　　　　　jar
    maina　　　　　　　　ṁahyinah
    mur　　　　　　　　　ṁiɫ
    kamlo　　　　　　　　kaṁɫ&w

7. <u>Emman</u> ainikien.　　 <u>Yeṁṁan</u> hayinikiyen.
    enana　　　　　　　　yenahnah
    ettʉ　　　　　　　　 yettay
    eutiej　　　　　　　 yewity&j
    ellaaj　　　　　　　 yeɫɫahaj
    ebʉna　　　　　　　　yebenah
    eblʉʉt　　　　　　　 yebiɫyat
    eaidrik　　　　　　　yehayidik
    ebboʜ　　　　　　　　yeppeǯ
    ebon　　　　　　　　 yebeṅ

8. *(Teacher looks at a student and makes requests like
    the following. Students carry out the request to
    show that they have understood. Later individual
    students make similar requests of each other.)*

    Kwʉn jutak mʉk.　　　Qen jiwtak ṁek.
    Kwʉn jijʉt mʉk.　　　Qen jiyjet ṁek.
    Kwʉn kotak mʉk beim.　Qen kewtak ṁek p&yiṁ.
    Kwʉn dror mʉk beim.　 Qen dewer ṁek p&yiṁ.
    Kwʉn kotak mʉk binjel　Qen kewtak ṁek pinjeɫ
    ne am.　　　　　　　　ney haṁ.
    *(etc.)*　　　　　　　*(etc.)*

*(Teacher makes similar requests of the whole class.)*

Kwomin jutak mük.          Q&ṁin jiwtak ṁek.
*(etc.)*                    *(etc.)*

9. *(Learn the following common sayings. Teacher should give the underlined words from both clauses as cues at first--later only those from the first clause.)*

Kwomin jab <u>keroro</u> bwe       Q&ṁin jab <u>k&yr&wr&w</u> bey
  elüṅ <u>dri naḧinmij</u>.          yeleg <u>rinahginm&j</u>.
Kwomin jab <u>büt</u>, bwe         Q&ṁin jab <u>b&t</u>, bey q&ṁ
  kwom naj <u>drüṅdrüṅ</u>.          nahaj <u>degdeg</u>.
Kwomin jab <u>wḁtowḁtak</u>,       Q&ṁin jab <u>wayt&w-waytak</u>,
  bwe elüṅ <u>dri nana</u>.          bey yeleg <u>rinahnah</u>.
Kwomin jab <u>etetal</u> in        Q&ṁin jab <u>yetyetal</u> yin
  boṅ, bwe elüṅ <u>timon</u>.        b&ǵ, bey yeleg <u>tiyṁeṅ</u>.
Kwomin jab <u>riab</u>, bwe        Q&ṁin jab <u>riyab</u>, bey q&ṁ
  kom naj <u>mij lüṅ</u>.            nahaj <u>m&j laq</u>.
Kwomin jab <u>iakwḁl</u>,          Q&ṁin jab <u>yiyhakwayal</u>,
  bwe <u>ejelok men</u> en           bey <u>yejjełaq men</u> yeṅ
  enaj <u>walok</u>.                 yenahaj <u>wahłaq</u>.
Kwomin jab <u>drike dron</u>,      Q&ṁin jab <u>dikey dewen</u>,
  bwe jej <u>jenkwon</u>.            bey jej <u>j&nq&n</u>.
Kwomin jab <u>utiej buruomi</u>,   Q&ṁin jab <u>wity&j biriwemiy</u>,
  bwe renaj <u>drike kwom</u>.       bey renahaj <u>dikey q&ṁ</u>.
Kwomin jab <u>kadrük</u>, bwe      Q&ṁin jab <u>kadek</u>, bey
  enana <u>kadrük</u>.               yenahnah <u>kadek</u>.
Kwomin jab <u>luṅ</u>, bwe kwom    Q&ṁin jab <u>ł&g</u>, bey q&ṁ
  naj <u>mij lüṅ</u>.                nahaj <u>m&j laq</u>.
Kwomin jab <u>jotal</u>, bwe       Q&ṁin jab <u>jewtal</u>, bey
  elüṅ <u>iroij</u>.                 yeleg <u>yirw&j</u>.

10. -<u>n</u> in future yes-no questions.

En w<u>it</u> ke ilju?      Yen w<u>&t</u> key yiljiw?
   <u>itok</u>                 <u>yiteq</u>
   iuwe                 wiw&y
   eṅwür                yaǵed
   ikkure               qqir&y
   mwij                 ṁ&j
   ketok                keyteq
   tübrak               teprak
   entak                y&ntak
   kümküm               keṁkeṁ
   okok                 wekwek

*(Substitute additional verbs. Substitute other subject pronouns before -<u>n</u>. Answer with the following (making the subject pronouns agree with the question).)*

93

    Aet, enaj.                    Hay&t, yenahaj.
    Jab, eban.                  Jahab, yeban.

11. -n kar in yes-no questions known to be contrary to fact (where there has been a change in plans.)

| En kar wit ke ilju? | Yen kar w&t key yiljiw? |
|---|---|
| ren itok inne | ren yiteq yinney |
| jen iuwe rainin | jen wiw&y rahyinyin |
| komin eHwŭr jŭklaj | q&ṁin yaǧed jekłaj |
| komro ikkure boH | q&ṁr&w qqir&y b&ǧ |
| en | yen |
| (etc.) (etc.) (etc.) | (etc.) (etc.) (etc.) |

12. (Answer questions like the above with answers like the following.)

    Aet, en kar.              Hay&t, yen kar.
    Aet, enaj kar.           Hay&t, yenahaj kar.
    Jab, eban kar.           Jahab, yeban kar.

(In this drill, the teacher gives the cues indicated. Three students then carry on conversations according to the pattern illustrated, making appropriate substitutions. (Assume that A and C cannot hear each other, but that B can hear and be heard by both.))

T: 'al'                          'hal'
A: Jen al ke?                  Jen hal key?
B: Aet, jenaj al.           Hay&t, jenahaj hal.
(B):Jab, jeban al.           Jahab, jeban hal.

T: 'rot'                        'łet'
A: Jenaj al al rot?          Jenahaj hal hal łet?
B: Ijaje. Ewi am           Yijahj&y. Yewiy haṁ
   lemnak?                     łemṅak?
A: Ṅa ibar jaje.            Gah yibar jahj&y.
   Kwŭn kajitŭk iben mŭk.   Qen kajjit&k yippan ṁek.
B: Jenaj al kain al rot?   Jenahaj hal kahyin hal łet?
C: Jen al in maina.         Jen hal yin mahyinah.
B: Ekŭnan bwe jen al in   Yekeṅhan bey jen hal yin
   maina.                      mahyinah.
A: Emman jen al in         Yeṁṁan jen hal yin
   maina.                      mahyinah.

T: 'Hŭŭt'                    'gayat'
A: Jenaj al Hŭŭt?          Jenahaj hal gayat?
B: Ijaje. Ewi am lemnak?  Yijahj&y. Yewiy haṁ
                                 łemṁak?

A: Ña ibar jaje.
   Kwƀn kajitƀk iben mƀk.
B: Ñüüt eo jenaj al?
C: Jen al kiƀ.
B: Ekƀnan bwe jen al kiƀ.
A: Emman jen al kiƀ.
T: 'ia'
A: Jenaj al ia?
B: Ijaje. Ewi am lemnak?
A: Ña ibar jaje.
   Kwƀn kajitƀk iben mƀk.
B: Ia eo jenaj al ie?
C: Jen al imwen imƀ.
B: Ekƀnan bwe jen al
   imwen imƀn.
A: Emman jen al imwen
   imƀn.
T: 'ippen wƀn'
A: Jenaj al iben wƀn?
B: Ijaje. Ewi am
   lemnak?
A: Ña ibar jaje.
   Kwƀn kajitƀk iben.
B: Wƀn en jenaj al iben.
(B): Wƀn ran jenaj al
     ibeir.
C: Jen al iben dri jikul
   ran.
B: Ekƀnan bwe jen al
   iben dri jikul ran.
A: Emman jen al iben dri
   jikul ran.

Gah yibar jahj&y.
Qen kajjit&k yippan ṁek.
Gayat yew jenahaj hal?
Jen hal kiyyeh.
Yekeṅhan bey jen hal
   kiyyeh.
Yeṁṁan jen hal kiyyeh.
'yi'yah'
Jenahaj hal yi'yah?
Yijahj&y. Yewiy haṁ
   ḻemṅak?
Gah yibar jahj&y.
Qen kajjit&k yippan ṁek.
Yi'yah yew jenahaj hal
   yi'y&y?
Jen hal yiṁeyeṅ yiṁ&h.
Yekeṅhan bey jen hal
   yiṁeyeṅ yiṁen.
Yeṁṁan jen hal yiṁeyeṅ
   yiṁen.
'yippan wen'
Jenahaj hal yippan wen?
Yijahj&y. Yewiy haṁ
   ḻemṅak?
Gah yibar jahj&y.
Qen kajjit&k yippan.
Wen yeṅ jenahaj hal
   yippan?
Wen raṅ jenahaj hal
   yippayy&r?
Jen hal yippan rijikiwiḻ
   raṅ.
Yekeṅhan bey jen hal
   yippan rijikiwiḻ raṅ.
Yeṁṁaṅ jen hal yippan
   rijikiwiḻ raṅ.

*(Continue, substituting qqir&y, jerbal, ṁegay, and beybeynahtew for hal. The following are sample substitutions for times, places, participants, and kinds of songs, games, work, food, and conversations or stories.)*

Times
kiƀ Iok jidrik        kiyyeh ḻaq jidik
ilju                  yiljiw
lalim awa             ḻal&m hawah

buHnin                          biǰniyin
Ήe eraeleb                      bey yerahyelep

## Places
iturin imŐn jikul kan           yitiťin yiṁen jikiwił kañ
iar                             yiyhar
ilo kiranto en                  yilew kirañtew yeñ
iumin mԒ en                     yiwṁin may yeñ
Mieco Beach                     Miyeykew Piyij

## Participants
ladrik ro nejin Ali             ładik rew najin Hałiy
kumi en an hospital             qimiy yeñ han hawijpiteł
dri jittaken                    rijittakyeñ
dri jittoen                     rijitt&wyeñ
Tom                             Tawaṁ

## Kinds of songs
al in maina                     hal yin ṁahyinah
*(see Drill 6)*

## Kinds of games
iakiu                           yi'yakiyiw
anidreb                         haniydep
bile                            pil&y
kaj                             kahaj
balebol                         bahl&ybawał
turum                           tiťiṁ

## Kinds of work
kowainini                       kewwahyiniyniy
ekkal im                        kkal y&ṁ
amimŐno                         hamiyṁeñew
eHwŐr                           yaǰed
kŐmman wa                       keṁṁhan wah

## Kinds of food
mԒ                              may
ik                              y&k
bilawԒ                          pilahway
raij                            rahyij
waini                           wahyiniy

## Kinds of beyebeyenaatew
inoH                            yinaǰ
bwebwenato bajjik               beybeynahtew bajjik
bwebwenato in etto              beybeynahtew yin yettew
bwebwenato in BaibŐl            beybeynahtew yin bahyibeł
lekŐto bajjik                   l&yk&t&w bajj&k

## GRAMMATICAL NOTES

1. This lesson concentrates primarily on the -n which may be suffixed to subject prefixes in the same slot of the verb phrase as the -j 'progressive'. The meaning of -n can be best understood by translating it as *be + to*, since it is used both for mild commands and in future questions. Thus:

Yen yiteq.           'Let him come.'     or 'He is to come.'
Yen yiteq key?       'Will he come?'     or 'Is he to come?'

2. The introduction of <u>kar</u> into the above examples gives:

    Yen kar yiteq.           'Would that he had come.'
    Yen kar yiteq key?       'Would he have come?'

3. <u>Bey</u> is often followed by -n with the meaning 'so that':

    Yen yiteq bey yin           'Let him come so that
      lewey.                    I can see him.'
    Yen kar yiteq bey           'Would that he had come
      yin lewey.                so that I could have
                                seen him.'

*Note the 4th and 5th Commandments on this matter.* The Ten Commandments are included here because they fit in well with the grammar of this lesson. The Marshallese translation of the Bible constitutes the main portion of Marshallese literature. Many people know large portions of it by heart and it is often quoted or alluded to in daily idiom. The student who hopes to get at all close to Marshallese life and thought is advised to learn some of this language. Other quotations will be included in later lessons.

4. Note from Drill 12 that although simple future yes-no questions (those with <u>key</u>) use -n, the where, when, what kind, and with whom questions all use <u>nahaj</u>. The use of <u>n</u> in these latter meanings is restricted to dependent clauses:

    Yekeṅhan bey jeṇ           'Where does he want us
      qqir&y yi'yah?            to play?'

5. The word for 'house' is irregular in several ways:
(a) the original word was *<u>yiṁe</u>. This has become <u>y&ṁ</u> with the loss of the final vowel when the stem stands alone without suffixes.
(b) with suffixes, the original stem is preserved: <u>yiṁe-</u>, which gives:
        yiṁ&h           'my house'

                    yiṁeṁ          'your house'
                    yiṁen          'his house'
                    (etc.)
(c) instead of being separate particles following the
    word, the demonstratives fuse with the last part
    of the original stem ṁe-, giving:

        ṁiyin                      ṁ&k&yin
        ṁ&y                        ṁekay
        ṁ&yiy&h                    ṁekaykay
        ṁeñey                      ṁekañey
        ṁeñeyñey                   ṁekaykañey
        ṁeyeñ                      ṁekañ
        ṁeyiyeñ                    ṁekaykañ
        ṁeyew                      ṁekew
        ṁewiweyew                  ṁekewkew
        ṁet(ah)?

## SOUND DRILL

Learn to hear and produce the following sound distinctions:

| | | | | | | |
|---|---|---|---|---|---|---|
| lij | lij | 'pandanus keys falling out of ripe fruit' | lij | ḷij | from *lijlij* 'nibble (of fish)' |
| lḠ | lay | 'to rock or bank, a boat or plane' | lḠ | ḷay | 'pebble, gravel' |
| laH | lag | 'sky, heaven' | laH | ḷag | 'storm' |
| le | ley | 'ma'am' | le | ḷey | 'sir' |
| al | hal | 'to sing, song; sp. of fish (Hawaiian *ono*)' | al | haḷ | 'sun' |
| jol | jewel | 'alone, abandoned' | jol | jeweḷ | 'sol of the musical scale' |
| Hl | yal | 'to shave' | Hl | yaḷ | 'coconut milk' |
| kil | kiyil | 'to close' | kil | kiyiḷ | 'keel' |

Since it happens that these two l-sounds occur in many
pairs of words distinguishing men from women, it may
be helpful to refer to them as 'the man l' (ḷ) and
'the woman l' (l). In addition to the two *le*'s above,
you are referred to numerous other examples in the
reference section of Lesson Nine among the personal
demonstratives.

## SHORT PROSE SELECTIONS

### Kamlo
### Kaṁl&w

    if        stranger
Elañe   kwŏj  ruamaejet    ilo    ailiñ   in   Majŏl
Yelaggey qej riwahmayej&t yilew hay&l&g yin Mahjel
        get together  bring  you        gifts
armij  ro   rej  koba    im   bŏkwŏj  mŏñǎ  im  men -
harm&j rew  rej  k&wbah  yim  bekw&j  megay yim  men -
                          this  thing  'make cool'
in - lelok  ko  ñan yok.  Etan   men  jab in: kamlo.
yin - leylaq kew gan y&q.  Yetan  men  jab yin: kaml&w.
           chickens    pigs    breadfruit   all
Rej bokwŏj bao    im   biik  im    mǎ    im  aolep
Rej bekw&j bahwew yim piyik yim   may  yim hawelep
kinds             handicrafts
kain   mŏñǎ,  kab amimŏnŏ.    Rej al  im  eb  ñan yok
kahyin ṁegay, kab hamiyṁeñew.  Rej hal yim yeb gan y&q
                                              thank
im kwŏj aikuj  in  jutak  im  jibiij  im  kamolol
yim qej hayiqij yin jiwtak yim jipyij yim kaṁṁewelwel
ir.  Rej kamlo wŏt ñan ruamaejet    kab iroij,   ñe
y&r.  Rej kaṁl&w wet gañ riwahmay&j&t kab yirw&j,  gey
ej wŏr kemem,     kab ñe  ewŏr  dri-lotok.
yej wer keyemyem, kab gey yewer rilewteq.

### Kien Ko Joñoul
### Kiyen Kew J&g&wil

              gods            before me
1. En  ejelok    bar anij  ran ibŏm  ijilokio.
   Yen y&jj&laq bar hanij rañ yippaṁ yij&llaqih.
            create   chop to shape idols
2. Kwŏn jab komŏnmŏn im jekjek  ekjŏp  ñan yuk.
   Qen  jab kaṁanṁan yim j&kj&k  yekjap gan y&q.
          say common            for, because
3. Kwŏn jab ba  bata   etan  Jeova   am  Anij;  bwe
   Qen  jab bah pahtah yetan Jiy&wbah haṁ Hanij;  bey
         will never consider not any  his guilt, the
  Jeova    yejjamin  likit  ejelok   ruŏn,  eo
  Jiy&wbah  yejjamin  likit  yejjelaq  riwen,  yew

```
                       one who
                           ej  ba   bata    etan.
                           yej bah  pahtah  yetan.
                  remember                              make it
         4. KwÖn kememej     ran   in   JabÖt,  bwe kwÖn kokojar-
            Qen  k&y&my&m&j  rahan yin  Jabet,  bey qen  keqqejar-
            holy
            jare.
            jarey.
                  show obedience                            long
         5. KwÖn kiblie      Han jemÖm im  jinÖm, bwe en   eto
            Qen  kipliyy&y   gan jeṁaṁ yim jineṁ, bey yen yettew
                                on   the islet
            ran   ko   am   ion       eneo    Jeova    am  Anij
            rahan kew  haṁ  yi'yewen  yanyew  Jiy&wbah haṁ Hanij

            ej  lewoj  HÖn yuk.
            yej l&yw&j gan y&q.
                        murder
         6. KwÖn jab uror.
            Qen  jab wirw&r.
                         lust
         7. KwÖn jab lÜH.
            Qen  jab ɬ&g.
                         steal
         8. KwÖn jab kwot.
            Qen  jab kawat.
                      utter words false words        against
         9. KwÖn jab kennan    nan   in   riab   nae
            Qen  jab kennahan  nahan yin  riyab  ṅahyey

            your neighbor
            dri turum.
            ritiɬiṁ.
                       covet
         10. KwÖn jab ankwÖnak  imÖn  dri turum, kwÖn jab ankwÖnak
             Qen  jab haṅgeṅak yiṁen ritiɬiṁ,   qen  jab haṅgeṅak
                  spouse of              servant    male
             lio   belen  dri turum,  jab   karijeran   man,
             liyew palyen ritiɬiṁ,    jahab kar&yjeran  ṁahan,
                                                    cow
             jab   karijeran   kÖra,  jab   an  kau,    jab
             jahab kar&yjeran  keray, jahab han kahwiw, jahab
```

```
                          anything
     an   ass, jab    men eo    jabrewŭt   dri turum.
     han haj, jahab   men yew jabdeywet   ritiḷiṁ.
```

PROVERB

    Jab likten beke.        Jab likten peykey.

Contraction of:
    Jab likit bwe en bebe     Jab likit bey yen peypey
    kake.                        kahkey.

        Literally: 'Don't leave it so that
            he decides about it.'
        Equivalent: 'Don't leave the decision to
            others.'
        (or)      'Take the initiative.'
        (or)      'He who hesitates is lost.'

VOCABULARY

| | | |
|---|---|---|
| aidrik | hayidik | thin, narrow |
| akwǎl | haqayal | (see *iakwǎl*) |
| al | hal | sing, song |
| anidreb | haniydep | Marshallese kickball game |
| aoleb | hawelep | all |
| baaj | bahaj | hesitate, pass up (from *pass*) |
| Baibŭl | Bahyibeł | Bible |
| bajjik | bajjɛk | just (postposed to verbs) |
| balebol | bahlɛybawał | volley ball (from Engl.) |
| bebe | peypey | decide, decision |
| bikŭt | pikɛt | afraid to do something, cowardly |
| bile | pilɛy | play poker (from *play*) |
| blǎǎt | biłyat | flat (musically) (from English) |
| Bŭlau | Bełahwiw | Palau (from English) |
| bon | beń | clogged up, obstructed, constipated |
| bŭna | benah | off-key |
| Bonbe | Bɛwɛnpɛy | Ponape (from English) |
| bŭt | bɛt | naughty |
| buru, buruo- | bɛrɛw, biriwe- | throat; front of neck; heart (seat of emotions) |
| bwebwenato | beybeynahtew | (tell) a story, converse, conversation |
| dri lotok | rilewteq | visitor: <u>ri-</u> person, <u>lewe-</u> see, + directional |

| | | |
|---|---|---|
| drike | dikey | hate |
| drőHdrőH | degdeg | slap, pound |
| dror | dewer | put down |
| ebboH | ppeǧ | throaty (voice) |
| eb | yeb | dance |
| elaHe | yelaggey | if |
| ellaaj | ɫɫahaj | melodious and sonorous voice |
| ettᵾ | ttay | low |
| etetal | yetyetal | walking about (distributive of yetal) |
| iakwᵾl | yiyhaqayal | quarrel, argue (RᵾI., Rat. aqayal) |
| imȪ, -m, -n | yiṁ&h, -ṁ, -ṅ | my (your, his) house |
| imwen | yiṁeyeṅ | at that house: fusion of yiy, ṁe-, yeṅ |
| iturin | yitiɫin | near it (him, her): yiy at + tiɫi- |
| iroij | yirw&j (Rat.) yirwej (RᵾI.) | king, chief |
| jar | jar | pray, go to church |
| jenkwon | j&nq&n | related to each other (from niqiyik dewen) |
| jibiij | jipyij | (make a) speech (from English) |
| jijȪt | jiyjet | sit (down) |
| jittoen | jitt&wyeṅ | the west end of the island |
| jok | jewek | ashamed, embarrassed, shy |
| jotal | jewtal | eat while walking |
| jutak | jiwtak | stand (up) |
| kadrȪk | kadek | drunk |
| kain | kahyin | kind (from English) |
| kaj | kahaj | play cards (from *cards*) |
| kajitȪk | kajjit&k | ask, question |
| kake | kahkey | about it (pl. kahkiy about them) |
| kamolol | kaṁṁewelwel | thank |
| kauboe | kahwiwbewey | cowboy (from English) |
| keroro | k&yr&wr&w | (make) noise |
| kiȪ lok jidrik | kiyyeh ɫaq jidik | in a little bit |
| kiranto | kiraṅtew | playground (from *ground* via Japanese) |
| koba | k&wbah | add, put together, get together, common-law marriage |

| | | |
|---|---|---|
| koleiat | q&ł&yiyahat | nude, half-nude |
| kȯmman | keṁṁhan | make, do |
| kȯnan | keṅhan | like, want (to) |
| kotak | kewtak | raise |
| kumi | qimiy | team (from Japanese) |
| lamȯj | laṁ&j | call, shout |
| lekȯto | l&yk&t&w | light conversation, soft sell (from l&y&- use, k&t&w wind) |
| lemnak | łemṅak | think, thought |
| lȯḧ | łag | sky, heaven |
| lüḧ | l&g | commit adultery, lust |
| makoko | ṁak&wk&w | be unwilling, refuse |
| men | men | thing |
| maina | ṁahyinah | love song |
| mij | m&j | die, dead |
| mij lȯḧ | m&j lag | go to hell: 'dead from heaven' |
| mijak | mijak | fear, be afraid |
| mȯk | ṁek | please (used following -n̄) |
| mur | ṁił | ancient chant |
| nana | nahnah | bad, evil |
| naḧinmij | nahginm&j | be sick: 'almost dead' |
| nukwi(k) | niqiy(ik) | family, related to |
| okok | wekwek | pick pandanus |
| riab | riyab | false(hood), lie |
| rot | łet | what kind of? |
| ruamaejet | riwahmay&j&t | stranger (ri- person of, wah canoe, may&- come (?), j&t ocean) |
| Ruk | Riq | Truk |
| tabur | tabił | reluctant, hesitate to |
| timon | tiyṁeḧ | demon (from English) |
| turin | tiłin, tiłi- | near it (him, her) |
| turum | tiłiṁ | (play) trump--a card game (from English) |
| utiej | wity&j | high |
| utiej buru | wity&j b&r&w, wity&j biriwe- | proud: 'high throat, heart' |
| walok | wahlaq | appear |
| wätowätak | wayt&w-waytak | go back and forth: 'go west, go east' |
| wit | w&t, wite- | rain |
| wȯt | wet | only, just; continue |

## LESSON ELEVEN

Foods and eating;
transitives and intransitives;
the causative prefix.

### DIALOGUE

A: Emat ke mөHи?            Yemat key megay?

B: Aet, kwo kөnan ke        Hay&t, qekeńhan key
    mөHи?                     ṁegay?

A: Inaj mөHи lalim awa.     Yinahaj ṁegay ɬal&m hawah.

B: Eokwe emman.             Yeqey yeṁṁan.

A: Is the food cooked?
B: Yes, would you like to eat?
A: I'll eat at five o'clock.
B: Fine.

### SUBSTITUTION DRILL

1. Kwo kөnan ke <u>mөHи</u>?        Qekeńhan key <u>ṁegay</u>?
           tutu                                 tiwtiw
           kiki                                 kiykiy
           ikkure                               qqir&y
           iakiu                                yi'yakiyiw
           aluij pija                           halw&j pijah

2. Aet, ikөnan mөHи.         Hay&t, yikeńhan ṁegay?
            *(follow Drill 1)*

3. <u>Kwo</u> kөnan ke mөHи?        <u>Qekeńhan</u> key ṁegay?
   e                                ye
   re                               re
   komro                            q&ṁrew
   komeaḣ                           q&ṁyag
   komjel                           q&ṁj&y&l
   kom                              q&ṁ
   komwij                           q&ṁw&j

4. Inaj mөHи <u>lalim awa</u>.      Yinahaj ṁegay <u>ɬalem hawah</u>.
              jiljino awa                         jiljinew
                                                    hawah

103

```
              jiljilimjuŋn awa         jiljilimjiwen hawah
              rualitok awa            riwahliyt&k hawah
              ruo awa                 riwew hawah

5. Inaj mŏŋŋ lalim awa.       Yinahaj ṁegay ɫal&m hawah.
   kimro                      k&mrew
   kimjel                     k&mj&y&l
   kimeaṅ                     k&myag
   kim                        k&m
   kimuij                     k&mw&j

6. Emat ke mŋ ko?             Yemat key may kew? (mat
                                   cooked)
              kanniek eo               kanniy&k yew
              ieraj ko                 yi'yaraj kew
              ik ko                    y&k kew
              raij eo                  rahyij yew
              bilawŋ ko                pilahway kew
              jokkob eo                jeqqep yew

7. Aet, remat mŋ ko.          Hay&t, remat may kew.
       e    kanniek eo          ye      kanniy&k yew
       re   ieraj ko            re      yi'yaraj kew
   (etc., using the words from Drill 6.)
```

*(At first, give only* may kew, kanniy&k yew, *etc.
as cues, making sure the students put the proper
prefix on* mat *in the responses; then later give
only* may, kanniy&k, yi'yaraj, *etc. as cues and
make sure the students put the proper prefix on*
mat *and the proper particle* yew *or* kew *after the
cue words.)*

```
8. Enno ke mŋ ko?             Yennaw key may kew?
                              (follow Drill 6)

   Aet, renno...              Hay&t, rennaw....
        enno....                     yennaw....
                              (follow Drill 7)

9. Emat ke mŋ ko?             Yemahat key may kew?
                              (follow Drill 6)

10. Aet, remat....            Hay&t, remahat.... (mahat
         or                       all gone) or
    e mat....                     yemahat....
                              (follow Drill 7)
```

11. *(All sentences in this drill are not completely written out--only the parts of those that involve changes from the one preceding. At first the teacher should give each entire sentence as a cue; after students begin to learn the pattern, underlined portions are to serve as cues.)*

 Ear eḧwŭr.     Yehar ya̰ğed.
 Ear <u>eḧwŭre</u> ik eo.  Yehar <u>ya̰ğedey</u> y&k yew.
    <u>juŭn</u> ik       <u>jiwen</u> y&k
    <u>ruo</u> ik       <u>riwew</u> y&k
    <u>jet</u> ik       <u>jet</u> y&k
    <u>elŭḧ</u> ik      <u>yeleg</u> y&k

 Ear <u>eḧwŭri</u> ik ko.  Yehar <u>ya̰ğediy</u> y&k kew.
    ik <u>kḁ</u>        y&k <u>kay</u>
    ik <u>kan</u>       y&k <u>kaṅ</u>

 Ear <u>karun</u> ik.    Yehar <u>karwin</u> y&k.
 Ear <u>karuni</u> ik eo   Yehar <u>karwiniy</u> y&k yew
  (<u>konan</u>).      (<u>qeṅan</u>).
    <u>juŭn</u> ik       <u>jiwen</u> y&k
    <u>ruo</u> ik       <u>riwew</u> y&k
    <u>jet</u> ik       <u>jet</u> y&k
    <u>elŭḧ</u> ik      <u>yeleg</u> y&k
    ik <u>ko</u>        y&k <u>kew</u>
     (<u>konan</u>)      (<u>qeṅan</u>)
    ik <u>kḁ</u>        y&k <u>kay</u>
     (<u>konan</u>)      (<u>qeṅan</u>)
    ik <u>kan</u>       y&k <u>kaṅ</u>
     (<u>konan</u>)      (<u>qeṅan</u>)

 Ear <u>jetjet</u> ik.    Yehar <u>j&jj&t</u> y&k.
 Ear <u>jitik(i)</u>     Yehar <u>jitik(iy)</u>
  ik eo (<u>konan</u>).   y&k yew (<u>qeṅan</u>).
  <u>juŭn</u> ik       <u>jiwen</u> y&k
  <u>ruo</u> ik       <u>riwew</u> y&k
  <u>jet</u> ik       <u>jet</u> y&k
  <u>elŭḧ</u> ik      <u>yeleg</u> y&k
  ik <u>ko</u> (<u>konan</u>)   y&k <u>kew</u> (<u>qeṅan</u>)
  ik <u>kḁ</u> (<u>konan</u>)   y&k <u>kay</u> (<u>qeṅan</u>)
  ik <u>kan</u> (<u>konan</u>)  y&k <u>kaṅ</u> (<u>qeṅan</u>)

 Ear <u>kŭmat</u> ik.    Yehar <u>kemat</u> y&k.
 Ear <u>kŭmatte</u>     Yehar <u>kemattey</u>
  ik eo (<u>konan</u>).   y&k yew (<u>qeṅan</u>).
  <u>juŭn</u> ik       <u>jiwen</u> y&k
  <u>ruo</u> ik       <u>riwew</u> y&k
  <u>jet</u> ik       <u>jet</u> y&k
  <u>elŭḧ</u> ik      <u>yeleg</u> y&k

    Ear kŭmatti                    Yehar kemattiy
     ik ko (konan).                 y&k kew (qeñan).
     ik kŭ (konan)                  y&k kay (qeñan)
     ik kan (konan)                 y&k kañ (qeñan)
    Ear mŭŋŭ ik.                   Yehar ṁegay y&k.
    Ear kaŋ(e)                     Yehar kag(&y)
     ik eo (konan).                 y&k yew (qeñan).
     juŏn ik                        jiwen y&k
     ruo ik                         riwew y&k
     jet ik                         jet y&k
     elŭŋ ik                        yeleg y&k
    Ear kaŋ(i)                     Yehar kag(iy)
     ik ko (konan).                 y&k kew (qeñan).
     ik kŭ (konan)                  y&k kay (qeñan)
     ik kan (konan)                 y&k kañ (qeñan)
    Ear wia kola.                  Yehar wiyah k&wɫah.
    Ear wiaik(i)                   Yehar wiyahyik(iy)
     kola eo (limen).               k&wɫah yew (limen).
     juŏn kola                      jiwen k&wɫah
     ruo kola                       riwew k&wɫah
     jet kola                       jet k&wɫah
     elŭŋ kola                      yeleg k&wɫah
     kola ko (limen)                k&wɫah kew (limen)
     kola kŭ (limen)                k&wɫah kay (limen)
     kola kan (limen)               k&wɫah kañ (limen)
    Ear idrak kola.                Yehar yidahak k&wɫah.
    Ear ilim(i)                    Yehar yilim(iy)
     kola eo (limen).               k&wɫah yew (limen).
     juŏn kola                      jiwen k&wɫah
     ruo kola                       riwew k&wɫah
     jet kola                       jet k&wɫah
     elŭŋ kola                      yeleg k&wɫah
     kola ko (limen)                k&wɫah kew (limen)
     kola kŭ (limen)                k&wɫah kay (limen)
     kola kan (limen)               k&wlah kañ (limen)

*(Continue the above pattern with the following material.)*

    Ear kokweet.                   Yehar kaq&y&t.
    Ear kokweete kweet             Yehar kaq&y&t q&y&t
     eo (konan).                    yew (qeñan).
    Ear kokweeti kweet             Yehar kaq&y&t q&y&t
     ko (konan).                    kew (qeñan).
    Ear entak ni.                  Yehar y&ntak niy.
    Ear entake ni eo.              Yehar y&ntakey niy yew.
    Ear entaki ni ko.              Yehar y&ntakiy niy kew.

Ear kŭmkŭm mŭ.
Ear kŭmŭj(e) mŭ eo.
Ear kŭmŭj(i) mŭ ko.
Ear okok bŭb.
Ear okaj(e) bŭb eo.
Ear okaj(i) bŭb ko.
Ear kajukkwe.
Ear kajukkweik(i)
  jukkwe eo (kijen).
  jukkwe ko (kijen)
Ear dŭñdŭñ kweet.
Ear dŭñŭt(e) kweet eo.
Ear dŭñŭt(i) kweet ko.
Ear kaiuiu.
Ear kaiuik(i) iu eo.
          iu ko
Ear wia juka.
Ear wiaik(i) juka eo.
  lalim baun
  in juka
  juon bek
  in juka
Ear juka.
Ear jukaik(i)
  ti eo limen.
  ti ko limen
Ear jol.
Ear jole ik eo kijen.

Ear joli ik ko kijen.

Ear umum pilawŭ.
Ear umin(i) pilawŭ
  eo (kijen).
  pilawŭ ko (kijer)
Ear mwijmwij pilawŭ.
Ear mwijit(i) pilawŭ
  eo (kijen).
  pilawa ko (kijer)

Yehar keṁkeṁ may.
Yehar keṁej(ey) may yew.
Yehar keṁej(iy) may kew.
Yehar wekwek beb.
Yehar weqaj(&y) beb yew.
Yehar weqaj(iy) beb kew.
Yehar kajiqq&y.
Yehar kajiqq&yik(iy)
  jiqq&y yew (kijen).
  jiqq&y kew (kijen)
Yehar degdeg q&y&t.
Yehar d&g&t(&y) q&y&t yew.
Yehar d&g&t(iy) q&y&t kew.
Yehar kayiwyiw.
Yehar kayiwik(iy) yiw yew.
                 yiw kew
Yehar wiyah jiqah.
Yehar wiyahyik jiqah yew.
  łal&m bawin
  yin jiqah
  jiwen payak
  yin jiqah
Yehar jiqah.
Yehar jiqahyik(iy)
  tiy yew limen.
  tiy kew limen
Yehar jawał.
Yehar jawałey y&k yew
  kijen.
Yehar jawałiy y&k kew
  kijen.
Yehar wiṁwiṁ pilahway.
Yehar wiṁin(iy) pilahway
  yew (kijen).
  pilahway kew (kijed)
Yehar ṁijṁij pilahway.
Yehar ṁijit(iy) pilahway
  yew (kijen).
  pilahway kew (kijed)

Ear ajij mṹñṹ.
Ear ajije mṹñṹ eo
 (kijer).
Ear ajiji mṹñṹ ko
 (kijer).
Ear kwalkwol pilej.
Ear kwal(e) pilej eo
 (ñin).
Ear kwal(i) pilej ko
 (ñir).
Ear kṹmṹrṹ jibun.
Ear kṹmṹrṹik(i) jibun
 eo (ñin).
 jibun ko (ñir).
Ear kakonkon pilej.
Ear kakon(e) pilej eo
 (ñin).
Ear kakon(i) pilej ko
 (ñir).
Ear rarṹ.
Ear rakij(i) melan eo.
 nabṹjen mweo (imṹn)

Yehar hajy&j ṁegay.
Yehar hajy&j&y ṁegay yew
 (kijed).
Yehar hajy&jiy ṁegay kew
 (kijed).
Yehar qałq&ł pilyej.
Yehar qał(&y) pilyej yew
 (giyin).
Yehar qał(iy) pilyej kew
 (giyid).
Yehar keṁeray jibwin.
Yehar keṁerayik(iy) jibwin
 yew (giyin).
 jibwin kew (giyid)
Yehar kaqqeṅqeṅ pilyej.
Yehar kaqeṅ(ey) pilyej
 yew (giyin).
Yehar kaqeṅ(iy) pilyej
 kew (giyid).
Yehar rahr&h.
Yehar rakij(iy) melan yew.
 nabejan ṁeyew (yiṁen).

12. Ne ij mṹñṹ in jibboñ,
 ij kañ(e) wṹt ruo
 tonaj.
 Ne ij idrak kobe,
 ij ilim(i) wṹt ruo
 kab.

Gey yij ṁegay yin jibb&ğ,
 yij kag(&y) wet riwew
 tewnahaj.
Gey yij yidahak kawp&y,
 yij yilim(iy) wet riwew
 kab.

*(Use the same pattern with the following.)*

...wia in Jadredre,
...wṹt juṹn bek in
 raij.
...wia karjin,
...wot juṹn kalan.
...kwalkwol,
...wṹt takin kan aṹ.
...aen,
...wṹt jṹt kan aṹ.
...aluij pija,
...wṹt pija in kauboe.
...eñwṹr,
...wṹt jet ik.

...wiyah yin Jadeydey,
...wet jiwen payak yin
 rahyij.
...wiyah karjin,
...wet jiwen kałan.
...qałq&ł,
...wet takin kañ hah&h.
...hayen,
...w&t jehet kañ hah&h.
...halw&j pijah,
...wet pijah yin kawiwbe-
 wey.
...yağed,
...wet jet y&k.

```
...juka kobe,            ...jiqah kawp&y,
...wöt kin ruo jibun.    ...wet k&n riwew jibwin.
...mönü tonet,           ...ṁegay tawnet,
...wöt juön.             ...wet jiwen.
...kömköm,               ...keṁkeṁ,
...wöt juön bek.         ...wet jiwen payak.
...okok,                 ...wekwek,
...wöt juön böb.         ...wet jiwen beb.
...entak,                ...y&ntak,
...wöt jet.              ...wet jet.
...kokweet,              ...kaq&y&t,
...wöt juön.             ...wet jiwen.
...rarö,                 ...rahr&h,
...wöt naböjen mwen.     ...wet nabejan ṁeyen.
...kömat ik,             ...kemat y&k,
...wöt ruo.              ...wet riwew.
```

## GRAMMATICAL NOTES

1. Some Marshallese verbs, those of motion for example (yiteq *come*, tt&r *run*, etc.), are only intransitive; they never take objects. But other verbs may have both transitive and intransitive forms. For such verbs you will have to learn both forms separately, since they often cannot be derived or predicted one from the other.

Some show complete suppletion; there is no formal resemblance between the two forms:

| Intransitive | Transitive | |
|---|---|---|
| ṁegay | kag(&y) (Rȧl.), kan(&y) (Rat.) | eat |
| yidahak | yilim(iy) | drink |

Many show reduplication in the intransitive, and some vowel differences between the two forms:

| | | |
|---|---|---|
| j&kj&k | jek(ey) | chop |
| b&nb&n | biney | count |

Some show simply a vowel increment in the transitive form:

| | | |
|---|---|---|
| yaǧed | yaǧedey | fish |
| karwin | karwiniy | scale fish |

(When the vowel increment is iy as in karwinIY (as it usually is for verbs that have i's earlier in the stem), this one transitive form serves for both singular and plural objects. When, however, the vowel increment is another vowel (ey or &y) as in yaǧedey, this transitive form serves only for objects thought of in a singular sense, and ey is changed to iy for plural objects: see yaǧediy in Drill 11, for example.)

Some show consonant material (a so-called thematic consonant) in the transitive form which is not present in the intransitive:

  jag    jagit(iy)   cry (for)
  kemat   kemattey   cook

Almost all those that end in h or y or w in the intransitive form add the increment -(y)ik(iy) to form the transitive:

  wiyah   wiyahyik(iy)  buy
  jiqah   jiqahyik(iy)  sugar
  kawp&y  kawp&yik(iy)  (put) coffee (in)

(The vowel increments in parentheses are optional when the object is stated, but obligatory when the object is deleted: implied or clear from earlier context.)

Some forms show combinations of some or all of these processes (reduplication, vowel change, thematic consonant, vowel increment):

  j&jj&t (<j&tj&t) jitik(iy)  clean fish
  jałjał    jełat(&y)  unsnarl

2. The meaning distinction between intransitive and transitive is not a simple one, and your understanding of it will have to grow with your learning of the language. The reference section lists both forms for verbs for which you have met one or the other in earlier lessons, together with a translation. The parts of the translations in parentheses are those which need to be added for the transitive forms.

The following additional observations can be made for the moment. Consider the following sentences, some of which are similar to those of Drill 11.

  Yehar ihegay y&k.   'He was eating fish.'
  Yehar ihegay y&k yew. 'He ate *at* the fish (but did not consume all of it).'
  Yehar ihegay y&k kew. 'He ate at the fish (pl.) (but did not consume all of them).'
  *yehar kag(&y) y&k  (not a complete sentence)

|  |  |
|---|---|
| Yehar kag(&y) y&k yew. | 'He ate the fish (all of it).' |
| Yehar kag(iy) y&k kew. | 'He ate the fish (pl.) (all of each one of them).' |

Note from the first example above that even the intransitive form m̧egay can have an object stated (y&k), but that the meaning is then generic and never a specific item or quantity.

You will find, too, that the intransitive form is often not especially marked as active or passive from an English point of view. Thus in the second sentence of Drill 9 of Lesson Ten:

|  |  |
|---|---|
| Q&m̧in jab b&t bey q&m̧ nahaj degdeg. | 'Don't be naughty or you'll get slapped.' |

the intransitive degdeg could mean either 'slap' or 'get slapped', and that the latter is intended is clear only from the context. Similarly:

Jawan yenahaj m̧ijm̧ij rahyinyin.

can mean either 'John will be operated on today.' or '(Dr.) John will operate today.' (Mi̧jm̧ij is intransitive of the transitive m̧ijit(iy) 'cut'.)

3. In the lessons thus far you have met a number of examples of the causative prefix ka-, (ke-). Some have been so analyzed for you in the vocabulary sections:

|  |  |
|---|---|
| kadik | make little |
| katt&r | cause to run, drive |
| kewwahyiniyniy | make copra |

and others were left unanalyzed for the moment:

|  |  |
|---|---|
| kejagjag | cause to cry (play a musical instrument) |
| kabirehreh | make red (wear lipstick) |
| kagaj(ey) | make (something) fragrant (tr.) (put on perfume) |
| kam̧m̧ewelwel | thank, tell someone he is generous |
| kekkeyłaq | cause to fly |

You should begin to be on the lookout for other examples, and subject all words that begin with ka- or ke- to scrutiny in this regard from this point on. Usually the meaning of the causative prefix added to a stem will be clear if you know the meaning of the stem itself, but there are cases where the causative shifts the meaning somewhat further from an English point of view. One good example of this is:

>  ke- + jerbal 'work', which means 'use'

Some other examples are introduced in this lesson, where the causative plus the names of specific plants and animals means 'to look for', 'catch', or 'gather such'.

| | |
|---|---|
| kaq&y&t | 'fish for octopus' |
| kayiwyiw | 'look for or gather yiw' |
| kajiqq&y | 'look for or gather jiqq&y' |

Another special use is in the formation of ordinal numbers, where the causative is used after k&yin 'tool, utensil, thing for' and preceding the cardinal:

| | |
|---|---|
| k&yin kajiwen | 'first' ('thing for making one') |
| k&yin kariwew | 'second'   (etc.) |
| k&yin kajiliw | 'third' |
| k&yin kayeman | 'fourth' |
| (etc.) | |

SOUND DRILL

The word mat 'cooked', in Drills 6 and 7, and the word mahat 'all gone', in Drills 9 and 10 above, point up the need for mastering the vowel length contrast. Practice identifying and making the contrast between the following words:

| | | | | | | |
|---|---|---|---|---|---|---|
| mat | mat | 'cooked' | mat | mahat | 'all gone' | |
| man | mag | 'coconut about to fall' | maH | mahag | 'pandanus leaf' | |
| jok | jeq | 'to land, alight' | jook | jewek | 'ashamed' | |
| jen | jen | 'let's' | jeen | jeyen | 'chain' | |
| jen | jan | 'from' | jHn | jayan | 'cent(s)' | |
| bat | bat | 'hill; slow, late' | bat | bahat | 'smoke' | |

SHORT PROSE SELECTION

Ejjab kanuij lUH mUHH ilo ailiH in MajUl.
Yejjab kahn&w&j leg rhegay yilew hay&l&g yin Mahjeł.

Elab an lUH ek ak ejjab bwe mH im men ko jet.
Yełap han leg y&k hak yejjab bey may yim men kew jet.

Raij im pilawH, juka im mUHH ko jet iloan
Rahyij yim pilahway, jiqah yim rhegay kew jet yilewwahan

kŭŭn rej itok jen Amerka, Australia, kab
kayan rej yiteq jan Hamedkah, Hawijterełiyah, kab
Jeban. Elab aer kadrelołtok mweiuk im mŭŧŭ jen
Jepahan. Yełap hay&r kadd&yłaǧteq ṁeyiq yim ṁegay jan
aer kadriojlok waini.
hay&r kaddiyw&jłaq wahyiniy.

## PROVERB

(Bwidrikdrik marołroŧ)      (Bidikdik mareǧreǧ)
 kandrikdrik kin yokwe.       kandikdik k&n yi'yaqey.

'Share whatever small food you have with love.'

## VOCABULARY

| | | |
|---|---|---|
| bek | payak | bag (from English) |
| bwidrikdrik | biddikdik | an aggregate of tiny things |
| drŭŧŭt(e) | d&g&t&y(Rat.) degetey(Rŭl.) | (tr. of <u>degdeg</u>) slap, pound something |
| enno | nnaw | delicious, taste good |
| idrak | yidahak | drink (intr.) |
| ieraj | yi'yaraj | taro (general term) |
| ik | y&k, yike- | fish (general term) |
| ilim | yilim | (tr. of <u>yidahak</u>) drink something |
| iu | yiw | spongy meat of sprouted coconut |
| jetjet | j&jj&t | clean fish (intr.) |
| jitik(i) | jitik(iy) | clean a/some fish (tr.) |
| jokkob | jeqqep | soft rice or breadfruit |
| jol(e) | jawał(ey) | salt (intr.) (something (tr.)) (from English) |
| juka(ik(i)) | jiqah(yik-(iy)) | sugar (intr.) (something (tr.)) (from English) |
| jukkwe | jiqq&y | a clam--lives in sand |
| kŭŭn | kayan | can, tin (from English) |
| kadrelołtok | kadd&yleǧteq | import, bring in (ka- causative + <u>d&yleǧ</u> enter + directional) |
| kadriojlok | kaddiyw&jłaq | export, take out (ka- causative + <u>diy&w&j</u> go out + directional) |
| kaiuiu | kayiwyiw | gather sprouted coconuts (<u>ka</u>- causative + <u>yiw</u> (spongy meat of) sprouted coconuts) |
| kajukkwe | kajiqq&y | gather <u>jiqq&y</u> clams |

| | | |
|---|---|---|
| kakweet(e) | kaq&y&t(&y) | fish for q&y&t octopus (catch (tr.)) |
| kakon(e) | kaqeń(ey) | tr. of kaqqeńqeń |
| kakonkon | kaqqeńqeń | put away (intr.) |
| kalan | kaɫan | gallon (from English) |
| kanniek | kanniy&k | meat |
| kañ(e) | kag(&y)(Rñl.) kan(&y)(Rat.) | eat something (tr. of ṁegay) |
| karjin | karjin | kerosene (from English) |
| karun(i) | karwin(iy) | scale (a/some (tr.)) fish |
| kin | k&n | with, about, concerning |
| kola | k&wɫah | a bottle/can of soft drink (general term) |
| kŭmat(te) | kemat(tey) | cook (something (tr.)) (ka- causative + mat cooked) |
| kŭmŭj(e) | keṁej(ey) | picked a breadfruit (tr. of keṁkeṁ) |
| kŭmŭrŭ(ik (iy)) | keṁeray(ik (iy)) | (make) (something (tr.)) dry |
| kwal(e) | qaɫ(&y) | tr. of qaɫq&ɫ |
| kwalkwol | qaɫq&ɫ | wash clothes or dishes |
| kweet | q&y&t | octopus |
| limen | limen, lime- (Rñl.) nimen, nime- (Rat.) | (his) drink |
| mat | mahat | all gone |
| mat | mat | cooked |
| mŭñŭ | ṁegay | food, eat (intr.) |
| mŭrŭ | ṁeray | dry |
| mweiuk | ṁeyiq, ṁeyiye- | goods, provisions, wealth, gift |
| mwijit(i) | ṁijit(iy) | cut something (tr. of ṁijṁij) |
| mwijmwij | ṁijṁij | cut (intr.), operate (surgery) |
| okaj(e) | weqaj(&y) | pick a pandanus (tr. of wekwek) |
| rakij(i) | rakij(iy) | clean up, tidy something (tr. of rahr&h) |
| rarŭ | rahr&h | clean up, tidy (intr.) |
| tonaj | tewnahaj | doughnut (with hole) (from English) |
| tonet | tawnet | doughnut (without hole) (from English) |
| umin(i) | wiṁin(iy) | bake something in an earth oven (tr. of wiṁwiṁ) |

REFERENCE

*Here are both the intransitive and transitive forms of words introduced in the first ten lessons, most of which you have met only in the intransitive form to date. Parts of meanings in parentheses are those needed to translate the transitive (as opposed to the intransitive). Note that occasionally the causative prefix must be used with the transitive.*

| Intransitive | Transitive | Meaning |
|---|---|---|
| ban | baney | unable, weak (to do something) |
| bahaṁ | bahaṁey | bomb (something) |
| bahyiybeł | bahyiybełey | (teach) Bible |
| benah | benahyik(iy) | (sing) off-key |
| b&nb&n | biney | arithmetic, count (something), (take inventory of) |
| b&ÿ | b&ÿ&y | (become) night (on someone) |
| bilbil | biliy | (put) gum (on) |
| biwj&k | biwj&k&y | (tie) wear hair in knot |
| degdeg | d&g&t(&y) | slap, pound (something) |
| dewer | dewerey | put (something) down |
| diy&d&y | diy&k(&y) | earring, wear (something) on ear |
| haheh | hahin(iy) | swim (somewhere) |
| hajy&j | hajy&jiy | divide, divide up, distribute |
| (yiy)haqayal | (yiy)haqayaley (Rł1.) | quarrel, argue (with someone) |
| halw&j | haliwjey | look at (something) |
| haniydep | haniydepey | Marshallese kickball game (kick the ball) |
| hawah | hawahyik(iy) | (become the) hour (for) |
| hawelep | hawelepey | (take) all (of something) |
| jałjał | jełat(&y) | loosen, unwind, unsnarl (something) |
| jar | jarey | pray (for someone), go to church |
| jařem | jařemey | lightning, electricity, (get shocked) |
| jerak | jerakey | leave, hoist sail--canoes |
| jeray | jerahyik(iy) | be(friend) |
| jerbal | jerbaley | work (it out) |

| | | |
|---|---|---|
| j&wtah | j&wtahyik(iy) | (become) evening (on someone) |
| jibb&ǧ | jibb&ǧ&y | (become) morning (on someone) |
| jibwin | jibwiniy | (use a) spoon |
| jikiwił | jikiwiłiy | (teach in) school |
| kahaṁteh | kahaṁtehyik(iy) | (construct by) carpentry, work as carpenter |
| kahtak | kahtakey | study (teach) |
| kadek | kadekey | (become) drunk (from) |
| kajj&wj&w | kajj&wj&wyik(iy) | each, (take one by one) |
| kajjit&k | kajitikin(iy) | ask, question (someone) |
| kaṁtheweIwel | kaṁtheweIweley | thank (someone) |
| kawp&y | kawp&yik(iy) | (put) coffee (in) |
| kejagjag | kejag(ey) | play a musical instrument |
| kajjit&k | | |
| keṁkeṁ | k&ṁ&j(&y) (Rat.) keṁej(ey) (Rål.) | pick breadfruit with a stick |
| kewtak | kewtakey | raise (something) |
| keṁṁhan | keṁṁhaney | make, do (something) |
| kewwahyiniyniy | kewwahyiniyniyik(iy) | make copra (on a tract) |
| keyemyem | keyemyemey | feast--traditional for first birthday |
| k&wbah | k&wbahyik(iy) | add, put together, get together, common-law marriage |
| kkal | kalek(ey) | build (something) |
| qqir&y | kaqqir&yik(iy) | play (with) |
| łemṁak | łemṁakey | think (about something) |
| laṁ&j | laṁ&j&y | shout (call someone) |
| l&yk&t&w | l&yk&t&wyik-(iy) (Rat.) ley... (Rål.) | light conversation, (proposition someone) |
| liwij | liwijiy | lose (a game or contest) |
| ṁak&wk&w | kaṁak&wk&wyik(iy) | be unwilling, refuse (force against one's will) |
| ṁarṁar | ṁarek(ey) | (wear a) necklace |
| ṁarey | ṁareyik(iy) | marry (someone) |
| ṁegay (Rål./Rat.) kkan (Rat.) | kag(&y) (Rål.) kan(&y) (Rat.) | food, eat (something) |
| ṁuṁar | ṁarek(ey) | (wear a) fish basket |
| mareǧ | mareǧey | can, be (able to do something), ability, power |

| | | |
|---|---|---|
| nahnah | kanahnahyik(iy) | bad, evil, (put blame on someone), (speak evil of) |
| payagkeł | payagkełey | (put on a) bracelet |
| peyij | peyijiy | (write) page (number on) |
| pijah | pijahyik(iy) | picture, movie, draw a picture (of something), (take a picture of someone/thing with camera) |
| pp&q | piqet/piq&t&y | look for (something) |
| rahan | rahaney | (become) day (on someone) |
| rahyelep | rahyelepey | (become) noon (on someone) |
| riwiṁ | riwiṁiy | (make) room(s in) |
| riyab | riyabey | (tell) falsehood, lie (to someone) |
| takteh | taktehyik(iy) | be a doctor (for someone), see a doctor |
| teyej | teyejey | test (someone) |
| teyegkiy | teyegkiyik(iy) | (shine) flashlight (on) |
| tiłiṁ | tiłiṁiy | (play) trump--a card game |
| tirak | tirakey | (carry on a) truck |
| tirahyip | tirahyipiy | drive (a vehicle) |
| tiwtiw | katiwtiwik(iy) | wet, bathe (someone) |
| tiy | tiyik(iy) | (put) tea (in) |
| tiyṁah | tiyṁahyik(iy) | ship-metal hulled (send by surface mail) |
| wahyiniy | wahyiniyik(iy) | (grind) copra (into food) |
| w&t | witey | rain (on someone/thing) |
| wetewbahyiy | wetewbahyik(iy) | (give ride on) motor bike, scooter |
| wiṁwiṁ | wiṁin(iy) | bake (something) in earth oven |
| wity&j | kawity&j&y | (make something) high |
| wiyah | wiyahyik(iy) | buy (something) |
| yaǧed | yaǧedey | go fishing, to fish (for some kind of fish) |
| yetal | yetaley | go (over something) |
| y&ntak | y&ntakey | climb a coconut tree and pick coconuts (from it) |
| yinjiniyah | yinjiniyahyik-(iy) | (be) engineer (of a vessel) |

117

## LESSON TWELVE

Health and sicknesses; different
people's medicines; some superlative
idioms; similarities and differences;
and being careful.

### DIALOGUE

A: Emman ke am mour?  Yeṁhan key haṁ mewir?
B: Ejjab kanuij.  Yejjab kahn&w&j.
A: Kwo naḧinmij ke?  Qenahginm&j key?
B: Jidik, ibʉk mejin.  Jidik, yibek m&jyin.
A: Ewʉr ke limʉm uno?  Yewer key liṁeṁ winew?
B: Aet, ewʉr jet limʉ  Hay&t, yewer jet lim&h
 aspirin.  hajbiryin.

A: Are you feeling fine?
B: Not exactly.
A: Are you sick?
B: A little.
A: Do you have any medicine?
B: Yes, I have some aspirin.

### DRILLS

1. Emʉn ke <u>am</u> mour?  Yeṁhan key <u>haṁ</u> mewir?
    <u>am</u>iro  <u>ham</u>iyrew
    <u>am</u>ijel  <u>ham</u>iyj&(y&)l
    <u>am</u>ieaḧ  <u>ham</u>iyyag
    <u>am</u>iwʉj  <u>ham</u>iyw&j

2. Ejjab kanuij emman  Yejjab kahn&w&j yeṁhan
    <u>aʉ</u> mour.  <u>hah&h</u> mewir.
    <u>am</u>ro  <u>ham</u>rew
    <u>am</u>jel  <u>ham</u>j&(y&)l
    <u>am</u>eaḧ  <u>ham</u>yag
    <u>am</u>wʉj  <u>ham</u>w&j

3. Ewʉr ke limʉm uno?  Yewer key liṁeṁ <u>winew</u>?
    <u>bia</u>  <u>piyah</u>
    wʉjke  w&jk&y

118

|   |   |
|---|---|
| aspirin | hajbiryin |
| kola | k&wɫah |
| kobe | kawpey |
| ti | tiy |
| aibʉj | hay&b&j |
| kadʉk | kadek |
| dren | dan |

4. Ewʉr jet <u>limʉ</u> uno.   Yewer jet <u>lim&h</u> wiɦew.
    <u>limemro</u>                   <u>limemrew</u>
    <u>limemjil</u>                  <u>limemj&(y&)l</u>
    <u>limemeaɦ</u>                  <u>limemyag</u>
    <u>limemwʉj</u>                  <u>limemw&j</u>

5. Emat <u>limʉm</u> bia.    Yemahat <u>liɦeɦ</u> piyah.
    <u>limemiro</u>                   <u>limemiyrew</u>
    <u>limemijil</u>                  <u>limemiyj&(y&)l</u>
    <u>limemeaɦ</u>                   <u>limemiyyag</u>
    <u>limemiwʉj</u>                  <u>limemiyw&j</u>

6. Ej wʉr wʉt ke           Yej wer wet key
    <u>limʉm</u> kobe?              <u>liɦeɦ</u> kawb&y?
    <u>limeirro</u>                   <u>lim&yy&rrew</u>
    <u>limeirjil</u>                  <u>lim&yy&rj&(y&)l</u>
    <u>limeireaɦ</u>                  <u>lim&yy&ryag</u>
    <u>limeirwʉj</u>                  <u>lim&yy&rw&j</u>

7. *(Teacher gives underlined portion of desired response as cue, and then asks the question. For example:*
    *Teacher:* 'M&jyin'...qenahginm&j key?
    *Student:* J<u>idik</u>, yibek m&jyin.*)*

|   |   |
|---|---|
| Kwo naɦinmij ke? | Qenahginm&j key? |
| Jidrik, ibʉk | Jidik, yibek |
| <u>mejin</u>. | <u>m&jyin</u>. |
| <u>ilok loje in</u> | <u>yilaq lawj&y yin</u> |
| <u>bokbok in</u> | <u>peqpeq yin</u> |
| <u>bilo in</u> | <u>pil&w yin</u> |
| <u>bio in</u> | <u>piyaw yin</u> |
| <u>metak ob in</u> | <u>metak w&b yin</u> |
| <u>libbʉr in</u> | <u>ɫ&pp&r yin</u> |
| <u>mijen alliɦ</u> | <u>mijen hall&g</u> |
| Jidrik, emetak bʉra. | Jidik, yemetak <u>berah</u>. |
| <u>ʉtʉ</u> | <u>yatih</u> |
| <u>lojiʉ</u> | <u>lawjiy&h</u> |
| <u>enbwinʉ</u> | <u>yanibinnih</u> |

                Hiŭ                    giyih
                ubŭ                    wib&h
                Iojilhŭ                lawjilgih
                neiŭ                   ney&h

*(After the above have been learned fairly well in the order given, the teacher should mix up the cues requiring <u>yibek</u> and <u>yemetak</u>.)*

8. *(After Drill 7 has been well learned, add two more lines to each response for those using <u>yemetak</u>: a confirming question and answer. Be careful to change the possessive suffixes as necessary.)*

    T: 'Berah'...qenahginm&j key?
    A: Jidik, yemetak berah.
    B: Yeliqqiwin metak b&raṁ key?
    A: Hay&t, yeɬap han metak berah.
                *(or)*
       Jahab, jidik wet han metak berah.

    T: 'Yatih'...qenahginm&j key?
    A: Jidik, yemetak yatih.
    B: Yeliqqiwin metak yatiṁ key?
    A: Hay&t, yeɬap han metak yatih.
                *(or)*
       Jahab, jidik wet han metak yatih.

              *(etc.)*

9. *(Repeat the above, choosing from among the following confirming replies:)*

    A: Hay&t, yeliqqiwin metak berah.
                *(or)*
       Hay&t, yekahn&w&j yin metak berah.
                *(or)*
       Jahab, yejjab liqqiwin metak berah.
                *(or)*
       Jahab, yejjab kahn&w&j yin metak berah.

10. *(Now, learn the following two patterns of intensifying responses for use in the above drill. Then as a culminating exercise, repeat the drill, choosing at random from among all the possible responses you have learned.)*

    Yejjelaq wet metakin berah!
                    yatih
                    lawjiy&h
                    *(etc.)*

Yemak&y metak berah!
    yatih
    lawjiy&h
    (etc.)

11. Same, similar, and different.

*(Learn the following expressions well enough so that one of each set of three can be used as a cue for the other two.)*

'*Those two canoes are the same.*'
Einwöt juön wa kan         Yayinwet jiwen wah kañ
  (ruo).                     (riwew).
Einlokwöt juön wa          Yayinłaqwet jiwen wah
  kan (ruo).                 kañ (riwew).
Einjuön wa kan (ruo).      Yayinjiwen wah kañ (riwew).

Ein wa kan (ruo)           Yayin wah kañ (riwew)
  wöt juön.                  wet jiwen.
Ein wa kan (ruo) lok       Yayin wah kañ (riwew) laq
  wöt juön.                  wet jiwen.
Einjuön wa kan (ruo).      Yayinjiwen wah kañ (riwew).

'*You are like that fellow.*'
Eimwöt leen.               Yayiṁwet łeyeñ.
Eimlokwöt leen.            Yayiṁłaqwet łeyeñ.
Eim juön jen leen.         Yayiṁ jiwen jan łeyeñ.
Ein kwe wöt leen.          Yayin qey wet łeyeñ.
Ein kwe lok wöt leen.      Yayin qey łaq wet łeyeñ.
Einjuön kwe jen leen.      Yayinjiwen qey jan łeyeñ.

'*You are like me.*'
Ein kwe wöt ña.            Yayin qey wet gah.
Ein kwe lok wöt ña.        Yayin qey łaq wet gah.
Einjuön kwe jen ña.        Yayinjiwen qey jan gah.

'*The two of us are the same.*'
Eirro wöt juön.            Yayirrew wet jiwen.
Eirro lok wöt juön.        Yayirrew łaq wet jiwen.
Ejjab eirro wöt juön.      Yejjab yayirrew wet jiwen.

Ein kijro wöt juön.        Yayin k&jrew wet jiwen.
Ein kijro lok wöt juön.    Yayin k&jrew łaq wet jiwen.
Einjuön kijro jen dron.    Yayinjiwen k&jrew jan
                             dewen.

'*They are like the two of us.*'
Eierwöt kijro.             Yayiy&rwet k&jrew.
Eierlokwöt kijro.          Yayiy&rłaqwet k&jrew.
Ejjab eierwöt kijro.       Yejjab yayiy&rwet k&jrew.

'*I am like you.*'
Eiũ wõt kwe.                     Yayiyih wet qey.
Eiũ lok wõt kwe.                 Yayiyih łaq wet qey.
Ejjab eiũ wõt kwe.               Yejjab yayiyih wet qey.

'*The boy is like his father.*'
Ein ladrik eo wõt jemen.         Yayin ładik yew wet jeman.
Ein ladrik eo lok wõt            Yayin ładik yew łaq wet
  jemen.                           jeman.
Einjuõn ladrik eo jen            Yayinjiwen ładik yew jan
  jemen.                           jeman.

Ladrik eo einwõt jemen.          Ładik yew yayinwet jeman.
Ladrik eo einlokwõt              Ładik yew yayinłaqwet
  jemen.                           jeman.
Ladrik eo einjuõn jen            Ładik yew yayinjiwen jan
  jemen.                           jeman.

'*The boys are like their father.*'
Ein ladrik ro wõt                Yayin ładik rew wet
  jemãir.                          jemayy&r.
Ein ladrik ro lok                Yayin ładik rew łaq
  wõt jemãir.                      wet jemayy&r.
Einjuõn ladrik ro                Yayinjiwen ładik rew
  jen jemãir.                      jan jemayy&r.

Ladrik ro eierwõt                Ładik rew yayiy&rwet
  jemãir.                          jemayy&r.
Ladrik ro eierlokwõt             Ładik rew yayiy&rłaqwet
  jemãir.                          jemayy&r.
Ladrik ro ejjab                  Ładik rew yejjab
  eierwõt jemãir.                  yayiy&rwet jemayy&r.

12. (*Substitute in the following. Be sure to include ñey at the end of each response.*)

Kejbarok bwe en jab              Kejpareq bey yen jab
  wõtlok ajiri ne.                 w&tlaq hajiriy ñey.
  rub bato                         ŕip batew
  lutõk dren                       liwt&k dan
  bwil nuknuk                      bil niqniq
  botak nuknuk                     pewtak niqniq
  loḧloḧ mõḦã                      łaǵłaǵ ḿegay
  tutu buk                         tiwtiw b&q
  jorren radio                     jeŕŕayan r&ytiy&w
  etton nuknuk                     tt&w&n niqniq

GRAMMATICAL NOTES

1. The Ratak form of lime- 'my drink' is nime- and may be substituted in Drills 3 through 5 at the discretion of your teacher.

2. The words for *stomach* and *ear* begin with a special formative law- to which it is difficult to attach any particular meaning. Later you will learn other body parts with the same formative:

  lawǰiy     'mouth'
  lawberin pay   'palm'
  lawberin ney   'sole'
  lawdigiy (Rat.)  'posterior'
  lawtegay    'inside of thigh'

(Note that in jiy&metak the formative is left off of *stomach*.)

The same formative is sometimes used with two different words for *ocean* (and sometimes left off):

  (law)metew
    and
  (law)j&t

and also occurs with a number of land tract names, seemingly with a locative meaning:

  Lawkid&n   'at the kiden tree'
  Lawpigpig  'at the pigpig tree', etc.

3. The words introduced in this lesson exhibit a fairly widespread pattern of stem vowel change parallel in a way to that discussed in Grammatical Note 3 of Lesson Six:

| Unpossessed form | Stem that combines with possessive or other suffixes | Meaning |
|---|---|---|
| w&b | wibe- | chest |
| j&y | jiye- | stomach |

The same pattern occurs in several words introduced in earlier lessons:

| y&ṁ | yiṁe- | house |
| b&r&w | biriwe- | throat |
| w&t | wite- | rain |
| y&k | yike- | fish |

From these examples we can see that when a final *e* of the stem is dropped in the unsuffixed forms, preceding *i*'s are changed to *&*. This is a pattern to watch for in subsequent vocabulary.

4. Two words introduced in this lesson have a double *n* in the combining stem, one of which is dropped from the free form, together with the final vowel:

|            |              |        |
|------------|--------------|--------|
| dan        | danni-       | water  |
| yanbin     | yanbinni-    | body   |

5. Drill 10 introduces two idiomatic superlative expressions which are extremely common in many contexts:

| yejjelaq | wet | metakin... | 'nothing hurts more |
|----------|-----|------------|---------------------|
| nothing  | just | its pain  | than...'            |

| yemak&y    | metak... | 'its pain is out- |
|------------|----------|-------------------|
| it alone   | hurts    | standing...'      |

6. Drill 11 gives practice on several patterns with yayi- too complex to attempt to generalize in any space shorter than that of the drill itself. The first line of each triplet should be translated with 'the same as', the second 'similar to', and the third 'different from'. Note that yayi- always occurs with one of the possessive suffixes or the construct particle fused so as to be identical in form with the 3rd person singular suffix.

It may help you to get a feel for these constructions if you translate them something like this:

| Yayin | wah kañ riwew | wet | jiwen. |
|-------|---------------|-----|--------|
| (The) likeness of | those two canoes | (is) only | one. |

| Yayin | wet | jiwen | wah kañ riwew. |
|-------|-----|-------|----------------|
| (The) likeness of | only | one: | those two canoes. |

| Yayin | łaq | wet | jiwen... |
|-------|-----|-----|----------|
| (The) likeness of | (a little) away (from) | (being) only | one: |

| Yayin | jiwen... | (Note that this jiwen-- |
|-------|----------|-------------------------|
| (The) likeness of | (something) other: | the one in the third line of each triplet in Drill 11--behaves differently from those above, and should be translated differently, as indicated.) |

| Yayiṁ | wet | łeyeñ. |
|-------|-----|--------|
| Your likeness | (is) just | (that of) that fellow. |

| Yayiṁ | jiwen | jan | łeyeñ. |
|-------|-------|-----|--------|
| Your likeness | (is something) other | than | (that of) that fellow. |

7. Drill 12 gives practice on <u>kejpareq</u> with <u>bey</u>...-<u>n</u> in cautionary sentences.

8. The human head is very sacred in Marshallese culture--one never pats a person on the head, walks near the head of someone sleeping on a mat, or even walks around the east side of a house (if he is extremely careful), since people usually lie with their heads toward the east when sleeping, or in final rest. This attitude extends to a certain taboo on the word <u>bar</u>, <u>bera</u>- itself, and there are euphemisms which have developed, one of which is <u>wily&j</u>, <u>wiliyeje</u>-, the basic meaning of which is *cemetery*. However, <u>bar</u> itself is used rather than any euphemism in discussing sickness or pain, as in Drill 7.

## SOUND DRILL

Learn to hear and produce the following sound distinctions:

| | | | | | |
|---|---|---|---|---|---|
| drak | dak | 'duck' | rak | rak | 'south' |
| dra | dah | 'blood' | ra | rah | 'branch' |
| dran | dahan | 'his (her, its) blood or portion of pandanus' | ran | rahan | 'day; his (her, its) branch; on top of' |
| dak | dahak | 'fm. *idak* 'to drink'' | rak | rahak | 'to move over' |
| dri | diy | 'bone' | ri- | riy... | 'person prefix (as pronounced before light consonant stems)' |
| adr | had | 'our (incl.)' | ar | har | 'lagoon side; lagoon beach' |
| wȍd | wed | 'coral' | wȍr | wer | 'to have; there is' |
| wir | wid | 'piece' | wir | wir | 'swollen lymph gland' |
| madr | mad | 'spend time on something' | mar | mar | 'bushes, vines' |
| pidr | pid | 'buttocks' | pir | pir | 'to slip or slide down' |

## SHORT PROSE SELECTION

### Jerbal in Ajmour
### Jerbal yin Yajmewir

Ilo ailiñ in Majõl, kien ej bõk edro in
Yilew hayel&g yin Mahjeł, kiyen yej bek ddew yin
                                        responsible for
                          regarding caring for    preventing
aoleb jerbal ko kijjien kejbarok im bõbrae
hawelep jerbal kew kijjiyen kejpareq yim bebrahyey
          sickness      accidents
armij jen nañinmij im jorren. Ejelok wõnen
harm&j jan nahginm&j yim jełłayan. Yejjełaq weñyan
see a doctor               others
taktõ ñan dri jikul im ñan armij ro jet, ewõr
takteh gan rijikiwił yim gan harm&j rew jet, yewer
         small
wõnen ak edrik. Aoleb taktõ rej jerbal ñan kien,
weñyan hak yedik. Hawelep takteh rej jerbal gan kiyen,
        like                  most
ejjab einwõt Amerka. Elab tata ilo Majõl
yejjab yayinwet Hamedkah. Yełap tahtah yilew Mahjeł
             coryza, coughing,    stomach ache
nañinmij in uwir, bokbok, kab jiemetak. Nañinmij
nahginm&j yin wwir, peqpeq, kab jiy&metak. Nahginm&j
ko rellab rej aoleb itok jen ailiñ in belle,
kew rełłap rej hawelep yiteq jan hay&l&g yin palley,
          polio        tuberculosis
einwõt polio kab tiipi.
yayinwet beliy&w kab tiypiy.

### PROVERB

Mõman mone dron.          Mṁahan ṁeñey dewen.

Roughly: 'Men fool each other.'

### VOCABULARY

| | | |
|---|---|---|
| aibõj | hay&b&j | cistern, well, fresh water from either |
| ãt, -ũ, -im, -in | yat, yati- | eyebrow, (sinus) |
| bato | batew (intr.) batewik(iy) (tr.) | bottle (from English) be cut by broken glass |

| | | |
|---|---|---|
| bia | piyah | beer (from English) |
| bilo | pil&w (intr.) | blind |
| | kapil&w&k(iy) (tr.) | make someone blind |
| bilo in | pil&w yin | pink eye |
| bio | piyaw (intr.) | feel chilly, feverish |
| | kapiyawik(iy) (tr.) | make someone chilly |
| bokbok | peqpeq (intr.) | cough |
| | ka...ey (tr.) | make someone cough |
| bŭbrae | bebrahyey | prevent (intr.) + ik(iy) (tr.) |
| bŭk edro | bek ddew | take responsibility for, take care of |
| botak | pewtak | torn |
| dren | dan, danni- | water, general term for liquids |
| edro | ddew | heavy, weight |
| einwŭt | yayinwet, yayi-...wet | as, like |
| enbwin, -ŭ, -im, -in | yanbin, yanbinni- | body |
| etton | tt&w&n (intr.) ka...&y (tr.) | dirty |
| ilok loje | yilaq lawj&y | diarrhea: 'stomach is diluted' |
| jiemetak | jiy&metak | stomach ache |
| jorren | jeɫɫayan (intr.) ka...ey (tr.) | broken, no good, accident (has a wide range of meaning like German *kaput*.) |
| kejbarok | kejpareq | protect, take care (intr.) + ey (tr.) |
| kijjien | kijjiyen, kijjiye- | regarding it, opposite |
| libbŭr | ɫ&pp&r | mumps |
| loje | lawj&y, lawjiye- | stomach |
| loji-, -ŭ, -ŭm, -en | lawjiy&h,...eṁ, ...en | (see *loje*) |
| loḧloḧ | ɫaǵɫaǵ | covered with flies (distributive of ɫaǵ *housefly*) |
| lukkun | liqqiwin | really |
| lutŭk | liwt&k (intr.) liwtekey (tr. sg.) liwt&kiy (tr. pl.) | spill |
| make | mak&y | alone, by...self |
| mejin | m&jyin | common cold (m&j sickness + yin demonstrative) |

| | | |
|---|---|---|
| metak | metak, metaki- (intr.) ka....ey (tr.) | pain, hurt |
| mijen alliḧ | mijen halleg | menstrual period: 'sickness of the month' |
| mŏman | [ṁeṁahan] | Ratak pronunciation of ṁṁahan *man*, *men* |
| mone | ṁeṅey (tr.) ṁeṅ (intr.) | deceive, lie, fool, trick (someone) |
| mour | mewir (intr.) ka...iy (tr.) | live, life, health make someone live |
| naḧinmij | nahginm&j (intr.) ka...&y (tr.) | sick(ness) (literally: 'almost dead') make someone sick |
| ne | ney, neye- | leg, foot |
| ob | w&b, wibe- | chest |
| rub | ṫip(ey) (tr.) ṫipṫip (intr.) | shatter, break (of glass, stones, coconuts, houses, vessels, etc.) |
| ubŏ, -m, -n | wib&h, wibeṁ, wiben | (see *ob*) |
| uwir | wwir (intr.) | nasal mucous, coryza, have a runny nose |
| | wwiriy (tr.) | blow nose on someone |
| wŏjke | w&jk&y | whiskey (homophonous with the word for *tree*) |
| wŏtlok | w&tlaq (intr.) ka...ey (tr.) | fall cause something to fall |

## LESSON THIRTEEN

More health problems; by (one's) self;
the lost has been found; general vs.
specific statements.

### DIALOGUE

A: Emetak bɵra, ewɵr ke  Yemetak berah, yewer key
   uno ibbam?  winew yippaṁ?

B: Ejelok. Bwɵlen emman  Yejjeɫaq, bɛlɛn yeṁṁan
   ḧe kwo kakkije.  gey qekakkijɛy.

C: Jab. Emmanlok ḧe  Jahab. Yeṁṁan ɫaq gey
   kwo ilen taktɵ.  qeyilan takteh.

A: Renaj letok wɵt  Renahaj leyteq wet
   aspirin.  hajbiryin.

B: Emman tata aspirin  Yeṁṁan tahtah hajbiryin
   ḧan metak bar.  gan metak bar.

A: I have a headache. Do you have any medicine?
B: None. Maybe you should rest.
C: No. You'd better see a doctor.
A: They'll only give me aspirin.
B: Aspirin is the best thing for a headache.

### DRILLS

1. Ewɵr ke uno in  Yewer key winew yin
   <u>metak bar</u> ibbam?  <u>metak bar</u> yippaṁ?
   metak loje  metak lawjɛy
   metak lojilḧi  metak lawjilgiy
   metak ḧi  metak giy
   mej metak  mɛj metak
   metak ob  metak wɛb

2. Ej kabbok uno bwe  Yej kappɛq winew bey
   emetak <u>bɵran</u>.  yemetak <u>beran</u>.
   lojien  lawjiyen
   lojilḧin  lawjilgin
   ḧiin  giyin
   mejen  mejan
   ubɵn  wiben

3. Letok limŭ uno bwe emetak bŭra.
   lojiŭ
   lojilĦŭ
   Ħiŭ
   meja
   ubŭ

Leyteq lim&h winew bey yemetak berah.
   lawjīy&h
   lawjilgih
   giyih
   mejah
   wib&h

4. Kwŭn idrak uno bwe en jab metak boram.
   lojiŭm
   lojilĦum
   Ħiim
   mejam
   ubŭm

Qen yidahak winew bey yen jab metak beraṁ.
   lawjīyeṁ
   lawjilgiṁ
   giyiṁ
   mejaṁ
   wibeṁ

5. Emman Ħe kwo kakkije.
   emmanlok
   emmantata
      ilen taktŭ
      idrak uno
      kiki
      kabbok aspirin

Yeṁṁan gey qekakkij&y.
yeṁṁan ɫaq
yeṁṁan tahtah
      yilan takteh
      yidahak winew
      kiykiy
      kapp&q hajbiryin

6. Letok pinjel ne iturum.
   buk
   pen
   beba
   jook

Leyteq pinjeɫ ṅey yitiɾiṁ.
   b&q
   peyen
   p&ybah
   jawak

7. Ijjab lewŭj pinjel e iturŭ.
(repeat Drill 6)

Yijjab leyw&j pinjeɫ y&y yitiɾih.

8. Litok pinjel kane iturum.
(repeat Drill 6)

Liyteq pinjeɫ kaṅey yitiɾiṁ.

9. Ijjab liwŭj pinjel kŭ iturŭ.
(repeat Drill 6)

Yijjab liyw&j pinjeɫ kay yitiɾih.

10.
A: NaĦinmij rot eo an leo?
B: Ebŭk naninmij in T.B.

Nahginm&j ɫet yew han ɫeyew?
Yebek nahginm&j yin tiypiy.

```
        tŭHal                     tegal
        leba                      lebah
        kirro                     kirr&w
        polio                     bewłiyew
        ilok loje                 yilaq lawj&y
        jeblij                    jeplej
        ruk                       łik
        metak je                  metak j&y
        metak bar                 metak bar
        metak Hi                  metak giy
        libbŭr                    l&pp&r
```

11.
A: EnaHinmij rot lio?          Yenahginm&j łet liyew?
B: Ebokbok.                    Yepeqpeq.
```
        bakke                     bakkey
        bilo                      pil&w
        bio                       piyaw
        mij rŭjitin               m&j rayjitin
        bon                       beH
        drekH                     dekay
        wŭt                       wet
        jaroHroH                  jarreǵreǵ
        rajjia                    rajjiyah
        mijin alliH               mijen hall&g
        mijin pitpit              mijen pitpit
```
*(Continue, substituting all the words from Drill 10.)*

12. *'He ate by himself.'* : *'He ate alone.'* OR *'He fed himself.'*
```
     Ear make mŭHŭ.            Yehar mak&y ḿegay.
              al                          hal
              jar                         jar
              ettŭr                       tt&r
              jerak                       jerak
              jerbal                      jerbal
              eHwŭr                       yaǵed
              entak                       y&ntak
              kŭmkŭm                      keḿkeḿ
              okok                        wekwek
```

13. Ear make kaH ik eo.        Yehar mak&y kag y&k yew.
```
              al al eo                   hal hal yew
              jare dri mij               jarey rim&j
                 eo                         yew
              kattir wa                  katt&r wah
                 eo                         yew
```

jerake wa eo                jerakey wah yew
jerbale wa eo               jerbaley y&k yew
eħwŭre ik ko                yaǧedey y&k kew
entake ni ko                y&ntakey niy kew
kŭmŭj ṁa ko                 k&ṁ&j may kew
okaj bŭb ko                 wekaj beb kew

14. '*Division of labor.*'

Jerbal in an <u>jejjo wŭt</u>.   Jerbal yin han <u>j&jj&w wet</u>.
 jabdrewŭt                       jabdeywet
 kŭrŭ wŭt                        keray wet
 jet wŭt                         jet wet
 dri belle wŭt                   ripalley wet
 eman wŭt                        ṁṁahan wet
 taktŭ wŭt                       takteh wet
 lŭllab wŭt                      łełłap wet
 aoleb                           hawelep
 dri kaki wŭt                    rikakiy wet
 kirijin wŭt                     kirijin wet

15. (*At first, the teacher should give all of each line as a cue, later only the possessive and what follows, and finally only the first word. Responses should always be the complete sentence.*)

Ejjab <u>erreo aer kŭmman</u> uno.   Yejjab <u>rreyew hay&r keṁṁan</u> winew.
 bwe aŭ jelŭ kajin Majŭl             bey hah&h jełay kajin Mahjeł
 lab an metak bŭra                   łap han metak berah
 etton aer kŭmat mŭħŭ                tt&w&n hay&r kemat ṁegay
 emman am jerbal                     ṁṁan haṁ jerbal
 mŭkaj an kattŭr wa en               ṁekaj han katt&r wah yeṅ
 lab an jelŭ kamtŭ                   łap han jełay kahaṁteh
 makijkij an lotok kij               makijkij han lewteq k&j
 mŭkaj an ettŭr leen                 ṁekaj han tt&r łeyeṅ

16. (*Do this drill in the same way as the preceding one.*)

Ebwe kijŭ mŭħŭ.              Yebey kij&h ṁegay.
 lŭħ nejin mak                leg najin ṁahak
 nana kijŭm mŭħŭ              nahnah kijeṁ ṁegay
 iet nejŭ jeen                'yiy&t najih jayan
 utiej imŭn im                wity&j yiṁen y&ṁ
 enno kijŭ mŭħŭ               nnaw kij&h ṁegay
 lŭħ kona ik                  leg qeṅah y&k

```
        bil limŭ kobe              bil lim&h kawp&y
        bwe kijer mŭHü             bey kijed ṁegay
        tŭHal nimen ti             tegal nimen tiy
        erreo imŭm im              rreyew yiṁeṁ y&ṁ
        etton imŭ im               tt&w&n yiṁ&h y&ṁ
        mŭkaj wan wa               ṁekaj wahan wah
        emman am nuknuk            ṁuhan haṁ niqniq
        aibŭjbŭj nimer kobe        hay&b&jb&j nimed kawp&y
        ettü imŭn im               ttay yiṁen y&ṁ
        mŭlo nimŭ kola             ṁ&l&w nim&h k&w⁺ah
        bat waan wa                bat wahan wah
        jabwe Hiü kab              jabey giyih kab
```

17. *(Teacher should give full statements from Drills 15 and 16 as cues, and students should give yes-no questions for which the statements are appropriate responses, then answer their own questions.)*

    T: Ejjab erreo aer kŭmman uno.      Yejjab rreyew hay&r keṁuhan winew.
    A: Erreo ke aer kŭmman uno?      Yerreyew key hay&r keṁuhan winew?
    B: Jab, ejjab erreo aer kŭmman uno.      Jahab, yejjab rreyew hay&r keṁuhan winew.

    T: Ejjab bwe kijŭ mŭHü.      Yejjab bey kij&h ṁegay.
    A: Ebwe ke kijŭm mŭHü?      Yebey key kijeṁ ṁegay?
    B: Jab, ejjab bwe kijŭ mŭHü.      Jahab, yejjab bey kij&h ṁegay.
    (etc.)      (etc.)

18. Alternative questions.
*(This exercise should be done in the same way, except that the questions should be formulated as follows:)*

    Erreo ke etton aer kŭmman uno?      Yerreyew key y&tt&w&n hay&r keṁuhan winew?
    Ebwe ke ejabwe am jelü kajin Majŭl?      Yebey key yejabey haṁ je⁺ay kajin Ṁahje⁺?
    Elab ke edrik an metak bŭram?      Ye⁺ap key yedik han metak beraṁ?

*(Other opposite pairs of adjective-like words you will need are:)*

    Emman ke enana...?      Yeṁuhan key yenahnah...?
    Emŭkaj ke ebat...?      Yeṁekaj key yebat...?
    Emakijkij ke ejamakijkij...?      Yemakijkij key yejammakijkij...?

El̈n̈ ke eiet...?          Yeleg key yeyiy&t...?
Eutiej ke ettü...?         Yewity&j key yettay...?
Enno ke enana...?          Yennaw key yenahnah...?
Ebil ke emül̈o...?         Yebil key y&ṁ&l&w...?
Etül̈al ke eaibüj-         Yetegal key yehay&b&j-
 büj...?                    b&j...?

19. The lost has been found: *'Here is the book you were looking for [it].'* (After this drill has been well modeled and partially learned, use only the underlined words as cues.)

Bin̄jel eo in kwar          Pin̄jeł yew yin qehar
 bukote.                     piq&t&y.
Eḧin binjel eo kwar        Y&gyin pinjeł yew qehar
 bukote.                     piq&t&y.

Buk eo en kwar bukote.     B&q yew yeṅ qehar piq&t&y.
Eḧen buk eo kwar           Yegyeṅ b&q yew qehar
 bukote.                     piq&t&y.

Beba ko kan kwar           P&ybah kew kaṅ qehar
 bukoti.                     piq&tiy.
Erkan beba ko kwar         Yerkaṅ p&ybah kew qehar
 bukoti.                     piq&t&y.

Armij ro rein kwar         Harm&j rew r&yin qehar
 bukot ir.                   piq&t y&r.
Irrein armij ro kwar       Y&rr&yin harm&j rew qehar
 bukot ir.                   piq&t y&r.

Ladik eo uweo kwar         Ładik yew wiweyew qehar
 bukote.                     piq&t&y.
Eḧuweo ladik eo            Y&gwiweyew ładik yew
 kwar bukote.                qehar piq&t&y.

*(Continue, changing the following according to the above pattern.)*

Jook ko kü kwar            Jawak kew kay qehar
 bukoti.                     piq&tiy.
Binjel eo ne kwar          Pin̄jeł yew ḣey qehar
 bukote.                     piq&t&y.
Ledrik eo in kwar          Ledik yew yin qehar
 bukote.                     piq&t&y.
Lümaro ran kwar            Łeṁahrew raṅ qehar
 bukot ir.                   piq&t y&r.
Buk ko kein kwar           B&q kew k&yin qehar
 bukoti.                     piq&tiy.
Buk eo eo kwar             B&q yew yew qehar
 bukote.                     piq&t&y.

Buk eo in kwar bukote.   B&q yew yin qehar piq&t&y.
Buk eo e kwar bukote.    B&q yew y&y qehar piq&t&y.

20. *(Change the sentences of Drill 16 in the following way:)*

Ebwe mᵿH̋ᵿ eo kijᵿ.      Yebey ṁegay yew kij&h.
ElᵿH̋ mak eo nejin.       Yeleg ṁahak yew najin.
Enana mᵿH̋ᵿ eo kijᵿm.    Yenahnah ṁegay yew kijeṁ.
*(etc.)*                  *(etc.)*

*(Do the same for the questions you built in Drill 18 as you have just done for sentences of Drill 16.)*

Ebwe ke ejabwe mᵿH̋ᵿ    Yebey key yejabey ṁegay
eo kijᵿ?                 yew kij&h?
*(etc.)*                 *(etc.)*

### GRAMMATICAL NOTES

1. In Drill 16, the statements should be translated very generally:

Yebey kij&h ṁegay.        'I have an adequate diet.'
Yeleg najin ṁahak.        'He always has lots of money.'
Yetegal nimen tiy.        'He drinks his tea sweet.'
Yeṁekaj wahan wah.        'He always has fast canoes.'
                          *(etc.)*

The change effected by Drill 20, however, gives much more specific meanings:

Yebey ṁegay yew          'The food I have is suffi-
kij&h.                    cient.'
Yeṁekaj wah yew          'His canoe is fast.'
wahan.
                          *(etc.)*

2. The underlined portions of sentences in Drill 19 may by themselves constitute complete sentences:

<u>Pinjeł yew</u>                <u>yin</u>.
The pencil (formerly) not visible is here between us.

The sentences of the drill have a dependent clause added:

...<u>qehar piq&t&y</u>
---'the one you were looking for'

Note that <u>piq&t&y</u> is the transitive form of <u>pp&q</u> listed in the reference section of Lesson Eleven, on page 117. While in some sentences the final <u>&y</u> is optional:

135

Yihar piq&t(&y) pinjeł yew.

In the sentences of Drill 19 it (or one of its replacements) is obligatory. The replacements are iy for plural non-human objects:

Pinjeł kew kań qehar piq&tiy.

and y&r for plural human objects:

Badik rew rań qehar piq&t y&r.

This is the pattern for all transitive vowel increments, except that the singular-plural distinction is not made for transitives that already have an iy increment for singular objects.

| Object | Transitives in -&y and -ey | Transitives in -iy | |
|---|---|---|---|
| sg. | -&y / -ey | -iy | --- (no dis- |
| pl. non-human | -iy | -iy | tinction) |
| pl. human | y&r | y&r | |

Note that the second of the two demonstratives in the cues of Drill 19 is changed to the comparable *sentence* demonstrative when it is shifted to the beginning of the sentence:

```
_____ pinjeł yew yin...
y&qyin pinjeł yew _____...
```

3. The last three lines of Drill 19 exhibit some subtle meaning distinctions:

| | |
|---|---|
| b&q yew yew... | (book brought into view while speaking) |
| b&q yew yin... | (book already in view of both speaker and addressee) |
| b&q yew y&y... | (book near and in view of speaker but remains out of view of addressee) |

## SOUND DRILL

In addition to the *l* and *r* sounds drilled on in Lessons 10 and 12, there is a third kind of each, of the *w*-variety: ł and ɍ.

| lwe | ł&y | pond | rwe | ɍey | to put a hand in |
| lwit | łiyit | to slurp | ruj | ɍij | to wake up |
| lot | łet | top of mast | rot | ɍet | what kind? |
| tol | teł | mountain | mor | meɍ | worn out |
| | | | mur | miɍ | ancient chant |

Note that l̠ and r̠ at the end of a syllable give the
preceding vowel an [u] or [o] sound. The same is true
of q, g̠ and n̠.

| tok | teq | hither | bol̠ | b&g̠ | night |
| jok | jeq | alight | rol̠ | reg̠ | hear |
| ruk | riq | Truk | bon | ben̠ | clogged up |

SHORT PROSE SELECTION

## Uno in Majôl
### Winew yin Mahjel̠

before
Mokta     jen an dri belle bôktok uno   ko   aer
M̂eqtah   jan han ripalley bekteq winew kew hay&r

       themselves                              leaves
dri-Majôl rar  make  kômman aer   uno  jen bwilôk,
riM̂ahjel̠ rehar mak&y ken̠un̠an hay&r winew jan b&l&k,

grass    roots                        treat (medically)
ujoj,    okar im men ko  jet.  Jerbal in  unoik
wijw&j, wekar yim men kew jet. Jerbal yin winewik

       few   only                    hide
armij  an  jejjo wôt.  Dri uno rein rar  noj  uno
harm&j han j&jj&w wet. Riwinew r&yin rehar n̠ewej winew

       the manner of         reveal
ko  aer    im  wâwin    kômmani   im  kwalok wôt n̠an ro
kew hay&r yim wayw&y&n ken̠un̠aniy yim qahl̠aq wet gan rew

their relatives     because     missionaries
nukier im  jer̠l̠ir.     Kin an  kar missionary ro
niqiyy&r yim jerayy&r. K&n han kar mejinedey rew

                          witchcraft
lemnak bwe uno   in  Majôl   ej  jerbal kin anijnij,
l̠emn̠ak bey winew yin M̂ahjel̠ yej jerbal k&n hanijnij,

       happy              allow
rar  jab kanuij   mônônô  in  kôtlok an  armij
rehar jab kahn&w&j n̠en̠ehn̠eh yin ketl̠aq han harm&j

use them
kejerbali.  Taktô ro  rej jab bar kôtlok an  dri Majôl
kejerbaliy. Takteh rew rej jab bar ketl̠aq han riM̂ahjel̠

             sanitary
make  uno   bwe ejjab erreo   aer   kômman uno   im
mak&y winew bey yejjab rrewyew hay&r ken̠un̠an winew yim

```
                              take power
bar juőn elab   aer     bŭk maroH jen armij.   Kin men
bar jiwen yełap hay&r   bek mareǧ jan harm&j.  K&n men
         there are hardly any               still
in,  mottan jidrik ejelok  dri uno ej  mour  wŏt kiŏ.
yin, ṁettan jidik yejjełaq riwinew yej mewir wet kiyyeh.
```

<u>PROVERB</u>

    Jiner ilo kŏbo,        Jined yilew k&b&w,
   jemer im jemen ro jet.   jemad yim jeman rew jet.
       'Our mother forever, our father
        and the father of others.'

<u>VOCABULARY</u>

| | | |
|---|---|---|
| aibŏjbŏj | hay&b&jb&j (intr.) | bland, little taste; |
| | ka...&y (tr.) | not sweet, sour or salty (related to <u>hay&b&j</u> *fresh water*) |
| anijnij | hanijnij (intr.) | witchcraft, magic |
| | ...iy (tr.) | |
| aoleb | hawelep, hawelepa- (intr.) | all (of) |
| | ...ey (tr.) | |
| bakke | bakkey | yaws (ulcerated); a large sore |
| bilo | pil&w (intr.) | blind, see poorly, have cataracts, trachoma |
| | kapil&wyik(iy)(tr.) | make someone... |
| bwilŏk | b&l&k, bilike- | leaf |
| drekH | dekay | stone, rock; yaws, skin ulcers |
| dri mij | rim&j | dead person |
| erreo | rr&y&w (intr.) | clean, pure, clear, sanitary |
| | karr&y&wik(iy)(tr.) | |
| iet | 'yiy&t (intr.) | few |
| | ka...&y (tr.) | |
| iturŭ | yitiłih | near me |
| jabdrewŏt | jabdeywet | any, each, every, all |
| jamakijkij | jammakijkij (intr.) | not often, seldom, infrequent <u>ja-</u> + <u>makijkij</u> |
| | ka...ey | |
| jaroHroH | jarreǧreǧ (intr.) | deaf, hard of hearing (distributive of <u>reǧ</u> *hear* + <u>ja-</u> negative prefix) |

| | ka...ey (tr.) | pretend to be... make someone... |
|---|---|---|
| jeblij | jeplej (intr.) ka...ey (tr.) | veneral disease (general term) (from *syphilis*) |
| jejo | j&jj&w | a few |
| kakkije | kakkij&y (intr.) ...ik(iy) (tr.) | rest, vacation, holiday |
| kejerbal | kejerbal | use (causative + *work*) |
| kirijin | kirjin (intr.) ...iy (tr.) | a Christian make someone Christian |
| kirro | kirr&w (intr.) ka...&y(iy) (tr.) | arthritis, rheumatism, gout make someone... |
| kŭbo | k&b&w | forever |
| kŭtlok | k&tɬaq | release, allow, permit, free |
| leba | lebah (intr.) ka...yik(iy) (tr.) | leprosy (from English) |
| makijkij | makijkij | often, frequent |
| mijen pitpit | mijen pitpit | sickness: abdominal pain and swelling |
| missionary | mejinedey (intr.) ...ik(iy) (tr.) | missionary, convert (from English) |
| mij rŭjitin | m&j rayjitin | paralysis from stroke ('his one side is dead') |
| mokta | ṁeqtah ṁeqtahtah | before first of all |
| mŭlo | ṁ&ɬ&w (intr.) ka...ik(iy) (tr.) | cool |
| mŭnŭnŭ | ṁeṅehṅeh (intr.) ka...yik(iy) (tr.) | happy |
| mŭttan jidrik | ṁettan jidik | soon, almost |
| noj | ṅewej (intr.) ...&y (tr.) | hide, conceal |
| okar | wekar, wekara- | root |
| pitpit | pitpit (intr.) pit(iy) (tr.) | traditional medicine (secret) which involves rubbing with coconut oil |
| rajjia | rajjiyah | yaws, skin ulcers |
| ruk | riq | yaws, sores on bottom of feet |
| tŭṅal | tegal | sweet; diabetes |

| | | |
|---|---|---|
| ujoj | wijw&j | grass (general term) |
| unoik | winewyik (tr.) | treat with medicine; |
| | winew (intr.) | paint |
| wʊt | wet | have a boil |

## LESSON FOURTEEN

Occupations; adjective-like words;
and singular-plural forms
of such dimensional words;
the reflexive **katey**.

### DIALOGUE

A: Kwȯj jerbal rot?         Qej jerbal ɫet?
B: Ij dri kaki iben kien.    Yij rikakiy yippan kiyen.
A: High School ke ta?        Hayey jikiwiɫ key tah?
B: Jab, elementary.          Jahab, yeɫemeyenter&y.
A: Kwȯj jokwe ia?            Qej j&q&y yi'yah?
B: Ij jokwe Rita. Ak         Yij j&q&y Riytah. Hak
   kwȯj et bajjȯk ran        qej y&t bajj&k rahan
   kein.                      k&yin.
A: Ejaḧin mȯj aȯ jikul,      Yejjagin ṁ&j hah&h jiki-
   mȯttan juȯn yiȯ.           wiɫ, ṁettan jiwen 'yiyeh.
B: Kate wȯt yok, ejjab       Katey wet y&q, yejjab
   to.                        tew.

A: What kind of work do you do?
B: I am a teacher with the government.
A: High School, or what?
B: No, elementary.
A: Where do you live?
B: I live in Rita. What are you doing these days?
A: My schooling is almost finished--one more year.
B: Work hard. It won't be long.

### DRILLS

1. Kwȯj jerbal rot?              Qej jerbal ɫet?
   Ij <u>dri kaki iben kien</u>.    Yij <u>rikakiy yippan kiyen</u>.
      dri kaki in mission      rikakiy yin miyjen
      taktȯ                    takteh
      kamtȯ                    kahaṁteh
      injinia                  yinjiniyah
      dri wia                  riwiyah
      jela                     jeyɫah
      nȯj                      nehej

dri iʊk pilawʜ		riyiy&k pilahway
dri eʜwʊr		riyaǧed
dri kallib		rikallib
dri jarom		rijaɫem
dri mwijbar		riṁijbar
dri jeje		rij&yj&y
dri ekajet		riyakajet
bilijmen		pilijmayan
dri katu		rikatiw
dri meto		rimetew
kaben		kapen
mej		meyej
dri kʊmman baib		rikeṁṁan bahyib
dri jojomar		rij&wj&wmar
komja		qeṁjah
dri jʊkjʊk wa		rij&kj&k wah
dri kowainini		rikewwahyiniyniy
dri lale bao		rilahley bahwew
dri lale bik		rilahley piyik
dri liaklok		riliyahakɫaq

2. Emʊj ke am jikul?   Yeṁ&j key haṁ jikiwiɫ?
   Jab, ejaʜlin mʊj aʊ   Jahab, yejjagin ṁ&j hah&h
   <u>jikul</u>.   <u>jikiwiɫ</u>.
   jerbal   jerbal
   mʊʜʜ   ṁegay
   jeje   j&yj&y
   kiki   kiykiy
   ikkure   qqir&y
   jerakrʊk   jerakr&k
   kowainini   kewwahyiniyniy
   rarʊ   rahr&h
   dri kaki   rikakiy
   tutu   tiwtiw
   kakkije   kakkij&y

3. E mʊj ke an jikul?   Yeṁ&j key han jikiwiɫ?
  Mʊttan juʊn yiʊ.   Ṁettan jiwen 'yiyeh.
  Enaj mʊj an jikul   Yenahaj ṁ&j han jikiwiɫ
  lokin <u>juʊn yiʊ</u>.   ɫaqin <u>jiwen 'yiyeh</u>.
    ruo alliʜ   riwew hall&g
    jilu wik   jiliw wiyik
    emen ran   yeman rahan
    lalim awa   ɫalem hawah
    joʜoul minit   j&g&wil minit

4. Ej jab to im enaj mōj      Yejjab tew yim yenahaj ṁ&j
   an John <u>jikul</u>.            han Jawan <u>jikiwił</u>.

   *(Use the cues from Drill 2 in this and the following drill.)*

5. Mōttan wōt jidik emōj      Mettan jidik yeṁ&j han
   an Miten <u>jikul</u>.           Miyten <u>jikiwił</u>.

6. Ewi <u>pinjel</u> eo?              Yewiy <u>pinjeł</u> yew?
   Uweo ion tabel             Wiweyew yi'yewen teybeł
   en.                        yeṅ.
   Iiō ion tabel              'Yiy&h yi'yewen teybeł
   e.                         y&y.
   Iien ion tabel             'Yiyen yi'yewen teybeł
   en.                        yeṅ.
   Ełenene ion tabel          Yegṅeyṅey yi'yewen teybeł
   ne.                        ṅey.

      buk                     b&q
      ben                     peyen
      beba                    p&ybah
      jook                    jawak

7. <u>Singular-plural changes in six pairs of dimensional words</u>.

   *(Change the following sentences from singular to plural by changing <u>yew</u> to <u>kew</u>, changing the subject prefix from <u>ye-</u> to <u>re-</u>, and by doubling the proper (underlined) consonants of the dimensional words. (Since this doubling is often not represented in traditional spelling, the drill is given only in phonetic spelling.) Use the first of each pair of sentences as the cue. Ignore for the moment the words in parentheses to the right.)*

   <u>The school is large</u> *(in size or high in level)*.
   Yełap jikiwił yew.         (łapłap)
   Rełłap jikiwił kew.        (łłap)

   <u>The school is small</u> *(in size or low in level)*.
   Yedik jikiwił yew.         (dikdik)
   Reddik jikiwił kew.        (ddik)

   <u>The school is large</u> *(in size)*.
   Yekilep jikiwił yew.       (kileplep)
   Rekkillep jikiwił kew.     (killep)

   <u>The school is small</u> *(in size)*.
   Yedik jikiwił yew.         (jidikdik)
   Reddik jikiwił kew.        (jiddik)

*The book is thick.*
Yemij&l b&q yew.                          (mij&lj&l)
Remmij&l b&q kew.                         (mmij&l/mijj&l)

*The book is thin.*
Yemaniy b&q yew.                          (maniyniy)
Remmanniy b&q kew.                        ((m)manniy)

*The rope is thick.*
Yehayiłip tew yew.                        (hayiłipłip)
Rehayiłłip tew kew.                       (hayiłłip)

*The rope is thin.*
Yehayidik tew yew.       (Rạlik)          (hayidikdik)
Rehayiddik tew kew.                       (hayiddik)

Yehayinig tew yew.       (Ratak)          (hayinignig)
Rehayinnig tew kew.                       (hayinnig)

*The channel is wide.*
Yedepakpak tew yew.                       (depakpak) *(no change)*

Reddepakpak tew yew.                      (ddepakpak/ deppakpak)

*The channel is narrow.*
Yehayidik tew yew.                        (yehayinig...)
*(Repeat hayidik from above, since it is the opposite of depakpak as well as of hayiłip.)*

*The rope is long.*
Yehayeteq tew yew.       (Rạlik)          (hayeteqteq)
Rehayetteq tew kew.                       (hayetteq)

Yehayiteq tew yew.       (Ratak)          (hayiteqteq)
Rehayitteq tew kew.                       (hayitteq)

*The rope is short.*
Yekadiw tew yew.                          (kadiwdiw)
Rekkaddiw tew kew.                        ((k)ka(d)diw)
                                          *(either k or d or both are doubled)*

*(Now repeat the above using other singular demonstratives in the cues and their plural counterparts in the responses:* yin, yeñ, ñey, y&y, wiweyew. *Continue until the singular-plural single-double consonant distinction for this small set of words has become second nature.)*

8. *(Proceed with this drill as with the preceding one. These adjective-like words show no comparable singular plural distinction, however. Ignore for the moment the words in parentheses.)*

| | | |
|---|---|---|
| Ebat wa eo. | Yebat wah yew. | (batb&t) |
| Emŏkaj wa eo. | Yemekaj wah yew. | (mekajk&j) |
| Enno ik eo. | Yennaw y&k yew. | (nnawn&w) |
| Enana ik eo. | Yenahnah y&k yew. | (nahnah) *(no change)* |
| Emman mweo. | Yemhan meyew. | (mhanm&n) |
| Enana mweo. | Yenahnah meyew. | |
| Etŏlial ti eo. | Yetegal tiy yew. | (tegalg&l) |
| Eaibŏjbŏj ti eo. | Yehay&b&jb&j tiy yew. | (hay&b&jb&j) *(no change)* |
| Ejol ik eo. | Yejawał y&k yew. | (jawałw&ł) |
| Eaibŏjbŏj ik eo. | Yehay&b&jb&j y&k yew. | |
| Emŏli mŭ eo. | Y&m&g may yew. | (m&gm&g) |
| Enno mŭ eo. | Yennaw may yew. | |
| Eliaj ut eo. | Yegaj wit yew. | (gajg&j) |
| Enana bwin ut eo. | Yenahnah biyin wit yew. | (biynahnah) |
| Eriab jibij eo. | Yeriyab jipyij yew. | (riyab&b) |
| Emol jibij eo. | Yemewel jipyij yew. | (mewelwel) |
| Eouwi ik eo. | Yewwiy y&k yew. | (wwiywiy) |
| Eaibŏjbŏj ik eo. | Yehay&b&jb&j y&k yew. | |
| Erreo mweo. | Yerreyew meyew. | (rreyewyew) |
| Etton mweo. | Y&tt&w&n meyew. | (tt&w&nw&n) |
| Edro bek eo. | Yeddew payak yew. | (ddewdew) |
| Emera bek eo. | Yemerah payak yew. | (merahrah) |
| Etutu nuknuk eo. | Yetiwtiw niqniq yew. | (tiwtiw) *(no change)* |
| Emŏrŭ nuknuk eo. | Yemeray niqniq yew. | (merayr&y) |
| Ebin nuknuk eo. | Y&p&n niqniq yew. | (p&np&n) |
| Ebiroro nuknuk eo. | Yepid&wd&w niqniq yew. | (pid&wd&w) *(no change)* |

| | | |
|---|---|---|
| Emwilal aibŭj eo. | Yeṁilaḷ hay&b&j yew. | (ṁilaḷḷaḷ) |
| Ebijbij aibŭj eo. | Y&p&jp&j hay&b&j yew. | (p&jp&j) *(no change)* |
| Eutiej armij eo. | Yewity&j harm&j yew. | (wity&jy&j) |
| Ettṵ armij eo. | Yettay harm&j yew. | (ttayt&y) |

*(Repeat, using other demonstratives as in Drill 7.)*

9. *(Build sentences based on those of Drills 7 and 8 like the following--similar to the first sentence of the prose selection. Use the underlined words, and other similar ones, as cues.)*

   Yewer jiwen <u>jikiwiḷ</u> <u>yeḷap</u>, kab jet re<u>dd</u>ik.
   Yewer jiwen <u>b&q</u> <u>mij&l</u>, kab jet <u>mm</u>a<u>nn</u>iy.
   Yewer jiwen <u>b&q</u> <u>maniy</u>, kab jet <u>mm</u>ij&l.
   Yewer jiwen <u>wah</u> <u>bat</u>, kab jet ṁekaj.
   *(etc.)*

10. <u>Adjective-like verbs as post-position modifiers.</u>

    *(Using the sentences of Drills 7 and 8 as cues, ask questions with <u>pad</u> <u>yi'yah</u> as responses, using the forms of the adjective-like words given in parentheses in the earlier drills. For example:)*

    | Cue: | Response: |
    |---|---|
    | <u>Yeḷap</u> jikiwiḷ yew. | <u>Yepad</u> <u>yi'yah</u> jikiwiḷ <u>ḷapḷap</u> yew? |
    | Re<u>ḷḷap</u> jikiwiḷ kew. | Repad yi'yah jikiwiḷ <u>ḷḷap</u> kew? |
    | Ye<u>kilep</u> jikiwiḷ yew. | Yepad yi'yah jikiwiḷ <u>kileplep</u> yew? |
    | Rek<u>killep</u> jikiwiḷ kew. | Repad yi'yah jikiwiḷ <u>killep</u> kew? |

    *(Note the contrast between the pattern of the dimensional words above, and that of the non-dimensional words which follow:)*

    | | |
    |---|---|
    | Ye<u>bat</u> wah yew. | Yepad yi'yah wah <u>batb&t</u> yew? |
    | Re<u>bat</u> wah kew. | Repad yi'yah wah <u>batb&t</u> kew? |
    | Yeṁ<u>ekaj</u> wah yew. | Yepad yi'yah wah ṁ<u>ekajk&j</u> yew? |
    | Reṁ<u>ekaj</u> wah kew. | Repad yi'yah wah ṁ<u>ekajk&j</u> kew? |

11. The reflexive katey.

| Kwɵn kate wɵt yok jerbal. | Qen katey wet y&q jerbal. |
|---|---|
| komin    kom | q&rhin    q&rh |
| ren    ir | ren    y&r |
| en    e | yen    y&y |
| jen    kij | jen    k&j |
| in    iɵ | yin    y&h |
| komro en    komro | q&rhrew yen    q&rh |
| (etc.) | (etc.) |

Kwɵj kate wɵt yok jerbal.    Qej katey wet y&q jerbal.
(etc.)    (etc.)

Kwar kate wɵt yok jerbal.    Qehar katey wet y&q jerbal.
(etc.)    (etc.)

Kwɵn kar kate wɵt yok
jerbal.
(etc.)

Qen kar katey wet y&q
jerbal.
(etc.)

Kwɵnaj kate wɵt yok
jerbal.
(etc.)

Qenahaj katey wet y&q
jerbal.
(etc.)

(*Continue, substituting other verbs such as* jikiwił,
kahtak, kerhɨhan wah, kerhɨhaney, *etc.*)

### GRAMMATICAL NOTES

1. The set of six pairs of dimensional opposites in Drill 7 are unique in having distinct plural forms with doubled consonants. You may find the single-double consonant contrast difficult to hear and produce smoothly at first, but should work on Drill 7 and the relevant portions of Drills 9 and 10 intensively until you have mastered the matter.

Note that words having more than one consonant in addition to the final one such as kilep, kadiw, and maniy, may double both to form kkillep, kkaddiw, and mmanniy, while others double only one--the first one not counting a y.

Later you will meet different doubled *and* reduplicated forms of the same words, such as:
                 jjidikdik
                 kkileplep
                 mmij&lj&l
                    (*etc.*)

but forms such as these should not be confused with the double-consonant plurals drilled in this lesson, since they make a different meaning distinction which will be introduced in a later lesson.

2. ḷap and kilep, and dik and ji(d)dik have a great deal of overlap in meaning and, as the drills show, some overlap in use within a paradigm, but as their use with jikiwiḷ demonstrates partially, kilep and ji(d)dik are usually restricted to references to size, while ḷap and dik are more general and can refer as well to level, intensity, status along time or social dimensions.

3. In Drill 10, where the adjective-like verbs are shifted to a position immediately following the word they modify and preceding a demonstrative, note that there is a special post-positional form for each such verb that is not already reduplicated, and that the dimensional words carry a singular-plural contrast over into the post position, while non-dimensional words use the same special post-positional form for both singular and plural.

4. Note that in at least some contexts dik is the opposite of both ḷap and kilep, and hayidik is the opposite of both hayiḷip and depakpak. This should not seem strange when one recalls that in English *light* is the opposite of both *dark* and *heavy*, *short* of both *long* and *tall*, and *narrow* of both *wide* and *broad*. Later we will learn that dik is also the opposite of rittew 'old': that is, 'young'.

5. The verb jerakr&k, although related to jerak, has certain differences in meaning. The transitive forms of each help to make this clear:

    Wen har jerakr&k&y teq wah yeṅ?   'Who sailed that canoe here?'
    Wen har jerakey w&jḷay yeṅ?   'Who hoisted that sail?'

Note the difference in objects. A few more examples may help:

    Rejerakr&k ḷeṁahrew.   'The fellows are sailing.'
    Rejerak ḷeṁahrew.   'The fellows have hoisted sail (departed).'

    Q&ṁ nahaj jerakr&k gayat?   'When will you be sailing?'
    Wiyik yin laḷ.   'Next week.'

149

  Q&ṁ nahaj jerak    'When will you (hoist)
  gayat?         sail?'
  Ḅal&m hawah.     'Five o'clock.'

SOUND DRILL

In Lesson Eleven we noted that vowel sounds in
Marshallese may be distinctively short or long. The
same is true of consonants; for example, the length
of the consonant sounds is the only difference between the following pairs of words:

eta yetah my name  etta yettah to be in the
                 early months
                 of pregnancy
ebat yebat he is slow ebbat yebbat he is late
elaḧ yeḷag squall   ellaḧ yeḷḷag to spread
                 something
                 apart
ele yeley possessed elle yelley to bear fruit
      by a            or flowers;
      demon          serves you
                 right
ewi yewiy where is  eouwi yewwiy taste of
      it?             fatty fish
kiŮ kiy&h laws that kiŮ  kiyyeh now
      apply to
      me

Long consonants are always written doubly in our phonetic spelling.

SHORT PROSE SELECTION

     Jikul ko ilo Majŭl
    Jikiwiḷ kew yilew Ṁahjeḷ

                 small
Ewŭr juŭn high school kab jejo jikul jidrik
Yewer jiwen hayey jikiwiḷ kab j&jj&w jikiwiḷ <u>jiddik</u>

        almost
ilo ailiḧ in Majŭl. Enaḧin aoleb jikul
yilew hayel&g yin Ṁahjeḷ. <u>Yenahgin</u> hawelep jikiwiḷ

     though
kein an kien botab ebar wŭr an katilik im
k&yin han kiyen <u>bethab</u> yebar wer han katilik yim

brotijen. Ewŭr emen an brotijen jikul kab
birewtiyjen. Yewer yeman han birewtiyjen jikiwiḷ kab

ruo   an  katilik.  Eloñ  rikaki  in  belle  ilo
riwew han katilik.  Yeleg rikakiy yin palley yilew
jikul   kein   rellab  ak   enañin   aoleb   jikul   ko
jikiwił k&yin rełłap hak yenahgin hawelep jikiwił kew
redrik  ilo    ailiñ   ko   ilikin  dri-Majől  wőt  rej
reddik yilew hay&l&g kew yilikin riMahjeł wet rej
rikaki.   Buk,  pinjel  im   mwein   jikul   ko   jet,
rikakiy.  B&q, pinjeł yim m&yiyen jikiwił kew jet,
                  easy  find them
ejjab  kanuij    bidodo   loi.    Kin men in  jerbal
yejjab kahn&w&j pid&wd&w lewiy.  K&n men yin jerbal
in  rikaki  ilo    ailiñ   ko   ilikin  ej  juőn  jerbal
yin rikakiy yilew hay&l&g kew yilikin yej jiwen jerbal
hard       trying
ebin   im  kaboubub.
yep&n yim kapewibwib.

**PROVERB**

    Bőtőktők ej kur.        Betektek yej kir.
        Literally: 'Blood calls.'
    Equivalent: 'Blood runs thicker than water.'

**VOCABULARY**

| | | |
|---|---|---|
| aetok | hayeteq (Rál.) | long; tall (of people) |
|  | hayiteq (Rat.) |  |
| aidik | hayidik | narrow; thin (of long, round objects) |
| ailib | hayiłib | thick (of long, round objects) |
| baib | bahyib | pipe (from English) |
| bilijmen | pilijmayan | policeman (from English) |
| biroro | pid&wd&w | soft, easy |
| bijbij | p&jp&j | shallow |
| bin | p&n | hard, difficult |
| bőtab | bethab | although, nevertheless |
| bőtőktők | betektek | blood, bleed |
| drebakbak | depakpak | wide, broad |
| ekajet | yakajet | to interrogate (+ *ri-* = *judge*) |
| enañin | yenahgin | almost, nearly |
| eouwi | (ye) + wwiy | delicious smell of fatty fish cooking |

| | | |
|---|---|---|
| iūk | 'yiy&k(&y) | mix |
| jeje | j&yj&y | write |
| jela | jey£ah | sailor (from English) |
| jerakrūk | jerakr&k (intr.) ...&y (tr.) | go sailing |
| jojomar | j&wj&wmar | intercede, defend (+ <u>ri</u> = *public defender*) |
| kaben | kapen | captain (from English) |
| kallib | kallib (intr.) kalibin(iy) (tr.) | to plant, bury plant something |
| kate | katey (tr.) kattikat (intr.) | apply...self to something |
| katu | katiw | meteorology, predict weather (cf. <u>k&t&w</u> *wind*) |
| kiki | kiykiy | sleep |
| komja | qeṁjah | district administrator, magistrate (from German *commissar*) |
| kūr | kir | call |
| lale | lahley (sg.) (...iy(pl.)) | look at, look after |
| liaklok | liyahak£aq | lead astray (+ <u>ri</u> = *prosecutor*) |
| lokin | £aqin | after |
| mej | meyej | mate on ship (from English) |
| meni | maniy | thin (of flat objects) |
| mera | merah | light (not heavy) |
| meto | metew | ocean, navigation |
| mijil | mij&l | thick (of flat objects) |
| mūj | ṁ&j | finish, end |
| mūrū | ṁeray | dry |
| mwijbar | ṁijbar | cut hair |
| mwilal | ṁila£ | deep |
| ḥaj | gaj | fragrant |
| to | tew | channel, pass; rope, string; long time |

## LESSON FIFTEEN

Additional greetings; requests
and polite refusals; the coconut.

### DIALOGUE

A: Yokwe dri mwin.　　　　　　Yi'yaqey riṁiyin.
B: Yokwe yok, dreloḧtok...　　Yi'yaqey y&q, d&yla𝑔teq...
　　jijʊttok joujo.　　　　　　jiyjetteq jewijew.
A: Erri ajiri ro?　　　　　　　Yerriy hajiriy rew?
B: Remot in tutu iar,　　　　　Remewet yin tiwtiw yiyhar,
　　mʊttan jidrik re roltok.　　ṁettan jidik rerawalteq.
A: Ak emman ke ami mour　　　　Hak, yeṁṁan key hamiy
　　imwin?　　　　　　　　　　　m&wir yiṁiyin.
B: Ej bwe wʊt, ak kwe?　　　　　Yej bey wet, hak qey?
A: O, ej emman wʊt.　　　　　　Wew, yej ṁṁan wet.
B: Kwʊn ber in kʊjota,　　　　 Qen pad yin k&j&wtah,
　　ewʊr ik im kwanjin.　　　　 yewer y&k yim qanjin.
A: Kommol a ijja ikiḧ.　　　　 Qeṁṁewel hah yijjah
　　　　　　　　　　　　　　　　 yik&g.

A: Hello folks (of this house).
B: Hello, come in... sit here.
A: Where are the children?
B: They've gone swimming; they'll be back soon.
A: And how are you all (here, in this house)?
B: Oh, so-so. And you?
A: Oh, fine.
B: Stay for dinner, there is some fish and breadfruit.
A: Thanks, but I guess not this time.

### DRILLS

1. Remot in <u>tutu</u> iar, mʊ-　　Remewet yin <u>tiwtiw</u> yiyhar,
　　ttan jid<u>rik</u> reroltok.　　　ṁettan jidik <u>rerawalteq</u>.
　　　　jikul　　　　　　　　　　　　　　jikiwił
　　　　kakijen　　　　　　　　　　　　　kakijen
　　　　eḧwʊr　　　　　　　　　　　　　　ya𝑔ed
　　　　kakkʊr　　　　　　　　　　　　　kakk&r
　　　　kemeem　　　　　　　　　　　　　keyemyem

2. Mōttan jidrik i etal.        Mettan jidik yiyetal
   Han Rita.                    gan Riytah.
            kwe                           qe
            e                             ye
            re                            re
            kim                           k&m
            kom                           q&ṁ

3. Ne kwe etal, inaj            Gey qeyetal, yinahaj
   buromōj.                     bir&wṁ&j.
   Ne kwo itok, inaj            Gey qeyiteq, yinahaj
   mōnōnō.                      ṁeṅehṅeh.
        (repeat the words in Drill 2)

4. Kwōn ber in kōjota.          Qen pad yin k&j&wtah.
     etal     mōḣū                yetal    ṁegay
     itok     uwe                  yiteq    wiw&y
     roltok   kōmat                rawalteq kemat
     rollok   rarō                 rawałłaq rahr&h
              mabuḣ                         ṁahbiḡ

5. Kwōn jab ikōḣ.               Qen jab yik&g.
           keroro                       keyr&wr&w
           ettōḣ                        tt&g
           kōbatat                      kebahathat
           emakitkit                    ṁuṁakitkit

6. Yokwe dri mwin.              Yi'yaqey riṁiyin.
         lōmaro                         łeṁahrew
         limaro                         liṁahrew
         lōllab ro                      łełłap rew
         lellab ro                      l&łłap rew
         dri wa ne                      riwah ṅey
         likao ro                       likahwew rew
         jiroḣ ro                       jireḡ rew
         dri mōne                       riṁeṅey
         dri wa in                      riwah yin
         dri'inin                       riyinyin
         dri en'ne                      riyaṅṅey
         dri mōkane                     riṁekaṅey
         dri mōkein                     riṁ&k&yin
         dritto ro                      rittew rew
         komeaḣ                         q&ṁyag
         ruamaejet eo                   riwamay&j&t yew
         ruamaejet ro                   riwamay&j&t rew
         yok baba                       y&q bahbah
         yok mama                       y&q ṁahṁah
         yok jera                       y&q jerah

```
            yok nejŭ                    y&q najih
            yok jibŭ                    y&q jibih
            yok jimma(ŭ)                y&q jiṁṁah(&h)
            yok lajimma(ŭ)              y&q łajiṁṁah(&h)
            yok jeiŭ                    y&q j&yih
            yok jatŭ                    y&q jatih
            yok lajjibŭbŭ               y&q łajjibihbih
            yok lijjibŭbŭ               y&q lijjibihbih

7. Kwŭn ber wŭt in              Qen pad wet yin
   kŭjota.                      k&j&wtah.
   mabuḧ                        ṁahbiğ
   mŭḧḧ in raelep               ṁegay yin rahyelep
   jerbal                       jerbal
   jikul                        jikiwił
   bwebwenato                   beybeynahtew
   eḧwŭr                        yağed
   uno                          winew
   al                           hal
   kwalkwol                     qałq&ł
   aen                          hayen
   kŭmkŭm                       keṁkeṁ
   entak                        y&ntak

8. Kommol a ijja ikŭḧ.          Qeṁṁewel hah yijjah yik&g.
            ejja bwe                    yejjah bey
            imat                        yimat
            ej kab mwij                 yej kab ṁ&j
            aŭ mŭḧḧ                     hah&h ṁegay
            kobbat                      qebbat
            ejja bwe                    yejjah bey
             mokta                       ṁeqtah
            ij kaiur                    yij kayił
            erumwij                     yeł'iṁij

9. Ṅe ejjab                     Gey yejjab
   ni, dri-Majŭl reban kar      niy, riṀahjeł reban kar
          marŭn mour.                  mareğ m&wir.
   wa           itoitak         wah          yit&wyitak
   waini        wia             wahyiniy     wiyah
   bŭb          kŭmman jaki     beb          keṁṁan jakiy
   mḧ           kŭmman wa       may          keṁṁan wah
   missionary   jelḧ Anij       mejinedey    jełay Hanij
   wit          kadrŭk ieraj    w&t          kaddek yi'yaraj
   dri belle    lolokjen        ripalley     lewłaqjeṅ
   ik           jalele          y&k          jal&yl&y
```

10. *(Teacher gives the response as cue, then asks the question.)*

    Emman ke am(i) mour?    Yeṁhan key haṁ/hamiy m&wir?
    Ej bwe wɵ̄t.    Yej bey wet.
    Ebwe.    Yebey.
    Emman.    Yeṁhan.
    Ejjab kanuij.    Yejjab kahn&w&j.
    Ebwe jidrik.    Yebey jidik.
    Ej emman wɵ̄t.    Yej ṁhan wet.
    Jidrik.    Jidik.
    Jimettan.    Jimettan.
    Ibok mejin jidrik.    Yibek m&jyin jidik.
    Emmanlok jen ran ko lok.    Yeṁhanłaq jan rahan kew łaq.
    Ij kab kajur lok.    Yij kab kajw&r łaq.

*(Practice also these alternative questions with the above responses.)*

    Ej it am(i) mour?    Yej y&t haṁ/hamiy m&wir?
    Emman ke am(i) mour bajjik?    Yeṁhan key haṁ/hamiy m&wir bajj&k?
    Ekijkan am(i) mour?    Y&k&jkan haṁ/hamiy m&wir?

11.  Drelottok.    D&yłagteq.
    jijɵ̄t    jiyjet
    jirak    jirhak
    urak    wirhak
    babu    bahbiw
    walok    wahłaq

12. The parts of the coconut tree. (See illustration, page 156.)

*(Teacher draws a coconut tree on the blackboard, including a bunch of nuts on the tree, a bottle to tap the sap, a fallen nut on the ground cut away in cross section to expose husk, shell, meat, and liquid, and a sprouted nut on the ground. Then teacher and students proceed to discuss the tree and its parts as follows:)*

T: John, etan mɵ̄ttan jab eo?    Jawan, yetan ṁettan jab yew?
J: <u>Kimij</u>.    <u>K&m&j</u>.    *frond or leaf of frond*
   Nok.    Neq.    *midrib of leaf*
   Beb.    Pap.    *midrib of frond*
   Jinibrałł.    Jinniprag.    *stem of bunch*

|   |   |   |
|---|---|---|
| Kwalini. (Rat.) | Qałiyniy. | *small nut* |
| Kwalinni. (Rʉl.) | Qałinniy. | *small nut* |
| Kʉn. | Kayan. | *trunk* |
| Utak. | Witak. | *shoot, sheath* |
| Okar. | Wekar. | *roots* |
| Jubub. | Jiwibwib. | *new shoot* |
| Jiab. | Jiyab. | *heart* |
| Uror. | Wirw&r. | *bunch (drinking stage)* |
| Jekaro. | Jekar&w. | *sap* |
| Inbil. | Yinp&l. | *'cloth'* |
| Drebdreb. | Dapd&p. | *base of trunk and root system* |
| Jakaiej. (Rat.) | Jakayiy&j. | *cut steps* |
| Jakairo. (Rʉl.) | Jakayir&w. | *cut steps* |
| Bweo. | Beyaw. | *husk* |
| Lat. | Łat. | *shell* |
| Latjim. | Łajjim. | *bottom half of shell* |
| Latmij. | Łatm&j. | *top half of shell* |
| Medre. | M&d&y. | *soft meat* |
| Dren in ni. | Dannin niy. | *juice* |
| Iu. | Yiw. | *sprouted nut and meat* |

13. *(Teacher has a student, or different students go to blackboard and point out different parts of the drawing.)*

T: John, kwalok mʉk      Jawan, qahłaq mek
   kimijen ni ne.             kimejan niy hey.
   nokin                     heqin
   bebin                     papin
   jinibraHin              jinnipragin
   kwalinin                qałiyniyin
   kwalinnin              qałinniyin
   kʉn                       kayan
   utakin                    witakin
   okarin                    wekarin
   jububin                  jiwibwibin
   jiabin                    jiyabin
   uror eo urorin         wirw&r yew wirw&rin
   jekaro eo jekaron     jekar&w yew jekar&win
   inbilin                  yinp&lin
   drebdrebin             dapd&pin
   jakaiejin              jakayiyejin
   jakairon               jakayir&win
   bweo'n                  beyawan
   latin                     łatin

```
          latjimin                   łatjiṁin
          latmijin                   łatm&jin
          medrein                    m&d&yin
          drenin                     dannin
          iuin                       yiwin
       J: EHeo kimij eo kimijen      Yegyew k&m&j yew kimejan
          ni e eo.                   niy y&y yew.
             nok       nokin            ṅeq       ṅeqin
               (etc.)                     (etc.)
```

14. Stages of coconut growth--jaw yin niy.

*(Teacher asks these questions of students; later students ask them of each other. At first the questions about each stage are kept in order; later they are intermixed.)*

```
    T: Kwalok mŭk jo eo edrik       Qahłaq ṁek jaw yew yedik
       tata ilo an walok               tahtah yilew han wahłaq
       juŏn ni?                        jiwen niy.
    A: Kwalinni. (Kwalini.)          Qałinniy. (Qałiyniy.)

    T: Kwalok mŭk jo eo elab         Qahłaq ṁek jaw yew yełap
       lok jen kwalinni.                łaq jan qałinniy.
       (kwalini).                      (qałiyniy).
    B: Ubleb.                        Wiblep.

    T: Kwalok mŭk jo eo jemarŏn      Qahłaq ṁek jaw yew jemareǧ
       kŏjerbal aulaklak, im           kejerbal hawiłakłak, yim
       eban edrŏb.                     yeban dd&b.
    C: Äjin aulaklak.                Yajin hawiłakłak.

    T: Kwalok mŭk jo eo joun         Qahłaq ṁek jaw yew jawin
       edrŏb.                          dd&b.
    D: Urŏnni.                       Wirenniy.

    T: Kwalok mŭk jo eo joun         Qahłaq ṁek jaw yew jawin
       jekŏbwa.                        j&k&bwah.
    E: Mejoub.                       Mejewib.

    T: Kwalok mŭk jo eo eoublok      Qahłaq ṁek jaw yew yewib-
       jen waini.                      łaq jan wahyiniy.
    F: MaHbŏn.                       Magben.

    T: Kwalok mŭk jo eo joun         Qahłaq ṁek jaw yew jawin
       kowainini.                      kewwahyiniyniy.
    G: Waini.                        Wahyiniy.

    T: Kwalok mŭk jo eo ejjino       Qahłaq ṁek jaw yew yejji-
       an eoH mejen.                   new han yaǧ mejan.
    H: Iu.                           Yiw.
```

## GRAMMATICAL NOTES

1. Some of the expressions in Drill 6 require comment. There are several contractions:

| | | | | |
|---|---|---|---|---|
| dri'inin | riyinyin | < ri + yan&y + yin | people of this islet |
| dri en'ne | riyahhey | < ri + yan&y + hey | people of that islet |
| dritto ro | rittew rew | < ri + rittew rew | elderly people |

Q&ihyag, literally 'you four' is often used to address more than four people in order to give the effect of intimacy.

Riwamay&j&t 'stranger' is used with the same connotations as in English.

Jihhhah(&h) and łajihhhah(&h) are both used to address grandfathers; the ła- is the male personal name prefix.

łajjibihbih and lijjibihbih are used to address grandchildren; the ła- and li- are the male and female personal name prefixes, and -jjibihbih is the distributive form of jibi- 'grandmother, grandchild'.

## PROVERB

Kojab kiki aneen emman.   Qejab kiykiy yanyeh hihahan.

'Don't sleep on men's islets (islets where one goes only to work).'

Be industrious. (Men shouldn't sleep late in the morning, and should never sleep too soundly, but should always be ready to rise and fight at a moment's notice.)

## SHORT PROSE SELECTION

```
                        fortunate         grow
Elab  an dri-MajØl  jeramÖn   kin an  edrØk ni ilo
Yełap han riMahjeł  jerahahuhan k&n han ddek niy yilew

                                                drink
ailih    ko air.    Ni  ej  lelok  Han ir  limeir,
hay&ł&g  kew hay&r. Niy yej leyłaq gan y&r lim&yy&r,

food       house      bedding     transportation
kijier,    imweir,    kinier,     kab wair.    Rej kØmman
kij&yy&r,  yih&yy&r,  kin&yy&r,   kab wahy&r.  Rej kehuhan
```

```
                                    need
enaḧin   aoleb    men ko   rej   aikuiji   ḧan mour jen
yenahgin haweḷep  men kew  rej   hayiqijiy gan mewir jan
                           fruits
ni  im  men ko  leen.    Ñe ejjab ni, dri-Majŭl reban
niy yim men kew leyen.   Gey yejjab niy, riṁahjeł reban
kar maroḧ mour.
kar mareg̈ mewir.
```

VOCABULARY

```
aikuij       hayiqij (intr.)         need
             ...iy (tr.)
aulaklak     hawiłakłak (intr.)      chip of green coconut
                                        husk used as spoon
             ...ey (tr.)             use a spoon to scoop
                                        out
babu         bahbiw                  lie down, rest
buromŭj      bir&wṁ&j                (be) sorry
ebbat        bbat                    (be) late
edrŭb        dd&b (intr.)            to husk
             dibej(ey) (tr.)
edrŭk        ddek                    grow
ekijka-      y&k&jka-                how?
emakitkit    ṁṁakitkit               unstable, moving (dis-
                                        tributive of ṁṁakit,
                                        keṁakitiy) move
emmol        ṁṁewel                  be thanked; be generous
ene          yan&y                   islet in an atoll
eoḧ          yag̈                    grow
ettŭḧ        tt&g                    laugh
ijjino       jjinew (intr.)          begin
             jinew(ey) (tr.)         begin something
ikŭḧ         yik&g                   keep silent; used with
                                        -ja as polite refusal
                                        of food, drink, or
                                        tobacco
jaki         jakiy                   mat
jekobwa      j&k&bwah                meat of mejewib coconut
                                        mixed with sap or sugar
jalele       jal&yl&y (intr.)        meat or sauce for rice
                                        or other staples
             jaleyek(ey) (tr.)       eat sauce with staples
jeramŭn      jerahaṁṁan              fortunate, lucky,
                                        blessed
jimma        jiṁṁah(a-)              grandfather
jirak        jirhak (intr.)          move
```

|  |  |  |
|---|---|---|
|  | ...ey (tr.) | right here |
| joujo | jewijew |  |
| kadrʉk | ka(+)ddek | cause to grow |
| kajur | kajw&r | strength, strong |
| kakijen | ka(+)kijen | gather food |
| kakkʉr | ka(+)k(i)k&r | gather clams (kik&r is Rat., for Rāl. jiqq&y) |
| kʉjota | k&j&wtah | (eat) supper |
| kʉbatat | ke(+)bahathat | to smoke |
| lee- | ley- | fruit |
| lolokjen | lewɬaqjeń | have broadened horizons: 'visit there' |
| mabuḧ | m̈ahbiǧ | (eat) breakfast |
| mat | mat | full of food or drink: satiated |
| ritto | rittew | old, elderly |
| ub | wib | soft |
| urak | wiṛhak | move |

## LESSON SIXTEEN

'Do you know how?';
'I used to.'; 'Teach me.';
nowadays and in the olden times.

### DIALOGUE

A: Kwo jela ke kŭjaḧjaḧ?        Qejełay key kejagjag?
B: Ta?                           Tah?
A: Kita.                         Kitah.
B: Aet, ijelŭ kita.              Hay&t, yijełay kitah.
A: Kwo maroḧ ke katakin iŭ?      Qemareğ key kahtakin y&h?
B: Aet, ḧe kwo kŭnan.            Hay&t, gey qekenhan.
A: Kejro maroḧ ke jino ilju?     K&jrew mareğ key jinew yiljiw?
B: Emman ibba, itok in jota bwe ij jerbal in ran.   Yeṁhan yippah, yiteq yin j&wtah bey yij jerbal yin rahan.

A: Do you know how to play (an instrument)?
B: What (instrument)?
A: Guitar.
B: Yes, I know how to play a guitar.
A: Could you please teach me?
B: Yes, if you like.
A: Could we start tomorrow?
B: Fine by me. Come in the evening--I work during the day.

### DRILLS

1. Kwo jela ke <u>kŭjaḧjaḧ</u>?    Qejełay key <u>kejagjag</u>?
                aŭ                                  haheh
                jerakrŭk                            jerakr&k
                eb                                  yeb
                al                                  hal

162

2. I jelā kita.                    Yijełay kitah.
       ukelele                         wikileyley
       piano                           piyanew
       robba                           łebbah
       okōn                            waqen

3. Kwo maroń ke katakin             Qemareġ key kahtakin y&h
   iō kita?                          kitah.
              (repeat Drill 2)

4. Ńe I kōnan jelā, John            Gey yikeńhan jełay, Jawan
   enāj katakin iō.                  yenāhaj kahtakin y&h.
       kwo       yok                     qe         y&q
       e         -i                      ye         -iy
       kom       kom                     q&rh       q&rh
       kim       kim                     k&m        k&m
       re        ir                      re         y&r

5. Itok in jota bwe ij              Yiteq yin j&wtah bey yij
   jerbal in ran.                    jerbal yin rahan.
       kiki                              kiykiy
       rikaki                            rikakiy
       ikkure                            qqir&y
       eńwōd                             yaġed

6. Emman ke ibbam ńe                Yeńhhan key yippańh gey
   kejro jino ilju.                  k&jrew jinew yiljiw.
       jako                              jak&w
       jerak                             jerak
       bojak                             pewjak
       emakit                            mhakit

7. In maroń ke katakini?            Yin mareġ key kahtakiniy?
       kwōn                              qen
       en                                yen
       komin                             q&rhin
       kimin                             k&min
       jen                               jen
       ren                               ren

8. Kwo maroń ke katakini?           Qemareġ key kahtakiniy?
       I                                 Yi
       e                                 ye
       kom                               q&rh
       je                                je
       re                                re

9. Eor ke am kein　　　　　　Yewer key haṁ k&yin
    kȯjaḧjaḧ?　　　　　　　　　kejagjag?
    jerbal　　　　　　　　　　　jerbal
    eoḧwȯr　　　　　　　　　　　yaǧed
    jaljal injin　　　　　　　jałjał yinjin
    iȯk pilawḧ　　　　　　　　'yiy&k pilahway
    liklik pilawḧ　　　　　　liklik pilahway
    tutu　　　　　　　　　　　　tiwtiw
    irir makmȯk　　　　　　　　yiryir ṁakṁ&k
    kwekwe mḧ　　　　　　　　　q&yq&y may
    kȯbatat　　　　　　　　　　kebahathat

10. Ikȯn kȯbatat, ak　　　　　Yik&n kebahathat, hak
    kiȯ ijjab.　　　　　　　　kiyyeh yijjab.
    kadȯk　　ij kirijin　　　kadek　　　yij kirijin
    kileb　　iaidrik　　　　　kilep　　　yihayidik
    bakij　　ijabbakij　　　　pakij　　　yijappakij
    mȯkaj　　ibat　　　　　　　ṁekaj　　　yibat
    katlik　 ij birotijen　　katilik　　yij birewtiyjen
    takȯtȯ　 ij dri kaki　　　takteh　　 yij rikakiy
    mej　　　ij kaben　　　　　meyej　　　yij kapen
    jeramȯl　imwȯie　　　　　 jeraṁel　　yiṁeyiyey
    eḧwȯr　　ijeḧwȯr　　　　　yaǧed　　　yijayaǧed
    jikul　　ij jerbal　　　　jikiwil　　yij jerbal

11. *(At first teacher should give all of each line as
    cue, later he should give only the underlined por-
    tion, and finally the order of the items should be
    intermixed.)*
    Ekȯn jab kȯbatat, ak　　　Y&k&n jab kebahathat, hak
    kio ej kȯbatat.　　　　　　kiyyeh yej kebahathat.
        ej kadȯk　　　　　　　　　　yej kadek
        ej kirijin　　　　　　　　　yej kirijin
        e aidik　　　　　　　　　　 yehayidik
        e kileb　　　　　　　　　　 yekilep
        ej katilik　　　　　　　　　yej katilik
        ej birotijen　　　　　　　　yej birewtiyjen
        ej dri kaki　　　　　　　　 yej rikakiy
        ej takȯtȯ　　　　　　　　　 yej takteh
        ej kaben　　　　　　　　　　yej kapen
        ej jikul　　　　　　　　　　yej jikiwił
        e jeramȯl　　　　　　　　　 yejeraṁel
        e mwȯie　　　　　　　　　　 yeṁeyiyey

12. *(Use as cues the two words from the second clause:
    for example: 'ładdik...p&nawiyy&y'.)*

| | | | |
|---|---|---|---|
| Ladrik en ebinawia, ak ladrik eo juŏn ebinawie. | | Ḻadik yeṅ yep&nawiyyah, hak ḻadik yew jiwen yep&nawiyy&y. | |
| wa | jalie | wah | jahaliyy&y |
| ledrik | kibilie | ledik | kipiliyy&y |
| wa | atakie | wah | hatakiyy&y |
| mŏHḄ | alakie | ṁegay | haḻakiyy&y |
| ladrik | roḦie | ḻadik | reǰiyy&y |
| bao | awie | bahwew | hawiyy&y |
| wŏn | mijjie | w&n | m&jjiyy&y |
| mḄ | mattie | may | mattiyy&y |
| kijak | mattie | kijak | mattiyy&y |

13. *(Use the same cues as in Drill 12, but now form sentences on the following pattern:)*

   Ladrik en ekŏn binawia, ak kiŭ ebinawie.

   Ḻadik yeṅ y&k&n p&nawiyyah, hak kiyyeh yep&nawiyy&y.

   Wa en ekŏn jalia, ak kiŭ ejalie.
   *(etc.)*

   Wah yeṅ y&k&n jahaliyyah, hak kiyyeh yejahaliyy&y.
   *(etc.)*

14. *(Using the cues on each line below, form sentences like the first three examples:)*

   T: 'Bao...riḦ nen'
   A: Bao rot en?
   B: Bao rot en me eor riḦ nen.

   'Bahwew...riyig neyen'
   Bahwew ḻet yeṅ?
   Bahwew ḻet yeṅ mey yewer riyig neyen.

   T: 'Boj...injinin'
   A: Boj rot en?
   B: Boj rot en me eor injinin.

   'Bewej...yinjinin'
   Bewej ḻet yeṅ?
   Bewej ḻet yeṅ mey yewer yinjinin.

   T: 'Otobai...jilu nen'
   A: Otobai rot en?
   B: Otobai rot en me eor jilu nen.

   'Wetewbahyiy...jiliw neyen?
   Wetewbahyiy ḻet yeṅ?
   Wetewbahyiy ḻet yeṅ mey yewer jiliw neyen.

   Ik...eotin.
   Pinjel...kein ejjeor ie.
   MḄ...kole ie.
   Mubi...mŏrŭ ie.
   Bade...eb ie.
   Madre...kḄjin.
   Bik...nejin.

   Y&k...yawatin.
   Pinjeḻ...k&yin jjeyeḻ yi'y&y.
   May...qeley yi'y&y.
   Ṁiwpiy...ṁehreh yi'y&y.
   Bahd&y...yeb yi'y&y.
   Ṁad&y...kayajin.
   Piyik...najin.

|  |  |  |  |
|---|---|---|---|
| Wut...lŭklŭkin. | | Wit...leklekin. | |
| Ene...tolin. | | Yan&y...telin. | |
| Balun...bikbikin. | | Bałwin...pikpikin. | |

15. Ilo ran kein i Majŭl,  ekanuij in <u>jeja</u> elolo aer kŭjerbal <u>aje</u>.  
    Yilew rahan k&yin yiy Mahjeł, yekahn&w&j yin j&yjah llewlew hay&r kejerbal haj&y.

| emakijkij | kita | mmakijkij | kitah |
|---|---|---|---|
| alŭkia | aje | hałakiyyah | haj&y |
| alŭkie | kita | hałakiyy&y | kitah |
| emelo | aje | ṁṁhełew | haj&y |
| ikkutkut | kita | qqitqit | kitah |

(*Continue, making meaningful sentences by substituting the above words.*)

Ilo ran ko etto, ekŭn jeja kŭjerbal <u>kita</u>.  
  emakijkij    aje  
     (etc.)

Yilew rahan kew yettew, y&k&n j&yjah kejerbal <u>kitah</u>.  
  ṁṁhakijkij    haj&y  
     (etc.)

## GRAMMATICAL NOTES

1. The <u>k&n</u> of Drills 10 and 11 is best translated 'used to'.

2. The words <u>jappakij</u> and <u>jayaǧed</u> of Drill 10, and <u>jarreǧreǧ</u> and <u>jammakijkij</u> introduced in Lesson 13, all contain the negative prefix <u>ja-</u>, which is obviously related to <u>jahab</u> and <u>jab</u>. There are a sizable number of such negations or opposites formed with this prefix in the language; you will be meeting more in later lessons. The form of the stem to which this <u>ja-</u> prefix is attached often has doubled consonants and reduplication. Such doubled and/or reduplicated forms are called 'distributive' forms. The meanings of distributives (without <u>ja-</u>) will be discussed in Lesson 20.

3. Drill 12 introduces a pair of suffix-like elements used to form opposite pairs of words. If one attempts to extract a common meaning element for each it would probably be something like the following:

>   -iyyah  'intractable'  
>   -iyy&y  'tractable'

The number of such pairs is limited, and you are introduced to a majority of them in this lesson.

4. The <u>mey</u> practiced in Drill 14 is a relative to be translated 'which', 'that', or 'who(m)'. As in English, it can often be omitted:

```
            ...harm&j   yew      (mey)    yihar  lewey
            ...the      people   (whom)   I      saw
```

5. The -<u>n</u> suffix in some of the words in Drill 14 is
the 3rd person singular possessive: ne<u>yen</u> 'its wheels
(legs)', <u>yinjinin</u> 'its engine', <u>yawatin</u> 'its stripes',
te<u>l</u>in 'its mountains', etc.

SHORT PROSE SELECTION

```
                                almost
Aje  ej   juŭn   kein  kejaḧjaḧ  im   eiten    einlok  wŭt
Haj&y yej jiwen  k&yin kejagjag  yim  yeyiten  y&yinḷaq wet
drum                                  only this
tiram.  Ej  kar  kein  kejaḧjaḧ eo  drein  ilo   ailiḧ
tiraṁ.  Yej kar  k&yin kejagjag yew d&yin  yilew hayel&g
                                          country
in  Majŭl  mokta  jen  an  dreloḧ  tok  lal  ko   jet.  Aje
yin Mahjeḷ ṁeqtah jan  han d&yḷagteq laḷ  kew  jet.  Haj&y
                shark skin                          tied
ej  kŭman  jen  kilin  bako.  Kilin  ik  in  ej  eloktok
yej keṁṁhan jan kilin  pakew. Kilin  y&k yin yej ll&qteq
on  at  the  end  of    piece    log
na  imejin  juŭn  mŭttan  wijike  rot  ne   me   ewŭr
ṅah yimejan jiwen ṁettan  w&jk&y  ḷet  ḥey  mey  yewer
hollow                used  to   use             time
loan.    Men in aje  ekŭn  jerbal   ilo   ien   rot
lewwahan. Men yin haj&y yek&n jerbal yilew 'yiyen ḷet
           dance  war          meeting       alarm
ne  an  eb,  tarinae    im  kwelok  ak  iruj  elab  ko
ḥey han yeb, tariyṅahyey yim q&ylaq hak yiḷij  ḷḷap  kew
           long ago
an  alab  ro  etto.    Ilo  ran   kein   i   Majŭl
han haḷap rew yettew.  Yilew rahan k&yin  yiy Mahjeḷ
                seldom see
ekanuij   in  jeja   elolo    aer  kŭjerbal  aje.
yekahn&w&j yin j&yjah llewlew hay&r kejerbal  haj&y.
           also      few
Im  bareinwot   eiet    ro   me   rej  kŭmane   menin
Yim barayinwet  yeyiy&t rew  mey  rej  keṁṁhaney menyin
aje.
haj&y.
```

## PROVERB

Uddrik kije.  Widdik kijey.
   'Small but mighty.'

## VOCABULARY

| | | |
|---|---|---|
| alakia | hałakiyyah | scarce, hard to find |
| ...ie | ...iyy&y | plentiful, easy to find |
| atakia | hatakiyyah | hard to drag in water |
| ...ie | ...iyy&y | easy to drag in water |
| aje | haj&y | aboriginal drum |
| awia | hawiyyah | wild |
| ...ie | ...iyy&y | tame, domesticated |
| bade | bahd&y | party (from English) |
| bakij | pakij | able to stay under water long |
| bako | pakew | shark |
| bareinwöt | barayinwet | also |
| bikbik | pikpik | propeller; kick feet in swimming, flap wings in flying |
| drein | d&yin | only this |
| drekein | d&k&yin | only these |
| eiten | yeyiten | (contraction of ye + yiteq + yin) almost |
| elok | ll&q (intr.) liqej(ey) (tr.) | tie |
| emelo | mmełew | spread apart, seldom, infrequent |
| eot | yawat, yawati- | stripe |
| etto | yettew | long time, a long time ago |
| ikkutkut | qqitqit | very close together, frequently (distributive of qit 'close together') |
| irir | yiryir (intr.) yir(iy) (tr.) | wipe, scrape; grind arrowroot with stone |
| iruj | yiłij | alarm, excitement |
| jal | jahał | turn to one side |
| jalia | jahałiyyah | hard to steer |
| ..ie | ...iyy&y | easy to steer |
| jeja | j&yjah | seldom |
| jeramöl | jerameł | poor |
| kÿj | kayaj | hook, barb |
| katakin | kahtakin | teach (a subject) |
| | kahtakiniy | teach (a subject) to someone |

| | | |
|---|---|---|
| kibil | kkipil (intr.) | force (someone) |
| | kipil (tr.) | |
| kibilia | kipiliyyah | disobedient |
| ...ie | kipiliyy&y | obedient |
| kil | kil, kili- | skin |
| kole | qeley | testicle, large seed |
| kwekwe | q&yq&y (intr.) | scratch, scrape, scrape |
| | qey (sg.) (tr.) | breadfruit with a clam (jiqq&y or kik&r) |
| | q&yiy (pl.) (tr.) | shell, or a piece of glass |
| kwelok | q&yłaq | meet, meeting |
| liklik | liklik (intr.) | strain, sift |
| | ...iy (tr.) | |
| lŭklŭk | l&kl&k, l&kl&ki- | be thorny, thorns |
| | l&k&y (tr.) | to scratch someone with thorns |
| madre | ṁad&y | spear |
| mattia | mattiyyah | hard to cook; hard to satisfy with food |
| ...ie | ...iyy&y | easy to cook; easy to satisfy with food |
| me | mey | which, that, who(m) (relative) |
| mijjia | m&jjiyyah | hard to kill |
| ...ie | ...iyy&y | easy to kill |
| mŭrŭ | ṁehreh (intr.) | murder (from English) |
| | ṁehrehik(iy) (tr.) | |
| mwŭie | ṁeyiyey | wealthy (cf. ṁeyiq ṁeyiye- 'goods') |
| na | ṅah | on, in, at |
| okŭn | waqen | organ (from English) |
| robba | łebbah | trumpet |
| roħia | reǰiyyah | hard of hearing |
| ...ie | ...iyy&y | having good hearing |
| tarinae | tariyṅahyey (intr.) | fight, battle |
| | ...ik(iy) (tr.) | |
| tiram | tiraṁ | drum (from English) |
| tol | teḷ, teḷi- | mountain |
| wijike | w&jk&y | tree |

## LESSON SEVENTEEN

Siblings and cousins; after graduation; more on foods; at the store.

### DIALOGUE

A: Ewi leo jeim?  
Yewiy ḷeyew j&yiṁ?

B: Ejelok jeiü. Leo jatü eber Hawaii.  
Yejjeḷaq j&yih. Ḷeyew jatih yepad Hawahyiy.

A: Ej jikul ke?  
Yej jikiwiḷ key?

B: EmÖj an jikul, ej jerbal ijen.  
Y&ṁ&j han jikiwiḷ, yej jerbal yijeṅ.

A: Ñe emöj am jerbal ijin, kwönaj et?  
Gey y&ṁ&j haṁ jerbal yijin qenahaj y&t?

B: Inaj rol Ḧan Hawaii im bar jikul.  
Yinahaj rawal gan Hawahyiy yim bar jikiwiḷ.

A: Where is your older brother?  
B: I don't have any older brother. My younger brother is in Hawaii.  
A: Is he going to school?  
B: He has finished school. He's working there.  
A: When you finish working here, what are you going to do?  
B: I am going back to Hawaii and go to school again.

### DRILLS

1. Eber <u>leo jatin</u> i Erikub.  
Yepad <u>ḷeyew jatin</u> yiy Yadqip.

 lio jatin     liyew jatin  
 leo jein      ḷeyew j&yin  
 lio jeiü      liyew j&yih  
 leo jeim      ḷeyew j&yiṁ  
 lio jatier      liyew jatiyy&r  
 leo jeid      ḷeyew j&yid  
 lio jeimi      liyew j&yimiy  
 leo rilikin     ḷeyew riylikin  
 lio jeir      liyew j&yiyy&r

2. Ewi leo jatim?
   Ijaje ewi leo.

   Eber ia lio jatim?
   Ijaje ebed ia lio.

   Ewi ledrik eo jeim?
   Ijaje ewi lio.
   Eber ia ladrik eo
     jeim?
   Ijaje ebed ia leo.
   Ewi jiroñ eo jatŭm?
   Eber ia likao eo
     jatŭm?
   Ewi John?
   Eber ia jibŭm?
   Ewi jimmam?
   Jinŭm eber ia?

   Yewiy ḻeyew jatiṁ?
   Yijahj&y yewiy ḻeyew.

   Yepad yi'yah liyew jatiṁ?
   Yijahj&y yepad yi'yah
     liyew.

   Yewiy ledik yew j&yiṁ?
   Yijahj&y yewiy liyew.
   Yepad yi'yah ḻadik yew
     j&yiṁ?
   Yijahj&y yepad yi'yah ḻeyew.
   Yewiy jireğ yew jatiṁ?
   Yepad yi'yah likahwew yew
     jatiṁ?
   Yewiy Jawan?
   Yepad yi'yah jibiṁ?
   Yewiy jiṁṁahaṁ?
   Jineṁ yepad yi'yah?

3. Emŭj an jikul, ej
     jerbal kiŭ.
            driwŭjlok
            mare
            wḁ
            kŭllḁ

   Y&ṁ&j han jikiwiḻ, yej
     jerbal kiyyeh.
            diyw&jḻaq
            ṁarey
            way
            keḻḻay

4. Ñe emŭj am jikul
     kwonaj et?
            kŭllḁ
            mare
            rikaki
            jerbal

   Gey y&ṁ&j haṁ jikiwiḻ,
     qenahaj y&t?
            keḻḻay
            ṁarey
            rikakiy
            jerbal

5. Ñe emŭj aŭ jikul,
     inaj kakkije.
            kŭllḁ
            mare
            rikaki

   Gey y&ṁ&j hah&h jikiwiḻ,
     yinahaj kakkij&y.
            keḻḻay
            ṁarey
            rikakiy

6. Itok in mŭḦḁ.
            tutu
            aluij
            mubi
            mwijbar
            eḦwŭr
            uwe

   Yiteq yin ṁegay.
            tiwtiw
            halw&j
            ṁiwpiy
            ṁijbar
            yağed
            wiw&y

*(The above sentences can all be contracted ones like the following:*
   Iten mőHŭ.   Yiten ṁegay.
*Practice producing them in this form as well.)*

7. Itok in jota.            Yiteq yin j&wtah.
      jiboH                         jibb&ğ
      raeleb                        rahyelep
      Mandre                        Ṁandey
      marok                         mareq
      meram                         meram
      wit                           w&t
      dret                          det
      Janodre                       Janewdey
      mŐlo                          ṁ&ł&w
      bwil                          bil
      eHat                          ggat
      lur                           liŕ

*(These sentences cannot be contracted like those in Drill 6 above, but only as given in the phonetic spelling or contracted to* yiteqin. *After you have practiced Drills 6 and 7 thoroughly separately, mix cues from each and make the appropriate contractions for each:*
   Yiten tiwtiw. *but* Yiteqin w&t.*)*

8. Aje ej kŐman jen          Haj&y yej keṁḧan jan
      kilin bako.                  kilin pakew.
   madre in    Hin bako       ṁad&yin       giyin pakew
    tarinae                    tariyṅahyey
   drekenin    adred in       d&k&ynin      hadedin
               kabor                         kapw&r
   juj         kilin kau      jiwij         kilin kahwiw
   nuknuk      kilin wijike   niqniq        kilin w&jk&y
   bol in      Hin elŐbŐn     bawałin       giyin yełeben
    biliet                     biliyet
   wa          kŐn mŐ         wah           kayan may
   jaki        maH            jakiy         mahag
   eokkal      bweo           qqał          beyaw
   binieb      waini          pinniyep      wahyiniy
   jŐnkwin     mejwan emmed   jayanqin      m&jwahan mmed
   kein        inbel          k&yin         yinp&l
    liklik                     liklik
   bwŐ         kar            bay           kahar

9. Eor ruo kain jenkun, juōn ej kōmman jen bōb, im eo juon ej kōmman jen mā.

Yewer riwew kahyin jayanqin, jiwen yej keṁuhan jan beb, yim yew jiwen yej keṁuhan jan may.

jenkun...bōb...mā
tibṅōl...rā...mā
bwā...kar...koba
juj...kau...kanbōj
at...kimej...maṅ
drun...alal...māl
im...tin...aj
drila...aen...kōba
bet...kol...kotin
bok...beba...rā
bakōj...bilajtik...tin
car...Japan...America
kab...kilaaj...drōkā

jayanqin...beb...may
tipgel...ray...may
bay...kahar...kewbah
jiwij...kahwiw...kanbej
hat...kim&j...mahag
d&w&n...hałhał...mayal
y&ṁ...tiyin...haj
diylah...hayen...kebah
p&t...keweł...qetin
bawak...p&ybah...ray
bakej...biłajtiyik...tiyin
kahar...Jepahan...Hamedkah
kab...kilhaj...dekay

10. *(Practice short conversations along the following lines. Be guided by your teacher.)*

A: Kwar et boṅ?
  inne
  jiboṅnin
  jota
B: Iar etal ṅan MIECO in wia nuknuk.
  jikka
  kiaj
  oil
  mejen dret
  alkot
  karjin
  tuna
 ...in kaikuijkuij.
  kulab
  mubi
  mōṅā
  biliet
  mwijbar
  aluij bajjik
  restaurant
Ejelok.
Iar ber bajjik.
  ber wōt mweo imō
  kabwil
  aujbitōl

Qehar y&t b&ɉ?
  yinney
  jibb&gniyin
  jewtah
Yihar yetal gan Miyeykew yin wiyah niqniq.
  jikkah
  kiyhaj
  weyił
  ṁejan det
  hałkewet
  karjin
  tiwnah
 ...yin kahayiqijqij.
  qiłab
  ṁiwpiy
  ṁegay
  piliyet
  ṁijbar
  halw&j bajj&k
  rejteren
Yejjełaq.
Yihar pad bajj&k.
  pad wet ṁeyew yiṁ&h
  kabil
  hawijpitel

jambo bajjik                    jaṁb&w bajj&k
kwalkwol                        qaɨq&ɨ
jerbal bajjik                   jerbal bajj&k

11. *(Practice asking questions like the following, with and without the quantity words:)*

| Jete wŭnen (juŭn kej in) kola? | | | Jetey weñyan (jiwen k&y&j yin) k&wɨah? | |
|---|---|---|---|---|
| * kej in) | kola? | ($4.80) | k&y&j yin) | k&wɨah? |
| baun | raij | (.15) | bawin | rahyij |
| bek | juka | (.80) | payak | jiqah |
| bekij | jikka | (.25) | pakij | jikkah |
| bok | jikka | (2.50) | bawak | jikkah |
| * kᵾn | kon bib | (.60) | kayan | kawan piyip |
| * bato | joiu | (.35) | batew | jewyiw |
| kᵾn | kola | (.20) | kayan | k&wɨah |
| * iat | nuknuk | (.60) | yi'yahat | niqniq |
| * kuat | jatin | (.30) | qiwat | jahtiyin |
| kalan | karjin | (.80) | kaɨan | karjin |
| * bek | bilawɨ | (4.50) | payak | pilahway |
| baun | bik | (.40) | bawin | piyik |
| baun | biteto | (.28) | bawin | piteytew |
| baun | anien | (.27) | bawin | haniyen |
| * bok | majet | (.02) | bawak | majet |

*(The starred items above can also be asked about according to the following pattern, sometimes with a change in meaning, as with **niqniq** and **pilahway**:
Jete wŭnen juŭn kola?     Jetey weñyan jiwen k&wɨah?

*(Teacher may write the prices on the blackboard and point to them, or give them in English as cues.)*

12. *(By substituting other items from above, practice producing store requests like the following:)*

Letok juŭn kalan in             Leyteq jiwen kaɨan yin
karjin.                         karjin.
ruo baun...kanniek              riwew bawin...kanniy&k
jilu kᵾn...kon bib              jiliw kayan...kawan piyip
(etc.)iat...nuknuk              (etc.) yi'yahat...niqniq
bato...joiu                     batew...jewyiw
(etc.)                          (etc.)

## SHORT PROSE SELECTION

Ewŭr ruo kain jenkun, juŭn ej kŭmman jen bŭb
Yewer riwew kahyin jayanqin, jiwen yej keṁhan jan beb

im eo juŋn ej kŋmman jen mŭ.   Wŭwen    kŋmman
yim yew jiwen yej keṁṁan jan may.  Wayw&y&n keṁṁan
                              ripe
jenkun   jen bŋb in,  Ħe   ej   ewat bŋb jej bŋktok im
jayanqin jan beb yin, gey yej <u>wwat</u> beb jej bekteq yim
boil it         bake it    press out
aintini       ak  umini.   Kilokwe im  ej  walok  mokan.
<u>hayintiyiniy</u> hak wiṁiniy.  <u>Kilaqey</u> yim yej wahłaq meqań.
                              dried    fold it
Jej kejeke    mokan en  im  Ħe  emŋrŭ,   limi   na
Jej kejeyekey meqań yeń yim gey <u>yeṁeray</u>, limiy ńah
                          it is ready
iloan       maĦ.    Kiŋ    ebojak   Ħan mŋĦŭ  jabdrewŋt
yilewwahan mahag.   Kiyyeh <u>yepewjak</u> gan ṁegay jabdeywet
ien.     Jenkun   in mŭ, ej  kŋmman jen mejwan.
'yiyen.  Jayanqin yin may, yej keṁṁan jan m&jwahan.
      ripe
Ńe ej  emmed,  kwŋj umini  im  ewalok    libed ak
Gey yej <u>mmed</u>, qej wiṁiniy yim yewahłaq liped hak
                                      wrap it in leaves
jŋkaka.   Kejeke    im  Ħe  emerŭ,  tirtiri  na
jekahkah. Kejeyekey yim gey yeṁeray, <u>tirtiriy</u> ńah
                 tie    sennit
ilo   maaĦ im  lukoj kin ekkwal im ebojak  Ħan mŋĦŭ.
yilew mahag yim <u>liqej</u> k&n <u>qqał</u> yim yepewjak gan ṁegay.

<u>PROVERB</u>
    KŋrŭĦ jeltan bwij.      Keray jełtan bij.
    'Woman is the core of the lineage.'
    (This proverb reflects the custom of
     matrilineal descent.)

<u>VOCABULARY</u>
adred     haded              white shell of certain
                              clams, especially of
                              large ones
aen       hayen              iron rods
aintin    hayintiyin (intr.) boil (pandanus only)
          (...iy) (tr.)
aj        haj                a section of thatch pre-
                              pared for building

| | | |
|---|---|---|
| alkot | haɫkewet | raincoat: ('sun coat') |
| aujbitɵl | hawijpiteɫ | hospital (from English) |
| bakɵj | bakej | bucket (from English) |
| baun | bawin | pound (of weight) (from English) |
| bekij | pakij | pack (gum, cigarette, candy) |
| biliet | piliyet | billiards, pool |
| binieb | pinniyep | coconut oil |
| biteto | piteytew | potato (from English) |
| bojak | pewjak | ready |
| bok | bawak | box (from English), carton |
| bol | bawaɫ | ball (from English) |
| bwǎ | bay | fishpole |
| bwij | bij, bijji- | lineage |
| drila | diylah (intr.) ...yik(iy) (tr.) | nail, screw |
| drekenin | d&k&ynin | pandanus leaf pounder made from shell |
| elebɵn | yeɫeben | elephant (from English) |
| emmed | mmed | ripe (of breadfruit, papaya, lime, pandanus) |
| eȟat | ggat | windy, stormy |
| eokkwal | qqaɫ | coconut sennit |
| ewat | wwat | ripe (pandanus only) |
| iat | yi'yahat | yard (measure) (from English) |
| jambo | jaȟb&w | walk or travel for a change of scene |
| jatin | jahtiyin | sardine (in cans only) (from English) |
| jeltan | jeɫtan | core of |
| jenkun | jayanqin | dried pandanus or breadfruit |
| joiu | jewyiw | soy sauce |
| jɵkaka | jekahkah | preserved pandanus chips |
| kabor | kabw&r | giant clam |
| kabwil | kabil | night fishing method using torch |
| kalan | kaɫan | gallon (from English) |
| kǎn | kayan | can (from English) |
| kǎn | kayan | its trunk |
| kanbɵj | kanbej | canvas (from English) |
| kar | kahar | a tree: *Premna corymbosa (obtusifola)* |
| karjin | karjin | kerosene (from English) |

| | | |
|---|---|---|
| kau | kahwiw | cow; beef (from English) |
| kej | k&y&j | case |
| kejek(e) | kejeyek(ey) (tr.) kejeyjey (intr.) | to dry under sun |
| kiaj | kiyhaj | gasolene (from English) |
| kilok | kilaq (intr.) ...ey (tr.) | press juice from boiled pandanus |
| koba | kewbah | bamboo |
| kŭba | kebah | copper, brass (from English) |
| kol | kewel, kewela- | hair, feather |
| kŭllŭ | kellay (intr.) ...ik(iy) (tr.) | pay |
| kon bib | kawan piyip | corned beef (from English) |
| kotin | qetin | cotton (from English) |
| kuat | qiwat | tin can |
| kulab | qilab | club (from English); drink at a club |
| libed | liped | baked breadfruit |
| limlim limi | l&ml&m (intr.) limiy (tr.) | fold |
| lur | lil | shade, shady |
| majet | majet | match |
| mŭl | mayal | iron (metal), axe |
| maH | mahaq | pandanus leaf |
| marok | mareq | dark(ness) |
| mejwan | m&jwahan | breadfruit variety with large seeds |
| mokan | meqañ | pandanus pudding |
| rŭ | ray | board |
| rilikin | riyliki- | cross cousin |
| tibHŭl | tipgel | sailing canoe |
| tin | tiyin | tin (roofing or metal) (from English) |
| tirtir | tirtir (intr.) ...iy (tr.) | wrap in basket or leaves |
| wŭ | way (intr.) ...ik (tr.) | injection, shot; stab with spear |

## LESSON EIGHTEEN

'You and who else?'
'By myself alone';
'Why?'; 'Because.'.

## DIALOGUE

A: Wǒn ar kǒmmane bǒram?        Wen har kerhrhaney berarh?
B: Ña make.                      Gah mak&y.
A: Ejelok en ear jibaň           Yejjełaq yeň yehar jipag
   yok ke?                          y&q key?
B: Iar make wǒt imwen.           Yihar mak&y wet yirheyeň.
A: Emake emman am kǒmmane.       Yemak&y rhrhan harh kerhrhaney.

A: Who fixed your hair?
B: I (did it) myself.
A: Didn't anyone help you?
B: I was alone in the house.
A: You really did a good job!

## DRILLS

1. Wǒn ar kǒmmane bǒram?         Wen har kerhrhaney berarh?
   Ña make. Iar make             Gah mak&y. Yihar mak&y
   kǒmmane bǒra.                 kerhrhaney berah.
   Wǒn ar kǒmmane bǒrřir?        Wen har kerhrhaney berayy&r.
   Ir make. Rar make             Y&r mak&y. Rehar mak&y
   kǒmmane bǒrřir.               kerhrhaney berayy&r.
   Wǒn ar kǒmmane bǒran?         Wen har kerhrhaney beran?
   Wǒn ar kǒmmane bǒrami?        Wen har kerhrhaney beramiy?
   Wǒn ar kǒmmane bǒra?          Wen har kerhrhaney berah?

2. Ij make wǒt <u>imwin</u>.     Yij mak&y wet <u>yirhyin</u>.
             <u>enin</u>                     yanyin
             wa in                            wah yin
             rum in                           riwirh yin
             tebǒl in                         teybeł yin

3. Ij make wǒt <u>drikaki</u>    Yij mak&y wet <u>rikakiy</u>
   enin.                         yanyin.
             dribelle                         ripalley
             drijikul                         rijikiwił

178

```
              drikadŭk              rikadek
              drieĦwŭr              riyağed
              dritarinae            rittariyńahyey

4. E make emman bŭram!     Yemak&y ŕhŕhan berańh!
              mejam                 mejańh
              botim                 bawtińh
              beim                  p&yińh
              nem                   neyeńh
              kămm                  kayańh
              tiem                  tiyeńh

5. E make bwil.            Yemak&y bil.
              molo                  ńh&ł&w
              eketoto               kk&t&wt&w
              lur                   liŀ
              meram                 meram
              marok                 mareq
              mŭĦ                   m&g
              tŭĦal                 tegal

6. I buromij kin Ħa make.  Yibir&wńh&j kin gah mak&y.
    kwo           kwe        qe            qey
    e             e          ye            y&y
    je            kij        je            k&j
    kim           kim        k&m           k&m
    kom           kom        q&ńh          q&ńh
    re            ir         re            y&r

7. Ij make wŭt bwebwe      Yij mak&y wet b&yb&y
    ilo kilaj in.            yilew kilhaj yin.
              meletlet              maletlet
              mŭjŭno                ńhejeńaw
              driben                diyp&n
              aitok                 hayiteq
              kadu                  kadiw
              kileb                 kilep
              aidik                 hayidik
              wŭlio                 wiliy&w
              drakelkel             dak&lk&l

8. Maroħ ko an rekanuij    Mareğ kew han rekahn&w&j
    in kabwilŭĦlŭĦ.          yin kabilegleg.
    juj ko an...rabŭlbŭl   jiwij kew hań...rabelbel
    jerbal eo air...kauwa- jerbal yew hay&r...kawi-
         tata                    watahtah
    wăto en aŭ...kimur     wayt&w yeń hah&h...kimiwir
```

```
        mweo imʉn...lap             m̧eyew yim̧en...ḷap
        wa ko waʉ...ellap           wah kew wah&h...ḷḷap
        wut ko kʉtʉkan...           wit kew ketkan...
          aibuijuij                   hayib&w&jw&j
        kidru eo nejin...           kidiw yew najin...
          kamijak                     kamijak
        ladrik eo jibwin...         ḷadik yew jibin...
          meletlet                    maletlet
        ok en amro...konkon         w&k yen hamrew...qeñqeñ
        ene eo enen...itti-         yan&y yew yanyen...ttiy-
          monmon                      m̧em̧m̧eñ
```

9.
A: Taunin am <u>rumij tok</u>?         Tahwinyin ham̧ <u>ḷim̧ij teq</u>?
B: Unin aʉ <u>rumij tok</u>            Winin hah&h <u>ḷim̧ij teq</u>
   kinke <u>ear wit</u>.                  k&nkey <u>yehar w&t</u>.

A: Taunin am <u>mʉkaj tok</u>?         Tahwinyin ham̧ <u>m̧ekaj teq</u>?
B: Unin aʉ <u>mʉkaj tok</u>            Winin hah&h <u>m̧ekaj teq</u>
   kinke <u>ij teej</u>.                  k&nkey <u>yij teyej</u>.

```
        kaiur tok...ij uwe          kayiḷ teq...yij wiw&y
        jab mʉñḷ...emetak ñiḷḷ      jab m̧egay...yemetak giyih
        jab tutu...ibio             jab tiwtiw...yipiyaw
        jab jikul...inañinmij       jab jikiwiḷ...yinahginm&j
        jab jar...ejelok aʉ         jab jar...yejjeḷaq hah&h
          nuknuk                       niqniq
        mʉjurleb...iar eñwʉr        majiḷlep...yihar yaĝed
          boñ                          b&ĝ
        to wʉt...eobrak wa eo       t&w wet...yewebrak wah yew
        ettʉr...ij kaiur iʉ         tt&r...yij kayiḷ y&h
        jañ...emetak neiʉ           jag...yemetak ney&h
```

10. '*Isn't that chicken finished cooking yet?*'

```
        Enañin mat ke bao           Yenahgin mat key bahwew
          eo?                          yew?
        Enañin bal ke um eo?        Yenahgin bal key wim̧ yew?
        Enañin jukok ke um          Yenahgin jiqeq key wim̧
          eo?                          yew?

        mat...pilawḷ eo             mahat...pilahway yew
        tutu...ladrik eo            tiwtiw...ḷadrik yew
        botok...wa eo               pewteq...wah yew
        uno...mweo                  winew...m̧eyew
        mwijbar...leo               m̧ijbar...ḷeyew
        taktʉ...ajiri ro            takteh...hajiriy rew
        jimjim...binjel ne          j&mj&m...pinjeḷ ñey
```

(Note that in the following, key splits the verb phrase.)

| | |
|---|---|
| Enaḧin jelü ke amimŭno lio? | Yenahgin jełay key hamiyṁeṅew liyew? |
| jelü kattŭr...leo | jełay katt&r...łeyew |
| jelü kajin Majŭl...lien | jełay kajin Ṁahjeł...liyeṅ |
| jelü bwinbwin...leen | jełay b&nb&n...łeyeṅ |
| jelü jeje...kijaken | jełay j&yj&y...kijakyeṅ |
| jelü konono...ajiri ne | jełay qenewnew...hajiriy ṅ&y |
| kŭnan mŭḧü...lŭllabeo | keṅhan ṁegay...łełłapyew |
| kŭnan jikul...ledrikeo | keṅhan jikiwił...ledikyew |

(Now intermix the two sets of cues above, taking care to insert key at the proper place.)

11. 'This shirt is awfully big.'

| | |
|---|---|
| Enaḧin kileb jŭt e. | Yenahgin kilep jehet y&y. |
| tŭḧal ti ne | tegal tiy ṅey |
| bin un ne | p&n win ṅey |
| meram teḧki ne | meram teyegkiy ṅey |
| bat wa en | bat wah yeṅ |
| enno mŭḧü in | nnaw ṁegay yin |
| bakij leen | pakij łeyeṅ |
| mat mŭkaj pilawü eo | mahat ṁekaj pilahway yew |
| mat bat mü kane | mat bat may kaṅey |
| uwi ik rot ne | wwiy y&k łet ṅey |
| rumij am itok | łiṁij haṁ yiteq |
| marok loan mwin | mareq lewwahan ṁiyin |
| to ien kŭllü | tew 'yiyen kełłay |
| drik wŭnen | dik weṅyan |
| ritto mŭkaj | rittew ṁekaj |
| likao eo | likahwew yew |

12. 'Why is this shirt so big?'

(In the statements of Drill 11, the voice falls at the end of the sentence. By raising the voice instead, one can form questions with the change in meaning indicated. Mimic your teacher's intonation closely, using the cues from above to form questions.)

*(Now the teacher should intermix statement and question forms of the sentences from Drills 11 and 12, and students should respond with either 'statement' or 'question'.)*

13. *(Continue as in the last part of Drill 12, but now students should respond to statements as follows:)*

| Kwōj mol ke ekileb. | Qej ṁewel key yekilep. |
|---|---|
| etōḥal | yetegal |
| ebin | yɛpɛn |
| emeram | yemeram |
| ebat | yebat |
| enno | yennaw |
| ebakij | yepakij |
| emat mōkaj | yemahat ṁekaj |
| remat bat | remat bat |
| eouwi | yewwiy |
| erumij | yeṛimij |
| emarok | yemareq |
| eto | yetew |
| edrik | yedik |
| eritto | yerittew |
| mōkaj | ṁekaj |

*(And to questions, students should respond with answers made up like the following, beginning with kɛnkey:)*

| Kinke an leo jeim. | Kɛnkey han łeyew jɛyiṁ. |
|---|---|
| elab am kar jukaiki | yełap haṁ kar jiqahyikiy |
| kwojaje bwinbwin | qejahjɛy bɛnbɛn |
| rekḷl būtōre kū | rekayal paytɛrɛy kay |
| edrik injin en | yedik yinjin yeṅ |
| ejelū iōk lien | yejełay 'yiyɛk liyeṅ |
| emminene in tulok | yemminɛynɛy yin tiwłaq |
| elab air kōmat | yełap hayɛr kemat |
| emattia leen mū en | yemattiyyah leyen may yeṅ |
| ikōn wōd | yiken wed |
| ear wit | yehar wɛt |
| ejelok wintō | yejjełaq winteh |
| ejaḥin wōr mak | yejjahgin wer ṁahak |
| mweiuk in Jepan | ṁeyiq yin Jepahan |
| edrik an jerbal | yedik han jerbal |

14. *'Your feet don't seem to hurt from going barefoot.'*

| Emake jab metak nem in jintōb. | Yemakɛy jab metak neyeṁ yin jintɛb. |
|---|---|

```
mʊk nem...jutak            m̃&k neyem̃...jiwtak
abnʊnʊ nem...jujuj         habm̃ehm̃eh neyem̃...jiwijwij
mʊk bein...jeje            m̃&k p&yin...j&yj&y
bwil elikin...kejeje       bil yalikin...kejeyjey
mʊlo loHin...mʊHʉ          m̃&ɫ&w lawǧiyin...m̃egay
  ice.                       hay&j
mʊk loHin...al             m̃&k lawǧiyin...hal

Kwomake jab bio in         Qemak&y jab piyaw yin
  turʊn in boH.              tiwraǧ yin b&ǧ.
ekkil...talliH             kk&l...tall&g
ekkil...bul otobai         kk&l...biwiɫ wetewbahyiy
abinmake...make iam        habinimak&y..mak&y yi'yaham̃
mʊk...jerbal               m̃&k...jerbal
mʊnʊnʊ...katak kajin       m̃em̃ehm̃eh...kahtak kajin
 Majʊl                       Mahjeɫ
abnʊnʊ...jujuj             habm̃ehm̃eh..jiwijwij
```

15. **'You and who else?'**

```
A: Iar eHwʊr boH.          Yihar yaǧed b&ǧ.
B: Kwe ʉt iam?             Qey yat yi'yaham̃?
A: Na wʊt iaʊ.             Gah wet yi'yah&h.

A: Tony ear eHwʊr boH.     Tewniy yehar yaǧed b&ǧ.
B: E ʉt ian?               Y&y yat yi'yahan?
A: E wʊt ian.              Y&y wet yi'yahan.

A: Tony in Ali rar...      Tewniy yim Haɫiy rehar...
B: Erro ʉt iairro?         Y&rrew yat yi'yahay&rrew?
A: Erro wʊt iairro.        Y&rrew wet yi'yahay&rrew.

A: Kimro Tony ar...        K&mrew Tewniy har...
B: Komro ʉt iamiro?        Q&m̃rew yat yi'yahamiyrew?
A: Kimro wʊt iamro.        K&mrew wet yi'yahamrew.
```

'One share for every two people.'  'Who should I share with?'

```
A: Ruo armij juʊn kij.     Riwew harm&j jiwen k&j.
B: Na ʉt iaʊ?              Gah yat yi'yah&h?
A: Kwe im lio ibʊm.        Qey yim liyew yippam̃.

B: E ʉt ian?               Y&y yat yi'yahan?
B: Kwe ʉt iam?             Qey yat yi'yaham̃?
```

'I saw you last night.'  'Me and who else?'

```
A: Iar lo yok boH.         Yihar lew y&q b&ǧ.
B: Kar Ha ʉt eo iHo?       Kar gah yat yew yi'yah&h?
A: Kwe wʊt iam.            Qey wet yi'yaham̃.
```

A: Iar lo e boṅ.　　　　　Yihar lew y&y b&g̣.
　　ḳomro　　　　　　　　　q&ṁrew
　　erro　　　　　　　　　　y&rrew
　'*What did you say?*'　'*Say that again.*'
　　Ej iam?　　　　　　　　Yej yi'yahaṁ?
　　　 ia̱n　　　　　　　　　　yi'yahan
　　　iamiro　　　　　　　　yi'yahamiyrew
　　　iairro　　　　　　　　yi'yahay&rrew
　　　iaʉ　　　　　　　　　 yi'yah&h
　　　iamro　　　　　　　　 yi'yahamrew
　'*What are you going to say?*'
　　Enaj iam?　　　　　　　Yenahaj yi'yahaṁ?
　(*Substitute the words immediately above for*
　yi'yahaṁ *here and below.*)
　'*What did you say (some time ago, or before we*
　*were interrupted)?*'
　　Ekar iam?　　　　　　　Yekar yi'yahaṁ?
　'*What were you supposed to say?*'
　　En kar iam?　　　　　　Yen kar yi'yahaṁ?
　'*What would you have said?*'
　　Enaj kar iam?　　　　　Yenahaj kar yi'yahaṁ?

GRAMMATICAL NOTES

1. The drills of this lesson show some of the uses of words like mak&y, kahn&w&j yin, tahwinyin: winin... k&nkey, nahgin, yat, and yi'yaha-, many of which seem idiomatic from an English point of view. There is little more that can be said beyond what is brought out by the organization of the drills. Learn them well!

SHORT PROSE SELECTION

　　　　　　　　Legends
　　　　　　Inoṅ in Majʉl
　　　　　　Yineg̣ yin M̊ahjeł

　　　　　　　　　　　　　　　　　　　　until
Kinke　kajin Majʉl　ear　jab　ber ilo　beba　mae
K&nkey kajin M̊ahjeł yehar jab pad yilew p&ybah ṁahyey

ien　eo　ear　itok dri belle,　ejjab kanuij　loṅ
'yiyen yew yehar yiteq ripalley, yejjab kahn&w&j leg

armij    rej  mour   wõt  kiõ     rejelũ  inoH  ko   an
harm&j   rej  m&wir  wet  kiyyeh  rejełay yinag̃ kew  han

dri Majõl.   Botab ewõr  jet inoH  rej ber wõt Han
riMahjeł.    Bethab yewer jet yinag̃ rej pad wet gan

rainin     im  jej maroH wõt roH ilo    ien   kiki.
rahyinyin  yim jej mareg̃ wet reg̃ yilew 'yiyen kiykiy.

           most famous
BuHbuHtata    ilo    inoH  in  Majõl,  l'Etao.
Big̃big̃tahtah yilew yinag̃ yin Mahjeł, łeYetahwew.

                         rascal
Etao     kar lukun   dri nana   im  maroH ko  an
Yetahwew kar liqqiwin rinahnah yim mareg̃ kew han

            amazing                            fire
rekanuij  in  kabwilõHlõH.  E  eo  ear  lo  kijeek,
rekahn&w&j yin kabilegleg.  Y&y yew yehar lew kijyek,

                         reason              smart
im  inoH ko rej ba  bwe unin    an dri Amerka meletlet,
yim yinag̃ kew rej bah bey winin han riHamedkah maletlet,

           fled
Etao     ear  ko  jen Majõl im  bõklok an  meletlet
Yetahwew yehar kew jan Mahjeł yim bekłaq han maletlet

                         try
Han Amerka.   Jenaj  kajjioH in lale   jet inoH
gan Hamedkah. Jenahaj kajjeyeg̃ yin lahley jet yinag̃

          lessons
ilo    leejen  kein lal.
yilew  leyjen  k&yin lał.

## PROVERB

Jeblab dejlok.           Jebłap dejłaq.

'People shy away from one who has
                too much.'

## VOCABULARY

| | | |
|---|---|---|
| abinmake | habinmak&y | fear being alone |
| abonono | habñehñeh | (be) uncomfortable |
| aibuijuij | hayib&w&jw&j | beautiful |
| ãt | yat | and who else? |
| bal | bal | cover an earth oven |
| bãtõre | payt&r&y | battery (from English) |
| boti | bawtiy, bawati- | nose |

| | | |
|---|---|---|
| bul | biwił (intr.) ...iy (tr.) | go at full speed |
| bultbult | biğbiğ | famous |
| bwilŮlt | bileg | (be) surprised |
| drakelkel | dak&lk&l | ugly |
| ekkil | kk&l | (be) afraid of speed or heights |
| ekŮtoto | kk&t&wt&w | windy (distributive of k&t&w) |
| eminene | mmin&yn&y | (be) accustomed, used to |
| Etao | Yetahwew | name of legendary trickster; sly |
| ia- | yi'yaha- | with..., said by... |
| ittimonmon | ttiymeltmelt | full of demons (distributive of tiymelt) |
| iur | yił | fast |
| jaltin | jahgin | not yet |
| jimjim | j&mj&m (intr.) j&m(&y) (tr.) | sharpen |
| jukok | jiqeq | open an earth oven |
| kaiur | ka + yił(iy) | hurry |
| kŮl | kayal | new |
| kŮm | kayam, kaya- | (your) figure |
| kij | k&j | a share |
| kimur | kimiwir | productive (of plants or land) (cf. m&wir) |
| kinke | k&nkey | because |
| konkon | qeltqelt | able to catch many fish |
| loltі | lawğiy lawğiyi- | mouth |
| majur | majił | sleep (Rat.) |
| majurleb | majiłlep | sleep a long time |
| meletlet | maletlet | smart |
| mŮjŮno | mejeñaw | weak |
| naltin | nahgin | almost |
| obrak | webrak | overloaded |
| ok | w&k, wike- | net |
| rabŮlbŮl | rabelbel | shiny |
| rumij | łimij (intr.) ...iy (tr.) | late (for something) |
| taunin | tahwinyin | why?, what is the reason? |
| tallilt | tall&g | climb up |
| teej | teyej | (have a) test (from English) |
| tie | tiyey, tiye- | lips |
| to | t&w | get off, not ride (opposite of wiw&y) |

| | | |
|---|---|---|
| to | tew | (be) a long time |
| tulok | tiwłaq | dive |
| turoħ | tiwrag̈ | fishing method: skin diving with spear, shooting fish in hole (<u>reg̈</u>) |
| wäto | wayt&w | land tract |
| wŭlio | wiliy&w | handsome |
| wŏd | wed | coral |
| un | win, wini- | reason; base, foundation; problem |

## LESSON NINETEEN

More store scenes;
double consonant intransitives;
kab and hawelep...yem; colors.

### DIALOGUES

1.
A: I maroń ke kejerbal
waj ne am?

Yimareǧ key kejerbal
waj ńey hań?

B: Ejelok aʉ waj. Ete-
ke kwʉj jab wia am?

Yejjeɫaq hah&h waj. Yet-
key qej jab wiyah hań?

A: Ewʉr ia waj in
wia?

Yewer yi'yah waj yin
wiyah?

B: Ewʉr ilo mʉn wia
en an Jelba.

Yewer yilew ńen wiyah
yen han Jelbah.

A: Inaj wia ńe ewʉr
aʉ mak.

Yinahaj wiyah hah&h gey
yewer hah&h ńahak.

B: Emman bwe en wʉr am
make.

Yeńńan bey yen wer hań
mak&y.

A: May I use your watch?
B: I don't have a watch. Why don't you buy one (for yourself)?
A: Where do they have watches for sale?
B: There are some at Jelba's store.
A: I'll buy one for myself when I have money.
B: It'll be good for you to have one of your own.

2.
A: Ewʉr ke jatin mwin?

Yewer key jahtiyin ńiyin?

B: Aet, ewʉr. Jete eo
kwo kʉnaan?

Hay&t, yewer. Jetey yew
qekeńhan?

A: Letok ruo kuat kab
lalim baun in juka.

Leyteq riwew qiwat kab
ɫal&m bawin yin jiqah.

B: Kwʉj ebbok ke kon bib
im tuna?

Qej pp&q key kawan piyip
yim tiwnah?

188

A: Aet, ka-ruo tok.  O,     Hay&t, kariwew teq.  Wew,
   kab juɐn bok in             kab jiwen bawak yin
   jikka.                      jikkah.
B: Jikka rot?                Jikka ƚet?
A: Salem ɦe ejab Kool,       Jeyƚeṁ gey yejjab Qiwiƚ,
   einwɐt juɐn.                yayinwet jiwen.
B: Ebar wɐr ke ta?           Yebar wer key tah?
A: Ejja mɐj.  Jete wɐnen     Yejjah ṁ&j.  Jetey weṅyan
   aolep?                      hawelep?
B: Lalim tala jonɐul-ruo     ƚal&m tahƚah j&g&wil-riwew
   jeen.                       jayan.
A: Ejelok aɐ jɐɐn jeb-       Yejjeƚaq hah&h jayan jep-
   leklek, joɦoul eo           leklek, j&g&wil yew
   tala.                       tahƚah.
B: Bwe eo am eo.  Kommol     Bey yew haṁ yew.  Qeṁṁewel
   tata.                       tahtah.
A: Kommol.                   Qeṁṁewel.

A: Do you have any sardines?
B: Yes, how many do you want?
A: Give me two cans and five pounds of sugar.
B: Do you want any corned beef or tuna?
A: Yes, give me two of each.  Oh, a carton of ciga-
   rettes, too.
B: What brand?
A: Salems or Kools.  Either one.
B: Anything else?
A: That's all.  How much for everything?
B: Five dollars and twelve cents.
A: I don't have any coins.  Here's a ten dollar bill.
B: Here's your change.  Thanks.
A: Thank you.

3.
A: Ewɐr ke bilawɐ in         Yewer key pilahway yin
   wia?                        wiyah?
B: Kwo rumij.  Ej kab mat.   Qeƚiṁij.  Yej kab mahat.
A: Enaj bar wɐr ɦɐɐt?        Yenahaj bar wer gayat?
B: Ilju ej jibboɦ.           Yiljiw yej jibb&ǧ.
   Kwo maroɦ roltok.           Qemareǧ rawalteq.

A: Ekwe ij likit juōn	Yeqey yij likit jiwen
   dollar, kab kakon ruo	   tahłah, kab kaqeñ riwew
   aō lob.	   hah&h łeweb.
B: Ekwe, kommol.	Yeqey, qeṁṁewel.
A: Kommol tata. Inaj	Qeṁṁewel tahtah. Yinahaj
   itok ilju.	   yiteq yiljiw.

A: Do you have any bread for sale?
B: You're late; we just ran out.
A: When will you have more?
B: Tomorrow morning. You can come back.
A: OK. I'll give you a dollar now. Please save two
   loaves for me.
B: Fine. Thank you.
A: Thank you. I'll come tomorrow.

## DRILLS

1. I maroñ ke kejerbal	Yiṁareğ key kejerbal <u>waj</u>
   <u>waj</u> ne am?	   ñey haṁ?
   Ejelok aō <u>waj</u>. Ewōr	Yejjełaq hah&h <u>waj</u>. Yewer
   an Meri	   han Meydiy.
      binjel	      pinjeł
      ben	      peyen
      buk	      b&q
      job	      jeweb
      jea	      jeyah
      tebel	      teybeł
      mej in dret	      maj yin det

2. Iar kejerbal <u>wa</u> eo	Yihar kejerbal <u>wah</u> yew
   waan.	   wahan.
      tirak	      tirak
      car	      kahar
      kōrkōr	      kerker
      balun	      bałwin
      wōtobai	      wetewbahyiy
      bajikōl	      bahajkeł
      drieka	      diyyakah
      tibñel	      tipg&l
      boj	      bewej

3. Ewōr ia <u>waj</u> in wia?	Yewer yi'yah <u>waj</u> yin wiyah?
   Mieco. Ewōr waj in	Miyeykew. Yewer waj yin
   wia Mieco.	   wiyah Miyeykew.

   *(Repeat Drill 1.)*

4. Ewʊr aʊ maak.        Yewer hah&h ṁahak.
   am                   haṁ
   an                   han
   ad                   had
   am                   ham
   ami                  hamiy
   air                  hay&r

5. I naj wia aʊ bwe      Yinahaj wiyah hah&h bey
   en wʊr aʊ make.       yen wer hah&h mak&y.
   kwo...am...am         qe...haṁ...haṁ
   e...an...an           ye...han...han
   je...adr...adr        je...had...had
   kim (etc.)            k&m (etc.)
   kom                   q&ṁ
   re                    re

6.
A: Ewʊr ke jatin mwin?   Yewer key jahtiyin ṁiyin?
B: Aet, ewʊr. Jete eo    Hay&t, yewer. Jetey yew
   kwo kʊnan?            qekeṅhan?
         kon bib                kawan piyip
         bao                    bahwew
         ik                     y&k
         kanniek                kanniy&k
         tuna                   tiwnah
         anien                  haniyen
         biteto                 piteytew

7. 'We just ran out of it.'
   Ej kab maat.          Yej kab mahat.
        mat                   mat
        itok                  yiteq
        etal                  yetal
        dreloḥtok             d&yɬaǥteq
        driwʊjlok             diyw&jɬaq
        ijjino                jjinew
        jemlok                jeṁɬaq

8. 'And give me a loaf of bread.'
   Kab letok juʊn bilawᵾ.  Kab leyteq jiwen pilahway.
        kon bib                  kawan piyip
        jikka                    jikkah
        mᵾjet                    majet
        jatin                    jahtiyin
        tuna                     tiwnah

|  |  |
|---|---|
| jamŏn | jaṁeṅ |
| job | jeweb |
| kanamnam | kaṅaṁṅaṁ |
| jakŏlkŏl | jakk&lk&l |
| jormŏta | jeṁṁetah |
| jiḦilij | jiyiglij |
| teinam | teyiṅaṁ |

9. *All the things you wanted have been achieved.*

| Aoleb men ko kwar | Hawelep men kew qehar |
|---|---|
| kŏnaan em | keṅhan yem |
| tŏbrak. | teprak. |
| mat | mahat |
| jako | jak&w |
| jorren | jeṁṁayan |
| mŏj aŏ kŏmmani | ṁ&j hah&h keṁṁhaniy |
| dredrelok air keboji | d&yd&y±aq hay&r kepewejiy |

(Change each of the above to the following patterns:)

Reteprak hawelep men kew qehar keṅhan.
Hawelepem teprak.

10. *All these cases are full of corned beef.*

| Aoleb bok ka em bol | Hawelep bawak kay yem b&w&± |
|---|---|
| kin koonbib. | k&n kawan piyip. |
| bek...drekⱨ | payak...dekay |
| tiroot...mŏḦⱨ | tirwet...ṁegay |
| ekekak...buk | kkeykahak...b&q |
| bⱨntŏre...pilej | payant&r&y...pilyej |
| tibtib...mweiuk | t&pt&p...ṁ&yiq |
| kabaḦ...nuknuk | kabag...niqniq |
| kalan...karjin | ka±an...karjin |
| bakŏj...dren | bakej...dan |

(Change each of the above to the following patterns:)

R&b&w&± k&n kawan piyip hawelep bawak kay.
Hawelepem b&w&± k&n kawan piyip.

11.

| I makoko in | Yiṁak&wk&w yin |
|---|---|
| baj bwe elab wŏnen. | baj bey ye±ap weṅyan. |
| bajinjea | bahjinjeyah |
| wia kanniek | wiyah kanniy&k |
| kelok ilo baluun | key±aq yilew balwin |
| idraak dren kajur | yidahak dan kajw&r |
| ebbŏk nejⱨ kirababon | bbek najih kirahbahbewen |

|  |  |
|---|---|
| mʉtʉ ekkan in belle | ṁegay kkan yin palley |
| jambo lok Han Jeban | jaṁb&w łaq gan Jepahan |

12. Komaroh ke elletok
    <u>jeen jebleklek</u>?
    jeen jiddik
    jeen in jaba
    konam Han kemeem en
    wʉnen aʉ mubi
    jidik aʉ muri Han
    kʉllʉ in lal
    jet aʉ aikuj im
    akkauni

    Qemareǥ key lleyteq
    <u>jayan jepleklek</u>?
    jayan jiddik
    jayan yin jahbah
    qeṅahaṁ gan keyemyem yeṅ
    weṅyan hah&h ṁiwpiy
    jidik hah&h ṁitiy gan
    kełłay yin lał
    jet hah&h hayiqij yim
    hakkawiniy

13. E make <u>lab</u> wʉnen <u>mʉtʉ</u>
    ailih <u>kein</u>!
    drik...kiaj
        mweiuk
        nuknuk
        taktʉ
        bajinjea

    Yemak&y <u>łap</u> weṅyan <u>ṁegay</u>
    hay&l&g <u>k&yin</u>!
    dik...kiyhaj
        ṁ&yiq
        niqniq
        takteh
        bahjinjeyah

14. Kwo maroh ke <u>janiji tok</u>
    <u>tala e nejʉ</u>.
    rube <u>lok mak</u> en nejin
    i....wʉj jeen ne nejim
    e........mani

    Qemareǥ <u>key janijiy teq</u>
    <u>tahłah y&y najih</u>?
    ṭipey łaq ṁahak yen najin
    yi....w&j jayan ṅey najiṁ
    ye........ṁaniy

15. *'I didn't bring rice.''So bring one bag.'*

    Iar jab ebbʉktok raij.
    Kab bʉktok juʉn bek.
    Iar jab ellelok kijen ik.
    Kab lelok juʉn kijen.
    Iar jab ekkʉlel am jʉt.
    Kab kʉlet juʉn aʉ.
    Iar jab ekkʉnak aʉ jʉt.
    Kab kʉnak juʉn am.
    Iar jab ebbok an ben.
    Kab bukot juʉn an.
    Iar jab edrʉb an waini.
    Kab diboj juʉn an.
    Iar jab ekkal imʉ im.

    Yihar jab <u>bbekteq rahyij</u>.
    Kab bekteq jiwen payak.
    Yihar jab <u>lleyłaq kijen y&k</u>.
    Kab leyłaq jiwen kijen.
    Yihar jab <u>kkayaly&l haṁ jehet</u>.
    Kab kaylet jiwen hah&h.
    Yihar jab <u>kkeṅak hah&h jehet</u>.
    Kab keṅak jiwen haṁ.
    Yihar jab <u>pp&q han peyen</u>.
    Kab piqet jiwen han.
    Yihar jab <u>ddeb han wahyiniy</u>.
    Kab dibej jiwen han.
    Yihar jab <u>kkal yiṁ&h y&ṁ</u>.

Kab kalek juön imöm.                Kab kalek jiwen yiṁeṁ.
Iar jab <u>eokkwal</u> an eo.       Yihar jab <u>qqa𝔩 han</u> yew.
Kab <u>kwa𝔩e</u> juön an.          Kab <u>qa𝔩ey</u> jiwen han.
Iar jab <u>ellok an</u>             Yihar jab <u>ll&q han</u>
    teinam.                             teyiṅaṁ.
Kab <u>lukoj</u> juön an.           Kab <u>liqej</u> jiwen han.
Iar jab <u>illik</u> konaö.         Yihar jab <u>llik</u> qeṅah&h.
Kab <u>likit</u> juön konam.        Kab <u>likit</u> jiwen qeṅahaṁ.
Iar jab <u>ekekak</u> aö            Yihar jab <u>kkeykahak</u> hah&h
    nuknuk.                             niqniq.
Kab <u>kekake</u> juön am.          Kab <u>keykahakey</u> jiwen haṁ.

16. '<u>Do you know where Tom is?</u>'  '<u>Do you know who Tom is?</u>'

A: Kwo jelṻ ke kajjien          Qeje𝔩ay key kajjiyen
     Tom?                           Tawaṁ?
B: E ber <u>möuweo</u>.         Yepad <u>ṁewiweyew</u>.

A: Kwo jelṻ ke kajjien          Qeje𝔩ay key kajjiyen
     Tom?                           Tawaṁ?
B: Aet, nejin <u>Ali</u> im         Hay&t, najin <u>Ha𝔩iy</u> yim
     men.                           men.

   (Substitute other personal names and locations in
   the above two conversations.)

A: Kwo jelṻ ke kajjien          Qeje𝔩ay key kajjiyen
     buk eo aö?                     b&q yew hah&h?
B: Buk öt?                       Biqet?

A: Buk <u>birörö</u> eo.         B&q <u>birehreh</u> yew.
B: E ber ion teböl en.          Yepad yi'yewen teybe𝔩 yeṅ.

   (Substitute the following words for <u>b&q</u>, and substitute other colors from the reference section for
   <u>birehreh</u>.)

<u>Other things to ask about
   (with possessing words
other than hah&h shown in              (Rṻlik)        (Ratak)
         parentheses)</u>

bik (najih, kij&h)      piyik     piyikit?       piyiktah?
beba                    p&ybah    p&ybahat?      p&ybahtah?
bao (jibih)             bahwew    bahwewet?      bahwewtah?
waj (najih)             waj       wajet?         wattah?
boj (wah&h)             bewej     bewejet?       bewettah?
ok                      w&k       wiket?         w&ktah?
bu  (najih)             biw       biwit?         biwtah?

```
wa      (wah&h)    wah       wahat?      wahtah?
pilej   (giyih)    pilyej    pilyejet?   pilyettah?
jibun   (giyih)    jibwin    jibwinit?   jibwintah?
ki                 kiy       kiyit?      kiytah?
bwḁ                bay       bayat?      baytah?
```

## GRAMMATICAL NOTES

1. Note the uses of kab in Drill 7: 'just' and Drill 8: 'and'.

2. Note the use of yem in Drills 9 and 10. It is related to yim 'and', and has a conjoining function, although it defies direct translation into some one English equivalent; note that hawelep always precedes it in the sentence. The first sentences of these two drills are the equivalents of the first of the two alternative patterns at the end of each of these two drills.

3. The lleyteq of Drill 12, and all of the verbs in the cues of Drill 15 are double consonant intransitives. Their transitive counterparts are called for in the responses to Drill 15.

4. The last part of Drill 16 gives a new pattern, one for asking 'What book?' or 'Which book?'. It consists of adding a suffix which consists of the repetition of the last vowel of the stem + t, or the adding of tah, depending on the dialect. Some stems with & as the vowel change in the western dialect, as in b&q and w&k. *House* and *fish* also change:

```
y&ṁ     yiṁet?     y&ṁtah?
y&k     yiket?     y&ktah?
```

Note also the change from j to t in the Ratak forms for words that end in j like waj and bewej.

## SHORT PROSE SELECTION

Ilomij<br>Yil&wm&j

```
                                                 relatives
Ne  juᵤn  armij  ej  mij  ilo  ailiḣ  in  Majᵤl  men
Gey jiwen harm&j yej m&j yilew hay&l&g yin Ṁahjeł men

in  ej  juᵤn  ien    kwelok tok an  ro  nukun, ro
yin yej jiwen 'yiyen q&ylaq teq han rew niqin, rew
```

jeran, im aoleb   ro  rejelŭ  kajien.     Rej bŭktok
jeran, yim hawelep rew rejeɫay kajjiyen.   Rej bekteq
men in lelok ko.    Men kein rej job,   jeen,  mŭttan
men yin leyɫaq kew. Men kₐyin rej jeweb, jayan, ṁettan
nuknuk im men ko  eirlokwŭt.      Men kein  rej
niqniq yim men kew yayiyₐrɫaqwet. Men kₐyin rej
kejerbali Ħan ien  eoreak,  jiljino  ran   elkin
kejerbaliy gan 'yiyen yeɫ'yak, jiljinₐw rahan yalikin
an armij en mij im   ien   eo rej tŭmak bwe dri mij
han harmₐj yeħ mₐj yim 'yiyen yew rej temak bey rimₐj
        rise (from the dead)
en  ej  jerkakbije.    Mweiuk kein rej likit  ion
yeħ yej <u>jerkakpₐjₐy</u>. Mₐyiq kₐyin rej likit yi'yewen
grave
leb eo Ħan an  armij  tebteb.  Elkin   eoreak eor
<u>lₐb</u> yew gan han harmₐj tₐptₐp.  Yalikin yeɫ'yak yewer
supper     bring to an end
kejota   in kejemlok ien  buromij en Ħan armij en.
<u>kₐjₐwtah</u> yin <u>kejeṁɫaq</u> 'yiyen birₐwṁₐj yeħ gan harmₐj yen.

## PROVERB

   An biliĦliĦ koba,        Han piliglig kₐwbah,
      kŭmman lometo.           keṁhan lawmetew.

   Roughly: 'Of the drops combined
             is the ocean made.'

   Equivalent: 'A penny saved is a
                 penny earned.'

## VOCABULARY

| | | |
|---|---|---|
| akkaun | hakkawin (intr.) ...iy (tr.) | buy on account |
| bajikŭl | bahajkeɫ (intr.) ...ey (tr.) | (go on a) bicycle carry on a bicycle |
| bajinjea | bahjinjeyah (intr.) ...yik(iy) (tr.) | (go as a) passenger take someone as a passenger |
| bantŭre | payantₐrₐy | pantry (from English) |
| biliĦliĦ | piliglig | drops of liquid (distributive of <u>pil(it)(iy)</u>) |
| boj | bewej | boat (from English) |
| bol | bₐwₐɫ | full (from English) |

| | | |
|---|---|---|
| bu | biw (intr.) | shoot gun |
| | biwik(iy) (tr.) | shoot it |
| ekkälel | kkayaly&l (intr.) | elect, chose |
| | kayalet (tr.) | |
| ekekak | kkeykahak (intr.) | pull; a drawer |
| | keykahakey (tr.) | |
| ekkan | kkan | food |
| eoreak | yełyak (intr.) | smooth out the ground; a service held at the grave six days after burial, in which the grave is smoothed out with gravel |
| | ...ey (tr.) | |
| eo | yew | fish line |
| illik | llik (intr.) | put, place, donate; consider...as |
| | likit(iy) (tr.) | |
| im men | yim men | and spouse |
| jaba | jahbah | church collection |
| janij | janij(iy) | change, exchange, make change (from English) |
| jamön | jaṁeṅ | salmon (from English) |
| jebleklek | j&pl&kl&k | scattered (a distributive) |
| jerkakbije | jerkakp&j&y | rise from the dead |
| kabaḧ | kabaq | suitcase |
| kajjien | kajjiye- | location of, the identification of (also k&yin kańaṁńaṁ) *mosquito coil* (cf. ṅaṁ *mosquito*) |
| kanamnam | kańaṁńaṁ | |
| keboji | kepewejiy | get them ready (causative + transitive of pewjak) |
| kirababon | kirahbahbewen | phonograph (from German *Grammophon*) |
| körkör | kerker | paddling canoe |
| kona- | qeńaha- (Rälh.) | duty, share of expenses |
| | qińaha- (Rat.) | |
| leb | l&b, libe- | grave, tomb |
| lob | łeweb | loaf (from English) |
| lometo | lawmetew | ocean, sea |
| makoko | ṁak&wk&w | refuse to |
| muri | miłiy(ik)(iy) | buy on credit, be in debt (to) |

| | | |
|---|---|---|
| nukun | niqin niqiy(i-) | (his) family, relatives |
| rubrub rube | ŧipŧip (intr.) ŧipey (tr.) | shatter, break |
| tebteb | t&pt&p (intr.) tep/t&p&y (tr.) (sg.) tepiy (tr.) (pl.) | gifts taken away from birthday party, wedding, or funeral |
| teinam | teyiṅaṁ | mosquito net (cf. ṅaṁ *mosquito*) |
| tibtib | t&pt&p (intr.) ...&y (tr.) | trunk, foot locker put something in a trunk |
| tŭmak | temak(&y) | believe, faith |
| tiroot | tirwet | cabinet, wardrobe, closet |

**REFERENCE** -- Colors

| | | |
|---|---|---|
| mouj | mewij | white |
| kilmej | kilmeyej | black |
| birŭrŭ | birehreh | red |
| maroro | mahrewrew | green |
| mŭnaknak | ṁeṅakṅak | brown |
| ubajaj | wipahajhaj | gray |
| mir | mir | red (of reddish coconuts) |
| kieo | kiyew | orange (also a name of a plant with orange flower) |
| kilmir | kilmir | black |
| ialo | yi'yał&w | yellow |
| bilu | biłiw | blue |
| biolet | piyewlet | violet |
| kirin | kiryin | green |
| biraun | birahwin | brown |
| kire | kir&y | gray |
| biḧ | piyig | pink |

## LESSON TWENTY

### More causatives; distributives; compound verbs.

DIALOGUES

1.
A: Ewör ke am buk in read?

Yewer key haṁ b&q yin riyit?

B: Aet, ewör jet. Kwo könaan ke lali?

Hay&t, yewer jet. Qekeṅhan key lahliy?

A: Letok mük juön bwe in lale.

Leyteq ṁek jiwen bey yin lahley?

B: Emman bwebwenato eo ak ekaburomijmij.

Yeṁṁan beybeynahtew yew hak yekabir&wṁ&jṁ&j.

A: Etke ekaburomijmij?

Yetkey yekabir&wṁ&jṁ&j?

B: Likao eo enaj mij jemlokin tata.

Likahwew yew yenahaj m&j jeṁłaqin tahtah.

A: Do you have any books to read?
B: Yes, I have some. Would you like to see them?
A: Give me one to look at.
B: This story is good but sad.
A: Why is it sad?
B: The hero dies at the end.

2.
A: Jen ilen kwelok.

Jen yilan q&ylaq.

B: Kwelok in ta?

Q&ylaq yin tah.

A: Kwelok an aoleb dri jikul.

Q&ylaq han hawelep rijikiwił.

B: Jenaj et ilo kwelok en?

Jenahaj y&t yilew q&ylaq yeṅ?

A: Rej ba jenaj ekkälel obija Ḣan iiü in.

Rej bah jenahaj kkayaly&l wepiyjah gan 'yiyeh yin.

A: Let's go to the meeting.
B: What's it for?
A: It's a meeting for all students.
B: What are we going to do there?
A: They say we'll have our annual election of officers.

DRILLS

1. Emman bwebwenato eo
    bwe ekaburomijmij.
    ekabwilŏhlŏh
    ekabalbal
    ekakŭmkŭm
    ekamŏnŏnŏ

   Yeṁṁan beybeynahtew yew
    bey yekabir&wṁ&jṁ&j.
    yeka(b)bilegleg
    yekappałpał
    yekakkiṁkiṁ
    yeka(ṁ)ṁeṅehṅeh

2. Jerbal kan an
    rekematŏrtŏr.
    rekaiḣtanan
    rekakitŏtŏ
    rekarubrub burŏ
    rekaitoktok limo
    rekamakoko

   Jerbal kaṅ han
    reka(m)materter.
    rekay&gtahanhan
    rekakit&ht&h
    reka(t̂)t̂ipt̂ip b&r&w
    rekayi(t)teqteq limew
    reka(ṁ)ṁak&wk&w

3. I matŏrtŏr kin jerbal
    kan an.
    i iḣtan
    i kotŏtŏ
    e rub buruŏ
    e itok limoŭ
    i makoko

   Yimaterter k&n jerbal
    kaṅ han.
    yiy&gtahan
    yikit&ht&h
    yet̂ip-biriw&h
    yeyiteq-limewih
    yiṁak&wk&w

4. Renaj mŏrŏik likao eo
    ḣe etak al.
    ḣe etulok al
    ilo takin alliḣ
    iumin meramin alliḣ
    ilo ran jidik en
     lokan al
    elkin an ettoḣ

   Renahaj ṁehrehyik likahwew
    yew gey yetak hał.
    gey yetiwlaq hał
    yilew takin hall&g
    yiwṁin meramin hall&g
    yilew rahan jidik yeṅ
     łeqan hał
    yalikin han tteğ

5. Likao eo enaj mij
    jemlokin tata.
    jinoin tata
    lukalban lok
    lukon lok
    iolaban lok

   Likahwew yew yenahaj ṁ&j
    jeṁłaqin tahtah.
    jinewin tahtah
    liqałpan łaq
    liqen łaq
    yewełepan łaq

6. Ta unin am ba          Tah winin haṁ bah
   ekaburomijmij?          yeka(b)bir&wṁ&jṁ&j?
   ekabwiIŬHIŬH            yeka(b)bilegleg
   ekabbalbal              yekappaɫpaɫ
   ekakŬmkŬm               yekakkiṁkiṁ
   ekamŬnŬnŬ               yeka(ṁ)ṁeṅċhṅeh
   ekaiHtanan              yekay&gtahanhan
   ekakitŬtŬ               yekakit&ht&h
   ekarubrub bŬrŬ          yeka(ɫ)ɫipɫip-b&r&w
   ekaitoktok limo         yekayi(t)teqteq-limew
   ekamakoko               yeka(ṁ)ṁak&wk&w
   ekamŬkmŬk               yeka(ṁ)ṁekṁek

7. Jen ilen kwelok.        Jen yilan q&ylaq.
   kulab                   qiɫab
   biknik                  piknik
   jambo                   jaṁb&w
   turoH                   tiwrag̊
   lŬkḦ                    lekay
   kŬmat                   kemat
   kalur                   kalw&r

8. Jenaj ekḦleel obija    Jenahaj kkayaly&l wepiyjah
   ilo kwelok en.          yilew q&ylaq yeṅ.
   idrak kobe              yidahak kawp&y
   mŬHḦ tonaj              ṁegay tewnahaj
   aluij bija              halw&j pijah
   le kŬto                 leyk&t&w
   al in maina             hal yin ṁahyinah

9. *(Be careful to substitute at the right place in
   these sentences. Two places are used.)*
   Rej ba jenaj ekḦlel     Rej bah yenahaj kkayaly&l
   obija buḦnin.           wepiyjah big̊niyin.
   idrak kobe              yidahak kawp&y
   jeklaj                  jekɫaj
   aluij bija              halw&j pijah
   kajukkwe                kajiqq&y
   kalur                   kalw&r
   wik in lal              wiyik yin laɫ
   jambo                   jaṁb&w
   le koto                 leyk&t&w
   kulab                   qiɫab
   iiŬ in lal              'yiyeh yin laɫ
   ilju ej jibboH          yiljiw yej jibb&g̊
   kiŬ eraeleb             kiyyeh yerahyelep
   kiŬ ejota               kiyyeh y&j&wtah

10. Kwo naj et ilju?                    Qenahaj y&t yiljiw?
    Inaj kakkonkon ilju.                Yinahaj kaqqeñgeñ yiljiw.
         katak                               kahtak
         kiki                                kiykiy
         kaikujkuj                           kahayiqijqij
         kakijen                             kakijen
         kakkije                             kakkij&y
         kakkÖr                              kakk&r
         kÖkkÖrÄrÄ                           kekkerayray

11. Wa en ej le injin                   Wah yeñ yej ley yinjin.
    Lam en ej le karijin.               Ɫahaṁ yeñ yej ley karjin.
         wa         wÖjelÄ                   wah         w&jɫay
         teiñki     bÄtere                   t&yigkiy    payt&r&y
         ratio      jarom                    reytiy&w    jaɫem
         injin      tijel                    yinjin      tiyjeɫ
         jitob      kiaj                     jitweb      kiyhaj
         le-        to ñan                   ɫe-         tew gan
                    talliñ                               tall&g
         ladrik     bwÄ                      ɫadik       bay
         lÖllab     kÖrkÖr                   ɫeɫɫap      kerker
         likao      eo im                    likahwew    yew yim
                    eñwÖr                                yağed
         kijak      mej im                   kijak       maj yim
                    tutu                                 tiwtiw

12. *This islet has lots of fish.*
    Cue:
        'ik'                                'y&k'
    Response:
        E ike ene in.                       Yeyikey yanyin.
    C: 'im'                                 'y&ṁ'
    R: E ime ene in.                        Yeyiṁey yanyin.
    C: 'armij'                              'harm&j'
    R: E armije ene in.                     Yeharmijey yanyin.
    C: 'mar'                                'mar'
    R: E mar(mar)e...                       Yemar(mar)ey...
    C: 'ujuij'                              'wijw&j'
    R: E ujuije...                          Yewijw&j&y...
    C: 'iu'                                 'yiw'
    R: E iui...                             Yeyiwiy...
    C: 'kijdrik'                            'kijdik'
    R: Ekkijdrikdrik(i)...                  Yekkijdikdik(iy)...

C: 'kuj'
R: Ekkujuj(i)...

'kiwij'
Yekkiwijwij(iy)...

C: 'kidru'
R: Ekkidrudru(i)...

'kidiw'
Yekkidiwdiw(iy)...

C: 'bako'
R: Ebbakoko(e)...

'pakew'
Yeppakewkew(ey)...

C: 'jojo'
R: E jojoe...

'jewjew'
Yejewjewey...

C: 'bik'
R: Ebbikik(i)...

'piyik'
Yeppiyikyik(iy)...

C: 'bao'
R: Ebbaoo(e)...

'bahwew'
Yebbahwewwew(ey)...

C: 'bŭb'
R: E bŭbe...

'beb'
Yebebey...

C: 'drekŭ'
R: E drekŭke...

'dekay'
Yedekayk&y...

C: 'bok'
R: E bokbok(e)...

'beq'
Yebeqbeq(ey)...

C: 'bar'
R: E barbar(e)...

'bar'
Yebarbar(ey)...

C: 'dret'
R: Edretdret(e)...

'det'
Yeddetdet(ey)...

C: 'wit'
R: E wituwit...

'w&t'
Y&w&tt&w&t...

C: 'makmŭk'
R: E makmike...

'ṁakṁ&k'
Yeṁakṁikey...

C: 'baru'
R: Ebbaruru(i)...

'bariw'
Yebbariwriw(iy)...

C: 'tol'
R: E toltol(e)...

'teĭ'
Yeteĭteĭ(ey)...

C: 'bat'
R: E batbat(e)...

'bat'
Yebatbat(ey)...

GRAMMATICAL NOTES

1. Sporadic references have been made in earlier lessons to a 'distributive' form of certain words. In this and following lessons you will now be given some drill and explanation of this very important category of Marshallese.

Drill 12 gives examples of how the distributive is formed for a number of noun-like words. Note the words for *dog, cat, rat, pig, shark, crab, mountain, hill* and *sunshine*. For these words the distributive is formed by reduplication of the final two historical syllables:

*kidiwi    >    ...*ki<u>diwidiwi</u>

and the doubling of the earlier consonant, in this case the <u>k</u>:

>    *<u>k</u>kidiwidiwi

The final vowel is then optionally either preserved by the addition of a <u>y</u>, or dropped, and the antepenultimate vowel is dropped:

kkidiwdiwiy
*or*   kkidiwdiw

This is the main pattern for forming distributives. In fact, whenever you find a word in Marshallese that has undergone both consonant doubling and final syllable reduplication like <u>KkidiwDIW</u> above, *you can be fairly sure it is a distributive.*

The remaining words in Drill 12 exemplify other minor patterns for forming distributives. These include some vowel changes in the base (which usually go back to the historical underlying form) and the obligatory preservation of a final vowel with the <u>y</u> increment. The words for *fish* and *house* exemplify both:

<u>Base vowel change</u>:   y&k   >   *yike...
                          y&ṁ   >   *yiṁe...

<u>Preservation of final vowel</u>:   yik<u>ey</u>
                                     yiṁ<u>ey</u>

The meaning difference signalled by distributive forms may seem quite diverse and wide in range from an English point of view, and it will be presented gradually in this and following lessons. In general it can be considered as a distributing or spreading out of the basic meaning of the stem in either time or space. For the words of Drill 12, the distribution is in space: 'The waters around this island are full of fish.'

Drills 1, 2, and 6 also contain some distributive forms used together with the causative <u>ka-</u>; here the meaning distinction is different, and more subtle. For example, consider the following:

Menyin yenahaj kabilegey.   'This thing will surprise him.' (transitive)

| | |
|---|---|
| Menyin yenahaj kabi-legleg. | 'This thing will cause surprise.' (intransitive) |
| Menyin yenahaj kabbi-legleg. | 'This thing will cause great surprise.' (distributive) |

Here the distributive seems to intensify. Similar intensification is effected by use of the doubled consonant forms shown in parentheses for (b)bilegleg and other words in Drills 1, 2, and 6.

In some contexts the distributive indicates the widespread nature or ease of an action. Consider a classic example:

| | |
|---|---|
| reǧ | 'hear' |
| jarreǧreǧ | 'deaf' |
| rreǧreǧ | 'able to hear well' |

There are a number of such pairs of opposites in the language: forms with and without the ja- negating prefix, and quite often the form without the prefix is a distributive.

Thus the following are possible:

| | |
|---|---|
| Yebbilegleg ɬeyeñ. | 'He is easy to surprise.' |
| Yejabbilegleg ɬeyeñ. | 'He is hard to surprise.' |

Finally, consider the following:

| | |
|---|---|
| Yibileg. | 'I'm surprised.' |

and the sarcastic:

| | |
|---|---|
| Jebar bbilegleg. | (literally:) 'Again we are greatly surprised.' (implication:) 'What else could we expect of you.' |

2. Yiteq-limew is one of a number of compound words, of which the first part behaves like a verb, taking subject prefixes (usually 3rd person), and the last part behaves like a noun, taking possessive suffixes. Thus:

| | |
|---|---|
| Yekayiteqteq-limew. | 'It causes interest.' (intransitive) |
| Yekayiteq-limewih. | 'It interests me.' (transitive) |
| Yeyiteq-limewih k&n pijah yew. | 'I am interested in the picture.' (literally: 'It comes: my interest...') |

rip-b&r&w in this lesson behaves in the same way.

## SHORT PROSE SELECTION

   conferees      Marshall Islands Congress
Dri bebe ro ilo ailiH in MajÜl rej kweloktok
Ripeypey rew yilew hay&l&g yin Mahjeł rej q&ylaqteq

                               go over
Han Majuro aoleb    iiÜ  im etali  kien ko im
gan Majr&w hawelep 'yiyeh yim yetaliy kiyen kew yim

bar kÜmman kien ekkar Han aikuj ko im kÜnan ko
bar keṁḣan kiyen kkar gan hayiqij kew yim keṅhan kew

                       leaders          Congress
an armij ro i MajÜl.  Dri tel ro an koHkirej
han harm&j rew yiy Mahjeł. Ritel  rew han qagkerej

in rej likao  ro rar jikul  im katak kin
yin rej likahwew rew rahar jikiwił yim kahtak k&n

wÜwen  kien.  EloH ian    dri bebe rein  rej
wayw&y&n kiyen.  Yeleg yi'yahan ripeypey r&yin rej

                         used to
alab im iroij  ro rej jaHin iminene  kin kilen
hałap yim yirw&j rew rej jahgin mmin&yn&y k&n kilen

kÜmakit ko an ran kein.  KoHkirej in ejjab
keṁḣakit kew han rahan k&yin. Qagkerej yin yejjab

                  however
lukkun  lab an maroH ijoke  elab an jibaH dri
liqqiwin łap han mareğ yijewkey yełap han jipag ri-

                             better (vt)
jikul  im dri naHinmij im Han kÜmanmanlok wÜwen
jikiwił yim rinahginm&j yim gan keṁanṁanłaq wayw&y&n

mour ko an dri MajÜl.
m&wir kew han riMahjeł.

## PROVERB

   Kijenmij bwe en am      Kijenm&j bey yen haṁ
     jemlok eo.               jeṁłaq yew.

    'Persevere and the reward shall be yours.'

## VOCABULARY

| | | |
|---|---|---|
| alab | haɫap | elder; lineage head |
| bar | bar | rocky formation, rocks along shore |
| bat | bat | hill |
| biknik | piknik | picnic (from English) |
| dri bebe | ripeypey | conferee; planner |
| dri tel | ritel | leader |
| ebbal | ppaɫ | absent minded |
| ettoḧ | tteǧ | fast asleep |
| iḧtan | y&gtahan | suffer |
| iolab | yewɫap, yewɫapa- | middle of |
| itok limo | yiteq-limew | be interested |
| jidbän | jidpan | saw |
| jitob | jitweb | stove (from English) |
| jojo | jewjew | flying fish |
| kabalbal | kappaɫpaɫ | fantastic |
| kaburomijmij | kabir&wṁ&jṁ&j (intr.) kabir&wṁ&j(&y) (tr.) | sad |
| kabwilöḧlöḧ | kabilegleg (intr.) kabileg(ey) (tr.) | surprising |
| kaiḧtanan | kay&gtahanhan (intr.) kay&gtahaney (tr.) | strenuous; requiring great effort |
| kakitötö | kakit&ht&h (intr.) ...ik (tr.) | tease; naughty; anger-provoking |
| kakümküm | kakiṁkiṁ (intr.) ...iy (tr.) | thrilling |
| kalur | kalw&r | hunt lobsters (cf. w&r _lobster_) |
| kemakoko | keṁak&wk&w (intr.) ...ik(iy) (tr.) | bothersome; force someone against will |
| kematörtör | kematerter (intr.) ...ey (tr.) | anger provoking |
| kijenmij | kijenm&j | persevere |
| kikör | kk&r | (Ratak only) clam (Rälik <u>jiqq&y</u>) |
| kitötö | kit&ht&h | angry |
| kökkörärä | kekkerayray | chase women (cf. <u>keray</u>) |

| | | |
|---|---|---|
| kŭmakitkit | keṁakitkit (intr.) keṁakit(iy) (tr.) | move; plan a move |
| kŭmanmanlok | keṁanṁanłaq | improve |
| koṅkirej | qagkerej | congress (from English) |
| kŭmkŭm | kiṁkiṁ | heart beat fast |
| lam | łahaṁ | lamp (from English) |
| le | ley | use |
| le kŭto | leyk&t&w | chat; soft sell; proposition |
| lokan | łeqan | after |
| lŭkḁ | lekay (Rḁl.), l&k&r (Rat.) | to surf |
| limo | limew, limewi- | interest |
| lukalban | liqałpan | middle of it |
| mar | mar | vines, bushes, boondocks |
| matŭrtŭr | materter | angry |
| mŭk | ṁek (Rat.) ṁ&k (Rḁl.) | tired |
| rub-bŭrŭ | łip-b&r&w | be broken hearted; be angry; be disappointed |
| tak | tak | rise; upward |
| tijel | tiyjeł | diesel (oil) (from English) |
| ujuij | wijw&j | grass |

## LESSON TWENTY-ONE

Flags and more on Congress;
distributives of color words;
'and then when'.

## DIALOGUES

1.
A: Bȫlȕk in ia ne?   Beɫyak yin yi'yah ney?
B: Bȫlak in Micronesia,   Beɫyak yin Mahyikrawnay-
   bwe ebilu kab          jiyah, bey yebiɫiw kab
   mouj.                  mewij.
A: Ñe ear wȫr birȫrȫ,   Gey yehar wer birehreh,
   enaj kar einwȫt       yenahaj kar yayinwet beɫ-
   bȫlȕk in Amedka.     yak yin Hamedkah.
B: Aet, ak bilu e,       Hayat, hak biɫiw yay,
   elab an mera.         yeɫap han merah.
A: Mol, edrolok bilu en   Mewel, yeddewɫaq biɫiw yen
   ilo bȫlȕk in Amedka.  yilew beɫyak yin Hamedkah.

A: What flag is that?
B: Micronesian, blue and white.
A: If it had red, it would've been like the American flag.
B: Yes, but this blue is much lighter.
A: That's right, the blue in the American flag is darker.

2.
A: Kwȫj et jiboñin Jabȫt?   Qej yat jibbañin Jabet?
B: Inaj ilen jar.           Yinahaj yilan jar.
A: A elkin raeleb?          Hah yalikin rahyelep?
B: Ij lemnak in etal in     Yij ɫemñak yin yetal yin
   ejerakrȫk, lak jota,     jjerakrak, ɫak jawtah,
   etal im mubi.            yetal yim ṁiwpiy.
A: Kwo kȫnaan ke itok in   Qekeñhan key yiteq yin
   eñwȫr boñin Jadredre?   yañed biñin Jadeydey?
B: Jete awa?                Jetey hawah?

A: Jen lukon boñ ñan          Jan liqen b&g̃ gan
   joraantak.                 jewrahantak.
B: Ekwe, kab bukŭt iŭ         Yeqey, kab piqet y&h
   imweñ imŭ.                 yiḿeyeñ yiḿ&h.

A: What are you doing Sunday morning?
B: I'm going to church.
A: How about in the afternoon?
B: I'm thinking of going sailing, then in the evening,
   going to a movie.
A: Would you like to go fishing Saturday night?
B: What time?
A: From midnight till dawn.
B: OK, pick me up at my place.

DRILLS
1. Ñe ear itok, enaj           Gey yehar yiteq yenahaj
      kar <u>tim</u>.                    kar <u>tiḿ</u>.
         bo                             pew
         jorŭŭn                         jeƚƚayan
         kadŭk                          kadek
         mat                            mat
         uwe                            wiw&y
         kalbuj                         kalbiwij
         kakkije                        kakkij&y
         mŭk                            ḿek
         mij                            m&j

2. Ñe rar jab itok,            Gey rehar jab yiteq,
   reban kar <u>tim</u>.                  reban kar <u>tiḿ</u>.

            *(Repeat Drill 1)*

3. E birŭrŭ nuknuk en          Yebirehreh niqniq yeñ
   an Betra.                   han Peyetrah.
      bilu                         biƚiw
      mouj                         mewij
      kirin                        kiryin
      kire                         kir&y
      bilu en emera                biƚiw yeñ yemerah
      kirin en emera               kiriyin yeñ yemerah
      kilmej                       kilmeyej
      ialo                         yi'yaƚ&w
      biñ                          piyig
      kieo                         kiyew
      biraun                       birahwin
      biñ en edro                  piyig yeñ yeddew
      maroro                       mahrewrew

4. Bḷlḷk in ia ne?      Beḷyak yin yi'yah ñey?
   Micronesia.  Bḷlḷk   Mahyikr&wn&yjiyah. Beḷyak
   in Micronesia men    yin Mahyikr&wn&yjiyah men
   e.                   y&y.
   Wūt in ia ne?        Wit yin yi'yah ñey?
   Likiep. Wūt in Likiep Likiyep. Wit yin Likiyep
   men e.               men y&y.
   Nuknuk in ia ne?     Niqniq yin yi'yah ñey?
   Hawaii.              Hawahyiy.
   Waj in ia ne?        Waj yin yi'yah ñey?
   Belle.               Palley.
   Retio in ia ne?      R&ytiy&w yin yi'yah ñey?
   Jeban.               Jepahan.

5. Ij ilen kajutak juōn    Yij yilan kajiwtak jiwen
   wōrwōr in bik.          werwer yin piyik.
              bao                     bahwew
              kau                     kahwiw
              koot                    kewet
              ooj                     wewaj

6. Ewōr kōtka ine in       Yewer ketkah yiney yin
   kotin.                  qetin.
   meria                   meyriyah
   mḍ                      may
   bōb                     beb
   makmōk                  ṁakṁ&k

7. Kwōj et jiboḧin Jabot.  Qej y&t jibb&ǧin Jabet.
        jotin     Mandre        jawt&y&n    Mandey
        raeleben  Juje          rahyelepen  Jiwjey
                  Wōnje                     Wenjey
                  Taije                     Tahyijey
                  Bōlaidre                  Beḷahyidey
                  Jadredre                  Jadeydey

8. Ṅe ijab boub, inaj      Gey yijab pewib, yinahaj
   ilen jar.               yilan jar.
        kadkad                  kadkad
        kōb                     k&b
        kadmuj                  kadimwij
        kabuḧ                   kabiǧ
        kattil                  kattil
        kallip                  kallib
        kajidul                 kajiddiwil
        kaladikdik              kalladikidik
        kakajriri               kkaha(j)jiriyriy
        karkar                  karkar
        kamaḧ                   kamahag

9.  Ij lɵmnak in etal in           Yij łemñak yin yetal yin
    ejerakrʉk, lak jota              jjerakr&k, łak j&wtah
    etal em movie.                   yetal yem ṁiwpiy.
            ilen                             yilan
            kab                              kab
            bar                              bar
            naj                              nahaj

10. Kokʉnan ke itok in             Qekeñhan key yiteq yin
    eołwod bułin Jadredre?           yaǧed biǧin Jadeydey.
            mubi                             ṁiwpiy
            badre                            bahd&y
            kemem                            keyemyem
            biknik                           piknik
            kulab                            qiłab

11. Eokwe kab bukʉt iʉ             Yeqey kab piqet y&h
    inwen imwʉ.                      yiṁeyeñ yiṁ&h.
            karuj                            kałij
            kiri                             kiriy
            lamije                           laṁ&j&y
            kajitʉk                          kajjit&k
            kabukʉt                          kappiqet

12. '*My clothing is redder than his, because his is
    (only) SPOTTED WITH RED on the surface.*'

    Ebirʉrʉ nuknuk eo              Yebirehreh niqniq yew
    aʉ jen nuknuk en                 hah&h jan niqniq yeñ
    an, bwe nuknuk en                han, bey niqniq yeñ
    an ebibbirʉrʉ mejen.             han yebibbirehreh mejan.

| Cue | Response | Cue | Response |
|---|---|---|---|
| mouj | emmoujuj | mewij | mmewijwij |
| kilmej | ekkilmejej | kilmeyej | kkilmeyejyej |
| maroro | emmaroro | mahrewrew | mmahrewrew |
| mʉnaknak | emmʉnaknak | ṁeñakñak | ṁṁeñakñak |
| ubajaj | ubajaje | wipahajhaj | wipahajhajey |
| kieo | ekkieoeo | kiyew | kkiyewyew |
| ialo | eialolo | yi'yał&w | yi'yał&wł&w |
| bilu | ebbilulu | biłiw | bbiłiwłiw |
| biolet | ebbioletlet | piyewlet | ppiyewletlet |
| kirin | ekkirinin | kiryin | kkiryinyin |
| biraun | ebbiraunun | birahwin | bbirahwinwin |
| kire | ekkirere | kir&y | kkir&yr&y |
| bił | ebbiłił | piyig | ppiyigyig |

13. *'I'm playing, and then when it's night, I'll come to you.'*
    *'I'm playing, and then when I'm tired, I'll rest.'*

    Ij ikkure em lak boħ i iwŭj.
    ilju...jerbal
    jota...badre
    raeleb...mŭħĦ
    boħ...kiki
    mŭk...kakkije
    menokaru...tutu
    kwole...mŭħĦ
    mwij...rolwŭj
    jemlok...mŭkajwŭj

    Yij qqir&y yem łak b&ǧ yiyiw&j.
    yiljiw...jerbal
    j&wtah...bahd&y
    rahyelep...ṁegay
    b&ǧ...kiykiy
    ṁ&k...kakkij&y
    menewkadiw...tiwtiw
    q&l&y...ṁegay
    ṁ&j...rawalw&j
    jeṁłaq...ṁekajw&j

14. *'The ship is leaving for Majuro and from there for Arno.'*

    Wa en ej jerak em lak Majuro, ejerak ħan Arno.

    Wah yeń yej jerak yem łak Majr&w, yejerak gan Harńew.

    *(Substitute other place names in the above frame.)*

15. *'Why don't you stop sleeping so late.'*

    Emwij ne am mejurleb.
       rumij
       kot
       rit
       kŭjaħjaħ
       ikkure
       abŭbleb
       tutu iar
       kakkije

    Y&ṁ&j ńey haṁ Majiłlep.
       Fiṁij
       kawat
       riyit
       kejagjag
       qqir&y
       hab&blep
       tiwtiw yiyhar
       kakkij&y

    *(Practice also the following:)*

    En mwij ne am mejurleb.    Yen ṁ&j ńey haṁ majiłlep.

    'I want your sleeping late to stop.'

16. *'Please help each other carry that bag.'*

    Komin maijŭk bek en em bŭke.
       kŭjerrĦik
       totoik
       inek
       kaabdrik

    Q&ṁin ṁahyij&k payak yeń yem b&k&y.
       kejerrayik
       tewtewyik
       yinyek
       kahapdik

|  |  |
|---|---|
| kabol | kab&w&ł |
| kanne | kanney |
| lutŭk | liwt&k |
| wiaik | wiyahyik |
| akkauni | hakkawiniy |

17. *'The bag he took was unopened.'*

| | |
|---|---|
| <u>Elikio</u> bek eo ear bŭke. | <u>Yelikiyy&w</u> payak yew yehar b&k&y. |
| jimettan | jimattan |
| drik | dik |
| kileb | kilep |
| jebolkwan | j&b&lqan |
| dro | ddew |
| mera | merah |
| bol | b&w&ł |
| jelok kobban | jjełaq qebban |
| jekaben | jekapen |

### GRAMMATICAL NOTES

1. In Drill 12 the distributive forms of color words are practiced. Note that they result in the spreading-out, thinning-out, or toning-down of the color. Thus <u>bibbirehreh</u> could be translated as in the drill as 'spotted with red', or as 'speckled with red', or simply as 'reddish'. The non-distributive forms of color words, on the other hand, generally refer to solid colors.

2. Drills 13 and 14 give practice on <u>yem łak</u>, which usually translates into English as 'and then when' or 'and then after'.

3. Drill 15 gives practice on two idiomatic exhortations, the second of which is stronger than the first.

### SHORT PROSE SELECTION

| | | | | | | | |
|---|---|---|---|---|---|---|---|
| Kwelok | eo | moktata | an | Congress | of | Micronesia | |
| Q&ylaq | yew | ṁeqtahtah | han | Qagqirej | wab | Ṁahyikr&wn&yjiyah | |

| | | | | | countries | | |
|---|---|---|---|---|---|---|---|
| ear | ilo | July | | 1965. | Aoleb | lal ko | rellab |
| yehar | yilew | Jiwłahyey | | 1965. | Hawelep | lal kew | rełłap |

| | | | interested | | | | |
|---|---|---|---|---|---|---|---|
| rar | kanuij | in | itok | limoier | kin men in | bwe | |
| rehar | kahn&w&j | yin | <u>yiteq</u> | <u>limewiyy&r</u> | k&n men yin | bey | |

|  | sign |  |
|---|---|---|
rar tŮmak bwe men in juŮn kŮkkale in an
rehar temak bey men yin jiwen **kake⅃⅃ey** yin han

progress
Micronesia jino wŮnmanlok Ĥan an make
Mahyikr&wn&yjiyah jinew **wenṁahan⅃aq** gan han mak&y

jutak im kejbarok jerbal ko an make. Ej kab
jiwtak yim kejpareq jerbal kew han mak&y. Yej kab

kar juŮn ien an dri MajŮl mat im ekkŮlel
kar jiwen 'yiyen han riṀahje⅃ mahat yim kkayaly&l

dri kwelok im ear kanuij lab iruj. Ear itok
riq&ylaq yim yehar kahn&w&j ⅃ap yiřij. Yehar yiteq

dri kaki jen University of Hawaii im rar
rikakiy jan Yiwinb&h&jt&y wab Hawahyiy yim rehar

katakin dri bebe ro wǎwen kwelok im bar men ko
kahtakin ripeypey rew wayw&y&n q&ylaq yim bar men kew

jet elab tokjeir Ĥan kŮmmani kwelok ko an kien.
jet ye⅃ap teqjay&r gan keṁṁaniy q&ylaq kew han kiyen.

first time
Ear jab kanuij lab tŮbrak kinke ej kab juŮn alen
Yehar jab kahn&w&j ⅃ap teprak k&nkey **yej kab jiwen halen**

pass
aer kwelok ak ewŮr ruo men ellab rar karŮki Ĥan
hay&r qeylaq hak yewer riwew men ⅃⅃ap rehar **karekiy** gan

follow
an dri Micronesia lor i. JuŮn, rar kowalok
han riṀahyikr&wn&yjiyah **⅃eweriy**. Jiwen, rehar kewwah⅃aq

bŮlǎk eo an Micronesia im ruo, rar kŮmman
be⅃yak yew han Ṁahyikr&wn&yjiyah yim riwew, rehar keṁṁan

bwe Julae 12 ran en an Micronesia
bey Jiw⅃ahyey 12 rahan yen han Ṁahyikr&wn&yjiyah

remembrance
holiday in kakememij jinoin Congress of
ha⅃&yt&y yin **kak&y&my&m&j** jinewin Qagqirej wab

Micronesia.
Ṁahyikir&wn&yjiyah.

## PROVERB

Ewǒr tarlik tarar in   Yewer tarlik tarhar yin
bǒkǎ.   bekay.

'The tide never ceases to go out and come in.'
(Commentary on the regularity and perpetuity
of nature.)

## VOCABULARY

| | | |
|---|---|---|
| abdrik | hapdik | less in quantity |
| abǒbleb | hab&blep | lazy |
| biĦ | piyig | pink (from English) |
| bo | pew | caught |
| bǒlǎk | beɫyak | flag (from English) |
| boub | pewib | busy |
| dimuj | dimwij | a clam shell |
| inek | yinyek | carry on shoulder, or on pole across shoulders of two men |
| jebolkwan | j&b&lqan | half |
| jekaben | jekapen | less than half (in container) |
| jidul | jiddiwil | a shell |
| kabǔn | kabiǧ | worship, religion |
| kakajiriri | kakahajjiriyriy | baby sit; adopt a child |
| kaladrikdrik | kallahdikidik | sit in shade and enjoy breeze |
| kalbuj | kalbiwij | (be in) jail (from *caIaboose*) |
| karkar | karkar | cut copra meat out of shell |
| karuj | kaɫij | wake someone |
| kattil | kattil | burn rubbish |
| kir | kir | call |
| koot | kewet | goat (from English) |
| kot | kawat | steal |
| kwole | q&l&y | hungry |
| lak | ɫak | then when, after |
| lamij | lam&j | shout |
| likio | likiyy&w | whole |
| lutǒk | liwt&k | pour out |
| maijǒk | m̂ahyij&k | help each other |
| menokaru | menewkadiw | sweat, perspiration |
| meria | meyriyah | plumeria |

| | | |
|---|---|---|
| ooj | wewaj/wawaj | horse (from English) |
| tim | tiṁ | break, to miss a ride |
| toto | tewtew | hang |
| wŏrwŏr | werwer | pen, fence, enclosure |

## LESSON TWENTY-TWO

### Relatives.

**DIALOGUES**

1.
A: Ewör ke belen Tom?  Yewer key palyen Tawaṁ?
B: Aet, ewör belen.  Hay&t, yewer palyen.
A: Ewör ke nejin?  Yewer key najin?
B: Ejelok, ejaḧin wör nejin.  Yejjełaq, yejjahgin wer najin.
A: Jen ḧüüt in an belele?  Jan gayat yin han pal&yl&y.
B: Elok ruo iiö in an belele.  Yełaq riwew 'yiyeh yin han pal&yl&y.

A: Is Tom married?
B: Yes, he's got a wife.
A: Does he have any children?
B: No, not yet. (He doesn't have children yet.)
A: How long has he been married?
B: Two years now.

2.
A: Obed, kwöj etal Ḧan ia?  Wepet, qej yetal gan yi'yah?
B: Ij ilen kemem, itok kejro etal.  Yij yilan keyemyem, yiteq kejrew yetal.
A: An wön en kemem?  Han wen yeṅ keyemyem?
B: An ajiri en nejin Mauro emmen.  Han hajiriy yeṅ najin Mawirew yemman.
A: Ledrik ke ladrik?  Leddik key ładdik?
B: Ladrik. Ejaḧin wör nejierro ledrik.  Ładdik. Yejjahgin wer najiyy&rrew leddik.
A: Etolok ke jikin kemem en?  Yettewłaq key jikin keyemyem yeṅ?
B: Jab ebak. Itok.  Jahab yepahak. Yiteq.
A: Iwöj, kejro etal.  Yiw&j, k&jrew yetal.

A: Obed, where are you going?
B: I'm going to a first birthday party; why don't the two of us go?
A: Whose birthday?
B: The baby of Mr. and Mrs. Mauro.
A: Girl or boy?
B: Boy. They don't have any girls.
A: Is it far from here?
B: No, it's close. Come.
A: I'm coming. Let's go.

3.
A: Enaj wŭr pade ilju.                    Yenahaj wer bahd&y yiljiw.
B: Pade in ta?                            Bahd&y yin tah?
A: Ledrik en jein Tommy ej driwŭjlok jen high school.   Ledik yeń j&yin Tewmiy yej diyw&jɫak jan hayey jikiwiɫ.
B: Wŭn iaer, Mila ke Mina?                Wen yi'yahay&r Miyɫah key Minah?
A: Mina.                                  Minah.
B: Wŭn ran rar kir ir?                    Wen rań rehar kir y&r?
A: Aoleb...Tommy ear ba kwŭn jab jako.    Hawelep...Tewmiy yehar bah qen jab jak&w.
B: Ekwe, inaj iwŭj.                       Yeqey, yinahaj yiw&j.
A: Lale kwar meloklok! Jiljilimjuŭn ilju ej jota.   Lahley qehar meɫaqlaq! Jiljilimjiwen yiljiw yej j&wtah.

A: There's a party tomorrow.
B: What's the occasion?
A: Tommy's daughter is graduating from high school.
B: Which one, Mila or Mina?
A: Mina.
B: Who's invited?
A: Everyone. Tom said for you to be there.
B: OK. I'll be there.
A: Don't forget now! Seven o'clock tomorrow evening.

DRILLS
1.
A: Ewŭr ke <u>belen</u> Tom?              Yewer key <u>palyen</u> Tawań?
         nejin                                       najin

```
                jatin                  jatin
                jein                   jeyin
                rilikin                riylikin
B: Aet, ewŏr belen.             Hay&t, yewer palyen.
B: Jab, ejelok, ejaHin          Jahab, yejjełaq, yejjahgin
   wŏr belen.                      wer palyen.

2.
A: Jen HŭHt in an               Jan gayat yin han
     belele?                      pal&yl&y?
     dri kaki                     rikakiy
     jikul                        jikiwił
     naHinmij                     nahginm&j
     kadŏk                        kadek
     bwebwe                       b&yb&y
     jako                         jakew
     jebel                        j&p&l
     birok                        birwek
     koba                         k&wbah
     kwole                        q&l&y
     maro                         mar&w

B: Ruo dre ran in an            Riwew d&y rahan yin han
     belele.                      pal&yl&y.
B: Elok ruo raan in an          Yełaq riwew rahan yin han
     belele.                      pal&yl&y.

3. (Be sure to substitute in the proper places.)
   Ruo dre raan in an           Riwew d&y rahan yin han
      jako.                        jak&w.
           allin                        hall&g
           jilu                         jiliw
           iiŏ                          'yiyeh
           wiik                         wiyik
           awa                          hawah
           lalim                        łal&m
           joHoul                       j&g&wil
           jilHoul                      jilgiwil
           eHoul                        yegewil
           minit                        minit

4. Ij ilen kemem, itok          Yij yilan keyemyem, yitkew
   kejro etal.                    k&jrew yetal.
           ilomij                       yil&wm&j
           enwŏr                        yaǧed
           kaikujkuj                    kahayiqijqij
```

221

```
             entak                      y&ntak
             okok                       wekwek
             kakijen                    kakijen
             taktŭ                      takteh
             kulab                      qiłab
             mŭHŭ                       ṁegay
             jambo                      jaṁb&w
```

5. Ejaḧin wŭr <u>nejierro</u>      Yejjahgin wer <u>najiyy&rrew</u>
   <u>ledrik</u>.                       <u>leddik</u>.
```
   waerro   wa                    wahy&rrew   wah
   enerro   ene                   yan&yy&rrew yan&y
   kijeero  biik                  kij&yy&rrew piyik
   imeerro  em                    yiṁ&yy&rrew y&ṁ
   kŭtkḧerro ni                   ketkayy&rrew niy
   limeerro bia                   lim&yy&rrew piyah
   kojeerro kooj                  kawaj&yy&rrew kawaj
   aerro    nuknuk                hay&rrew    niqniq
```

6. Some practice on opposites.
   *(In addition to doing the drill as outlined below,
   ask and answer questions like the following:*

              Yewer key najin hajiriy?
              Yewer najin hajiriy key yejjełaq?

   *Also, try composing similar questions using the
   pairs of opposites from Lesson Fourteen.)*

A: Ewŭr nejin ajiri.          Yewer najin hajiriy.
B: Ejelok...                  Yejjełaq...

A: ElŭH waan korkor.          Yeleg wahan kerker.
B: Eiet...                    Yeyiy&t...

A: Ebak eneen.                Yepahak yanyeṅ.
B: Etolok...                  Yettewłaq...

A: Ebwil rainin.              Yebił rahyinyin.
B: EmŬlo...                   Y&ṁ&ł&w...

A: Ebidodo nuknuk in.         Yepid&wd&w niqniq yin.
B: Ebin...                    Y&p&n...

A: EmŭH apel in.              Y&m&g habeł yin.
B: EtŭHal...                  Yetegal...

7. Kejro etal ḧan ijen        K&jrew yetal gan yijeṅ
   <u>jikŭ</u>.                      <u>jikih</u>.
   <u>jikŭm</u>                      <u>jikiṁ</u>
   jikin                      jikin
   jikid                      jikid

jikim          jikim
jikimi         jikimiy
jikier         jikiyyɛr

(Substitute the above words in each of the following:)

Kimro ar etal Han ijo jikü.
Kɛmrew har yetal gan yijew jikih.
Kimro ej iwōj Han ijōne jikü.
Kɛmrew yej yiwɛj gan yijeñey jikih.
Kimro ej bed wōt ije jikü.
Kɛmrew yej pad wet yijɛy jikih.
Kimro naj iwōj Han ijōkane jikü.
Kɛmrew nahaj yiwɛj gan yijekañey jikih.
Kimro ej bed wōt ijō-kein jikü.
Kɛmrew yej pad wet yijɛkɛ-yin jikih.
Kimro ar etal Han ijōko jikü.
Kɛmrew har yetal gan yijekew jikih.

8. 'I wish I knew Spanish.'

Yokwe bwe in kar jeḷä kajin Jibein.
Yaqey bey yin kar jeḷay kajin Jipeyin.
bed ibben Sophia Loren
pad yippan *Sophia Loren*
jikul in taktō
jikiwił yin takteh
mweie im einwōt kwe
meyiyey yim yayinwet qey
kakkije lok Han Paris
kakkijɛy łaq gan *Paris*
jimaat im einwōt Einstein
jimahat yim yayinwet *Einstein*

9. Ledrik en nejin Tommy ej driwōjlok iiō in.
Ledik yeñ najin Tewmiy yej diywɛjłak 'yiyeh yin.
mare ibben Dave jabōt in
marey yippan Tɛyɛb jabet yin
kelok Han Honolulu wiik in lal
keylaq gan Weñewłiwłiw wiyik yin lał
jino jerbal ilo obiij ilju
jinew jerbal yilew wepyij yiljiw
kamōj an jikul alliñ in lal
kamɛj han jikiwił hallɛg yin lał
rejetak kij ilo lemnak in
reyejtak kɛj yilew łemñak yin

10. Tommy ear ba kwōn jab jako.
Tewmiy yehar bah qen jab jakɛw.
bed
pad
jabwūbwe
jebaybɛy
rumij
łimij

```
          ko                       kew
          kabwir am ial            kab&d haṁ yiyaɫ
          kabwir am lemank         kab&d haṁ ɫemṅak
```

11. *'Don't do your work that way all the time.'*
    *(Teacher should mix the cues from the two slots in this drill.)*

```
     Kwɵn jab kɵnaan jerbal      Qen jab keṅhan jerbal
       rot ne.                      ɫet ṅey.
          kijoṅ lemnak rot            kijeğ ɫemṅak ɫet
          ekkein kɵmman kain          kk&yin keṁhan kahyin
                    kain rot                    kahyin ɫet
                    eindre                      yayin d&y
                    kain                        kahyin
                    men rot                     men ɫet
```

    *(Now make the same substitutions in the following:)*

```
     Emwij ne am kɵnaan          Y&ṁ&j ṅey haṁ keṅhan
       jerbal rot ne.              jerbal ɫet ṅey.
```

12. ```
    Kwɵn ḁjmour ke Ḣan         Qen yajmiwir key gan
      pade eo buḢnin?             bahd&y yew biǧniyin.
         emourur                     mmewirwir
         bojak                       pewjak
         mɵk                         ṁek
         rumij                       ɫiṁij
         ebbat                       bbat
    ```

13. *(Ask and answer questions like the following based on the diagram 'Some Marshallese Relatives.')*

```
    A: Teen Timɵj Tom?              Teyen Tiyṁej Tawaṁ?
    B: Nejin.      (his child)      Najin.
    B: Nejin Timɵj Tom.             Najin Tiyṁej Tawaṁ.

    A: Teen Tom Timɵj?              Teyen Tawaṁ Tiyṁej?
    B: Jemḁn.      (his father)     Jeman.
    B: Jemḁn Tom Timɵj.             Jeman Tawaṁ Tiyṁej.

    A: Teen Medri Mina?             Teyen Meydiy Minah?
    B: Jinen.      (her mother)     Jinen.
    B: Jinen Medri Mina.            Jinen Meydiy Minah.

    A: Teen Ali Tom?                Teyen Haɫiy Tawaṁ?
    B: Jḁtin.      (his younger     Jatin.
    B: Jḁtin Ali Tom.  brother)     Jatin Haɫiy Tawaṁ.

    A: Teen Alɵk Medri?             Teyen Haɫek Meydiy.
    B: Rilikin. (his cross cous-    Riylikin.
    B: Rilikin Alɵk Medri.   in)    Riylikin Haɫek Meydiy.
```
```

| | |
|---|---|
| A: Teen Tom Bokin? | Teyen Tawaṁ Bawakin? |
| B: Erro ej jimjăn jimjatin. *(siblings)* | Yerrew yej j&ṁjayan j&ṁjatin. |
| A: Teen Ali Bita? | Teyen Haɬiy Piytah? |
| B: Wileben (Rat.)/Rikorean (Răl.). | Willepan/Rikeweryan. |
| B: Wileben Ali Bita. | Willepan Haɬiy Piytah. |
| B: Rikorean Ali Bita. *(his mother's brother)* | Rikeweryan Haɬiy Piytah. |
| A: Teen Bita Ali? | Teyen Piytah Haɬiy? |
| B: Maḧden. *(his sister's son)* | Magden. |
| B: Maḧden Bita Ali. | Magden Piytah Haɬiy. |
| A: Teen Timŭj Rojita? | Teyen Tiyṁej Rewjiytah? |
| B: Jinen. *(his 'mother')* | Jinen. |
| B: Jinen lio iben. | Jinen liyew yippan. |
| A: Teen Ali Mitel? | Teyen Haɬiy Miyt&l. |
| B: Jemăn. Eritto jen lukkun jeman. | Jeman. Yerittew jan liqqiwin jeman. |
| B: Jemăn eo eritto. *(his older 'father')* | Jeman yew yerittew. |
| A: Teen Medri Mila? | Teyen Meyediy Miyɬah? |
| B: Jinen. Edrik jen lukkun jinen. | Jinen. Yedik jan liqqiwin jinen. |
| B: Jinen eo edrik. *(her younger 'mother')* | Jinen yew yedik. |
| A: Teen Ali Rubon? | Teyen Haɬiy Riwben? |
| B: Jimman. *(his grandfather)* | Jiṁṁahan. |
| B: Jimman Ali Rubon. | Jiṁṁahan Haɬiy Riwben. |
| A: Teen Rubon Ali? | Teyen Riwben Haɬiy? |
| B: Jibŭn. *(his grandchild)* | Jibin. |
| B: Jibŭn Rubon Ali. | Jibin Riwben Haɬiy. |
| A: Teen Medri Rojita? | Teyen Meydiy Rewjiytah? |
| B: Jibŭn. *(her grandmother)* | Jibin. |
| B: Jibŭn Medri Rojita. | Jibin Meydiy Rewjiytah. |
| A: Teen Rojita Medri? | Teyen Rewjiytah Meydiy. |
| B: Jibŭn. *(her grandchild)* | Jibin. |
| A: Teen Timŭj Bita? | Teyen Tiyṁej Piytah? |
| B: An emman. *(his wife's brother)* | Han ṁṁahan. |
| A: Teen Bita Timŭj? | Teyen Piytah Tiyṁej? |
| B: Jemăn lellab. *(his sister's husband)* | Jeman ɬeɬɬap. |

*Some Marshallese Relatives*

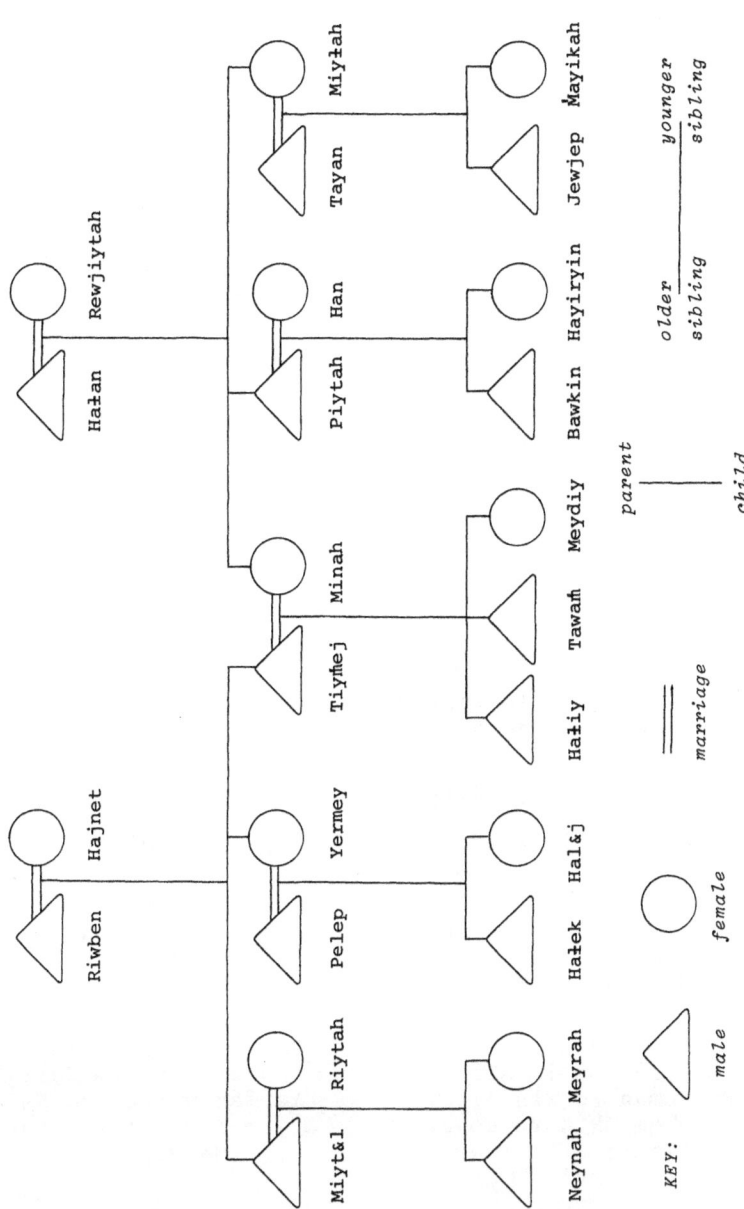

A: Teen Timüj Ten?    Teyen Tiyṁej Tayan?
B: Jemänjin. *(his wife's*    Jemanjin.
   *sister's husband)*

A: Teen Mina Rita?    Teyen Minah Riytah?
B: Jininjin. *(her husband's*    Jininjin.
   *brother's wife)*

14. *(Ask questions like the following based on the same diagram.)*

A: Rej teek dron Timüj    Rej teyek dewen Tiyṁej
   im Ali?    yim Haɫiy?
B: Rej jimnüjin. *(parent*    Rej J&ṁnajin.
   *and child)*

A: Medri im Alice rej    Meydiy yim Hal&j rej
   teek dron?    teyek dewen?
B: Rej rilikin dron.    Rej riylikin dewen.
   *(cross cousins)*

A: Rej teek dron Ali    Rej teyek dewen Haɫiy
   im Nena?    yim Neynah?
B: Rej jimjün jimjütin,    Rej j&ṁjayan j&ṁjatin,
   nejin emman erro    najin ṁṁahan yerrew
   jimor. *(brothers:*    jimeɫ.
   *children of brothers)*

A: Rej teek dron Bita    Rej teyek dewen Piytah
   im Tom?    yim Tawaṁ?
B: Laulleb im lojemmaüüd.    ɫawillep yim ɫejemmaged.
   *(brother and son of a*
   *woman)*

A: Medri im Rojita rej    Meydiy yim Rewjiytah rej
   teek dron?    teyek dewen?
B: Rej jim jibwik dron.    Rej j&ṁ jibiyik dewen.
   *(grandparent and*
   *grandchild)*

A: Rej teek dron Timüj    Rej teyek dewen Tiyṁej
   im Ten?    yim Tayan?
B: Rej jemünjik dron.    Rej jemanjiyik dewen.
   *(husbands of sisters)*

A: Ewi̱ kadkadin Medri    Yewiy kadkadin Meydiy
   kab Tom im Ali?    kab Tawaṁ yim Haɫiy?
B: Emman ro ran Ali im    Yeṁṁahan rew rañ Haɫiy
   Tom ak kürü eo en    yim Tawaṁ hak keray yew
   Medri. *(brothers and*    yeñ Meydiy.
   *sisters)*

A: Ewi kadkadin Ali, Tom,
im Medri Han Joseph
im Maika?
B: Nejin kŭrŭ aolepair.
Bwij eo edrik en an
Joseph im Maika.
*(children of sisters)*

Yewiy kadkadin Haɫiy, Tawaṁ,
yim Meydiy gaṅ Jewjep yim
Mayikah?
Najin keray hawelepayy&r.
Bij yew yedik yeṅ han
Jewjep yim Ṁayikah.

A: Ewi kadkadin Ali, Tom,
im Medri Han Nena im
Mera?
B: Nejin emman aolepair.
Eritto jeman Nena im
Mera. *(children of brothers)*

Yewiy kadkadin Haɫiy, Tawaṁ,
yim Meydiy gan Neynah yim
Meyrah?
Najin ṁṁahan hawelepayy&r.
Yerittew jeman Neynah yim
Meyrah.

## GRAMMATICAL NOTES

1. Drill 2 gives two ways for counting up until a given point: *(2)* d&y and yeɫaq *(2)*. D&y is related to d&yd&y-ɫaq 'completed', and ɫaq is the same word as in ɫaqin jet rahan 'after several days' and kiyyeh ɫaq jidik 'in a little bit' or 'a little after now'.

2. Marshallese kinship reckoning is quite complex, since lineage ties are of greater importance in Marshallese culture than in the more mobile Western world. You have already learned some of the basic kin terms in earlier lessons; Drills 13 and 14 now introduce a number of additional relationship terms. When you have mastered all these as there presented, you will be able to learn more about their application by asking questions of your teacher concerning other pairs of individuals shown on the diagram 'Some Marshallese Relatives.'

For a discussion of Marshallese kinship from an anthropological perspective, see Alexander Spoehr, Majuro: A Village in the Marshall Islands, Volume 39, Anthropological Series of Field Museum of Natural History, Chicago, 1949, Chapter VII and VIII, pp. 155-220.

## SHORT PROSE SELECTION

Field Trip
Piyiɫ Tiryep

```
                         field  trip  ship
Elkin  aolep    ruo    alliH,  wan   raun  en  ej  raun
Yalkin hawelep  riwew  hallⅇg, wahan rahwin yeṅ yej rahwin
```

Ḧan aolep     ailiḧ    in Majöl.    Wḧwen     raun,    wan
gan hawelep hay&l&g yin Ṁahjeł. Wayw&y&n rahwin, wahan
raun   en   ej   etal   Ḧan aolep   ene    in Relik,   Ḧe
rahwin yeñ yej yetal gan hawelep yan&y yin Raylik, gey
full      its contents
ebol      kobban kab Ḧe  emat     möḦḧ  im  mweiuk, erol
yeb&w&ł  qebban kab gey yemahat ṁegay yim ṁ&yiq, yerawal
            discharge    load     finish
Ḧan Majuro, ekto    im   ektak,   kamöjlok   trip  en   an.
gan Majr&w,  yakt&w yim yektak,  kaṁ&jłaq  tiryep yeñ han.
Ejja    wḧwen     drein wöt  an   raun  Ratak.   Unin
Yejjah wayw&y&n d&yin wet han rahwin Rahtak. Winin
trip  in   raun    kein,   kinke  en   böklok  möḦḧ   im
tiryep yin rahwin k&yin, k&nkey yen bekłaq ṁegay yim
mweiuk im ektak   waini     jen aolep    ailiḧ    ko
ṁ&yiq yim yektak wahyiniy jan hawelep hay&l&g kew
  ilikin Majuro.   Ilo    Majöl  kiö,     ewör    jilu
yilikin Majr&w. Yilew Ṁahjeł kiyyeh, yewer jiliw
wan    raun.    Militobi,    Mieco     Queen,  im  Rḧlik-
wahan rahwin.  Militewpiy, Miyeykew Qiyin, yim Raylik-
Ratak.
Rahtak.

**PROVERB**

  Edrik a ejatdrik.          Yedik hah yejatdik.
          'Small but mighty.'

**VOCABULARY**

belen         palyen           his wife, her husband; spouse
biil tirep    piyił tiryep     field trip
birok         birwek           broke
bwebwe        b&yb&y           crazy, foolish
bwir          b&d              mistake, sin, error, fault,
                                 wrong
dre           d&y              up until now, just, at his
                                 point as of now
dredrelok     d&yd&yłaq        completed
ebak          yepahak          close, near
jatdrik       jatdik           able, strong, with hidden
                                 resources
ektak         yektak           to load, carry
ekto          yakt&w           discharge, unload

| | | |
|---|---|---|
| emmourur | mmewirwir | energetic (distr.) |
| ial | yiyał | road, path |
| jabwäbwe | jebaybəy | lost |
| jebel | jəpəl | apart, divorced, separated |
| jimaat | jimahat | smart, wise, cunning (from English) |
| kadkadin | kadkadin | relationship of |
| kobban | qebban | its contents |
| lok | qebbałaq | after |
| mañden | magden | his sister's children |
| maro | marəw | thirsty |
| raun | rahwin | go around, make a field trip (from English) |
| rejetak | reyejtak | agree with, concur, to second |
| rilikin | riylikin | his cross cousin |
| rukorea | rikeweryah | my mother's brother (Rāl.) |
| teek | teyek | what relationship? |
| teen | teyen | what relative of? |
| wileba | willepah | my mother's brother (Rat.) |

## LESSON TWENTY-THREE

Yewen vs. rahan;
this particular one;
becoming; look alike.

**DIALOGUES**

1.
A: Ta ne beim?               Tah ñey p&yiṁ?
B: Libbuke.                  Libbiq&y.
A: Kwar bŭk ia?              Qehar bek yi'yah?
B: Iar lo ion bok.           Yihar lew yewen beq.
A: Kwo kŭnan ke wia kake?    Qekeñhan key wiyah kahkey?
B: Bwe kwo kŭnan ke wiai-    Bey qekeñhan key wiyahyi-
   ki?                          kiy?
A: Aet, ij ae nejŭ libbu-    Hay&t, yij hay&y n&jih libbi-
   ke.                          q&y.

A: What do you have in your hand?
B: A shell.
A: Where did you get it?
B: I found it on the sand.
A: Do you want to sell it?
B: Why, will you buy it?
A: Yes, I'm making a shell collection.

2.
A: Ewŭr ke imŭn mwijbar?     Yewer key yiṁen ṁijbar?
B: Ejelok. Ak eloH           Yejjełaq. Hak yeleg
   likao re kanoj jelŭ          likahwew rekahn&w&j
   mwijbar.                     jełay ṁijbar.
A: Kwo maroH ke bukot        Qemareğ key piqet teq
   tok juŭn.                    jiwen?
B: Aet, rainin wŭt.          Hay&t, rahyinyin wet.
A: Jete wŭnŭŭn mwijbar?      Jetey weñyan ṁijbar?
B: Ejelok. Kwŭj jab          Yejjełaq. Qej jab
   aikuj kŭllŭ.                 hayiqij kełłay.

A: Is there a barber shop (around here)?
B: No. But there are many fellows who know how to cut hair.
A: Can you find one for me?
B: Yes. I'll get one today.
A: How much for a haircut?
B: Nothing. You don't have to pay.

DRILLS

1. *'What's that in your hand, a cowrie?'*

   *(Teacher asks questions, students answer. Later teacher may give underlined cues, one student asks question, and another answers.)*

   | | |
   |---|---|
   | Ta ne beim, libbuke ke? | Tah ñey peyiṁ, libbiq&y key? |
   | Aet, libbuke men e beiŭ. | Hay&t, libbiq&y men y&y peyih. |
   | Ta ne turum, mŭjet ke? | Tah ñey tiřiṁ, majet key? |
   | Aet, mŭjet men e turŭ. | Hay&t, majet men y&y tiřih. |
   | Ta ne loñiim, lole ke? | Tah ñey lawɟiyiṁ, ławł&y key? |
   | Ta ne adrim, riiñ ke? | Tah ñey haddiyiṁ, riyig key? |
   | Ta ne iumŭm, jaki ke? | Tah ñey yiwṁiṁ, jakiy key? |
   | Ta ne likim, kulul ke? | Tah ñey likiṁ, qiłił key? |
   | Ta ne katŭm, jaki ke? | Tah ñey katiṁ, jakiy key? |
   | Ta ne yipim, bu ke? | Tah ñey yipiṁ, biw key? |
   | Ta ne bŭram, wŭt ke? | Tah ñey beraṁ, wit key? |
   | Ta ne lojilñŭm, diede ke? | Tah ñey lawjilgiṁ, diy&d&y key? |

2. *'I saw it on the sand.'*

   *(As the exercise is learned, teacher may give only the second part of cue, and students supply rahan or yewen as appropriate.)*

   | | |
   |---|---|
   | Iar loe ion bok. | Yihar lewey yewen beq. |
   |     raan bok en |     rahan bawak yeñ |
   |     raan mwen |     rahan ṁeyeñ |

```
            ion jimen en              yewen jimyeñ yeñ
            ion ujoj kan              yewen wijw&j kañ
            ion wa en                 yewen wah yeñ
              (raan)                    (rahan)
            ion tebel en              yewen tebeł yeñ
              (raan)                    (rahan)
            ion jaki en               yewen jakiy yeñ
            raan tol en               rahan teł yeñ
            raan mü en                rahan may yeñ
            ion jea en                yewen jeyah yeñ
              (raan)                    (rahan)
            ion bed en                yewen peyet yeñ
              (raan)                    (rahan)
```

3. *'Hatfield is going to buy a cowrie.'*

```
    T: Ejbil enaj wiaik           Yejpiyił yenahaj wiyahyik
       juön libbuke.                 jiwen libbiq&y.
    A: Enaj wiaiki.               Yenahaj wiyahyikiy.
    B: Kwo könan ke wia           Qekeñhan key wiyah
       libbuke.                      libbiq&y.
    T: Liiemjo ej biraeik         Liyeṁjew yej birahyeyik
       juön ik.                      jiwen y&k.
    A: Enaj biraeiki.             Yenahaj birahyeyikiy.
    B: Kwo könan ke birae         Qekeñhan key birahyey
       ik?                           y&k?
    T: Mönjob enaj dilaik         Menjeweb yenahaj diylahyik
       juön alal.                    jiwen hałhał.
       Bijja enaj jerdik          Pijjah yenahaj jerayik
       juön ledrik.                  jiwen leddik.
       Laji enaj jukaik           Łajiy yenahaj jiqahyik
       juön kobe.                    jiwen kawp&y.
       Embi enaj jikiruik         Yempiy yenahaj jikiriwik
       juön nat.                     jiwen ñat.
       Kijbal enaj lekötoik       Kiyijbahal yenahaj leyk&-
       juön jiroḧ.                   t&wyik jiwen jireġ.
```

4. *'Would you like to sell it?'*

```
       Kwo könan ke wia           Qekeñhan key wiyah
         kake?                       kahkey?
         joloke                      jewłaqey
         aje                         hajey
         kote                        kawatey
         kejerbale                   kejerbaley
```

233

```
wiaiki                    wiyahyikiy
kokone                    kaqeñey
kejbaroke                 kejpareq&y
kokkure                   kaqqirey
noje                      ñewejey
```

5. *'Is there a barber shop?'*

```
EwÖr ke imwen             Yewer key yiṁen
  mwijbar?                  ṁijbar?
  bijÖk                     pij&k
  bwirej                    bid&j
  kobej                     q&p&j
  kepojak                   keppewjak
  tutu                      tiwtiw
```

6. *'Can you find me a spear?'*

```
Kwo maroH ke bukot tok    Qemareÿ key piqet teq
  juÖn aÖ made?             jiwen hah&h ṁad&y?
      wiaik                     wiyahyik
      kajitÖk                   kajjit&k
      kÖmmane                   keṁṁaney
      jeme                      j&m&y
```

7. *'You don't need to pay for a haircut.'*

```
Kwojjab aikuj kÖllÖ       Qejjab hayiqij kełłay
  wonÖÖn mwijbar.           weñyan ṁijbar.
    uwe ibba                  wiw&y yippah
    kejerbal made ne aÖ       kejerbal ṁad&y ñey hah&h
    tak wa ne waÖ             tak wah ñey wah&h
    uwe ilo wa en waan        wiw&y yilew wah yeñ
      kien                      wahan kiyen
    taktÖ He kwe dri jikul    takteh gey qey rijikiwił
```

8. *'Give him my greetings when you write him.'*

```
Kab lelok aÖ yokwe He     Kab leyłaq hah&h yi'yaqey
  kwo jeje Han e.           gey q&j&yj&y gan y&y.
      lo                        qelew
      iion                      qeyiyewen
      telebon Han               qetalebewen gan
      wÖÖlej Han                qewayl&j gan
```

9. *'I was going to write, but I forgot his address.'*

```
I naj kar jeje ak i       Yinahaj kar j&yj&y hak yi-
  meloklok aterej eo an.    mełaqłaq hateryej yew han.
  jaje                      jahj&y
```

```
        jolok                      jewłaq
        kawitlok                   kaw&tlaq
        jaje i likit na ia         jahj&y yilikit ṅah yi'yah

10. 'Yes, today yet.'
        Aet, rainin wöt.           Hay&t, rahyinyin wet.
        kiö/kin                    kiyyeh/kiyin
        kiökiö/kinkin              kiyyeh-kiyyeh/kiyin-
                                     kiyin
        ilju                       yiljiw
        buṅnin                     biŋniyin
        jöklaj                     jekłaj
        wiik in                    wiyik yin
        alliṅ in wöt               hall&g yin wet
        awa in wöt                 hawah yin wet
        alliṅ kein lal             hall&g k&yin lał

11. 'That particular book is better than this particular
    one.'
        Buk jab en emman jen       B&q jab yeṅ yeṅṅhan jan
        buk jab in.                b&q jab yin.
        mwö                        ṁe-
        wa                         wah
        nuknuk                     niqniq
        teböl                      teybeł
        waj                        waj
        ratio                      r&ytiy&w
        kar                        kahar
        jikul                      jikiwił

12. 'This particular book is better than the one I read.'
        Buk jab in emman jen       B&q jab yin yeṅṅhan jan
        buk jab eo iar riti.       b&q jab yew yihar riytiy.
        mwö......jokwe             ṁe-........j&q&y
        wa.......kömmane           wah........keṅṅhaney
        nuknuk...wiaiki            niqniq.....wiyahyikiy
        teböl....köjerbale         teybeł.....kejerbaley
        waj......loe               waj........lewey
        ratio....wia kake          r&ytiy&w...wiyah kahkey
        jikul....jikul ie          jikiwił....jikiwił yi'y&y

13. 'He became a Protestant.'
        Emwij an erom              Y&ṅ&j han y&ł&m
         brotijen.                  birewtiyjen.
         katilik                    katilik
```

```
    dri nana                rinahnah
    dri kabatat             rikabahathat
    dri kadrok              rikadek
    kirijin                 kirijin
    takötö                  takteh
    dri kaki                rikakiy
    babbüb                  babbib
    bao                     bahwew
    jökmai                  jekṁayiy
    arkol                   harkeweł
```

14. *'She looks almost exactly like her sister.'*

```
    Enaḧin ein nemümin       Yenahgin yayin nemaym&y&n
      lien wöt lieo jein.      liyeṅ wet liyew j&yin.
      ładrik en...jemün        ładik yeṅ...jeman
      ledrik en...jinen        ledik yeṅ...jinen
      köröö en.....lieo nejin  keray yeṅ...liyew nejin
      kwe.........jimmam       qey.........jiṁṅahaṁ
      kuj en......taikö        kiwij yeṅ...tahyikeh
      kijak en....dri balle    kijak yeṅ...ripalley
      bao en......ak           bahwew yeṅ..hak
```

15. *'She looks almost exactly like her sister.'*

```
    Enaḧin ein nemümin       Yenahgin yayin nemaym&y&n
      lien wöt lieo jein.      liyeṅ wet liyew j&yin.
      wüwen                    wayw&y&n
      jökjökin                 j&kj&kin
      baotokin                 pahwewteqin
      ettöḧin                  y&tt&gin
      jorjorin                 jełjełin
      ainikien                 hayinikiyen
      mantin                   ṁantin
      rokojün                  reqejan
```

GRAMMATICAL NOTES

1. Yewen is used with objects like b&q, jimeyeṅ, jakiy, and, in general, flat surfaces. Rahan is used with w&jk&y, niy, kijiw, and, in general, when one wants to specify 'on top of' something high. Sometimes there are words that take either yewen or rahan such as wah, jeyah, teybeł, etc.

2. Jab is used between noun-like words and following demonstratives in singling out a particular or specific item from among others.

## SHORT PROSE SELECTION

### Coconut Oil
### Biniep
### Pinneyep

Mottan men ko rellab tokjeir im rej walok jen ni
Mettan men kew reḷḷap teqjayy&r yim rej wahḷeq jan niy

ej biniep. Binieb ej kōmman jen waini im
yej pinneyep. Pinneyep yej keṁṁan jan wahyiniy yim

dri Majōl rej kejerbale ḥan eloḥ men ko einwōt
riṀahjeḷ rej kejerbaley gan yeleg men kew yayinwet

      annoint       light
ekabit bar, enbwin, ḥan uno im ḥan romrom. Ewōr
<u>yekkapit</u> bar, yanbin, gan winew yim gan <u>ṛemṛem</u>. Yewer

ruo wāwen kōmman biniep. Wāwen eo mokta
riwew wayw&y&n keṁṁan pinneyep. Wayw&y&n yew meqtah

              grate it
rej kejeke. Moktata, elkin aer raankeik
rej kejeyekey. Meqtahtah, yalkin hay&r <u>rahank&yik</u>

    milk
waini en im bōk ḥl en jen e, rej kejeke im
wahyiniy yeṅ yim bek <u>yaḷ</u> yeṅ jan y&y, rej kejeyekey yim

  become     second
ej erom biniep. Kein karuo wāwen, rej kōmat e
yej <u>y&ṛ&m</u> pinneyep. K&yin kariwew wayw&y&n, rej kemattey

elkin aer bok ḥl in waini en. Wāwen jab in
yalkin hay&r bek yaḷin wahyiniy yeṅ. Wayw&y&n jab yin

               musty
elablok an mōkaj im biniep en ejjab kanoj lōl
yeḷapḷaq han ṁekaj yim pinneyep yeṅ yejjab kahn&w&j <u>ḷeḷ</u>

   that
im einwōt en me rej kejek wōt. Jet ien ilo
yim yayinwet yeṅ <u>mey</u> rej kejeyek wet. Jet 'yiyen yilew

     put in       fragrant
aer kōmatte rej illik wōt men ko re ḥaj nai ie
hay&r kemattey rej llik wet men kew <u>regaj</u> ṅahyiy yi'y&y

    its odor
bwe en enno bwin im jab lōl.
bey yen nnaw <u>biyin</u> yim jab ḷeḷ.

PROVERB

Ailiñ in Jaluit, ailiñ in jalele.   Hay&l&g yin Jalw&j, hay&l&g yin jal&yl&y.

'Jaluit is a rich island (where one can always have meat and gravy with his staples).'

VOCABULARY

| | | |
|---|---|---|
| ae | hay&y | collect, gather |
| ainikien | hayinikiyen | sound, voice |
| alal | haɬhaɬ | lumber, piece of wood |
| ʉl | yaɬ | coconut milk |
| arkol | harkeweɬ | alcohol (from English) |
| aterej | hateryej | address (from English) |
| baotok | pahwewteq | to appear |
| bijʉk | pij&k | defecate |
| biniep | pinneyep | coconut oil |
| birae(ik) | birahyey(ik) | fry |
| bwin | biyin | smell of, odor of |
| drila(ik) | diyɬah(yik) | nail |
| ekkabit | kkapit | annoint, massage, lubricate |
| erom | y&ɽ&m | become |
| iyon | 'yiyewen | meet |
| jab | jab | particular, specific |
| jeme | jemey | sharpen it (tr.) |
| jerʉ | jeray | a formalized friendship |
| jikiru(ik) | jikiriw(ik) | screw, to screw |
| jimen | jimyeñ | cement, concrete (from English) |
| jʉkjʉkin | j&kj&kin | (his) shape, the way he is hewn |
| jʉkmai | jekɱayiy | coconut syrup |
| jorjor | jeɽjeɽ | walk rapidly |
| jorjorin | jeɽjeɽin | the way he walks |
| kobej | q&p&j | garbage |
| kulul | qilil | cockroach |
| libbuke | libbiq&y | cowrie shell |
| lʉl | ɬeɬ | moldy, smell moldy |
| mʉjet | majet | matches |
| manit | ɱanit | custom, behavior, manner |
| nat | ɲat | nut (for bolt) (from English) |
| nemʉmin | nemaym&y&n | appearance |
| raanke | rahank&y | grate (coconut), coconut grater |
| rokojʉn | ɽeqejan | the shape of (his) body |
| romrom | ɽemɽem | light |
| talebon | taɬebewen | telephone |
| wʉlij | wayl&j | (send a) cable (from *wireless*) |

## LESSON TWENTY-FOUR

More past tense, contrary-to-fact,
and conditional practice; more on
the coconut; several idiomatic expressions.

DIALOGUES

1.
A: Kwar bed ia inne?     Qehar pad yi'yah yinney?
B: Iar bed imwen imʉ.     Yihar pad yiṁeyeṅ yiṁ&h.
A: Iar iwʉj in bukot yok     Yihar yiw&j yin piqet y&q
    ak kwar jako.     hak qehar jak&w.
B: Jete awa?     Jetey hawah?
A: Ruo jimettan.     Riwew jimettan.
B: O, iar bed imwen Are.     Wew, yihar pad yiṁen Har&y.
    Bwe Ḣan ta?     Bey gan tah.
A: Kejro en kar etal Ḣan     K&jrew yen kar yetal gan
    Rita in iakiu.     Riytah yin yi'yakiyiw.
B: Ak kwʉj et ilju, bwe     Hak qej y&t yiljiw, bey
    Ḣe men kejro etal?     gey men k&jrew yetal?
A: Ekwe ilju ej raeleb,     Yeqey yiljiw yej rahyelep,
    lale kwar jako.     lahley qehar jak&w.

A: Where were you yesterday?
B: At my place.
A: I came to see you but you were gone.
B: What time?
A: Two-thirty.
B: Oh, I was at Harry's. What did you want?
A: We were supposed to go to Rita to play baseball.
B: What are you doing tomorrow? Why don't we go then
    if it's convenient.
A: OK. Tomorrow at noon. Be there.

2.
A: Mokta jen an dri belle     Meqtah jan han ripalley
    itok ear wʉr ke dren     yiteq yehar wer key dannin
    in kadʉk ailiḣ kein?     kadek hay&l&g k&yin?

B: Aet, kim kein kōmman    Hayęt, kęm kęyin keṁṁhan
   jimaḥiḥ jen ni.            jimagig jan niy.
A: Ej baj lōḥ men en komij  Yej baj leg men yeṅ qęṁij
   kōmman jen ni!             keṁṁhan jan niy!
B: Mol...kimij bōk naḥin    Ṁewel...kęmij bek nahgin
   aoleḅ am aikuj jen         hawelep ham hayiqij jan
   ni...mōḤẸ, em, eo,         niy...ṁegay, yęṁ, yew
   uno, dren in kadōk im      winew, dannin kadek yim
   eloḤ men ko jet.           yeleg men kew jet.
A: Mol ke komij kejerbal    Ṁewel key qęṁij kejerbal
   aoleben ni en ke?          hawelepan niy yeṅ key?
B: Ejelok men en kimij jab  Yejjełaq men yeṅ kęmij jab
   kejerbale--jen okar Ḥan    kejerbaley--jan wekar gan
   jubub, ewōr tokjen.        jiwibwib, yewer teqjan.
A: Juōn ne ami jeraman      Jiwen ṅey hamiy jerahamman
   lablab.                    łapłap.
B: Mol...Ḥe ear jab wōr     Ṁewel...gey yehar jab wer
   ni, i jaje ewi wḤwen       niy, yijahjęy yewiy way-
   am naj kar mour.           węyęn ham nahaj kar mewir.

A: Did you have alcohol in these islands before the
   foreigners came?
B: Yes, we used to make toddy from coconut (sap).
A: You sure make a lot of things from coconut trees!
B: Right...we get practically everything we need from
   the coconut...food, housing, fishing lines, medi-
   cine, alcoholic beverages, and many other things.
A: Is it true that you make use of the entire tree?
B: There isn't a single thing we don't use--from roots
   to sprouts--all of it serves a purpose.
A: It's really a godsend for you!
B: That's right...if it hadn't been for the coconut,
   I don't know how we could have survived.

## DRILLS

1. '*Where were you yesterday?*'

   Kwar bed ia              Qehar pad yi'yah
   <u>inne</u>?                    <u>yinney</u>?
   ran eo lok juōn          rahan yew łaq jiwen
   Mandre eo                Ṁandey yew
   Bōlaidre eo              Bełahyidey yew
   ke ej raeleb             key yej rahyelep
   ke ej jota               key yej jęwtah

```
       wiik eo lok              wiyik yew łaq
       alliḧ eo lok             hallag yew łaq
       ekkein                   yakkayin

    2. 'I came to look for you.'
       Iar iwaj in              Yihar yiwaj yin
       bukot yok.               piqet yaq.
       ektake                   yektakey
       ḧḧin                     yagin
       lowaj                    lewwaj
       ukwe                     wiqey
       kajamboik                kejaṁbawyik
       kaaluje                  kahalwijey

    3. 'We'll go play baseball tomorrow.'
       Jenaj ilen iakiu         Jenahaj yilan yi'yakiyiw
       ilju.                    yiljiw.
       jekülaj                  jekłaj
       Mandre in                Mandey yin
       Bülaidre in              Bełahyidey yin
       kiü e raeleb             kiyyeh yerahyelep
       wik in lal               wiyik yin lał
       alliḧ in lal             hallag yin lał
       kiin lok jirik           kiyin łaq jidik

    4. 'Be sure not to be late.' ('Watch out that you
       don't be late.')
       Lale bwe kwün jab rumij. Lahley bey qen jab łiṁij.
       Lale kwar rumij.         Lahley qehar łiṁij.
                  jako                      jakaw
                  meloklok                  mełaqłaq
                  ebbat                     bbat
                  mad                       ṁad

    5. 'I wish there were only the two of us here.'
       En kar kejro wüt         Yen kar kajrew wet
       ijin.                    yijin.
       ijükein                  yijakayin
       ilalin                   yilałin
       ienin                    yiyanyin
       imwin                    yiṁiyin
       ienekein                 yiyeney kayin
       imükein                  yiṁakayin
```

6. *'We will need to look for some drinking water before we go.'*

Jenaj aikuj in kabbok dren in <u>idrak</u> mokta jen ad etal.
    amin
    tutu
    ormej
    kwalkwol
    kadrŏk

Jenahaj hayiqij yin kapp&q dannin <u>yidahak</u> ḿeqtah jan had yetal.
    haḿin
    tiwtiw
    w&rm&j
    qaɫq&ɫ
    kadek

7. *'<u>You are really fortunate</u>.'*

Ej baj lab am
  <u>jeraman</u>!
  jorren
  bul
  jerbal
  kijoH kadrŏk
  kein naHinmij
  kŏnan illu

Yej baj ɫap haḿ
  <u>jerahaḿuhan</u>!
  jeɫɫayan
  biwiɫ
  jerbal
  kijeǥ kadek
  k&yin nahginm&j
  keḿhan lliw

8. *'<u>You can build a house with coconut trees</u>.'*

KomaroH kŏmman <u>em</u> jen ni.
    kein liklik
    kein kauwe
    kein boktak
    kein arar Hi
    kein kŭre
    ieb
    at
    jeinae
    jor
    kijen ajiri
    jekmai
    bŏrwaj in em
    tererein em
    kein ikkure
    ametama

Kemareǥ keḿuhan y&ḿ jan niy.
    k&yin liklik
    k&yin kawiw&y
    k&yin p&qtak
    k&yin harhar giy
    k&yin kayrey
    yiyep
    hat
    jeyiynahyey
    j&w&r
    kijen hajiriy
    jekḿayiy
    berwaj yin y&ḿ
    t&r&yr&yin y&ḿ
    k&yin qqir&y
    hameyteḿah

9. *'<u>If there hadn't been trouble, the party would have been a good one</u>.'*

Ńe ear <u>jab wŏr tirabel</u>, enaj kar emman bade eo.

Gey yehar <u>jab wer tirabeɫ</u>, yenahaj kar ḿuhan bahd&y yew.

```
        loḧ lok jidrik ledrik          leg łaq jidik leddik
        lab lok jidrik dren in         łap łaq jidik dannin
          kadek                          kadek
        bol lok kain mṍḧạ             b&w&ł łaq kahyin ṁegay
        jab mat bia                    jab mahat piyah
        jino wṏt ke ej ran             jinew wet key yej rahan
        jemlok wṏt ke ej               jeṁłaq wet key yej
        jilu awa                       jiliw hawah
        kadek dri belle ro             kadek ripalley rew
```

10. *'We used to go skin diving only at night.'*

```
        Kim kein turoḧ wṏt in         K&m k&yin tiwrağ wet yin
        boḧ.                          b&ğ.
        mubi wṏt in ran                ṁiwpiy wet yin rahan
        entak wṏt in Jadede            y&ntak wet yin Jadeydey
        jar wṏt in jota                jar wet yin j&wtah
        jikul wṏt in jibboḧ            jikiwił wet yin jibb&ğ
        tutu wṏt in jota               tiwtiw wet yin j&wtah
        jerbal wṏt iben kien           jerbal wet yippan kiyen
        jikul wṏt iben dri             jikiwił wet yippan ri-
          belle                          palley
```

11. *'If it's convenient let's have the party next Saturday, because it's raining now.'*

```
        Ṅe men jebade Jadede          Gey men jebahd&y Jadeydey
          in łṻł bwe ewit.              yin lał bey y&w&t.
          iakiu                         jeyiyakiyiw
          eḧwṏr                         jeyağed
          jerak                         jejerak
          etal                          jeyetal
          mubi                          jeṁiwpiy
          kabiro                        jekabiyr&w
          entak                         j&y&ntak
          kwelok                        j&q&ylaq
```

12. *'There are many kinds of things coconut sap can be changed into.'*

   *'There is only one kind of thing coconut sap can be changed into.'*

   (Change each of these sentences to singular as is done for the first example.)

```
        Elṻḧ kain im jekaro           Yeleg kahyin yim jekar&w
          emaroḧ oktak ḧani.            yemareğ w&ktak ganiy.
```

| | |
|---|---|
| Ju�björn wöt kain im jekaro emaroň oktak ňane. | Jiwen wet kahyin yim jekar&w yemareğ w&ktak ganey. |
| Elöň jikin im armij remaroň etal ňani. | Yeleg jikin yim harm&j remareğ yetal ganiy. |
| Elöň buk im dri jikul remaroň katak jäni. | Yeleg b&q yim rijikiwił remareğ kahtak janiy. |
| Elöň mweiuk im dri wia remaroň wia kaki. | Yeleg ṁeyiq yim riwiyah remareğ wiyah kahkiy. |
| Elöň bebe im koňkurej remaroň lemnak kaki. | Yeleg peypey yim qagqirej remareğ łemṅak kahkiy. |
| Elöň kain im dri Majöl remaroň mour jäni. | Yeleg kahyin yim riṀahjeł remareğ mewir janiy. |
| Elöň job im ajiri remaroň tutu kaki. | Yeleg jeweb yim hajiriy remareğ tiwtiw kahkiy. |
| Elöň job im ajiri remaroň tutu eaki. | Yeleg jeweb yim hajiriy remareğ tiwtiw yahkiy. |

GRAMMATICAL NOTES

1. The gey men of the first dialogue and of Drill 11 is idiomatic and is best translated as 'if it is convenient' or 'if it suits'.

2. The k&yin of the second line of the second dialogue, and of Drill 10 is pronounced this way in the Rälik dialect, but [k(&)k&yin] in the Ratak dialect. It is practically synonymous with the k&n of Drills 10, 11, and 13 of Lesson 16, and is also translated 'used to'.

3. The final line of the second dialogue is a good example of a contrary-to-fact conditional sentence, and should be memorized thoroughly as a basis for constructing similar complex sentences in the future. Drill 9 furnishes additional practice on a very similar pattern.

4. The second line of Drill 4, even though it contains a form that is usually used for past tense (qehar), is synonymous with the first line, and must be considered idiomatic.

5. Drill 12 furnishes more practice on yim constructions which do not translate directly as 'and', and in addition gives practice on ganey, janey, kahkey and yahkey. (Yahkey is the Ratak form of the Rälik kahkey.) These words behave like transitive verbs in that their

*ey*-endings change to *iy* for plural objects, but differ from verbs in that they never take the subject prefixes. Ganey and janey are forms of *gan* 'to' and *jan* 'from' that have objects incorporated.

SHORT PROSE SELECTION

Coconut Toddy<br>Jekaro<br>Jekar&w

```
                     shoot
Jekaro  ej  walok  jen  witak  in   ni   ilo    ien    en
Jekar&w yej wahłaq jan  witak  yin  niy  yilew  'yiyen yeń
             break  spread apart
ejańin     rub  im jebbellok im walok kwalini.  Mokta,
yejjahgin  łip  yim j&płłaq  yim wahłaq qałiyniy. Meqtah,
         examine                      size         cut
jej  kakilen  witak eo,  bwe  ńe  emman  jońan, jej jebe
jej  kakilen  witak yew, bey  gey yeńńhan jeǵan, jej j&p&y
         bind it  peel off the end of it *bend it down
im   eouti,     kaudebake,    im *kietake     jidrik.  Aolep
yim  yawitiy,   kawidepakey,  yim kiy&ytakey  jidik.   Hawelep
              collect toddy
 ien   ar   jekaro,   ilo   jibboń im  jota   im  jet
'yiyen had  jekar&w,  yilew jibb&ǵ yim j&wtah yim jet
                                          little by
 ien   ilo  raelep,   jej jeb witak eo  jidrik illok
'yiyen yilew rahyelep, jej jep witak yew jidik yillaq
little                                  be unable to
jidrik, im bareinwöt   kietake     bwe en jab idrak
jidik,  yim barayinwet kiy&ytakey  bey yen jab yidahak
flow            ready for a bottle
bwijen.  Elańe  erani-bökań,          kiö  eien     an
bijen.   Yełaggey yerahaniy-bekayan,  kiyyeh yeyiyen han
fasten the bottle                       take down
kajokkwor.  Aolep jibboń im jota,  ej  ien   ekato
kaj&qq&r.   Hawelep jibb&ǵ yim j&wtah yej 'yiyen yakt&w
            replace the bottle
jekaro   im kökkäl  jeib.   Elöń kain  im jekaro
jekar&w  yim kekkayal j&yib. Yeleg kahyin yim jekar&w
emaroń  oktak  ńani.  Jemaroń kömatte    im ewalok
yemareǵ w&ktak ganiy. Jemareǵ kemattey yim yewahłaq
```

concentrate
jŭkajeje    (emman  Han limen niHniH).   ElaHe     eto
<u>jekajeyjey</u>   (yeṁhan gan limen nignig).   Yełaggey yetew
                                   syrup
lok wŏt   ar kŏmatte   enaj    walok  jekŏmai.     Bar
łaq wet had kemattey yenahaj wahłaq <u>jekeṁayiy</u>.  Bar
                             leave
juŏn,  elaHe    jenaj    kŏtlok jekaro  eo  bwe  en ber
jiwen, yełaggey jenahaj <u>ketłaq</u> jekar&w yew bey yen pad
                                wine
jilu  ran,   enaj    erom jimaHiH....dren in kadrŏk eo
jiliw rahan, yenahaj y&ł&m <u>jimagig</u>....dannin kadek yew

limen dri Majŏl.  Ňe  eto  lok wŏt  an ber jimaHiH  eo
limen riṀahjeł.  Gey yetew łaq wet han pad jimagig yew
                vinegar                           yeast
enaj    erom benŏkŏ.  Jekaro  ej  bar bŏk jikin iij
yenahaj y&ł&m <u>penkeh</u>.  Jekar&w yej bar bek jikin <u>yij</u>
ilo    iŏk   bilawH.
yilew 'yiy&k pilahway.

Men kein  rej kwalok    im  kalikar  joHan an  lab an
Men k&yin rej kewwahłaq yim kalikkar jeğan han łap han
ni   jibaH dri Majŏl.
niy  jipag riṀahjeł.

**PROVERB**
    Loje kŏlla.                  Lawj&y kellah.
             'Stomachs are dumps.'
    'Don't be particular about your food--your
        stomach is but a garbage pile.'

**VOCABULARY**

| | | |
|---|---|---|
| ametama | hameyteṁah | coconut candy |
| amin | haṁhin | wash hands (and mouth) (before and after eating) |
| aHin | yagin | get, pick up (a person) and take him somewhere |
| arar | harhar | pick (teeth, nose, etc.) |
| benŏkŏ | penkeh | vinegar (from English) |

245

| | | |
|---|---|---|
| bŭkŭ | bekay | bottle |
| boktak | p&qtak | stir |
| bŭrwaj | berwaj | roof |
| eake | yahkey (Rat.) | concerning it, about it (cf. kahkey) |
| ebbat | bbat | late |
| eoeu | yawy&w (intr.) | bind, lash |
| eouti | yawitiy (tr.) | bind it, lash it |
| ekkein | yekk&yin | a little while ago |
| jebjeb | j&pj&p (intr.) jep, j&p&y (tr.) | cut the end off; amputate |
| jeib | j&yip | bottle used for collecting coconut sap |
| jeinae | jeyinahyey | mat of fresh, green palm leaves |
| jekajeje | jekajeyjey | half-cooked coconut sap; concentrate |
| jekaro | jekar&w | coconut sap, toddy |
| jekmai | jekṁayiy | coconut syrup |
| jimaḧiḧ | jimagin | toddy wine |
| jor | j&w&r, jiwire- | post, pole; |
| kaaluje | kahalwijey (tr., causative) | to show someone around |
| kake | kahkey (Rŭl.) | about it, concerning it (cf. yahkey) |
| kabiro | kabiyr&w | to make preserved breadfruit |
| kajambo(ik) | kejaṁb&w(ik) | take (someone) for a change of scene |
| kajukwor | kaj&qq&r | fasten a bottle (q&r) for tapping coconut sap |
| kakilen | kakilen | examine |
| kalikar | kahalikkar | clarify |
| kaudbak(ey) | kawidpak | peel off the end of a coconut shoot |
| kauwe(ik) | kawiw&y(ik) | to make rise; leaven (cf. wiw&y) |
| kein kauwe | k&yin kawiw&y | yeast |
| kiele | kiyeley | to bend it |
| kietak | kiy&ytak | to bend down (coconut shoots only) |
| kiin | kiyin | now (Rat.) |
| kŭkŭŭl | kekayal | renew, replace |
| kŭlla | kellah | garbage, dump |
| liklik | liklik | strain, sift |
| lowaj | lewwaj | to visit (you) |
| mad | ṁad | be distracted, detained |

| | | |
|---|---|---|
| meloklok | mełaqłaq | forget |
| Ħe men | gey men | if it suits, if it is convenient |
| niĦniĦ | nignig | baby, infant |
| okar | wekar | root |
| ormej | w&rm&j | wash face |
| ranibŭkŭn | rahaniy-bekayan | ready for a bottle (<u>bekay</u>) (of coconut shoots only) |
| tererein | t&r&yr&yin | its side, edge, wall |
| toor | tawar | pour out, run, flow |
| ukwe | wiqey | to take out |
| witak | witak | coconut shoot |

## LESSON TWENTY-FIVE

Beverages; more distributives;
arrowroot and divination.

<u>DIALOGUES</u>

1.
A: I maro. EwOr ke           Yimar&w. Yewer key
   aibOj in drak?             hay&b&j yin dahak?
B: KOttar i ja lale.          Kettar yijjah lahley.
A: Ne ewOr, bOktok jidrik.    Gey yewer, bekteq jidik.
B: EwOr jekaro im aibOj.      Yewer jekar&w yim hay&b&j.
   Ta eo limOm?               Tah yew limem?
A: Ebwe aibOj, kommol.        Yebey hay&b&j. Qemhewel.

A: I'm thirsty. Do you have any water to drink?
B: Wait, let me see.
A: If there is any, bring me some.
B: There's toddy and water. Which do you want?
A: Water will do. Thank you.'

2.
A: EwOr ke kola mOlo?         Yewer key k&wlah m&l&w?
B: Emat, ak ewOr bia.         Yemahat, hak yewer piyah.
   KwOj idrak ke bia?         Qej yidahak key piyah?
A: Kommol a ij jab.           Qemhewel hah yijjab.
B: EwOr ban ak ejjab          Yewer ban hak yejjab
   kanuij mOlo.               kahn&w&j m&l&w.
A: Eokwe letok juOn....       Yeqey leyteq jiwen....
   kommol tata.               qemhewel tahtah.

A: Do you have any cold coke?
B: It's all gone, but we have some beer. Do you drink beer?
A: No, thank you.
B: There's some punch but it's not very cold.
A: That'll do, let me have one....thank you very much.

DRILLS
1. I maro.                  Yimar&w.
    kwole                    q&l&y
    bwil                     bil
    bio                      piyaw
    adreboulul               haddebewilwil
    mejki                    m&jkiy
    mÖk                      ṁ&k
    metak                    metak
    menokaru                 menewkadiw
    mÖlaHlÖH                 ṁełagł&g

2. EwÖr ke aibÖj in         Yewer key hay&b&j yin
    idrak?                   yidahak?
    tutu                     tiwtiw
    kwalkwol                 qałq&ł
    kamÖlo                   kaṁ&ł&w
    kabodren                 kab&wdan

3. KÖttar. Ij ja lale.      Kettar. Yijjah lahley.
    jerbal                   jerbal
    kiki                     kiykiy
    tutu                     tiwtiw
    kÖmrḦ                    keṁeray
    mÖHḦ                     ṁegay
    idrak                    yidahak
    kwalkwol                 qałq&ł
    kakije                   kakkij&y
    jeje                     j&yj&y

4. Ta eo limÖm?             Tah yew liṁeṁ?
    kijÖm                    kijeṁ
    jelem                    jaleyeṁ
    am                       haṁ
    kunam                    qiṅahaṁ

5. Kwo maroH ke bÖktok      Qemareǧ key bekteq jidik
    jidrik bia?              piyah?
    aiboj                    hay&b&j
    kanniek                  kanniy&k
    raij                     rahyij
    dren                     dan
    mḦ                       may
    jekaro                   jekar&w
    bilawḦ                   pilahway
    eal                      yał
    ik                       y&k

6. EwŏR ke kola mŏlo?          Yewer key k&wɨah ṁ&ɨ&w?
     kola in wia                     k&wɨah yin wiyah
     kola bwil                       k&wɨah bil
     kola in kŭre                    k&wɨah yin kayrey
     bia mŏlo                        piyah ṁ&ɨ&w
     wŏjke                           w&jk&y
     aibŏj in kŭre                   hay&b&j yin kayrey

7. Emat bia imwin.              Yemahat piyah yiṁyin.
     kola                            k&wɨah
     jodi                            jewdiy
     jatin                           jahtiyin
     konbib                          kawanpiyip
     wŏjke                           w&jk&y

8. Kwŏj idrak ke bia?           Qej yidahak key piyah?
   Aet, He ewŏr, letok          Hay&t, gey yewer, leyteq
   juŏn.                         jiwen.
     kola                            k&wɨah
     jekaro                          jekar&w
     jimaHiH                         jimagig
     jekmai                          jekṁayiy
     jŏkajeje                        jekajeyjey
     ni                              niy
     dren mŏlo                       dan ṁ&ɨ&w

9. Ejjab kanuij mŏlo bia        Yejjab kahn&w&j ṁ&ɨ&w piyah
   e limŏ.                       y&y lim&h.
             (Repeat Drill 8.)

10. Letok juŏn limŏ kola.       Leyteq jiwen lim&h k&wɨah.
     limen                           limen
     limŏm                           liṁeṁ
     limerjel                        lim&yy&rj&l
     limerwŏj                        lim&yy&rw&j
     limier                          lim&yy&r
     limemwŏj                        limemw&j

11. 'Who folded this MAT and folded it carelessly here?
    Could you fold it properly?'
     Wŏn e ear limlim im         Wen y&y yehar l&ml&m yim
     limlimi jaki e na           limlimiy jakiy y&y ṅah
     ije?                        yij&y?
     Kwo maroH ke kŏmanman       Qemareḡ key keṁanṁan haṁ
     am limi?                    limiy?

*'...lashed this COCONUT SHOOT...'* *(for tapping toddy)*

Wōn e ear eoeu im eoiuti <u>utak</u> e na ije?
Kwo maroñ ke kōmanman am <u>eouti</u>?

Wen y&y yehar yawy&w yim yawyiwitiy <u>witak</u> y&y ñah yij&y?
Qemareg̊ key keṁanṁan haṁ <u>yawitiy</u>?

*'...wound up this FISH LINE...'*

Wōn e ear bobu im bobuti <u>eo</u> e na ije?
Kwo maroñ ke kōmanman am <u>bouti</u>?

Wen y&y yehar pawp&w yim pawpiwitiy <u>yew</u> y&y ñah yij&y?
Qemareg̊ key keṁanṁan haṁ <u>pawitiy</u>?

*'...knotted this ROPE...'*

...bubu im bubuji <u>to</u>...
...<u>buji</u>?

...biwbiw yim biwbiwijiy <u>tew</u>...
...<u>biwijiy</u>?

*'...took apart this ENGINE...'*

...jaljal im jaljalate <u>injin</u>...
...<u>jalate</u>?

...jałjał yim jałjałatey <u>yinjin</u>...
...<u>jałatey</u>?

*'...turned this SEWING MACHINE...'*

...iñiñ im iñiñiti <u>mejin</u>...
...<u>iñiti</u>?

...yigyig yim yigyigitiy <u>meyjin</u>...
...<u>yigitiy</u>

*'...rolled this EMPTY DRUM...'*

...kajabilbil im kajjabilbili <u>kajliñ</u>...
...<u>kajabili</u>?

...kejabilbil im kejjabilbiliy <u>kahajliyig</u>...
...<u>kejabiliy</u>?

...kadrabilbil im kadrabilibili <u>kajliñ</u>...
...<u>kadrabili</u>?

...kadapilpil yim kaddapilpiliy <u>kahajliyig</u>...
...<u>kadapiliy</u>?

*'...opened this CASE...'*

...rubrub im irrubrube <u>bok</u>...
...<u>rube</u>?

...łipłip yim łłipłipey <u>bawak</u>...
...<u>łipey</u>?

*'...sliced this BREAD...'*

...mwijmwij im *(mwi-)mwijmwijiti <u>pilawā</u>...
...<u>mwijiti</u>?

...ṁijṁij yim *(ṁ)ṁijṁijitiy <u>pilahway</u>...
...<u>ṁijitiy</u>

(*part of word in parenthesis indicates Ratak pronunciation.)

'...<u>pounded this OCTOPUS</u>...'
...dreḧdreḧ im dreḧdre-      ...<u>degdeg</u> yim <u>degdegetey</u>
   ḧete <u>kwet</u>...            <u>q&y&t</u>...
...<u>dreḧete</u>?               ...<u>degetey</u>?

## GRAMMATICAL NOTES

1. Distributive forms of noun-like words and of certain verbs were practiced in Lesson 21. Now in Drill 11 of this lesson the distributive forms of verbs of *tying, binding, wrapping, rolling, opening, taking apart*, etc. are introduced. For words of this sort, the semantic element added by the distributive is one of carelessness, sloppiness, in every direction, all over the place, etc. It should not be too difficult to relate this concept to that of items that are widespread over an island, actions that are intensified or facilitated, and colors that are splattered about.

## SHORT PROSE SELECTIONS

1.　　　　　　　Starch
　　　　　　　　Makmȫk
　　　　　　　　M̌akṁ&k

```
          starch
Makmȫk  ej   juȫn    ian     mȫḧ&  ko  kijen  dri Majȫl.
M̌akṁ&k  yej  jiwen  yi'yahan ṁegay kew kijen  riM̌ahjeł.

Ekk&    wȫt  an  edrek  ilo    ailiḧ    ko  iȫḧ  kinke  makmȫk
Yekkay  wet  han ddek   yilew  hay&ł&g  kew y&g k&nkey ṁakṁ&k
                              dry (not rainy)
emman   an  edrek ilo  jikin  ko  rejawȫtwȫt  im
yeṁḧan  han ddek  yilew jikin kew rejaww&tw&t yim

  sandy                          dig up              after
kabokbok.  Kilen kȫmmane,      totake   mokta, mwijin kwale,
kabeqbeq.  Kilen keṁḧaney,  t&wtakey  ṁeqtah,  ṁ&jin qałey,

  then       grate  stone              then    strain
tokelik    iri    kin  dek&   bukor   inem    likliki    im
teqaylik  yiriy   k&n  dekay  piq&r   yinnam  liklikiy  yim

sun-dry
kejeeke.  Elaḧe       emwij,  likit  ilo    nuknuk  im
kejeyekey. Yełaggey  y&ṁ&j,  likit  yilew  niqniq  yim

hang it                    dry      finally     grind
totoiki     mae    ien     emor&.   Eliktata    rube
tewtewyikiy ṁahyey 'yiyen  yeṁeray. Yaliktahtah łipey
```

|  | | basket | |
|---|---|---|---|
| im likit na iloan | bŭjo. | Kiŭ ebojak Han |
| yim likit ńah yilewwahan | bejaw. | Kiyyeh yepewjak gan |

      to starch clothes
mŏHY, kŏmakmŏk nuknuk, im Han uno.
ṁegay, keṁakṁ&k niqniq, yim gan winew.

2.       Divination
        Bubu
        Biwbiw

Bubu ej juŏn maroH dri uno in etto ilo MajŭI
Biwbiw yej jiwen mareǰ riwinew yin yettew yilew Mahjeł

              wish
rar kejerbale He rej kŏnan jelY kin juŏn men
rehar kejerbaley gey rej keńhan jełay k&n jiwen men

eo rej jab melele kake. Men in kar mŏttan
yew rej jab mełeyłey kahkey. Men yin kar ṁettan

voodoo             important
ekŏbYl im uno. Bubu elab tokjen Han uno, Han
kkepal yim winew. Biwbiw yełap teqjan gan winew, gan

kabbok dri kot im Han kabbok men ko rej jako. Rar
kapp&q rikawat yim gan kapp&q men kew rej jak&w. Rehar

kejerbal Han uno He rej bukot naHinmij rot eo an
kejerbal gan winew gey rej piqet naginm&j łet yew han

juŏn armij, uno ta eo ekkar, ia eo uno
jiwen harm&j, winew tah yew yekkar, yi'yah yew winew

eo eber ie, kab wŏn eo ekkar Han lelok uno eo.
yew yepad y&y, kab wen yew yekkar gan leyłaq winew yew.

Ien eo ien uno ej bar juŏn ian men ko
'Yiyen yew 'yiyen winew yej bar jiwen yi'yahan men kew

bubu ej kwalok. Men ko rej kejerbali Han bubu
biwbiw yej qahłaq. Men kew rej kejerbaliy gan biwbiw

remaroH kimej, jubub, maaH, ekwal, drekY im bwelek.
remareǰ kim&j, jiwibwib, mahag, qqał, dekay yim b&l&k.

PROVERBS
1. Etetal mŏmŏHYHe.       Yetyetal ṁṁegayg&y.
      'Walking, eating.'

Note: When visitors are greeted in a Marshallese household the first thing that's offered is food. Thus: When you walk around visiting, you'll have to be ready to eat at each house you visit.

2. Kwe wɵt kwe, Ha wɵt Ha.  Qey wet qey, gah wet gah.
   Equivalent: 'Each man for himself.'

## VOCABULARY

| | | |
|---|---|---|
| adreboulul | haddebewilwil | dizzy (a distributive in form and meaning) |
| ban | ban | punch (from English) |
| bio | piyaw | to be cold, chilly |
| bobu | pawp&w (intr.) | wind up (as fish line) |
| bobouti | pawpiwitiy (distr.) | wind up carelessly |
| bouti | pawitiy (tr.) | wind it up |
| bɵjo | bejaw | basket, pocket |
| bubu | biwbiw (intr.) | to knot; divination, fortune teller, wizardism |
| bubuji | biwbiwijiy (distr.) | knot carelessly |
| buji | biwijiy (tr.) | knot it |
| drɵbilbil | dapilpil | roll |
| dri kot | rikawat | thief, robber |
| dri uno | riwinew | witch doctor, medicine man (woman) |
| eal | yaɬ | coconut milk |
| ekkar | kkar | fit, it is fitting, suitable |
| ekɵbɵl | kkepal | voodoo |
| elap tokjen | yeɬap teqjan | it is important |
| eliktata | yaliktahtah | finally, last of all |
| eo | yew | fish line |
| iHiH | yigyig | to wind, crank, cause to revolve |
| iHiHiti | yigyigitiy (distr.) | wind carelessly |
| iHiti | yigitiy (tr.) | wind it |
| jabilbil | jabilbil | roll |
| jawɵtwɵt | jaww&tw&t | not rainy (ja- + distributive of w&t rain) |
| jeleem | jaleyeṁ jaleye- | your meat course (cf. jaleyley) |
| jodi | jewdiy | zories (from Jap.) |
| jubub | jiwibwib | stem of coconut, pandanus, etc. |

| | | |
|---|---|---|
| kabokbok | kabeqbeq | sandy |
| kajliñ | kahajliyig | barrel, drum--gas, kerosene (from *gasolene*) |
| kŭre | kayrey | mix |
| kimej | kim&j | coconut leaves |
| kŭmrŭ | keṁeray | to dry |
| kŭmakmŭk | keṁakṁ&k | to starch (clothes) |
| limi | limiy (tr.) | to fold |
| limlim | limlim | fold |
| mejin | meyjin | sewing machine (from English) |
| mejki | m&jkiy | sleepy |
| melele | meɫeyɫey | understand |
| menokaru | menewkadiw | perspiration, to perspire |
| mŭk | ṁek (Rat.) ṁ&k (Rŭl.) | |
| mŭlañlŭñ | ṁeɫagɫ&g | nausea, nauseated |
| mŭmŭñŭñe | ṁuṁegayg&y | always eating (distributive of *ṁegay*) |
| mwijin | ṁ&jin | after (it) |
| tokelik | teqaylik | afterwards, then |
| totake | t&wtakey (tr.) | dig (it) up |
| totoiki | tewtewyikiy | hang (it) up |

255

## LESSON TWENTY-SIX

Working and getting accustomed;
more negatives with *ja-*.

### DIALOGUES

1.
A: Ij lŏmnak in jerbal jŏmar in.  Yij łemṁak yin jerbal jeṁar yin.
B: Kwo naj jerbal ia?  Qenahaj jerbal yi'yah?
A: Inaj dri wia ilo imŏn wia en an Mieco.  Yinahaj riwiyah yilew yiṁen wiyah yeṅ han Miyeykew.
B: Naj jete wŏnem?  Nahaj jetey weṅyaṁ?
A: LemHoul jeen juŏn awa.  L&mg&wil jayan jiwen hawah.
B: Emake naj lŏH am mak.  Yemak&y nahaj leg haṁ ṁahak.

A: I'm thinking of working this summer.
B: Where will you work?
A: I'll be a salesman at Mieco.
B: How much will you be making?
A: Fifty cents an hour.
B: You'll make a lot of money.

2.
A: Lina, emwij ke am karreoik rum en?  Liynah, y&ṁ&j key haṁ karr&y&wik riwiṁ yeṅ?
B: IjaHin. EjaHin mwij aŏ kwalkwol pileij.  Yijjahgin. Yejjahgin ṁ&j hah&h qałq&ł pilyej.
A: Lale kwar meloklok wintŏ kan.  Lahley qehar mełaqłaq winteh kaṅ.
B: Ewi Jomi?  Yewiy Jewmiy?
A: E kŏmat. Bwe?  Yekemat. Bey?
B: Ejelok. Ij baj kajitok.  Yejjełaq. Yij baj kajjit&k.

A: Lina, have you finished cleaning that room?
B: Not yet. I haven't washed the dishes yet.
A: Don't forget the windows.
B: Where's Jomi?
A: She's cooking. Why?
B: Nothing. I was just wondering.

3.
A: Emetak drill.                    Yemetak diyih.

B: Eita, elab am mŏk                Yeyitah, yeḷap haṁ ṁ&k
   ke?                              key?

A: Jab, I jaminene in               Jahab, yijammin&yn&y yin
   kiki ion jaki.                   kiykiy yewen jakiy.

B: Oh, eminene drim                 W&w&w, yemmin&yn&y diyiṁ
   ḥan bitoḥ ke?                    gan biteǧ key?

A: Aet, a ejab to im                Hay&t, hah yejjab tew yim
   inaj bar iminene kin             yinahaj bar mmin&yn&y k&n
   jaki.                            jakiy.

A: My back hurts.
B: What happened? Are you exhausted?
A: No. I'm not used to sleeping on mats.
B: Oh, you're used to mattresses.
A: Yes, but it won't take long for me to become
   accustomed to mats.

DRILLS

1. *'I plan to work during this summer vacation.'*
   Ij lŏmnak in jerbal           Yij ḷemḥak yin jerbal
   jŏmar in.                     jeṁar yin.
    kowainini              kewwahyiniyniy
    jikul                  jikiwiḷ
    dri kaki               rikakiy
    job                    jawab
    eḥwŏr                  yaǧed
    kabwiro                kabiyr&w
    jerakrŏk               jerakr&k

2. Kwo naj jerbal ia?            Qenahaj jerbal yi'yah?
   (*Repeat Drill 1.*)

3. I naj dri wia i               Yinahaj riwiyah yiy
   Mieco jŏmar in.               Miyeykew jeṁar yin.
    kamtŏ                  kahaṁteh

```
           wŏkin pade                wekin bahdɛy
           injinia                   yinjiniyah
           kuk                       qiq
           job                       jawab
           jerbal                    jerbal

4. 'You will earn a lot of money.'
       Emake naj loħ am mak!     Yemakɛy nahaj leg haṁ ṁahak!
                 iiet                            yiyɛt
                 lab                             ɬap
                 drik                            dik
                 bool                            bɛwɛɬ

5. 'How much will you get paid?'
       Naj jete wŏnem?           Nahaj jetey weñyaṁ?
                kunam                            qiñahaṁ
                waam                             wahaṁ
                bŭlem                            palyeṁ
                enem                             yanyeṁ

6. Lina, emwij ke am         Liynah, yɛṁɛj key haṁ
       karreoik rum en?              karrɛyɛwik riwiṁ yeñ?
       kabelok                       kabeɬɬaq
       karŏk                         karek
       kili                          kiyiliy
       kainŏknŏk                     kayinɛknɛk

7. Ijaħin. Ejaħin mwij        Yijjahgin. Yejjahgin ṁɛj
       aŏ kwalkwol pilej?            hahɛh qaɬqɛɬ pilyej?
          kŏmman                        keṁṁan
          kwalok                        kewwahɬaq
          kabojak                       keppewjak
          kŏmrŭ                         keṁeray
          kŏrol                         kerrawal

8. 'Don't forget the windows.'
       Lale kwar meloklok        Lahley qehar meɬaqɬaq
            wintŏ kane.                  winteh kañey.
            kejam                        kejam
            katiħ                        kahtɛyɛg
            kilaj                        kilahaj
            eteħak ne                    tteghak ñey
```

9. *'Don't forget that we have to go pick breadfruit.'*

 Komin lemnake ad ilen    Qemhin łemmakey had yilan
 <u>kömköm mü</u>.         <u>kemhkemh may</u>.
 <u>köb roH</u>           <u>k&b rag̃</u>
 jekjek kane        j&kj&k kan&y
 keke nuknuk        k&yk&y niqniq
 okok böb         wekwek beb
 entak ni          y&ntak niy

10. *'Watch out that you don't get burned.'*

 Lale kwo <u>bwil</u>.       Lahley qebil.
  okjak          <u>w&kjak</u>
  wutlok         w&tlaq
  maloH         małeg̃
  tibbok          tibbaq
  mwijmwij        mhijmhij
  tibjek          tipj&k
  jirilok         jiriylaq
  buH          big̃

11. *'What's the matter with your back?'*

 Eita <u>drim</u>?        Yeyitah <u>diyimh</u>?
 E joren driu.       Yejełłayan diyih.
  akküm         hakkiyimh
  kilüm          kilimh
  botüm         bawtimh
  ütüm          yatimh
  atüm          hatimh
  ürüm         yarimh
  enbwinüm        yanbinnimh
  Harüm         garimh
  lojilHüm         lawjilgimh
  Hatim          gatimh
  ittüm          yittimh
  katüm         katimh
  ajajüm         hajhajimh
  nem          neyemh
  Him          giyimh
  ibüm          yipimh
  alküm         yalkimh
  möjHalüm        mhejgalimh

(<u>Yeyitah</u> *above is a Ratak form; for the Rälik dialect, substitute* <u>yebaj y&t</u>.)

12. *'I haven't gotten used to sleeping on mats yet.'*

<table>
<tr><td>I jaminene in kiki ion <u>jaki</u>.</td><td>Yijammin&yn&y yin kiykiy yewen <u>jakiy</u>.</td></tr>
<tr><td>bet</td><td>peyet</td></tr>
<tr><td>bitoH</td><td>biteğ</td></tr>
<tr><td>tÜlao</td><td>teɫahwew</td></tr>
<tr><td>mÜterej</td><td>materej</td></tr>
<tr><td>jeinae</td><td>j&yinahyey</td></tr>
<tr><td>jebko</td><td>j&pkaw</td></tr>
<tr><td>rÜ</td><td>ray</td></tr>
<tr><td>jimen</td><td>jimyeń</td></tr>
<tr><td>ujoj</td><td>wijw&j</td></tr>
<tr><td>bok</td><td>beq</td></tr>
<tr><td>amak</td><td>hańak</td></tr>
</table>

13. *'He hasn't gotten used to sleeping on mats yet.'*

Ejaminene enbwinin Han kiki ion <u>jaki</u>.     Yejammin&yn&y yanbinnin gan kiykiy yewen <u>jakiy</u>.

*(Repeat the cues of Drill 12 for this and the following drill.)*

14. Ejaminene kin <u>jaki</u>.     Yejammin&yn&y k&n <u>jakiy</u>.

15. *(Practice negating the following by using the <u>ja</u>- prefix.)*

A: Iminene in kadÜk.     Yimmin&yn&y yin kadek.
B: Ijaminene in kadÜk.   Yijammin&yn&y yin kadek.
A: Ekkutkut an kadÜk.    Yeqqitqit han kadek.
B: Ejakutkut an kadÜk.   Yejaqqitqit han kadek.

Ebakij leen.         Yepakij ɫeyeń.
Eniknik leen.        Yeniknik ɫeyeń.
Emmourur leen.       Yemmewirwir ɫeyeń.
Ekon lowan mween.    Yeqeń lewwahan ńeyeń.
EuH bwinbwin eo.     Yewiğ b&nb&n yew.
Ekkijeje leen.       Yekkij&yj&y ɫeyeń.
ErroHroH leen.       Yerreğreğ ɫeyeń.
Eowan leen.          Yewwan ɫeyeń.
Eiur leen.           Yeyiɫ ɫeyeń.
Ejimat leen.         Yejińahat ɫeyeń.

## SHORT PROSE SELECTION

### Aibōj Lal
### Hay&b&j Laɫ

Mokta jen an itok armij in belle Han Majōl, dri
Meqtah jan han yiteq harm&j yin palley gan Mahjeɫ, ri-

Majōl rōkein kejerbal emmak, aibōj lal, kab lojet
Mahjeɫ rek&yin kejerbal ṁhak, hay&b&j laɫ, kab lawj&t

Han tutu, amwin, im idrak. Emmak im aibōj lal
gan tiwtiw, haṁin, yim yidahak. Ṁhak yim hay&b&j laɫ

ko etto rar jab kanuij in erreo. Ran kein
kew yettew rehar jab kahn&w&j yin rr&y&w. Rahan k&yin

ekanuij in emman lok im erreo lok aibōj lal.
yekahn&w&j yin ṁhan ɫaq yim rr&y&w ɫaq hay&b&j laɫ.
           dig them    caught
Wāwen aer kōmmani, rej kibwiji Han He ebo dren
Wayw&y&n hay&r keṁhaniy, rej kibijiy gan gey yepew dan
       its sides  protect (it)
inem jimeene tererein ak abare tererein kin
yinnam jimyeṅey t&r&yr&yin hak haparey t&r&yr&yin k&n
             crumble
kajliḢ ak drekḢ bwe en jab rōm tererein im
kahajliyig hak dekay bey yeṅ jab r&ṁ ter&yr&yin yim
            cover of
kōmman an etton. Kiō rej kōmman benjen mejen bwe
keṁhan han tt&w&n. Kiyyeh rej keṁhan p&njan mejan bey

en jab wōtlok menoknok ak jabrewōt men iloan
yen jab w&tlaq menaqnaq hak jabdeywet men yilewwahan

im kattone. Ear kanuij iiet aibōj lal
yim katt&w&n&y. Yehar kahn&w&j 'yiy&t hay&b&j laɫ

etto im jabrewōt armij rej kejerbali im kattoni.
yettew yim jabdeywet harm&j rej kejerbaliy yim katt&w&-

  Kiō enaḢin wōr aibōj lal iturin aolep
niy. Kiyyeh yenahgin wer hay&b&j laɫ yitiṛin hawelep

em. Elab lok an armij ro aer aibōj lal kein
y&ṁ. Yeɫap ɫaq han harm&j rew hay&r hay&b&j laɫ k&yin

karreoiki bwe ren erreo im jab kōmman naḢinmij
karr&y&wikiy bey ren rreyew yim jab keṁhan nahginm&j

Han ir He rej tutu, idrak, ak kōmman mōḢḢ ilo
gan y&r gey rej tiwtiw, yidahak, hak keṁhan ṁegay yilew

aibŏj    lal kein.
hayőbőj lał kőyin.

## PROVERB

Emŭnŭnŭ eo ej roH jen       Yeṁeṅehṅeh yew yej reǵ jan
   eo ej loe.                     yew yej lewey.

'He that hears is happier than he that sees.'

## VOCABULARY

| | | |
|---|---|---|
| abare | haparey | support; escort; outline (edges) |
| akki | hakkiy | fingernails, toenails, claws |
| amak | haṁak | hammock (from English) |
| amwim | haṁin | wash hands |
| at | hat | gall bladder |
| benjen | pőnjan, pőnja- | its cover |
| bitoH | biteǵ | mattress (from Jap.) |
| bool | bőwől | full; bowl |
| di, -ŭ, -im, -in | diy, diyi- | bone |
| ebo | yepew | reach, caught |
| eita | yeyitah | what happened to |
| ekkijeje | kkijőyjőy | gets tired easily |
| emmak | ṁṁak | a tree-hole water catchment |
| eowan | wwan | hard worker, industrious |
| eteHak | tteghak | porch |
| ib, -ŭ, -im, -in | yip, yipi- | waist |
| imminene | mminőynőy | be accustomed to; be used to |
| itti | yittiy, yitti- (RHl.) tittit, titti- (Rat.) | breast |
| jakkijeje | jakkijőyjőy | not tire easily |
| jamminene | jamminőynőy | not accustomed to |
| janiknik | janiknik | lazy |
| jirilok | jiriylaq | slip; accident |
| job | jawab | get a job; work for a salary (from English) |
| kainŭknŭk | kayinőknők | to decorate |
| karŏk | karek | to put things in order |

| | | |
|---|---|---|
| kat, -ŭ, -im, -in | kat, kati- | side |
| katiħ | kahtəyəg | curtain (from English) |
| kibwij | kibij (tr.) | to dig |
| kŭrol | kerawal | to return |
| maloħ | małeǧ | to drown |
| meloklok | mełaqłaq | forget |
| menoknok | menaqnaq | debris, litter |
| mŭjħal | ṁejgal | intestines |
| niknik | niknik | work hard |
| ħar | gad, gadi- | gums |
| okjak | wəkjak | capsize, fall, trip |
| rŭm | rəṁ | cave in; mud slide; crumble |
| tererein | tərəyrəyin | side, edge |
| tibbok | tibbaq | fall, trip |
| tibjek | tipjək | fall, trip |
| wŭkin bade | wekin bahdəy | stevedore; (working party) (from Engl.) |
| wutlok | wətlaq | fall down, drop |

## LESSON TWENTY-SEVEN

Animals;
more on directionals.

DIALOGUES

1.
A: Eamőn, elukun yokwe       Yeyameń yeliqqiwin yi'yaqey
   men in mour.                men yin mewir.

B: Mol, előH nejin bik        Mewel, yeleg najin piyik
   im bao.                     yim bahwew.

A: Koba ruo jibŭn bao         K&wbah riwew jibin bahwew
   in mejatoto.                yin mejatewtew.

B: Ebar wőr jilu nejin        Yebar wer jiliw najin kiwij
   kuuj kab juŏn kiru.         kab jiwen kidiw.

A: Jab meloklok dak kan       Jab me±aq±aq dak kań mey
   me elabtata an yokwi.       ye±aptahtah han yi'yaqiy.

A: Herman really loves animals.
B: That's right. He's got a lot of pigs and chickens.
A: Plus two birds.
B: He also has three cats and a dog.
A: Don't forget the ducks. He loves them most.

2.
A: Juŏn en nejŭ kiru.         Jiwen yeń najih kidiw.

B: Kwar bŭk ia?               Qehar bek yi'yah?

A: Baba ear bŭktok jen        Bahbah yehar bekteq jan
   Hawaii.                     Hawahyiy.

B: Kiru in belle ke?          Kidiw yin palley key?

A: Aet koman kilmej.          Hay&t, kewmahan kilmeyej.

B: Emman bwe ejeja en         Yemhan bey y&j&yjah yeń
   ekŏnaan nejnej kokŏrĦ.      yekeńhan najn&j kewkeray.

A: I have a dog.
B: Where did you get it?
A: Dad brought it down from Hawaii
B: An American dog?
A: Yes, a black male.
B: That's nice. Not many people like females as pets.

DRILLS

1.
A: Eamõn e yokwe men in mour.
Yeyaṁeñ yeyiyaqey men yin mewir.

B: Eamõn elukun yokwe men in mour.
Yeyaṁeñ yeliqqiwin yi'yaqey men yin mewir.

A: Eloḧ nejin bik im bao.
Yeleg najin piyik yim bahwew.

B: E lukun loḧ nejin bik im bao.
Yeliqqiwin leg najin piyik yim bahwew.

A: Kwo naḧinmij.
Qenahginm&j.

B: Kwo lukun naḧinmij.
Qeliqqiwin nahginm&j.

A: Re dreo.
Redeyew.

   I mõk.
Yiṁ&k

   E meletlet.
Yemaletlet.

   Ej kate ilo jikul.
Yej katey yilew jikiwił.

   Ear lab an naḧinmij.
Yehar łap han nahginm&j.

   E bwil rainin.
Yebil rahyinyin.

   I mõk in katak.
Yiṁ&k yin kahtak.

2. Eloḧ nejin bao.
Yeleg najin bahwew.
            kau                kahwiw
            biik               piyik
            kiru               kidiw
            dak                dak
            lolo               lawlaw
            kako               kahk&w
            kuj                kiwij
            kijidrik           kijdik
            koot               kewet
            jojo               j&wj&w

3. *(Substitute the pronouns indicated in the questions and be sure to make the pronouns of the response agree with those of the question.)*

A: Kwo meloklok iũ ke?
Qemełaqłaq y&h key?

B: Jab. Ij janin meloklok yok.
Jahab. Yij jahgin mełaqłaq y&q.
        e                     y&y
        ir                   y&r
        kim                 k&m
        ḧa                  gah

4. E bar wŏr juŏn aŏ piḣjel.  
   kijŏ jikka  
   nejŭ bik  
   jibŭ bao  
   waŏ wa  
   imŏ em  
   eneŏ ene  
   kŏtka ni  
   limŏ aspiriḣ  
   kona ek  
   kineŏ jaki  
   meja mej  
   kojŏ koj  

   Yebar wer jiwen hah&h pinjeł.  
   kij&h jikkah  
   najih piyik  
   jibih bahwew  
   wah&h wah  
   yiṁ&h y&ṁ  
   yan&y&h yan&y  
   ketkah niy  
   lim&h hajbiryin  
   qeṅah y&k  
   kiniy&h jakiy  
   mejah maj  
   kawj&h kawaj  

5. Kwar bŏk ia kiru en nejŭm?  
   penjīl...am  
   jikka....kijŏm  
   bao   (etc.)  
   wa  
   em  
   ene  
   ni  
   aspirin  
   jaki  
   mej  
   wŭt  

   Qehar bek yi'yah kidiw yeṅ najiṁ.  
   pinjeł...haṁ  
   jikkah...kijeṁ  
   bahwew  (etc.)  
   wah  
   y&ṁ  
   yan&y  
   niy  
   hajbiryin  
   jakiy  
   maj  
   wit  

6. Wŏn ekŏnan nejnij koman?  
   tutu iar  
   komat mŏḣŭ  
   iakiu  
   turoḣ  
   dri kaki  
   jerbal  
   katak kaamtŏ  

   Wen yekeṅhaṅ najn&j kewṁahan.  
   tiwtiw yiyhar  
   kemat ṁegay  
   yi'yakiyiw  
   tiwraǧ  
   rikakiy  
   jerbal  
   kahtak kahaṁteh  

7. Ear bŏktok juŏn aŏ jŏt.  
   Ear bŏklok juŏn an jŏt.  
   Ear bŏkwŏj juŏn am jŏt.  

   Yehar bekteq jiwen hah&h jehet.  
   Yehar bekłaq jiwen han jehet.  
   Yehar bekw&j jiwen haṁ jehet.  

*(Continue, substituting the other two directionals and the appropriate possessive:)*

```
letok                    leyteq
jilkintok                jilkinteq
buköttok                 piqetteq
wiaiktok                 wiyahyikteq
aenetok                  hayeneyteq
kwaltok                  qałteq
```

8. '*Move that table this way.*'

```
Kömakittok tebel ne.     Kemakitteq teybeł ney.
kömakitwöj               kemakitw&j
kömakitlok               kemakitłaq
iuntok                   yiwinteq
```
(*Substitute the other directionals, as above.*)
```
kebaktok                 keyepahakteq
wuraketok                wirahakeyteq
```

9. '*Laiben is going northward.*'

```
Laiben ej wäniHalok.     Łayipen yej waynigahłaq.
         wärö̈Halok                    wayr&gahłaq

         tarniHalok                   tarnigahłaq
         tarrö̈Halok                   tarr&gahłaq

         ettörniHalok                 tt&rnigahłaq
         ettörroHalok                 tt&rr&gahłaq

         malniHalok                   malnigahłaq
```
(*Continue, changing 'northward' to 'southward'.*)
```
         jorjorniHalok                jełjełnigahłaq
         ajäriknihalok                hajadiknigahłaq
```

(*The parts of the above words meaning 'northward' and 'southward' are Rälik forms; the Ratak equivalents and those for 'eastward' and 'westward' as practiced in the next drill are as follows:*)

```
         Rälik            Ratak
      waynigahłaq     waynigyagłaq     northward
      wayr&gahłaq     wayr&kyagłaq     southward
      yitahłaq        waytahłaq/
                      waytakłaq        eastward
      yit&właq        wayt&właq        westward
```

*Note the change of the root to* yi- *for Rälik 'eastward' and 'westward' (paralleling the dialectal pattern of* yiteq/wayteq*), and the optional substitution of* k *for* h *in the Ratak 'eastward'.*

10. *'Laiben is going eastward.'*

  Laiben ej italok.   Ḷayipen yej yitahḷaq.
      itolok         yit&wḷaq

      tartalok        tartahḷaq
      tartolok        tart&wḷaq

      ettörtalok       tt&rtahḷaq
      ettörtolok       tt&rt&wḷaq

  *(Continue, changing 'eastward' to 'westward'.)*

      maltalok        ṁaltahḷaq

      jorjortalok       jeŕjeŕtahḷaq

      ajäriktalok       hajadiktahḷaq

      kotalok        kewtahḷaq

  *(This and the following drills give Rälik forms. The Ratak equivalents can be derived from the information at the end of Drill 9.)*

11. *'Laiben is coming northward.'*

  Laiben ej wäniḧatak.  Ḷayipen yej waynigahtak.
      wäröḧatak       wayr&gahtak

      tarniḧatak       tarnigahtak
      tarröḧatak       tarr&gahtak

      ettörniḧatak      tt&rnigahtak

      malniḧatak       ṁalnigahtak

      jorjorniḧatak      jeŕjeŕnigahtak

      ajärikniḧatak      hajadiknigahtak

      koniḧatak       kewnigahtak

12. *'Laiben is coming eastward.'*

  Laiben ej itak.    Ḷayipen yej yitak.
      ito          yit&w
      tartak        tartak
      tarto         tart&w
      *(etc.)*         *(etc.)*

*(Note that in this drill the forms we might expect (\*yitahtak, \*yit&wtak, \*tartahtak, etc.) are shortened to those given above. Similarly, in the Ratak dialect, \*waytahtak becomes waytak, etc.)*

13. *'Laiben went away northward; he'll come (back) southward in a moment.'*

    Ewḁniḧalok Laiben,  
    mö̈ttan wö̈t jidrik  
    ewḁrö̈ḧatak.

    Yewaynigahłaq Ḻayipen,  
    ṁettan wet jidik  
    yewayr&gahtak.

    *(Continue, substituting tar, tt&r, ṁal, jeṙjeṙ, hajadik, and kew- in the above frame, and in the following one:)*

    *'Laiben went away eastward; he'll come (back) westward in a moment.'*

    Eitalok Laiben, mö̈ttan  
    wö̈t jidrik eito.

    Yeyitahłaq Ḻayipen, ṁettan  
    wet jidik yeyit&w.

14. *'Where did Laiben go?'*

    Ewaj jikit Laiben?  
      tar  
      ttö̈r  
      mal  
      jorjor  
      ajḁrik  
      ko  
      tö̈bal  
      wḁwe

    Yewa(j) j&k&t Ḻayipen?  
      tar  
      tt&r  
      ṁal  
      jeṙjeṙ  
      hajadik  
      kew  
      tebal  
      wayw&y

    *(Answer with appropriate statements from the preceding drills.)*

15. *'Where is Laiben going?'*

    *(Continue exactly as in Drill 14, but with the tense changed as indicated.)*

    A: Ej waj jikit Laiben?  
    B: Ej wḁniḧalok, mö̈ttan wet jidrik ewḁrö̈ḧatak.

        *(etc.)*

    Yej wa(j) jikit Ḻayipen?  
    Yej waynigahłaq, ṁettan jidik yewayr&gahtak.

        *(etc.)*

16. *(Practice the following, which can be added to the repertory of possible answers to the questions of Drills 14 and 15. Substitute other verbal roots from preceding lessons, and other directional combinations.)*

'*He went (is going) away northward; he'll come southward in your direction in a moment.*'

E(j) wŭniHalok, mŏttan      Ye(j) waynigahłaq, ṁettan
wŏt jīdrik ewŭrŏHawŏj.       wet jīdrik yewayr&gahw&j.

E(j) wŭniHawŏj, mŏttan      Ye(j) waynigahw&j, ṁettan
wŏt jīdrik ewŭrŏHatak.       wet jidik yewayr&gahtak.

(physically possible probably only by telephone.)

*(Ratak equivalents of the above would be:)*

E(j) wŭniHeaHlok, mŏttan    Ye(j) waynigyagłaq, ṁettan
wŏt jīdrik ewŭrŏkeaHwaj.    wet jidik yewayr&kyagwaj.

E(j) wŭniHeaHwaj, mŏttan    Ye(j) waynigyagwaj, ṁettan
wŏt jīdrik ewŭrŏkeaHtak.    wet jidik yewayr&kyagtak.

## GRAMMATICAL NOTES

1. The directionals <u>teq</u>, <u>łaq</u>, and <u>w&j/waj</u> were presented and discussed in Lesson 4, and have been met again in the lesson materials that followed. They form a set of three which can occupy certain post-verbal slots. With this lesson begins the presentation of *another set of directionals*, which occupy a different, preceding slot.

| Verbal Roots | DIRECTIONALS | |
|---|---|---|
|  | Slot I | Slot II |
| way- | -nigah-/-nigyag- | -teq(-tak) |
| tar- | -r&gah-/-r&kyag- | -łaq |
| tt&r- | -tah-/-tak- | -w&j/waj |
|  | -t&w- |  |
| (etc.) | (additional members of this set will be introduced in later lessons) | (a set consisting of only these three) |

Note that <u>teq</u> is replaced by <u>tak</u> when Slot I is occupied, but that this <u>tak</u> must be considered only as a homonym of (not identical with) the one in Slot I meaning 'eastward'. Note also the prohibition against the sequences -*tahtak, -*taktak and -*t&wtak referred to in Drill 12.

## SHORT PROSE SELECTIONS

1.                    Men in Mour
                 Men yin Mewir

Ilo   MajÜl,  kin an idrik ene    ko   ie      im  jabwe
Yilew Mahjeł, k&n han ddik yan&y kew yi'y&y yim jabwey

jikin men in  mour,  ejelok  men in  mour ellab.  EwÜr
jikin men yin mewir, yejjełaq men yin mewir łłap. Yewer

bik   im  bao,    ak  men kein ebbÜktok in dri belle
piyik yim bahwew, hak men k&yin bb&kteq yin ripalley

im  ejjab men in  mour  in  MajÜl.  Kar kijen dri MajÜl
yim yejjab men yin mewir yin Mahjeł. Kar kijen riMahjeł

wÜt ik Han jÜlele   im  Han Ün  ko  reaikuji    jen
wet y&k gan jal&yl&y yim gan h&n kew rehayiqijiy jan

kanniek.  Ekanuij   in   loH wÜwen    kÜmat im  keboj
kanniy&k. Yekahn&w&j yin leg wayw&y&n kemat yim kep&w&j

ik  Han mÜHÜ  im  jekdron  ewi ikutkut in  aer   mÜHÜ
y&k gan ṁegay yim jekdawan yewiy qqitqit yin hay&r ṁegay

ak  reban in  mÜk kake.
hak reban yin ṁ&k kahkey.

2.          Jikul ko ilo AiliH ko Ilikin
        Jikiwił kew yilew Hay&l&g kew Yilikin
                                    middle of
Jikul   ko   ilo    ailiH   ko   ilikin rej bed eolaban
Jikiwił kew yilew hay&l&g kew yilikin rej pad yewłapan
                    magistrate
jikin kwelok ko,  ijo  im  jonjo    ro  im alab  ro
jikin q&ylaq kew, yijew yim jewenjew rew yim hałap rew

rej jokwe    ie.      EkkÜ  aer  bed ijo  imÜn taktÜ
rej j&q&y yi'y&y.  Yekkay hay&r pad yijew yiṁen takteh

                  these houses       thatch
eo  ej  bed   ie.   MÜkein  kÜmman  jen  aj  im
yew yej pad yi'y&y. Mek&yin keṁṁan jan haj yim

              cement   gravel
iloair    ejab   jimeen   ak  lÜ.  Ran  kein  ewÜr
yilewwahy&r yejjab jimyeṁ hak łay. Rahan k&yin yewer

jet jikul kõmman in kien im ebo lok jirik lemḐir.
jet jikiwił keṁhan yin kiyen yim yep&właq jidik łemayy&r.
                                              better planned

Wõran dri jikul ilo jikul kein ekkḐ jen roḦoul
Weran rijikiwił yilew jikiwił k&yin yekkay jan r&g&wil
                                    class
Ḧan rualitõkḦoul       koba kilaj juõn Ḧan rualitõk.
gan riwahliyt&kg&wil, k&wbah kilhaj jiwen gan riwahliy-
     Elkin kilaj rualitõk      ro dri kaki ro  rej
t&k. Yalkin kilhaj riwahliyt&k, rew rikakiy rew rej
lemenak bwe remaroḦ etal Ḧan aer  jikul,   rej
łemḣak bey remareğ yetal gan hayey jikiwił, rej
 send                         well
jilkinlok ir Ḧan Majuro. Ro jet, ekwe, emwij aer
jilkinłaq y&r gan Majr&w. Rew jet, yeqey, y&ṁ&j hay&r
jikul.
jikiwił.

## PROVERB

  Kwojab inojeeklok jeni     Qejab yinewj&yikłaq janiy
  wa kein, ial in mour        wah k&yin, yiyał yin mewir
  ko kein.                        kew k&yin.

  'Don't drift away from these canoes, these
     are your passes to life.'
    'Don't take things for granted.'

## VOCABULARY

| | | |
|---|---|---|
| aen | hayen | iron, to iron |
| aj | haj | thatch |
| ajḐrik | hajadik | stroll |
| bolemḧn | pewłeman | well planned, well designed, perfect |
| bukottok | piqetteq | to look for and bring here |
| dak | dak | duck (from English) |
| dreo | deyaw | beautiful--woman only |
| ekkḐ | yekkay | usually, often |
| eolabḧn | yewłapan | in the middle of it |
| itak-/ita- | yitak-, yitah- | to go toward the east |
| iun | yiwin | to push |

| | | |
|---|---|---|
| jilkin-, -lok, -tok, -woj | jilkin- | send--it, her, him (with directional suffixes) |
| jojo | j&wj&w | chick |
| jonjo | jewenjew | magistrate (from Japanese) |
| jorjor | jeɫjeɫ | to walk fast and vigorously |
| kako | kahk&w | rooster |
| kebak | keyepahak | to move closer |
| kijidrik | kijdik | mouse, rat |
| kilaj | kilhaj | class |
| kiniŭ | kiniy&h, kiniye- | my mat |
| koj | kawaj | blanket |
| kojŭ | kawaj&h, kawaje- | my blanket |
| kŭmakit | kemhakit | to move |
| koman | kewmhahan | male |
| koot | kewet | goat (from English) |
| kuj | kiwij | cat |
| lŭ | ɫay | gravel |
| lolo | lawlaw | hen |
| mal- | mhal- | to lean toward (always used with directional suffix) |
| mejatoto | mejatewtew | air |
| nejnij | najn&j | to keep as a pet |
| tar | tar | to head (always used with a directional suffix) |
| tŭbal | tebal | to crawl |
| wŭ | way- | to proceed (always used with a directional suffix) |
| wŭwe | wayw&y | to go toward (used with directional suffix) |
| wurake | wirahkey | to move it |

## LESSON TWENTY-EIGHT

Drinking and eating; washing;
common questions; personal names;
ñah; more Slot I directionals.

### DIALOGUES

1.
A: I kwɵle.　　　　　　　　　Yiq&l&y.

B: Bar ña. Kejro ilen　　　Bar gah. K&jrew yilan
　 mɵñʉ.　　　　　　　　　　ñegay.

A: Ewɵr bik im mʉ imwen　　Yewer piyik yim may yiñeyeñ
　 imɵ. Jero naj idrak　　yiñ&h. Jerew nahaj yida-
　 ni.　　　　　　　　　　　　hak niy.

B: Ekwe kejro kaiur.　　　Yeqey k&jrew yetal.

A: Kwo mat ke?　　　　　　Qemat key?

B: I lukun mat, jej amwin　Yiɬiqqiwin mat, jej hañin
　 ia?　　　　　　　　　　　　yi'yah?

A: Ewɵr dren in amwin na-　Yewer dannin hañin nab&j,
　 bij, turin kejam en.　　tiɬin kejam yeñ.

B: Ko kanuij in emol.　　Qekahn&w&j yin ñuñewel.

A: I'm hungry.
B: Me too. Let's go eat.
A: There's some pork and some breadfruit at my house.
　 We'll drink coconut (juice).
B: Let's hurry.
A: Are you full?
B: I really am full. Where do we wash our hands?
A: There's water outside by the door.
B: Thanks.

2.
A: Enno ke mɵñʉ imwɵn　　Yennaw key ñegay yiñen
　 jikul kan?　　　　　　　　jikiwiɬ kañ?

B: Ebwe, ak awa in mɵñʉ　　Yebey, hak hawah yin
　 kan renana.　　　　　　　ñegay kañ renahnah.

A: Bwe?　　　　　　　　　　Bey?

274

B: Kimij mōḩḁ in jibboḩ           K&mij ṁegay yin jibb&g
   ilo jiljino awa                  yilew jiljinew hawah
   jimettan, lak mōḩḁ in            jimettan, łak ṁegay yin
   raeleb, joḩoul-ruo               rahyelep, jegewil-riwew
   awa jimettan.                    hawah jimettan.
A: Ak mōḩḁ in jota?                Hak ṁegay yin j&wtah?
B: Lalim awa. Emen im              Ḃal&m hawah. Yeman yim
   jimettan awa jen ien             jimettan hawah jan 'yiyen
   mōḩḁ in raeleb.                  ṁegay yin rahyelep.
A: Etke komij jab jṷnij            Yetkey q&ṁij jab janijiy
   i awa kan?                       hawah kań?
B: Kim ar kajjioḩ, ak              K&m har kajjiyeg̣, hak
   ejaḩin wōr tōbrak.               yejjahgin wer teprak.

A: Is the food at the school good?
B: Yes, but the meal times are bad.
A: Why?
B: We eat breakfast at 6:30 and lunch at 12:30.
A: How about dinner?
B: Five. Four and a half hours after lunch.
A: Why don't you change the time?
B: We tried but there have been no results.

DRILLS
1. *'When are you going to wash your hands?'*

   Kwonaj amwin ḩṷḁt?        Qenahaj haṁin gayat?
          kwalkwol                   qałq&ł
          ormij                      w&rm&j
          tutu                       tiwtiw
          karreo                     karr&y&w
          jokiiḩ                     jewkiyig
          biraj                      biraj
          rukruk                     riqriq
          kurkur                     kił̇kił̇
          namnam                     naṁnaṁ
          mukmuk                     ṁiqṁiq
          reja                       reyjah

2. *'There is some pork at my house.'*

   Ewōr bik imwen imō.        Yewer piyik yiṁeyeń yiṁ&h.
        bao                           bahwew
        ik                            y&k
        bwiro                         biyr&w
        kwanjin                       qanjin

          jenkun                      jayanqin
          raij                        rahyij
          jekkob                      jeqqep
          bʉb                         beb
          ni                          niy

3. *Are you full?*        *Yes, I'm really full.*
A: Kwo mat ke?                Qemat key?
B: Aet, ilukkun mat.          Hay&t, yiɫiqqiwin mat.
          maro                        mar&w
          kwole                       q&l&y
          ɖɧden                       yagden
          batur                       batiɫ
          aɧir                        hagir
          aɧaaɧe                      haghagey

4. *Mwejen craves chicken meat.*
     Elab an Mwejen ijol      Yeɫap han Ḿeyjen yijeɫ
          bao.                        bahwew.
          bwiro                       biyr&w
          kau                         kahwiw
          bʉb                         beb
          ieraj                       yi'yeraj
          ma                          may
          binana                      pinahnah
          ik                          y&k
          iu                          yiw
          baru                        bariw

5. *These foods are delicious.*
     Enno wʉt kein mʉɧɥ.      Yennaw wet k&yin ḿegay.
          etʉɧal                      tegal
          ekiriji                     kiryijiy
          edrendren                   dandan
          ebil                        bil
          emʉlu                       ḿ&ɫ&w
          ebin                        p&n
          ebidodo                     pid&wd&w
          ekʉmatmat                   kematmat
          ekʉjamjam                   kejaḿjaḿ
          emattia                     mattiyyah
          emattie                     mattiyy&y

6. *Is the food at school delicious?*
     Enno ke mʉɧɥ imʉn jikul       Yennaw key ḿegay yiḿen
          kan?                           jikiwiɫ kaɧ?

|  |  |
|---|---|
| ebin ke katak | yəpən key kahtak |
| elap ke katak | yełap key kahtak |
| elɵñ ke drijikul | yeleg key rijikiwił |
| eor ke kobe | yewer key kawpəy |
| emeram ke teñki | yemeram key teyegkiy |
| ebiroro ke katak | yepidəwdəw key kahtak |
| ebil ke loan | yebil key lewwahan |
| emolu ke loan | yəṁəłəw key lewwahan |

7. Some questions. *(Use English cues.)*

| | | |
|---|---|---|
| Bwe? | Why? | Bey? |
| Etke? | Why? | Yetkey? |
| Taunin? | What's the reason? | Tahwinin? |
| Bwe et? | So that what? | Bey yət? |
| Ebaj et? | What's the matter? | Yebaj yət? |
| Bwe eake? | Why do you ask? | Bey yahkey |
| En ta? | Why do you ask? | Yen tah? |
| Ta rot? | What for? | Tah łet? |
| Kein ta? | What's that for? | Kəyin tah? |
| Men ta? | Which thing? | Men tah? |
| Waj jikɵt? | Where to? | Wajjikət? |
| Tu ia? | Where exactly? | Tiw yi'yah? |

8. *'Translate your book.'*

| | |
|---|---|
| Kwɵn ukot buk ne am. | Qen <u>wiket</u> bəq ñey hañ. |
| <u>jɐniji</u> | <u>janijiy</u> |
| ikir | yikir |
| lale | lahley |
| kɵmanmanlok | keṁanṁanłaq |
| riti | riyitiy |
| kakɵleik | kakełłeyik |
| kejbarok | kejpareq |

9. *'We tried but haven't succeeded yet.'*

| | |
|---|---|
| Kim ar kajjioñ ak eja-ñin wɵr <u>tɵbrak</u>. | Kəm har kajjiyeğ hak yejjah-gin wer <u>teprak</u>. |
| oktak | wəqtak |
| irilok | yirlaq |
| jɐnij | janij |
| aineman | hayənəṁṁhan |
| melele | mełeyłey |
| walok | wahłaq |
| uak | wiwahak |
| alikkar | halikkar |

10. *'They named the boy Jori.'*
    (*Practice these names with and without the prefixes.*)

    T: Jori
    A: Rar na etan ladrik eo Jori.
    B: Rar na etan ladrik eo Lṳjori.

    Jewdiy
    Rehar ñah yetan ladik yew Jewdiy.
    Rehar ñah yetan ladik yew Lejewdiy.

    T: Mithen
    A: Rar na etan ladrik eo Mithen.
    B: Rar na etan ladrik eo Lamithen.

    Miyten
    Rehar ñah yetan ladik yew Miyten.
    Rehar ñah yetan ladik yew Lamiyten.

    T: Anwoj
       Katnar
       Jṳbro
       Rena
       Beia

    Hanwej (la-)
    Ketnar
    Jebraw
    Reynah
    Peyiyah

    (*Prefix is pronounced* le- *unless otherwise indicated.*)

11. *'They named the girl Almi.'*

    T: Almi
    A: Rar na etan ledrik eo Almi.
    B: Rar na etan ledrik eo Laalmi.

    Halmiy
    Rehar ñah yetan ledik yew Halimiy.
    Rehar ñah yetan ledik yew Lahalimiy.

    T: Tiblok
    A: Rar na etan ledrik eo Tiblok.
    B: Rar na etan ledrik eo Litiblok.

    Tiblaq
    Rehar ñah yetan ledik yew Tiblaq.
    Rehar ñah yetan ledik yew Litiblaq.

    T: Tokkwi
       Betra
       Ajenet
       Mina
       Witen
       Joubon
       Niba

    Teqqiy
    Peyetrah
    Hajenet (la-)
    Minah
    Wiytayan
    Jewiben
    Niybah

    (*Prefix is pronounced* li- *unless otherwise indicated.*)

12. *'Make room for that boy.'*

    Kwṳn kab <u>na</u> jikin ladrik ne.
          na mweien

    Qen kab <u>ñah</u> jikin ladik ñey.
          ñah ṁeyiyen

```
           na kinien              ñah kiniyen
           na biten               ñah piten
           na etan                ñah yetan
           na ballin              ñah ballin
           na kojen               ñah kawajen
           na kijen               ñah kijen
           na limen               ñah limen
```

13. *'Laiben went towards the ocean side; he'll come (back) to the lagoon side in a moment.'*

    (speaker and addressee(s) both near lagoon side of island)

    Laiben ewanliklok, mŭttan wŭt jidrik ewanartak.   Layipen yewanlikłaq, ṁettan wet jidik yewanhartak.

    ```
              tar                     tar
              ttŭr                    tt&r
              ko                      kew
              bul                     biwił
              jorjor                  jełjeł
              ajŭrik                  hajadik
              kkaiuriur               kkayiłyił
              tŭbal                   tebal
              ju                      jiw
    ```

    (Use the above cues with each of the following:)

14. *'Laiben went towards the ocean side; he'll come towards the lagoon beach to you in a moment.'*

    Laiben ewanliklok, mŭttan wŭt jidrik ewanarwŭj.    Layipen yewanlikłaq, ṁettan wet jidik yewanharw&j.

15. *'Laiben went towards the interior of the island; he'll come (back) to the lagoon side in a moment.'*

    (speaker and addressee(s) both near lagoon side of island)

    Laiben ewŭnojlok, mŭttan wŭt jidrik ewanartak.    Ƚayipen yewenwejłaq, ṁettan wet jidik yewanhartak.

16. *'Laiben went towards the lagoon side; he'll come towards the ocean side in a moment.'*

    (speaker and addressee(s) both in interior or near ocean side)

        Laiben ewanarlok,            Ḷayipen yewanharḷaq,
          mȫttan wōt jidrik            ṁettan wet jidik
          ewan̲liktak.                  yewan̲liktak.

17. *'The canoe went out toward the ocean; it'll come
    (back) toward the island soon.'*

        Wa eo ewanmetolok,           Wah yew yewanmetewḷaq,
          mȫttan wōt jidrik            ṁettan wet jidik
          ewanenetak.                  yewanyan&ytak.
          tar                          tar
          jejjej                       jajjaj
          tȫbtȫb                       tebteb
          be                           pey
          jerak                        jerak
          ttȫr                         tt&r
          bukarar                      biqaharhar
          le injin                     ley yinjin
          le wȫjlä                     ley w&jḷay

18. *'Laiben went up to the top of the mountain; he'll
    come down in a little while.'*

    (Learn each of the following well; then use the
    underlined words as cues.)

        Laiben ewanliḦlok Ḧan        Ḷayipen y̭ewanl&gḷaq gan
          ran tol en, mȫttan           rahan tel yeṅ, ṁettan
          wōt jidrik ewanlȫltak.       wet jidik yewanlaḷtak.

        Laiben euweliḦlok Ḧan        Ḷayipen yewiw&yl&gḷaq
          ran tima en, mȫttan          gan rahan tiyṁah yeṅ,
          wōt jidrik etolȫltak.        ṁettan wet jidik
                                       y&t&wlaḷtak.

        Bao eo ekeliḦlok Ḧan         Bahwew yew yekayl&gḷaq gan
          ran mä en, mȫttan wōt        rahan may yeṅ, ṁettan wet
          jidrik ekelȫltak.            jidik yekaylaḷtak.

        Ladrik eo etalliḦliḦlok      Ḷadik yew yetall&gl&gḷaq
          Ḧan ran ni en, mȫttan        gan rahan niy yeṅ, ṁettan
          wōt jidrik etolȫltak.        wet jidik y&t&wlaḷtak.

19. A classroom exercise in directionals, requiring two
    sitting mats.

    (A is standing, B is seated on a mat on the ground.)

    A: Kwȫn jutak mȫk lȫḦtak.      Qen jiwtak ṁek l&gtak.

    (while in the act of getting up, B says:)

    B: Ij jutak lȫḦwȫj.             Yij jiwtak l&gw&j.

*(when on his feet, B says:)*

B: Emwij aṇ jutak lōḥtak.  Y&ṁ&j hah&h jiwtak l&gtak.
A: Emwij am jutak lōḥtak.  Y&ṁ&j haṁ jiwtak l&gtak.
   Kiṇ kwōn bar jijōt mōk  Kiyyeh qen bar jiyjet ṁek
   lōllok.                 laḷḷaq.

*(while in the act of being seated, B says:)*

B: Ij jijōt lōllok.  Yij jiyjet laḷḷaq.

*(when seated, A says:)*

A: Emwij aṇ jijōt lōltak.  Y&ṁ&j hah&h jiyjet laltak.
B: Emwij am jijōt lōltak.  Y&ṁ&j haṁ jiyjet laltak.
   Kiṇ kwōn bar jutak      Kiyyeh qen bar jiwtak
   mōk lōḥlok.             ṁek l&gḷaq.

*(while in the act of getting up, A says:)*

A: Ij jutak lōḥlok.  Yij jiwtak l&gḷaq.

*(when on his feet, A says:)*

A: Emwij aṇ jutak lōḥtak.  Y&ṁ&j hah&h jiwtak l&gtak.
B: Emwij am jutak lōḥlok.  Y&ṁ&j haṁ jiwtak l&gḷaq.

*(Now repeat, trading roles.)*

20. Another classroom exercise in directionals using the same format as Drill 19.

    *(A is standing at the front of the classroom, B near the back.)*

    A: Kwōn wōnmantak mōk.       Qen wenṁahantak ṁek.
    B: Ij wōnmanwōj.             Yij wenṁahanw&j.
    B: Emwij aṇ wōnmantak.       Y&ṁ&j hah&h wenṁahantak.
    A: Emwij am wōnmantak.       Y&ṁ&j haṁ wenṁahantak.
       Kiṇ kwōn bar wōnliklok.   Kiyyeh qen bar wenlikḷaq.
    B: Ij wōnliklok.             Yij wenlikḷaq.
    B: Emwij aṇ wonliktak.       Y&ṁ&j hah&h wenliktak.
    A: Emwij am wōnliklok.       Y&ṁ&j haṁ wenlikḷaq.
    B: Kwōn wōnliktak mōk.       Qen wenliktak ṁek.
    A: Ij wōnlikwōj.             Yij wenlikw&j.
    A: Emwij aṇ wōnliktak.       Y&ṁ&j hah&h wenliktak.

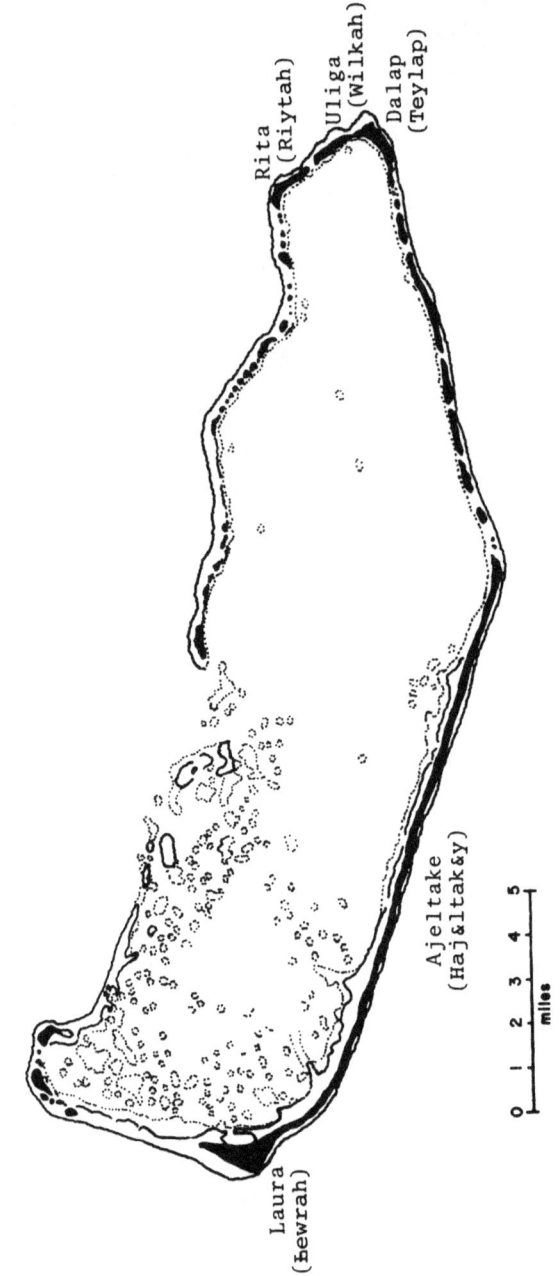

Majuro (Majr&w) Atoll

Note: The original names of the islets of Laura and Rita are Majuro (Majr&w) and Jarej (Jarej), respectively.

B: Emwij am wŏnliktak.  Y&ṁ&j haṁ wenliktak.
   Kiŭ kwŏn bar wŏn-  Kiyyeh qen bar wen-
   manlok.  ṁahanɫaq.

A: Ij wŏnmanlok.  Yij wenṁahanɫaq.

A: Emwij aŭ wŏnmantak.  Y&ṁ&j hah&h wenṁahantak.

B: Emwij am wŏnmanlok.  Y&ṁ&j haṁ wenṁahanɫaq.

(Now repeat, trading roles.)

21. (Establish an imaginary islet in the classroom, designating the oceanside, the interior and the lagoon side. Perform drills parallel to 19 and 20, with A and B positioned at various of the three locations.)

22. (Similarly, establish a map of Majuro Atoll on the classroom floor, showing the following five points along north-south and east-west axes:

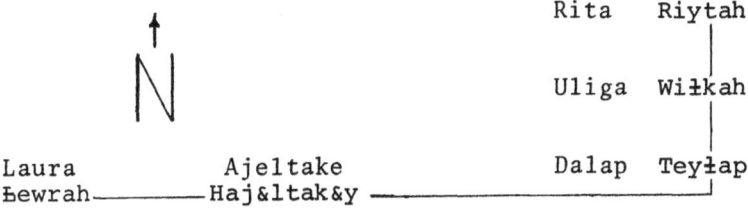

Perform drills parallel to those of Drills 19, 20 and 21, using the north-south and east-west directionals, and using various verb stems, including those for going (<u>yi-</u>, <u>way-</u>), running (<u>tt&r</u>), and driving or riding on a vehicle (<u>tar</u>).)

23. (Use an imaginary or model airplane, and have speakers stand near the east-west runway of the Dalap airstrip and discuss the arrivals and departures of the plane.)

A: Balun eo en ej ketak.  Baɫwin yew yeṅ yej kaytak.

B: Balun en enaj jok  Baɫwin yeṅ yenahaj jeq
   jikŭt?  j&k&t.

A: Bwe kŭto in eitok  Bey k&t&w yin yeyiteq
   ia?  yi'yah?

B: Eitok rear.  Yeyiteq r&yyahar.

A: Ekwe, balun en enaj　　　Yeqey, bałwin yeñ yenahaj
　　joktak.　　　　　　　　　　 jeqtak.

　　　*　*　*　*　　　　　　　　　*　*　*　*

A: Bwe kὃto in eitok　　　　Bey k&t&w yin yeyiteq
　　ia?　　　　　　　　　　　　 yi'yah?
B: Eitok rilik.　　　　　　　Yeyiteq riylik.
A: Ekwe, balun en enaj　　　Yeqey, bałwin yeñ yenahaj
　　jokto.　　　　　　　　　　 jeqt&w.

　　　*　*　*　*　　　　　　　　　*　*　*　*

A: Balun eo en ej keto.　　 Bałwin yew yeñ yej kayt&w.

　　　*　*　*　*　　　　　　　　　*　*　*　*

A: Balun eo en ebojak　　　 Bałwin yew yeñ yepewjak
　　in kelok.　　　　　　　　 yin kayłaq.
B: Balun en enaj kelok　　　Bałwin yeñ yenahaj kayłaq
　　jikὃt?　　　　　　　　　　 j&k&t?
A: Bwe kὃto in eitok　　　　Bey k&t&w yin yeyiteq
　　ia?　　　　　　　　　　　　 yi'yah?

　　　*　*　*　*　　　　　　　　　*　*　*　*

A: Ekwe, balun en enaj　　　Yeqey, bałwin yeñ yenahaj
　　ketaklok.　　　　　　　　　kaytakłaq.

　　　*　*　*　*　　　　　　　　　*　*　*　*

A: Ekwe, balun en enaj　　　Yeqey, bałwin yeñ yenahaj
　　ketolok.　　　　　　　　　 kayt&właq.

## GRAMMATICAL NOTES

1. Most Marshallese personal names may be used with or without the personal name prefixes, although there are a few that never occur without them.

The vowel of the male prefix is determined by the first vowel of the name:

| Prefix | First vowel | Example |
|---|---|---|
| ḷa- | i<br>initial a | ḷayinah<br>ḷahaḷiy |
| ḷa- or ḷe- | a | ḷatawam̧<br>ḷetawam̧ |
| ḷe- | e | ḷejebraw |
| ḷe̦- | e̦ | ḷe̦te̦we̦jiye̦w |

The vowel of the female prefix is i: (li-) except before names with initial h, where it is a; see the examples in Drill 11.

The situations in which the prefixes are used and the connotations of using them are not easy to define with a simple rule of thumb, but the following guides may be of some use:

Young children use them commonly.
Parents use them with children.
Children use them with parents.
Spouses use them with each other.
Men use them with non-taboo females.
Women use them with each other unless a taboo
 relationship is involved.
Women use them with non-taboo men.

Men do not use them with male taboo relatives.
Men do not use them with each other unless they
 are especially close friends.
No one uses them on formal occasions.

In short, they are marks of close, intimate, informal, and friendly relationships. Although it may be safest not to use them at all at first, their skillful use can be an asset at winning friends and influencing people Marshallese style.

2. Additional Slot I directionals introduced in this lesson include:

| | |
|---|---|
| -lik- | toward the ocean side of the islet |
| -har- | toward the lagoon side of the islet |
| -wej- | toward the interior of the islet (from the lagoon side only) |
| -metew- | toward the deep sea |
| -yan&y- | toward land |

    -l&g-      upward
    -laɫ-      downward
    -m̈ahan-    forward, toward the front
    -lik-      backward, toward the back

Note that -lik- is the opposite of both -har- and -m̈ahan-.

These, together with those presented in Lesson 27, complete the set of Slot I directionals.

SHORT PROSE SELECTIONS

1.    Abaḧ an Ial im Ratio in
     Hapag han Yiyaɫ yim Reytiy&w yin
             Konono ilo Majŭl
           Kenewnew yilew M̈ahjeɫ

Kin an jabwe wa im kein konono ilo ailiḧ in
K&n han jabey wah yim k&yin kenewnew yilew hay&l&g yin

Majŭl, jet ien ej wŭr Ḧita ilo ailiḧ ko
M̈ahjeɫ, jet 'yiyen yej wer gitah yilew hay&l&g kew

ilikin ak ejelok ejelẅ kake mae ien ej
yilikin hak yejjeɫaq yejeɫay kahkey m̈ahyey 'yiyen yej

etal wa ko Ḧani. Einwŭt ad kar ba mokta bwe
yetal wah kew ganiy. Yayinwet had kar bah m̈eqtah bey

dri Majŭl rainin elab wŭt aer lemnak kin mŭḦẅ in
riM̈ahjeɫ rahyinyin yeɫap wet hay&r ɫemn̈ak k&n m̈egay yin

belle einwŭt raij, bilawẅ, juka im men ko
palley yayinwet rahyij, pilahway, jiqah yim men kew

jet. Kin men in elab an wa lab tokjen Ḧan
jet. K&n men yin yeɫap han wah ɫap teqjan gan

dri Majŭl.
riM̈ahjeɫ.

ElaḦe enaj wŭr ratio in konono ilo
Yeɫaggey yenahaj wer reytiy&w yin kenewnew yilew

aolep ailiḧ, enaj kanuij in jibaḦ aolep
hawelep hay&l&g, yenahaj kahn&w&j yin jipag hawelep

ailiḧ ko ilikin. Men in ej juŭn ian         men
hay&l&g kew yilikin. Men yin yej jiwen yi'yahan men

                          give attention to
ko jej tŭmak bwe kien enaj   lolorjake         ilo
kew jej temak bey kiyen yenahaj l&wl&w&rjahakey yilew

alliH kein rej itok.
hall&g k&yin rej yiteq.

ElaHe ewŭr ratio in konono ilo aolep
Yełaggey yewer reytiy&w yin kenewnew yilew hawelep

ailiH in Majŭl, dri naHinmij reban aikuj in mij
hay&l&g yin Mahjeł, rinahginm&j reban hayiqij yin m&j

kin an ejelok taktŭ ak uno, im bareinwŭt jibaH
k&n han jjełaq takteh hak winew, yim barayinwet jipag

bŭbrae jen an walok Hita.
bebrahyey jan han wahłaq gitah.

2. Ratio
    Reytiy&w

Mŭttan men ko kien ear biktok Han dri Majŭl ej
Mettan men kew kiyen yehar bikteq gan riMahjeł yej

ratio. Kiŭ armij in ailiH ko ilikin rejjab
reytiy&w. Kiyyeh harm&j yin hay&l&g kew yilikin rejjab

    wait    find our news
aikuj in kŭttar wa bwe ren eoroH enaan. Ne
hayiqij yin kettar wah bey ren yawreğ nnahan. Gey

 typhoon  disaster
ewŭr taibun im jorren ko rellab, remaroH in
yewer tahyibiwin yim jełłayan kew rełłab, remareğ yin

    listen
jelŭ kake jen aer roHjake ratio. Bar juŭn
jełay kahkey jan hay&r reğjakey reytiy&w. Bar jiwen

     to make easier
men ratio emwij an kabidodolok Han dri Majŭl, ej
men reytiy&w y&m&j han kapid&wd&właq gan riMahjeł, yej

kijien al ko aer. Mokta ear kanuij bin an
kijjiyen hal kew hay&r. Meqtah yehar kahn&w&j p&n han

 famous  few
juŭn al buHbuH kin an iiet armij en ej roH.
jiwen hal biğbiğ k&n han 'yiy&t harm&j yeń yej reğ.

      played
Kiŭ aoleb al jen aoleb ailiH rej jaH ilo
Kiyyeh hawelep hal jan hawelep hay&l&g rej jaq yilew

air
mejatoto im armij remaroH in kŭlet ko rekŭnaan,
mejatewtew yim harm&j remareğ yin kaylet kew rekeńhan,

ko remman, ak ko renana.   Ratio ej juōn jibaĦ
kew reṁṁan, hak kew renahnah.   Reytiy&w yej jiwen yipag
elab.
yełap.

## PROVERBS

1. Wan kōjōban kij, wan      Wahan kejeban k&j, wahan
   kokkure kij.                kaqqirey k&j.
   'The same canoes that sustain us can also be
       the cause of our destruction.'

2. Rumij im lo leen.         Ŕiṁij yim lew leyen.
   'Be late and face the consequences.'
   'The early bird gets the worm.'

## VOCABULARY

| | | |
|---|---|---|
| abaĦ | hapag | inconvenience, barrier, hindrance |
| aĦaaĦe | haghagey | to be hungry to the point at which one feels weak and shaky |
| ūĦden | yagden | starved |
| aĦir | hagir | to crave cigarettes |
| batur | batił | to crave fish |
| biraj | biraj | brush (from English) |
| bukarar | biqaharhar | foam created by a vessel (at both bow and stern) |
| ebajet | yebajy&t | why? what's the matter with...? |
| ekiriji | yekiryijiy | greasy (distributive of <u>kiryij</u>) |
| ekōjamjam | yekejaṁjaṁ | it causes desire |
| ekōmatmat | yekematmat | it makes one's stomach full |
| iep | yiyep | basket |
| ikir | yikir | change |
| jejjej | jajjaj | to skim across the surface of the water |
| jokiĦ | jewkiyig | scrub |
| joone | jeweney (tr.) jewjew (intr.) | soak it |
| jukjuki | jiqjiqiy (tr.) | pound it |
| kakili | kakiliy | peel it |
| kalle | kalley | bear fruit; to punish |

| | | |
|---|---|---|
| kallib | kallib | buried, planted |
| kalbini | kalbiniy | bury it, plant it |
| kőborike | kebawrikey | wrap it |
| kőjem | kejam | door, doorway |
| kőtan | ketahan, ketaha- | between, dividing line |
| kurkur | qirqir | brush one's teeth |
| lojet | lawj&t | ocean |
| mukmuk | ṁiqṁiq | to rinse clothes |
| nabij | nab&j | outside |
| na biten | ṅah-piten | provide a pillow for |
| na etan | ṅah-yetan | to name |
| na jikin | ṅah-jikin | to make a room for |
| na kijen | ṅah-kijen | to provide food for |
| na kinien | ṅah-kiniyen | to provide a mat for |
| na limen | ṅah-limen | to provide drink for |
| na mweien | ṅah-ṁeyiyen | to enrish, give gifts to |
| namnam | naṁnaṁ | to wash bottles |
| Ḣita | gitah | famine |
| oktak | w&ktak | change, turn around |
| ormij | w&rm&j | to wash one's face |
| rukruk | riqriq | brush teeth, gargle |
| ta unin | tahwinyin | why?, what's the reason? |
| tőbtőb | tebteb | to run |

## LESSON TWENTY-NINE

Fishing; review of directionals;
some miscellaneous patterns.

### DIALOGUES

1.
A: Ewȫr ke am madre?  Yewer key haṁ ṁad&y?
B: Ejelok aȭ madre. N̈an ta?  Yejjełaq hah&h ṁad&y. Gan tah?
A: I kȭnan eḦwȫr.  Yikeṅhan yaǧed.
B: Ewȫr an Ejbi.  Yewer han Yejpiy.
A: Kommol. I naj ilen kajjitȭk iben.  Keṁṁewel, yinahaj yilan kajjit&k yippan.

A: Do you have a spear?
B: No. I don't have a spear. What for?
A: I want to go fishing.
B: Ejbi has one.
A: Thank you. I'll ask S.P.

2.
A: Ewȫr ke am madre?  Yewer key haṁ ṁad&y?
B: Ejelok. Bwe kwȭj ilen eḦwȫr ke?  Yejjełaq. Bey qej yilan yaǧed key?
A: Ij baj lale wȭt. N̈e emen i ilem turoḦ?  Yij baj lahley wet. Gey yemen yiyilam tiwraǧ?
B: Elab an bȭt Ḧan turoḦ. Kejro ilen kokweet.  Yełap haṅ payat gan tiwraǧ. K&jrew yilan kaq&y&t.
A: Ekwe, ak emmanlok Ḧe kejro bȭk wȭt juȭn madre in turoḦ.  Yeqey, hak yeṁṁanłaq gey k&jrew bek wet jiwen ṁad&y yin tiwraǧ.
B: Eokwe kȭttar bwe in ilẹn kajitȭk madre en an Ejbi.  Yeqey kettar bey yin yilan kajjit&k ṁad&y yeṅ han Yejpiy.

A: Do you have a spear?
B: No, I don't. Why, are you going fishing?
A: I'm thinking of going spear-fishing?

290

B: The tide's too low for spear-fishing. Let's go
   octopus hunting.
A: OK. But it'll still be a good idea to take a
   spear along.
B: Wait, I'll borrow S.P.'s.

DRILLS

1. *'Do you need a spear?'*

   Kwôj aikuj ke am           Qej hayiqij key haṁ
   madre?                     ṁad&y?
   ok                         w&k
   mejen turoḧ                mejan tiwraǧ
   bü                         bay
   küüj                       kayaj
   eo                         yew
   ok aitok                   w&k hayiteq
   ok kadkad                  w&k kadkad
   mwieo                      ṁiyew
   emmar                      ṁṁar
   roba in turoḧ              ɫebah yin tiwraǧ
   teiḧki in turoḧ            teyegkiy yin tiwraǧ

2. *'Let's go fishing instead of doing nothing.'*

   Jen ilen eḧwôr im jab      Jen yilan yaǧed yim jab
   ber wan.                   pad wahan.
           turoḧ                      tiwraǧ
           jabuk                      jabiq
           ok kadkad                  w&k kadkad
           alele                      haɫeyɫey
           ok aitok                   w&k hayiteq
           wurôk                      wir&k
           rube om                    ɫip&y w&ṁ
           eo lal                     yew laɫ
           eojojo                     yew jewjew
           kobabe                     kebayb&y
           latibün                    ɫatippan
           eojaak                     yewejjahak
           juunboḧ                    jiwinb&ǧ
           bobu                       bawb&w
           kabwil                     kabil
           ilarak                     yilahrak

3. Practice with the negative prefix.

   E ike.                     Yeyikey.
   E jaike.                   Yejayikey.
   E kik.                     Yekkik.

| | |
|---|---|
| E jakkik. | Yejakkik. |
| E konkon. | Yeqeṅqeṅ. |
| E jakonkon. | Yejaqeṅqeṅ. |
| E oda. | Yewedah. |
| E joda. | Yejewedah. |
| E möṅa. | Yeṁegay. |
| E jamöṅa. | Yejaṁegay. |
| E bakij. | Yepakij. |
| E jabakij. | Yejappakij. |
| E wälel. | Yewaylɛl. |
| E jowälel. | Yejewaylɛl. |

4. Tides, waves, and water.

| | |
|---|---|
| E bäät. | Yepayat. |
| E ibwij. | Yeyibij. |
| E idrik. | Yeyidik. |
| E eielab. | Yeyiyełap. |
| E bät mönaknak. | Yepayat ṁeṅakṅak. |
| E ibwij lebleb. | Yeyibij leplep. |
| E bäät lok. | Yepayat łaq. |
| E ibwij tok. | Yeyibij teq. |
| E buṅ no. | Yebig̈ ṅew. |
| E jej no. | Yɛjɛj ṅew. |
| E lim. | Yelim. |
| E jok. | Yejeq. |
| E mwilal. | Yeṁilał. |
| E bijbij. | Yɛpɛjpɛj. |

5. Conditionals--future and past contrary-to-fact.
   *'If the weather is good, we two can go fishing.'*
   *'If the weather had been good, we two could have gone fishing.'*

| | |
|---|---|
| Ne emman laṅ kejro maroṅ eṅwör. | Gey yeṁṁan lag kɛjrew mareg̈ yag̈ed. |
| Ne ear emman laṅ kejro maroṅ kar eṅwör. | Gey yehar ṁṁan lag kɛjrew mareg̈ kar yag̈ed. |

(The <u>har</u> in the first clause immediately above is
Rälik usage; Ratak would be <u>kar</u>.)

| | |
|---|---|
| Ne enana laṅ kejro ban eṅwör. | Gey yenahnah lag kɛjrew ban yag̈ed. |
| Ne ear nana laṅ kejro ban kar eṅwör. | Gey yehar nahnah lag kɛjrew ban kar yag̈ed. |

Ne eibwij, enaj emman
   Ḧan tutu iar.
Ne ear ibwij, enaj
   kar emman Ḧan tutu
   iar.
Ne ebät lok jidik,
   enaj ekkar Ḧan ok
   kadkad.
Ne ebuḦ no, enaj
   nana Ḧan ok aitok.
Ne elim, enaj jekkar
   Ḧan turoḦ.
Ne elab keto, enaj
   bin am latiben.
Ne kwojab anan, enaj
   jakkik ijen jikin am
   eḦwör.
Ne kwo eḦwör in boḦ,
   kwonaj aikuj teiḦki.
Ne elur, enaj lae
   lojet.

Gey yeyibij, yenahaj ṁhan
   gan tiwtiw yiyhar.
Gey yehar yibij, yenahaj
   kar ṁhan gan tiwtiw yiyhar.
Gey yepayat łaq jidik,
   yenahaj kkar gan w&k
   kadkad.
Gey yebiǧ ṅew, yenahaj
   nahnah gan w&k hayiteq.
Gey yeliṁ, yenahaj jekkar
   tiwrag̈.
Gey yełap k&t&w, yenahaj
   p&n haṁ łatippan.
Gey qejab hanhan, yenahaj
   jakkik yijeṅ jikin haṁ
   yag̈ed.
Gey qeyag̈ed yin b&g̈,
   qenahaj hayiqij teyegkiy.
Gey yelił, yenahaj łahyey
   lawj&t.

6. *'S.P. will lend me his spear for fishing in holes.'*

Ejbi enaj letok <u>madre</u>
   <u>in turoḦ eo an.</u>
   <u>mej in turoḦ</u>
   <u>roba in turoḦ</u>
   <u>teiḦki in turoḦ</u>
   <u>bu in turoḦ</u>

Yejpiy yenahaj leyteq ṁad&y
   <u>yin tiwrag̈ yeṅ han.</u>
   <u>maj yin tiwrag̈</u>
   <u>łebah yin tiwrag̈</u>
   <u>teyegkiy yin tiwrag̈</u>
   <u>biw yin tiwrag̈</u>

7. *'The men are going fishing with a net.'*

Lömaran rej ilen le
   ok.
   <u>bwä</u>
   <u>eo</u>
   <u>wa</u>

Ṡeṁahraṅ rej yilan l&y
   w&k.
   <u>bay</u>
   <u>yew</u>
   <u>wah</u>

8. *'If you have a canoe, you can troll on the ocean side.'*

Ne ewör wam wa, kwo
   maroḦ ilarak.
   <u>kökojekjek</u>
   <u>körajraj</u>
   <u>kökaboor</u>
   <u>kajilo</u>

Gey yewer wahaṁ wah,
   qemareg̈ <u>yilahrak.</u>
   <u>kekkawj&kj&k</u>
   <u>kerajraj</u>
   <u>kekapw&r</u>
   <u>kajil&w</u>

9. *'Wait while I go get a spear.'*
    Köttar bwe in ilen        Kettar bey yin yilan
      bŭktok juŏn <u>madre</u>.      bekteq jiwen ṁad&y.
           <u>ok</u>                        <u>w&k</u>
           käăj                      kayaj
           eo                          yew
           emmar                  ṁuṁar
           wea                       weyah
           bakbŭk                bakbek
           bwä                       bay

10. *'The tide is too low for spear fishing in holes.'*
    Elab an <u>bäăt</u> nan        Yełap han <u>payat</u> gan
      turoḧ.                        tiwrağ.
           ibwij                     yibij
           idrik                     yidik
           ialab                     yałap
           buḧ no                   biğ ṅew

11. *'The tide will start to come in at two o'clock.'*
    Enaj <u>ibwij</u> tok ilo       Yenahaj <u>yibij</u> teq yilew
      ruo awa.                     riwew hawah.
           ibwij lebleb             yibij leplep
           bäăt lok                   payat łaq
           bäăt mŏnaknak         payat ṁeṅakṅak

12. *'It is true that that fellow always catches lots of fish.'*
    Mol ke likao en          Ṁewel key likahwew yeṅ
      elab an <u>oda</u>.              yełap han <u>wedah</u>.
           jodra                     jewedah
           konkon                   qeṅqeṅ
           jakonkon               jaqeṅqeṅ
           ebakij                   yepakij
           jebakij                  jeppakij
           wälel                     wayl&l
           jewälel                  jewayl&l

13. *'That secondary lagoon is really deep!'*
    Ej make wŏt <u>mwilal</u>       Yej mak&y wet <u>ṁilał</u>
      loan nam en!                 lewwahan naṁ yeṅ!
           bejbej                   p&jp&j
           lim                       liṁ
           lab no                    łap ṅew
           lae                       łahyey
           jej no                    j&j ṅew

14. *'The breadfruit are baking.'*

  Mü ko kan rej umum.  May kew kañ rej wiṁwiṁ.
    *(oven not in view, but*
    *speaker knows location)*

   ko        kew
    *(speaker doesn't know location)*

   kein       k&yin
    *(oven in view)*

   kü        kay
    *(oven in view of speaker,*
    *but not of addressee)*

   kane       kañey
    *(oven not in view of speaker,*
  *but he knows it to be near addressee)*

*(Using the above sentences as cues, change each to singular.)*

Mü eo en ej umum.  May yew yeñ yej wiṁwiṁ.
 *(etc.)*      *(etc.)*

*(Now make parallel variations on each of the following sentences in both plural and singular.)*

Ladrik ro ran rej tutu.  Ḃadik rew rañ rej tiwtiw.
Bao ko kan rej toktok.  Bahwew kew kañ rej t&qt&q.
Ajri ro ran rej ikkure.  Hajiriy rew rañ rej qqir&y.
Limaro ran rej kaikikit.  Liṁahrew rañ rej kayikyikit.
Lümaro ran rej entak.  Ḃeṁahrew rañ rej y&ntak.
Ik ko kan rej kümat.  Y&k kew kañ rej kemat.

*(Now the teacher may use English to describe one of the above situations as a cue.)*

T: 'The breadfruit are baking. You can see the oven but I can't.'

A: Mü ko kü rej umum.  May kew kay rej wiṁwiṁ.

T: 'There is only one of them.'

B: Mü eo e ej umum.  May yew y&y y&j wiṁwiṁ.

T: *(etc.)*

15. *(Do this drill in precisely the same way as the last one.)*

    *'They are baking the breadfruit (pl.).'*

    Mḭ ko <u>kan</u> rej umuni.        May kew <u>kañ</u> rej wiminiy.
       <u>ko</u>                           <u>kew</u>
       kein                           k&yin
       kḭ                             kay
       kane                           kañey

    Mḭ eo <u>en</u> rej umini.         May yew <u>yeñ</u> rej wiṁiniy.
       eo                             yew
       in                             yin
       e                              y&y
       ne                             ñey

    *'They are bathing the boys.'*

    Ladrik ro <u>ran</u> rej           Ḷadik rew <u>rañ</u> rej
      katutuik <u>ir</u>.                katiwtiwik y&r.
    Ladrik eo en rej                   Ḷadik yew <u>yeñ</u> rej
      katutuik(i).                       katiwtiwik(iy).

    *'They are cooking the fish.'*

    Ik ko <u>kan</u> rej kḇmatti.      Y&k kew <u>kañ</u> rej kemattiy.
    Ik eo <u>en</u> rej kḇmatte.       Y&k yew <u>yeñ</u> rej kemattey.

16. *'I am proud of the canoe.'*

    Ebuḷ buruḇ kin wa eo.              Yebi&̰ biriw&h k&n wah yew.
      <u>utiej</u> -ḇn                    wity&j  -en
      metak  -eir                       metak   -&yy&r
      rup    -em                        ṭip     -em

    *'The canoe has been my good fortune.'*

    Ebo lem<u>a</u> kin wa eo.         Yepew ḷema<u>h</u> k&n wah yew.
         -<u>en</u>                         -<u>an</u>
         -eir                               -ayy&r
         -em                                -am

    *'I am interested in the canoe.'*

    Eitok limoḇ̱ kin wa eo.             Yeyiteq lime<u>wih</u> k&n wah yew.
         -<u>un</u>                         -<u>in</u>
         -eir                               -iyy&r
         -um                                -im

    *(Change each of the above possible sentences to the following pattern:)*

*'I am very proud of...'*

| | |
|---|---|
| Elab an buḧ buruȵ... | Yełap han biǧ biriw&h... |
| Elab an bo lema... | Yełap han pew łemah... |
| Elab an itok limoṳ... | Yełap han yiteq līmewih... |

*(Now change each by inserting* łaq jidik *as follows:)*

| | |
|---|---|
| Eitok lok jidrik limoṳ... | Yeyiteq łaq jidik limewih... |

17. *'The boy is (there) among all those people.'*

| Ladrik eo en | | Ƚadik yew yeṅ | |
|---|---|---|---|
| ibwiljin | armij ran wȫj. | yibilijin | harm&j raṅ w&j. |
| iben | joḧoul | ppan | j&g&wil |
| iturin | roḧoul | tiłin | r&g&wil |
| ikijien | jet | kijjiyen | jet |
| | otemjej | | w&t&mj&j |

*(Change* ...yeṅ...raṅ... *above to:)*

| | |
|---|---|
| ...ne...rane... | ...ṅey...raṅey... |
| ...e....rȕ..... | ...y&y...ray..... |
| ...in...rein... | ...yin...r&yin... |

18. *'Why are you crying?'*

| Kwo | jam jaḧ? | Qejahaṁ | jag? |
|---|---|---|---|
| e | etal | ye- | yetal |
| re | ko | re- | kew |
| kom | ettȫr | q&ṁ | tt&r |
| jero | | jerew | |
| erjil | | y&rj&l | |
| komeaḧ | | q&ṁyag | |

*(This use of* jahaṁ *(*jaham*) to form 'why' questions is a Rȁlik pattern.)*

19. *'I looked for it (him, her) without success.'*
*(literally...* 'and got tired.'*)*

| Iar bukote im mȫk. | Yihar piqetey yim ṁ&k. |
|---|---|
| bukoti | piqetiy |
| bukot ir | piqet y&r |
| kajjioḧ | kajjiyeǧ |
| ettȫr | tt&r |
| eḧwȫr | yaǧed |
| ekkatak | kkahtak |
| kate iȵ | katey y&h |
| turoḧ | tiwraǧ |

## SHORT PROSE SELECTION
### Wāwen Kejbarok Ik
### Wayw&yen Kejpareq Y&k

    refrigerator
Ejelok aij-bok ilo enaḧin aolep im i
Yejjełaq hayij-bawak yilew yenahgin hawelep y&ṁ yiy

Majŭl, bŭtab elak wŭr ilo jet wŭt im ko
Ṁahjeł, bethab yełak wer yilew jet wet y&ṁ kew

Kwajalein im Majuro kab jejjo ilo ailiḧ ko
Kiwajleyen yim Majr&w kab j&jj&w yilew hay&l&g kew

         increase time
ilikin. Ṅe armij rej kŭnan kato an ik ber,
yilikin. Gey harm&j rej keṅhan katew han y&k pad,

           smoke
rej jol im kŭmman ik jol ak atiti im kŭmman
rej jawał yim keṁṁhan y&k jawał hak hatiytiy yim keṁṁhan

  dried
ik mŭnaknak.
y&k ṁeṅakṅak.

Wāwen jol ik, mokta jej karreoik ik ko, im
Wayw&y&n jawał y&k, ṁeqtah jej karr&y&wik y&k kew, yim

               pieces
elaḧe ik killeb men ko jej mwijiti im kŭmman bukon
yełaggey y&k killep men kew jej ṁijitiy yim keṁṁhan biqen

            keep them as wholes
jidrik, ak elaḧe ik jidrik, jej kaieoki  wŭt im
jiddik, hak yełaggey y&k jiddik, jej kayiy&w&kiy wet yim

soak them   for
joni ilo dren-in-jol iumin juŭn boḧ. Mwijin.
jeweniy yilew daṅṅin-jawał yiwṁin jiwen b&ǧ. Ṁ&jin,

jej kŭjeki im ḧe rŭmŭrā, kakoni nai loan
jej kejeyekiy yim gey reṁeray, kaqeṅiy ṅahyiy lewwahan

ieb, bok, ak tin, mae ien jaikuji  Ḧan
yiyep, bawak, hak tiyin, ṁahyey 'yiyen jehayiqijiy gan

mŭḧā.
ṁegay.

Bar juŭn wāwen kejbarok ik bwe en to an ber,
Bar jiwen wayw&y&n kejpareq y&k bey yen tew han pad,

           smoke them
jej atiki       im kŭmman ik mŭnaknak.
jej hatiyikiy yim keṁṁhan y&k ṁeṅakṅak.

Ik jol kab ik mŭnaknak ekkŭ wŭt air kŭmman ilo
Y&k jawał kab y&k ṁeṅakṅak yekkay wet hay&r keṁṁhan yilew
ailiṄ ko ilikin me reike ak ejelok armij in
hay&leg kew yilikin mey reyikey hak yejjełaq harm&j yin
consume them
amŭni.
hamaniy.


VOCABULARY

| | | |
|---|---|---|
| aij | hayij | ice |
| alele | hałeyłey | net fishing (encircling the fish) |
| amŭn | haman | make use of |
| anan | hanhan | chum; attract fish by scattering bait |
| atiki | hatiyikiy (tr.) hatiytiy (intr.) | smoke it |
| bakbŭk | bakbek | knife |
| bŭt | payat | low tide |
| bobu | bawb&w | fishing by means of a scoop net and torch at night |
| bukon | biqen | portion, part; state, district |
| buṄ | biǧ | fall; lose virginity |
| bwiljin | biljin bilji- | among |
| ekkaṄ | kkag | sharp |
| ekkŭb | kk&b | dull |
| eo | yew | line, string, fishing line |
| eojaak | yewejjahak | fishing method--casting for fish from a boat |
| eojojo | yewjewjew | fishing method--casting for fish from land |
| ialab | yałap | spring tide |
| ibwij | yibij | high tide |
| ibwiljin | | (see *bwilijin*) |
| idrik | yidik | neap tide |
| ike | yikey (distr.) | full of fish, lots of fish |
| ikijien | | (see *kijien*) |

| | | |
|---|---|---|
| ilarak | yilahrak | fishing method--trolling (outside lagoon) |
| jabuk | jabiq | fishing method--net fishing |
| jakkik | jakkik | describes an area where fish are not biting |
| jakonkon | jaqeñqeñ | describes a man who never catches many fish |
| jej | j&j | none (Rat.) |
| jibke | jibk&y | a method of trapping porpoises |
| jidrikdrik | jidikdik | small (of singular things) |
| jodra | jewedah | describes a man who does not catch many fish |
| junboH | jiwinb&ğ | fishing method--pole fishing at night |
| kaikikit | kayikyikit | look for fish in pools on reef |
| kaioki | kayiy&w&kiy | leave whole |
| kajilo | kajil&w | tuna fishing--blue fin tuna |
| kato | katew | prolong |
| kijien | kijjiyen kijjiye- | direction of |
| kikik | kkik | bite; describes an area where fish are biting |
| kübwübwe | kebayb&y | fishing method--pole fishing |
| kükabor | kekapw&r | hunt giant clams |
| kokkojekjek | qakawj&kj&k | fishing method--trolling (inside lagoon) |
| konkon | qeñqeñ | describes a man who can catch lots of fish |
| kürajraj | kerajraj | whaling |
| lae | łahyey | smooth and shiny water |
| latiben | łatippan | fishing method--line fishing for tuna |
| lim | liṁ | murky |
| lojet | lawj&t | sea |
| maj | ṁaj | eel |
| mejün turoH | mejan tiwrağ | diving mask |
| meram | meram | light |
| münaknak | ṁeñakñak | dry, brown, withered |
| mwieo | miyew | palm leaves woven into a fishing net |
| no | ñew | wave(s) |

| | | |
|---|---|---|
| oda | wedah | describes a man who can catch lots of fish |
| ok | wɛk | net |
| roba | ɫebah | rubber (from English) |
| toktok | tɛqtɛq | scratch in ground for food--chickens only |
| walel | waylɛl | able to shoot straight |
| wea | weyah | wire (from English) |
| wöjaki | wejakiy | do them |
| wurök | wirɛk | fishing method--line fishing from a boat |

## LESSON THIRTY

More fishing; adjective-like
words with and without ka-;
directional locatives with tiw;
possessive suffixes on units
of time; miscellaneous patterns.

<u>DIALOGUES</u>

1.
A: Jero ilen enwŏr.                  Jerew yilan yaǧed.
B: Enana laH, enaj wŏt.              Yenahnah lag, yenahaj w&t.
A: Eban bwe elab kŏto.               Yeban bey yełap k&t&w.
   MŬttan jirik edret.               Mettan jidik yedet.
B: Ekwe He emman laH,                Yeqey gey yeṁhan lag,
   kejro etal.                       k&jrew yetal.
A: Ijja rol in ekebŭ.                Yijjah rawal yin yekepay.
   Kwŏnaj bed ia?                    Qenahaj pad yi'yah?
B: Inaj kŏttar yok iar.              Yinahaj kettar y&q yiyhar.

A: Let's go fishing.
B: The weather's bad. It's going to rain.
A: It won't (rain) because it's windy. The sun will
   come out soon.
B: Well, if the weather's fine, we'll go.
A: Let me go back and change. Where will you be?
B: I'll wait for you at the beach.

2.
A: EwŬr ke konam?                    Yewer key qeṅaṁ?
B: Ejelok kona. EwŬr                 Yejjełaq qeṅah. Yewer
   konan Aijin.                      qeṅan Hayijen.
A: I kŏnan wia kijŭ ek.              Yikeṅhan wiyah kij&h y&k.
B: Wia kijŬm ibben                   Wiyah kijeṁ yippan
   Aijin. Ear bol wa                 Hayijen. Yehar b&w&ł wah
   eo wan.                           yew wahan.
A: Eber ia Aijin kiŭ?                Yepad yi'yah Hayijen kiyyeh?

302

B: Eber imwen mŭn.          Yepad yiṁeyeṅ ṁen.
A: Kommol.                  Qeṁṁewel.

A: Did you catch anything?
B: I didn't catch any. Aijin got some.
A: I want to buy some fish.
B: Get some from Aijin. His boat was full (of fish).
A: Where is Aijin now?
B: He's at home.
A: Thank you.

DRILLS

1. *I'm going home to put on old clothes right now.*

    Ijja rol in ekebŭ.        Yijjah rawal yin yekepay.
       terejab                              tereyjab
       kebojak                              keppewjak
       jŭnij aŭ                             janij hah&h
       nuknuk                               niqniq

2. *I'll wait for you at the lagoon side.*

    I naj kottar yok          Yinahaj kettar y&q
      iar.                                  yiyhar.
      lik                                   lik
      ioj                                   yi'y&w&j
      tur                                   tił
      jittoen                               jitt&wyeṅ
      jittaken                              jittakyeṅ
      jeniŭṅ                                jeṅiy&g
      jenrŭk                                jeṅr&k

3. *Somebody cracked the pipe.*

    Emwij an kabŭlṅak baib    Y&ṁ&j han kabełgak bahyib
    eo.                       yew.
       kajar                                kajar
       karran                               karran
       kattal                               kattal
       kaib                                 kayip
       kabellok                             kapełłaq
       katoor                               katawar
       kalaṅ                                kalag
       katton                               katt&w&n
       kabolol                              kabewełweł

4. *'The pipe is cracked.'*

 Ebŭlḧak baib eo.      Yebeɫgak bahyib yew.
 ejar             yejar
 erran            yerran
 ettal            yettal
 eib             yeyip
 ebellok           yepeɫɫaq
 etor            yetawar
 elaḧ            yeɫag
 etton            y&tt&w&n
 ebolol           yebeweɫweɫ

5. *'What's the matter with the pipe?'*   *'Maybe somebody cracked it.'*

 Eita baib eo?        Yeyitah bahyib yew?
 ebajet           yebajy&t

 Wŭn ej jab ba rar      Wen yej jab bah rehar
  kabŭlḧake.          kabeɫgakey.
 bwelen...kajare       b&l&n...kajar&y
     karrane          karraney
     kattale          kattaley
     kabelloke        kapeɫɫaqey
     kattoore         katawarey
     kalaḧe          kaɫagey
     katoone         katt&w&n&y

6. *'What do you know! It's really raining!'*
 (See Grammatical Note 1.)

 Emwijlok! Ej kab naj    Y&ṁ&jɫaq! Yej kab nahaj
       wit!              w&t.
       bŭktak            bektak
       liboror            libewerwer
       letlet             l&tl&t
       kakkŭt            kakket
       kate             katey

7. *'Did you catch anything?'*   *'Yes, I caught a lobster/ some lobsters.'*

 Ewŭr ke konam?       Yewer key qeṅaṁ?
 Aet...ewŭr kona wŭr.    Hay&t, yewer qeṅah w&r.
        kweet             q&y&t
        ek               y&k
        wŭn              w&n
        jidrul            jiddiwil
        drimuj           dimwij

8. *'I want to buy some fish that I can eat.'*

| | |
|---|---|
| I kŭnan wia kijo ek | Yikeñhan wiyah kij&h y&k. |
| wŭr | w&r |
| kweet | q&y&t |
| wŭn | w&n |
| jidrul | jiddiwil |
| drimuj | dimwij |

9. *(Substitute in the appropriate slot.)*
   *'That canoe is full of fish.'*

| | |
|---|---|
| E bol wa en kin ek. | Y&b&w&ł wah yen k&n y&k. |
| wŭr | w&r |
| armij | harm&j |
| mwen | ḿeyeñ |
| rum en | riwiḿ yeñ |
| kweet | q&y&t |
| book en | bawak yeñ |
| wŭn | w&n |
| jidrul | jiddiwil |
| bek en | payak yeñ |
| drimuj | dimwij |
| waini | wahyiniy |
| kŭrkŭr en | kerker yeñ |

10. *'Where is Arjin?'*
    *'I don't know where he is. I don't know where Arjin is.'*

| | |
|---|---|
| Eber ia Arjin? | Yepad yi'yah Harjin? |
| Ijaje ia in eber ie. | Yijahj&y yi'yah yin yepad yi'y&y. |
| Ijaje ia in Arjin eber ie. | Yijahj&y yi'yah yin Harjin yepad yi'y&y. |
| Ijmeel | Yijmeyeł |
| Laukon | Lawiqeñ |
| Bijenta | Piyjentah |
| Kiijbaal | Kiyijbahal |
| Jolikiep | Jewlikiyep |
| Mŭnna | Ḿennah |
| Bijja | Pijjah |
| Kuma | Qimah |
| Jŭne | Jayn&y |
| Konet | Kawnet |
| Adiki | Hadikiy |
| Tareaḧ | Teryag |
| Jeita | Jeyitah |
| Neijon | Neyijawan |

11. I kŭnan bwebwenato          Yikeṅhan beybeynahtew
    ibam.                       yippaṁ.
       kŭmmao                       keṁṁahwew
       jerbal                       jerbal
       ber                          pad
       tanij                        tanij
       kejota                       k&j&wtah
       kŭnono                       kenewnew
       ire                          yirey
       kuku                         kiwkiw
       jaja                         jahjah
       leketo                       l&yk&t&w

12. *'Go talk to him.'*
    Etal im bwebwenato          Yetal yim beybeynahtew
    ibben.                      yippan.
    (Repeat substitutions from Drill 11.)

13. *'Buy your food from Arjin.'*
    Wia kijŭm ibben Arjin.      Wiyah kijeṁ yippan Harjin.
    ebbŭk                       bb&k
    kane                        kanney
    koot                        kawat
    kajitŭk                     kajjit&k
    uṅṅar                       wiggar

14. *'Which direction is the canoe (from here)?'*
    A: Tu ia eo wa eo eber      Tiw yi'yah yew wah yew
       ie?                      yepad yi'y&y.
          tima                        tiyṁah
          boj                         bewej
          kŭrkŭr                      kerker
          tibṅil                      tipg&l
          tirak                       tirak
          otobai                      wetewbahyiy
          inej                        yin&j
    *'It's toward the east of (from) this island.'*
    B: Eber turear in           Yepad tiwr&yyahar yin
       ene in.                  yan&y yin.
          rilik                       riylik
          iŭn                         y&g
          rŭk                         r&k
          ar                          har
          lik                         lik
          iolab                       yewɬap

15. *'Where is the canoe anchored?'*

A: Tu ia eo wa eo ej  aḧkü ie?  
Tiw yi'yah yew wah yew yej hagkeh yi'y&y?

*'It's anchored to the east of that coral head.'*

B: Ej aḧkü tu<u>rear</u> in wür en.  
  rilik  
  iüḧ  
  rük  
  meto  
  ene  
  lüḧ  

Yej hagkeh tiw<u>r&yyahar</u> yin wed yeñ.  
  riylik  
  y&g  
  r&k  
  metew  
  yan&y  
  l&g  

16. *'Where is the whale?'*

A: Tu ia eo raj eo eber ie?  
Tiw yi'yah yew raj yew yepad yi'y&y?

*'It's east of the (this) ship.'*

B: Eber tu<u>rear</u> in wa in.  
  rilik  
  iüḧ  
  rük  
  man  
  lik  
  meto  
  ene  

Yepad tiw<u>r&yyahar</u> yin wah yin.  
  riylik  
  y&g  
  r&k  
  ṁahan  
  lik  
  metew  
  yan&y  

17. *'Where is the book?'*

A: Tu ia eo buk eo eber ie?  
Tiw yi'yah yew b&q yew yepad yi'y&y?

*'It's above the table there by you.'*

B: Eber tulüḧ in tebül ne.  
  lül  
  iolab  
  rear  
  rilik  
  iüḧ  
  rük  

Yepad tiw<u>l&g</u> yin teybel ñey.  
  lal  
  yewlap  
  r&yyahar  
  riylik  
  y&g  
  r&k  

18. *'How many months have you been on this island?'*

A: Jete alliḧim nai ene in?  
Jetey <u>halligiṁ</u> ñahyiy yan&y yin.

```
                    ran                     rahan
                    wik                     wiyik
                    iiṭ                     'yiyeh
                    boḥ                     b&ǧ
                    awa                     hawah
        'I've been on this island about three months.'
B:  Eor jilu im men              Yewer jiliw yim men
       alliḥṳ...                    halligih...
       joḥoul jima                  j&g&wil jiṁah
       lalim im emen                ḻal&m yim yeman
       tarin lalim                  tarrin ḻal&m
        'How many months will you be...?'
A:  (E)naj jete alliḥim...?       (Ye)nahaj jetey halligiṁ...?
        'Probably about three months.'
B:  Emaroḥ jilu im men             Yemareǧ jiliw yim men
       alliḥṳ...                     halligih...
        'How many months were you supposed to have been...?'
A:  En kar jete alliḥim...         Yen kar jetey halligiṁ...
        'It was supposed to have been about three...'
B:  En kar jilu im men             Yen kar jiliw yim men
       alliḥṳ...                     halligih...
19. (Emphasis on naj and the word following it in the
    sentences below gives the meaning 'It has finally
    started to...' whereas no special emphasis, or a
    little on yej gives the meaning 'It's really...'.)
        Ej kab naj wit.            Yej kab nahaj w&t.
            'It has finally started to rain.'
        Ej kab naj wit.            Yej kab nahaj w&t.
            'It's really raining.'
    (Practice the above sentence and the following with
    both emphases.)
        Ej kab naj jorren.         Yej kab nahaj jeṟṟayan.
                mwij                        ṁ&j
                dret                        det
                bwil                        bil
                bwe                         bey
                jerbal                      jerbal
                emman                       ṁṁan
                mat                         mahat
                mat                         mat
```

20.
A: 'How is Tom related to you?'
　Teem Tom?　　　　　　　Teyem̂ Tawam̂?
A: 'How is Ali related to me?'
　Teʉ Ali?　　　　　　　T&y&h Haɬiy?

*(Substitute other names above as appropriate to your situation.)*

B: 'He's not related to you/me.'
　Ejelok.　　　　　　　Yejjeɬaq.
B: He's a male relative of my/your parents' generation.'
　Jemam.　　　　　　　Jem̂am̂.
　(etc.)　　　　　　　 (etc.)

21. *Tell me the names of your fingers.*
T: Kwalok mʉk etan adrin　Qahɬaq m̂ek yetan haddiyin
　 beim.　　　　　　　　p&yim̂.
A: *(touching each as he names it)*

　1. adri leb　　　　　haddiy lep
　2. adri kootut　　　 haddiy kawatw&t
　3. adri eolab　　　　haddiy yewɬap
　4. (adri riH)　　　　(haddiy riyig)
　5. adri drik　　　　 haddiy dik

GRAMMATICAL NOTES
1. Drills 6 and 19 contain examples of a meaning difference signalled by differences in the relative loudness of different words in sentences with the sequence

　　　　　yej kab nahaj...

Emphasis on yej gives the meaning 'It's really...', whereas emphasis on nahaj and the word following it gives the meaning 'It has finally started to...'
In Drill 6 the former emphasis is intended; in Drill 19 both are contrasted.

2. Comparing Drills 3 and 4, we note that the sentences of Drill 4 translate into English with pipe as subject, and comment on the state of the pipe:

　Yebeɬgak bahyib yew.　　'The pipe is cracked.'

Note that the intransitive form of beɬgak is used.

We could also say

 Y&ṁ&j han beɫgak bahyib  'The pipe has been
  yew.          cracked.'

with little change in meaning other than to emphasize that the state of being cracked has already been reached. In this last sentence, the fact that <u>han</u> refers to <u>bahyib</u> can be shown by pluralizing <u>bahyib</u>:

 Y&ṁ&j hay&r beɫgak   'The pipes have been
  bahyib kew.       cracked.'

Note that <u>han</u> is replaced by <u>hay&r</u>.

If, instead, ka- is inserted before <u>beɫgak</u>, the first sentence of Drill 3 is formed:

 Y&ṁ&j han kabeɫgak   'Someone has cracked
  bahyib yew.       the pipe.'

Now <u>han</u> no longer refers to <u>bahyib</u> but to an unspecified actor. Pluralizing <u>bahyib</u> does not affect <u>han</u>:

 Y&ṁ&j han kabeɫgak   'Someone has cracked
  bahyib kew.       the pipes.'

Actually these last two sentences are best interpreted as the results of deleting a specified actor:

 Y&ṁ&j han (Tawaṁ) kabeɫ-  'Tom has cracked the
  gak bahyib yew/kew.    pipe(s).'

3. The directional locatives with <u>tiw</u> in Drills 14 through 17 can be considered as counterparts to the Slot I directionals of Lessons 27 and 28:

| Slot I Directionals | | Locative Directionals with tiw |
|---|---|---|
| -nigah-/-nigyag- | north | -y&g |
| -r&gah-/-r&kyag | south | -r&k |
| -tak-/-tah- | east | -r&yyahar |
| -t&w- | west | -riylik |
| -har- | lagoon side | -har |
| -wej- | interior; middle | -yewɫap |
| -lik- | ocean side | -lik |
| -metew- | sea | -metew |
| -yan&y- | land | -yan&y |
| -l&g- | up, above | -l&g |
| -laɫ- | down, below | -laɫ |
| -ṁahan- | forward, front | -ṁahan |
| -lik | backward, behind | -lik |

## SHORT PROSE SELECTION

### Bwiro
### Biyr&w

Mü ej juön ian möHü ko elab tata an dri
May yej jiwen yi'yahan ṁegay kew yełap tahtah han ri-
Majöl kejerbale. Ej elle ilo enaHin aoleb
Ṁahjeł kejerbaley. Yej yelley yilew yenahgin hawelep
                                              between
alliH bötaab ewör juön ien, kötaan yen ilo
hall&g bethab yewer jiwen 'yiyen, <u>ketahan</u> yeh yilew
May im August, etan 'rak', im mü ej lukun lab
May&y yim Waqej, yetan 'rak', yim may yej liqqiwin łap
  bear fruit
an kalle. Ilo ien in, armij rej kömman bwiro.
han <u>kalley</u>. Yilew 'yiyen yin, harm&j rej keṁhan biyr&w.
                   peel it    soak it   ocean
Rej bök mü en, kakili im joone i lojet. Mwijin,
Rej bek may yeh, <u>kakiliy</u> yim j&w&n&y <u>yilawj&t</u>. Ṁ&jin,
   wrap it                           and then
rej köboreke kin bwilök in mü im kimej, inem rej
rej kebawar&k&y k&n b&l&k yin may yim kim&j, <u>yinnam</u> rej
pound it                       bury it
jukjuki im bar kitimi kin bwilök im kalbini. Ilo
<u>jiqjiqiy</u> yim bar kitimiy k&n b&l&k yim <u>kalbiniy</u>. Yilew
                                    little by little
wüwen in, ejjab joren ak rej kwalok jidik-jidik
wayw&y&n yin, yejjab jeŀŀayan hak rej qahłaq <u>jidik-jidik</u>
ekkar Han aer aikuji Han möHü. Nemen ilo an
yekkàr gan hay&r hayiqijiy gan ṁegay. Neman yilew han
buried
kallib, einwöt bwin *cheese* He rej kömmane. Kin men
<u>kallib</u>, yayinwet biyin jiyij gey rej keṁhaney. K&n men
                         name it
in, eloH dri belle rej na etan
yin, yeleg ripalley rej hah <u>yetan</u> '*Marshallese cheese*'.

### PROVERB

    Likiep kabin iep.      Likiyep kapin yiyep.

Likiep is the bottom of the basket. A saying resulting from belief that Likiep's cooking is the tastiest, stemming from legends that fire was discovered in Likiep by Etao. Also the idea that the best food is put at the bottom of the basket.

VOCABULARY

| | | |
|---|---|---|
| bŭlHak | beɫgak | spread apart; cracked |
| bŭktak | bektak | catching up--as in competitive games |
| ebolol | yebeweɫweɫ | (it is) loose |
| ekebŭ | yekepay | change clothes--from clean to dirty |
| erran | rran | dirty |
| ettal | ttal | leak |
| ib | yip | crooked, bent |
| inej | yin&j | fleet |
| ioj | yi'y&w&j (Rat.) yawaj (Rŭl.) | in the interior of the islet |
| ire | yirey | fight |
| jaja | jahjah | carry someone on the hips |
| janij | janij | change (from English) |
| jar | jar | torn off, ripped off (but not for clothes) |
| jeniŏH | jeñiy&g | north section of an island |
| jenrŭk | jeñr&k | south section of an island |
| jidrul | jiddiwil | a shell: 'top shell' |
| jittaken | jittakyeñ | east or south east section of an island |
| kanne | kanney | to fill |
| kŏmmao | keṁḣahwew | to converse |
| koot | kawat | steal |
| kootut | kawatw&t | (distr.) |
| kuku | kiwkiw | carry someone on the back |
| letlet | l&tl&t | 'high' (inebriated) a full, steady breeze |
| liboror | libewerwer | striving to catch up |
| terejab | tereyjab | dress up |
| toor | tawar | drip, flow |
| tur | tiɫ | at the end of an islet |
| uHHar | wiggar | beg for something |
| wŏr | wed | coral, coral head, reef |

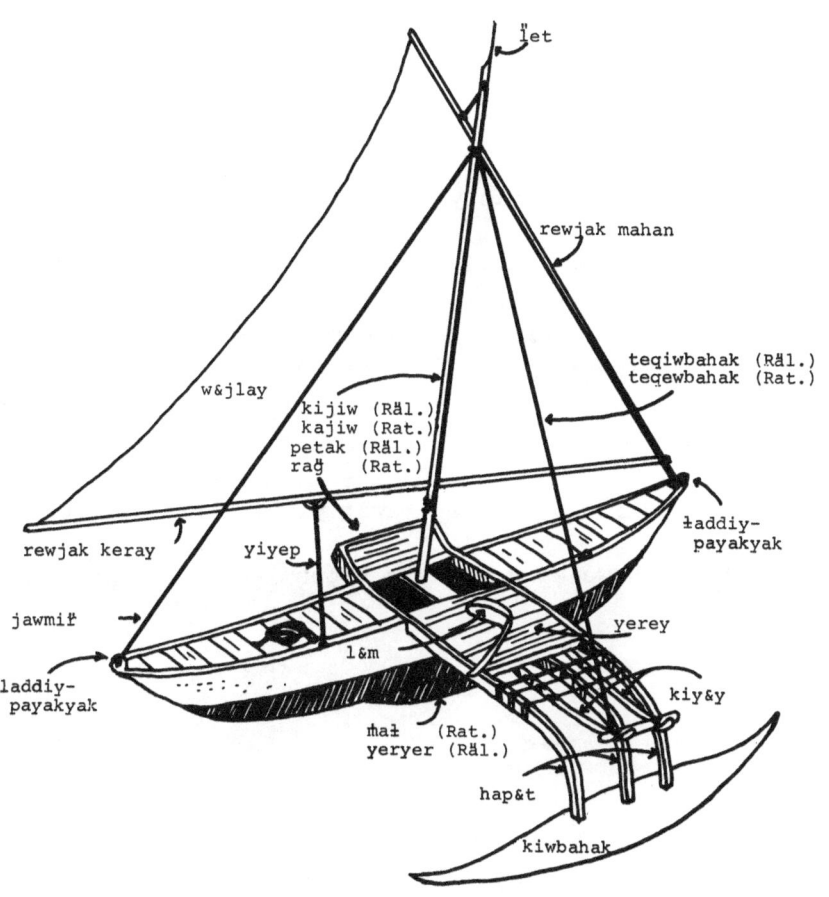

yetan mettan kew yilew jiwen tipg&l

## BONUS SELECTION

Yegyin yej jeṁłaq yew. Yełaggey qehar kij&nm&j jan jinewin, k&mij kejatdikdik bey yilew hawah yin qej riyitiy p&yij yin, qemareǧ kenewnew yim mełeyłey kajin Ṁahjeł. K&mij temak barayinwet, bey jan d&yd&yłaq yin y&ṁ&j haṁ teparey, yewer ṁettan haṁ mełeyłey k&n ṁanit yim wayw&y&n mewir han riṀahjeł.

Hawelepan kahtak k&yin yilew b&q yin, k&mij temak bey
                   they include
<u>rekepeweł</u> hawelep wayw&y&n kew gan haṁ jełay k&n wayw&-
                 structure
y&n mewir, yim <u>raypełtan</u> kajin Ṁahjeł. Jan b&q yin yim jipag han rikakiy yew haṁ yippan dewen, yegyin, y&ṁ&j haṁ teprak teq yijin. Yijewkey, yejjab mełeyłeyen bey
               you are completely finished
yilew haṁ kejeṁłaq b&q yin, <u>q&d&yd&y łaq</u>, hak k&mij temak bey yilew haṁ nahaj mewir yippan riṀahjeł, qenahaj
make grow
<u>kaddek</u> łaq hawelep men k&yin yippaṁ mak&y.

# GLOSSARY

## Marshallese-English

### B

b&d  mistake, error, wrong, fault, sin

b&ŋ  night, last night

b&jrak  stand still, pause, stop

b&k&y  cape--geographical; knot--in wood

b&l  taro patch

b&l&k  leaf

b&l&n  perhaps, probably, maybe

b&nb&n  arithmetic, count

b&q  bladder

b&q  book

b&q hayidik  prickly heat, heat rash, measles

b&q&y  knee

b&r&w  seat of emotions, throat, 'heart'

b&r&w-qiq  form a united group, agree among selves

b&t  disobedient, naughty, mischievous

b&w  missile--for throwing only

b&w&ł  filled up, full, lustful --males only

B&w&np&y  place name--Ponape

b&yb&y  crazy, silly, foolish; giddy

bab  fit tightly, full

babbib  butterfly

badik  duck, lower the head

bah  say

bah pahtah  say in vain

bahab  suppose, have an opinion, think

bahaj  taken aback, halted, give up; pass--in card games, surrender

bahajkeł  bicycle

bahar  crowbar

bahathat  smoke, steam

bahbah  father, daddy

bahbiw  lie down

bahjinjeyyah  passenger, go as a passenger

bahł&ybawał   to play volleyball, volleyball

bahtah   priest

bahwew   bird, chicken, fowl

bahwitah   powder

bahyey   bamboo

bahyib   pipe--plumbing

bahyibeł   Bible

bahyid   pipe--smoking

bahyijin   poison, harmful
  substances

baj   lower abdomen--triangu-
  lar area

baj   bus

bajj&k   a little, just, only--
  indicating relative unimpor-
  tance of verbal activity

bakej   bucket

bakkey   yaws--ulcerated type

bakt&k   small house on canoe

bal   covered over

bał   canoe part--end of yard-
  boom (łejak mahan)

bałwin   airplane

bam̂   pump, pulse, heart

ban   unable, cannot, impossible, weak, not have the
  ability to, never will do;
  negative future tense

ban   punch--beverage

baqej   embrace, hug

baqitag   bomb, dynamite

bar   rock

bar   again

bar   head

bar jet   other, others

bar jidik   a little more

bar jiwen   another

barayinwet   the same, also,
  likewise

bariw   crab--general term

bariw   bulldozer

bat   slow, late

bat   hill, mound, knoll

batew   bottle, jar, broken glass

batin   secret lover, sweetheart

batin   button, pill, tablet--
  medicine

bawak   box

bawał   ball

bawar   stopper, cork

bawb&w   fishing method--flying
  fish at night with torch and
  net

bawin   pound, scales; weight

bawir   catch with net or basket; lift, hold up or catch with both hands

bawtiy   nose

bay   fish pole

bbɛl   blossom

bbahyidyid   smell of smoke on breath or body or clothing, etc.

bbaq   swollen, swell

bbej   swollen, to swell

bbiddikdik mareɠreɠ   a proverb --'we share the little food we have, but thereby gain much power (many friends)'

bbidetdet   smell of clothing or mats under sun

beb   pandanus

bebrahyey   hinder, prevent, forbid, stop

bejaw   pocket; hand basket of fine weave

bek   take, carry, receive, get, capture, subtract

bek ddew   assume responsibility for, care for

bek qenaha-   participate, take part in, do one's duty

bekay   small bottle or jar, container for liquids-- coconut shell

bekay   tide

bekaygaj   perfume--imported only

bekkeray   carry female to or from vessel

bekłałłaq   take downwards

bekłɛgłaq   to take upwards

bektak   catch up--in a game

bełał   light--weight

Bełahyidey   Friday

bełgak   split open

bełyak   flag

Belahwiw   place name--Palau

beɦ   stymied, dumbfounded, blocked, obstructed

benah   flat--music, off-key-- voice

beq   sand

beqpay   fold arms in front

beqtak   protect from rain or spray at sea with mat, shelter with mat at sea

berawrɛw   pregnant

Berahyidey   Friday

berwaj   roof ridge

betah   butter

betektek   blood, bleed, menstruation

bethab   however, nevertheless

bettah    bat--baseball
bew    twins
bewbew    make balls
bewej    boat
bewelwel    poorly fitting, loose
bewliyew    polio
bey    left over, remainder, sufficient, enough
bey    because, so that, that, for
bey    divination--result of
bey    enough
bey betah    assuming that
beyaw    coconut husk, coconut fibre
beybey    tuna
beybeynahtew    talk, conversation, story, history
bid&j    earth, ground, soil
bidak    quarter prince--royal father but commoner mother
biŋ    fall down
biŋ    lose virginity, be excommunicated
biŋbiŋ    famous, fame
biŋ-b&r&w    happy, proud
biŋlaq    fall down

biŋlik    sail out to sea, depart
biŋñew    breaking waves, high surf
biŋniyin    tonight
bigal    dust, dusty
bihbih    grandmother, grandchildren
bij    lineage, crowd, family, tribe
bije-    navel
bijin    flock, a crowd of, school of fish, group
bil    burn, hot, fever, temperature
bil    sap, chewing gum
bilajtiyik    plastic
biliw    bluing, blue
bilyat    flat--music or voice
bilaq    break
bilbil    gummy, cover with gum
bileg    wonder, amaze, surprise
bilijmayañ    police, guard
bilji-    middle of many things or people, among
billaq    launch forth
bilm&ly&g    heartburn
biqabeq    cut, operate

biqaharhar wake--ship or fish--foam

biqen district, division of an atoll or islet

biqiy hundreds of

bił unripe

bir&wh&j sorrow, sadness, sorry, mourn

Birahnij France

birahwin brown

birahyey fry

biraj brush, scrub

birar smear

birar stains, remnants, traces

bireġ talk harshly

birehreh red

Birewtiyjen Protestant--religion

bireyjeten president

birwek broke--out of money

birwih broom

biteġ mattress

biw gun, shoot

biwbiw tie a knot--string or rope, divination method--using knots in pandanus leaf

biwbiw fortune teller, wizardism, divination

biwj&k knot of hair--women, twist the hair into a knot

biwjentehah balloon

biyar pierce--with knife, stab

biyi- smell, odor

biyr&w a food--preserved breadfruit

### D

d&bd&b to spear

d&k&ynin mallet made from clam shell

d&w&n sharp stick for husking coconuts

d&y just

d&yd&y ready, completed

d&yd&ylaq ready, prepared, entirely finished, completed

d&ylaġ enter

dah blood

daha- ...'s pandanus

dahwew first food after fast, break fast

dak duck

dak&lk&l ugly, homely

dah forehead

damdəm  lick

dan  water, liquid

dannin hayəbəj  rain water

dannin kadek  strong liquor

dannin kemjahaɫhaɫ  tears

dannin laɫ  well water

dannin lawjət  salt water

dannin niy  coconut juice

dannin wət  rain water

dannin yidahak  drinking water

dapdəp  trunk--of trees, stump

dapdəp  hold, grip, resist

dapilpil  roll

dawlel  serious illness

ddəb  husks--coconuts, pierce with husking stick or spear

ddap  cling to, stick to, sticky

ddek  grow

ddew  heavy

degdeg  spank, slap, pound

dekay  stone, rock, gravel

dekay  yaws, skin ulcers

depakpak  wide

det  sunshine

dewen  each other

dewen  subjects, followers

dewer  leave it, put

dewij  to ship water

dewilwil  round, circle, club of people

deyaw  pretty (of woman), beautiful

deyel  a fan

didəy  relay race

dik  small, young, little

dik weńya-  cheap, low salary

dikey  hate, abhor, strongly dislike

dim  tight

dimwij  a shell--clam--medium large

diw  boil, have convulsions

diwəj  get out, go out

diy  bone

diy  knife

diyədəy  wear earring

diyakah  push cart

diye-  possessive for earrings and other things worn on ear

diylah  nail

diylep   backbone, spine

diyley   damage caused by termites or bookworms

diyp&n   strong--physically

diypayakyak   canoe part--socket for end of boom

## G

gad   gums

gah   I--absolute

gaj   smell--fragrant

gak   not know

gan   to

gat   palate--of mouth

gayat   when?

gey   when, if

ggat   storm

giy   tooth

## H

h&n   nourishing, substance, vitamin

habaw   fender

habeł   apple

habentawin   teeter, see-saw

habinmak&y   afraid of ghosts, fear of being alone in the dark or at sea

habjey   shy, flirting

hablajtiyig   a plant--*Gomphrena globosa*

habñehñeh   nervous, upset, disturbed, uncomfortable

had&bd&b   move something closer by using a stick

haddebewilwil   rotate, whirl, dizzy, giddy

haddim&j   feeble, lethargic, sickly--chronic

haddiy   finger, toe

haddiy lep   thumb, big toe

haddiy yewłap   middle finger

haddiyṁak&wk&w   sluggishness, dullness (of people)

haded   clam shell--large, small tridachnus

hagenyag   wintertime; harvest time for arrowroot, windy season

haghagey   hungry

hagir   crave cigarettes

hagirlep   smoking addict

hagkeh   anchor

hagłap   exaggerate

hagtikliy   canoe part

hah&h   my soul, my, mine

haheh   swim

hahenhen   paddle, row

hahih   be dying, near death

haj   liver

haj   thatch

hajadik   walk slowly

hajełkay   weak feeling--usually from hunger, stiffness--of a corpse

hajey   give away without remuneration, devote presents to the gods

hajey   drum

hajhaj   calf of leg

hajiriy   child

hajweywey   whistle, whistling--long continued

hajyəj   divide, distribute

hak   but, or

hak   frigate bird

hakkəjdat   hate

hakkawin   charge on account

hakkiy   fingernail, toenail

hakkiyin ney   toenail

hakkiyin pay   fingernail

hal   song, music, sing

hał   sun

hałakiyyəy   plentiful, easy to find (opposite of hałakiyyah)

hałakiyyah   scarce, hard to find (opposite of hałakiyyəy)

hałap   lineage head; old man--term of respect

hałeyłey   fishing method--surround a school in shallow water using a coconut-leaf chain as scarer

hałhał   stick, wood, plank, lumber

halen   time, turn, or occasion; times, in multiplication; sheet of paper, page; rows of houses, story of a house

halikkar   clear, understandable

halin jar   hymn

halin ṁahyinah   love song

halin ṁił   steering song

haliw   white shell--used in head leis

haljək   carry, transport

halləg   month, moon

halləg yin lał   next month

hallew   stammer, tongue-tied

halwəj   watch, look at

halyak   wear the hair loose on one's back--women

ham   our soul, ours; ours--exclusive

haṁ   your soul, your; yours--singular

haṁhah   hammer

haṁhak   hammock

haṁhin   water for washing hands

haṁhin   wash hands

ham&j   raw, uncooked

haman   use, spend

Hamedkah   America

hameyteṁhah   coconut candy

hamiy   your souls, your, yours--plural

hamiyj&l   your, yours (three or more persons)

hamiyṁeṅew   handicraft, make handicraft

hamiyrew   your, yours (two persons)

hamiyw&j   your, yours (five or more persons)

hamiyyag   your, yours (four persons)

han   his soul, her soul, his, hers, her

hanbijban   left (opposite of right), left hand

hanbijmareg̊   right (opposite of left), right hand

hanek   trace, pattern; follow trail or track, imitate

hanhan   bait, lure, to chum for fish, attracted by bait

hanij   god

haniydep   ball made from pandanus leaves, native ball game

haniydep   a plant--pandanus cultigen--Eniwetok

haniyen   onion

haniylen   fate, destiny

hank&laha-   will, desire

hanmiyig   left hand, left hand of a human body

hannag   shadow, reflection, picture, diagram, plan, shape, silhouette, outline

hap&t   canoe part--curved piece connecting outrigger to hull

hapag   harass, hem in, crowded, cramped

hapar   put alongside, rim, edge, border--on mat, or stone edge of road

hapdik   less (quantity), diminish, lessen

hapkahaj   half-caste

har   past tense marker

harhar   pick out--food from teeth--splinters, extricate

harm&j   person, people, human being

Harṅew   place name--atoll--Ratak--Arno

harrew    our souls, ours, our--dual inclusive

hat    hat

hat&w    go or come out of water or fire

hatak    tow, pull

hatakiyy&y    easy to drag in water (opposite of hatakiyyah)

hatakiyyah    hard to drag in water (opposite of hatakiyy&y)

hatartar    lean upon, lean back, adjoining, rest on

hatbaqej    embrace, cuddle

hathat    wear a hat

hatiytiy    smoke, dry fish or copra by heat

hatrak    lean

hatreyej    address to, address --a letter

haw&j&k    stir

haw&r&k    valuable, precious

hawah    hour, clock

hawel    dispute, complain, bewail one's state

hawer    door

hawijpitel    hospital

Hawijtereliyah    Australia

hawilaklak    chip of green coconut husk used as spoon

Hawir    place name--atoll--Ratak--Aur

hawiyy&y    tame, domesticated

hawiyyah    wild, undomesticated

hay&b&j    rain water; well, drinking water

hay&j qiryiń    ice cream

Hay&l&q    place name--atoll--Ratak--Ailuk

hay&l&gin palley    land of the white man, Europe, America

hay&l&ginlag    heaven

hay&l&g-k&yin    a plant--banana variety--'these islands'

Hay&l&glaplap    place name--atoll--Ṟlik--Ailinglaplap

Hay&l&ginhayey    place name--atoll--Ṟlik--Ailinginae

hay&r    tight, stretched

hay&r    theirs

hay&rj&(y&)l    theirs (three persons)

hay&rw&j    theirs (five or more persons)

hay&ryag    theirs (four persons)

hay&t    yes

hay&y    gather, collect

hayekeray   canoe part--foot of sail--fastened to boom

hayeṁhan   good current

hayen   iron

hayeray   shoulder

hayetaw   small islets of an atoll, section of some atolls--windward--usually northeast

hayeteq   long, tall

hayib&w&jw&j   glorious, splendid, marvelous, pretty

hayik   cedar driftwood

hayiłip   thick--of long and round objects

hayinbat   iron pot

hayinig   thin, narrow

hayinikiye-   voice, sound, noise

hayintiyin   to boil pandanus

hayiqij   desire, need, lack, must

hilhil   side, edge

hilhil   axe, hatchet

hirej   provoke to a quarrel

J

j&bj&b   seize, hold, capture

j&jj&t   clean a fish or chicken

j&jj&w   few

j&kj&k   cut, hew, chop

j&kj&k wah   build a canoe or boat

j&lbah   silver

j&ṁnajin   parent-child relationship, sister-brother relationship

j&ṁnajin   examination day at end of term, review day

j&mj&m   whet, sharpen

j&n   shrink, grow smaller, fall short of--in length

j&nj&n   start a fire

j&nq&n   related to each other

j&p&l   apart, divorce, separate

j&pj&p   move away, change domicile

j&pkaw   floor mat--coarse

j&q&y   live somewhere, dwell

j&t&b   spirit

j&tteqja-   worthless, of no value, no good

j&tteqjan   unprofitable, of no use

j&wj&w   chick

j&wj&wmar   intercede, defend

j&wkay   chop down, cut down--trees

j&wtah evening

j&y belly, stomach

j&yban head of, at the top of

j&yib bottle used for collecting coconut sap

j&yj&y write

j&yjah scarce, seldom

j&ymetak stomach ache

jab not

jabdeywet any, anything, miscellaneous, whatever, each, every

jabdik after part of canoe when outrigger is on port side; starboard tack

jabeł shovel

jaben point, corner, at the end of

jabenkennahan proverb

Jabet Sunday, the sabbath

jabey not enough, insufficient

jabilbil roll back and forth

jabiq fishing method--using long net at day time along reef ridge

jabłap forward part of canoe when outrigger is on port side; port tack

jad&y appear

Jadeydey Saturday

jag cry, play music on radio or phonograph

jah still, for the time being, now

jahab no

jahad rather, fairly, somewhat

jahajmiy raw fish--edible

jahałiyy&y easy to turn

Jahṁiwwah place name--Samoa

jahap a fish--red snapper--*Lutjanus vaigiensis*

jahat chart

jahbahwet church offering

jahgin not yet, never

jahj&y not know

jahj&ylaqjeṅ ignorant, silly, innocent

jahjah carry a child on the hip

jahkey offer, hold out--as a baby for another to take

jahtiyin sardines

jahw&tw&t drought, dry spell, not rainy, seldom rains

jajiny&t unacquainted

jajjaj boast, boastful, brag (about one's self)

jajjewekwek  hard to embarrass

jak&w  gone, missing, lost

jakapen  less than half full

jakapyel  not skillful, not clever

jakiley  not recognize

jakiy  mat

jakk&l  not scared easily

jakk&lk&l  panties (women's)

jakkij&yj&y  seldom tire

jakkik  not biting--of fish

jaɬjaɬ  loosen, unwind, unsnarl, take apart

jaɬɬetak  facing east

jal&yl&y  meat course, sauce, gravy

jalet  not well-sifted, not well-cleaned, not thoroughly done

jalj&l  roll up--as fried pandanus leaves, coil

Jalw&j  place name--atoll--Rɇlik--Jaluit

jaṁb&w  hike, travel on a vacation, go away for a change of scene

jaṁeñ  a fish--salmon

jaṁjaṁ  desire more--of a delicious food, music, game, not satisfied, want more

Jameney  place name--Germany

jamin  will never, will not--determination or simple future

jan  since, from, than

Janewdey  January

janij  make change, trade, exchange

janiknik  not persevering

jap&y  wooden bowl, wooden tub

japakij  stay underwater long--inability to

jaqenqen  catch many fish--inability to

jaqqir&yr&y  seldom play

jar  pray, go to church

jar  crowd, any group of people --as a class, unit or division

jar  split, broke, torn off, ripped

jaɬem  electricity, lightning, electric shock

jati-  younger sibling, younger brother, younger sister, younger cousin (parallel)

jaw  run--of engines

jawab  get a job, work on a job

jawak  chalk

jawaɬ  salt

jawig  not complete, not enough --of counted things; not add up, not paired off jawiwatah   not scare easily

jawwiy   not tasty--of fish

jayan   cent(s), money

jayanqin   a food--dried over-ripe breadfruit (also in Rḁlik chain, dried pandanus paste)

jayibew   dumpling

jayidyig   siren

jayikey   fish--scarcity of

jayj&y   long knife, sword, machete

jeban   rich, well supplied with food and property

jebayb&y   stray, wander, be lost

jebey   oar, paddle, rudder

jebeybey   steer, rudder

jebłahak   return, go

jedawijij   trousers

jegaw   smell of fish--lingering on hands or utensils

jegewil   ten

jehet   shirt

jehethet   wear a shirt

jekahkah   a food--pandanus chip

jekajeyjey   a by-product of jekarew--coconut sap--white, keeps only two days without fermenting

jekak   copra pieces--taken out of the shell

jekapyel   unskillfull

jekar&w   coconut sap

jekayiyej   notches cut in a tree for climbing

jekaykay   anywhere around here

jekdawan   not matter, never mind

jekłaj   the day after tomorrow

jekeṁayiy   coconut syrup--boiled down from sap

jeken   a second--of time; second base

jekkar   ill matched, unbecoming, improper, contrary to, unsuitable

jełay   know, well-informed, know how to

jełłaq   face away from

jelṁahyey   face to face

jeṁar   summer, summer vacation

jeṁlaq   end, finish

jema-   father, uncle--father's brother

jemanji- one who has taken care of another's child; relation between two brothers-in-law who are married to two sisters

jempahan sampan

jep take sides

Jepahan place name--Japan

jeplahak sail away on a voyage

jeplej syphilis, gonorrhea, venereal disease

Jeptembah September

jeq to land, alight

jeqqep soup of soft rice or breadfruit

jeqqep yin may a food--breadfruit soup

jetjet walk fast and vigorously

jetmetah underpants--men's

jettayan broke, accident, damaged

jerahamhan wealthy, lucky, blessed, fortunate

jerakr&k go sailing

jeramel poor, lonely, poverty

jerawiywiy sin

jeray befriend, friend

jerbal work

jerkakp&j&y rise from the dead, resurrection

jerwahan prodigal, waste

jet few, several, a few others

jetey how many

jettal not leak, water-tight

jewdiy zorie(s)

jeweb soap

jewedah catch many fish--inability to

jew- throw

jewek ashamed, embarrassed, shy

jewenjew magistrate

jewet bullet

jewij kind, kindhearted

jewij canoe part--bottom part of canoe

jewijew right here

jewjew soak

jewjew a fish--flying fish--family *Exocoetidae*

jewkankan dress, to dress

jewkiyig scrub--using wet cloths

Jewnah person or thing that causes trouble or bad luck--Jonah jewrahantak   dawn

jewtah   last evening

jewwan   lazy

jeyah   chair, bench

jeyen   chain

jeyi-   older brother, older sister, older sibling

Jeyinah   place name--China

Jeyinah   a plant--banana variety--*Colocasia*

jeyinahyey   mat woven from coconut frond

jeyłah   sailor

Jeymaw   place name--atoll--Ratak--Jemo

jeyyahal   beckon with the hand--downward motion

jibadek   try to reach

jibbǝŋ   morning

jibi-   grandmother, grandchild

jibiqiy   hundred, one hundred

jibwin   spoon, fork

jiddiwil   a shell--top

jidpan   saw

jijilimjiwen   seven

jiki-   place, property, land

jikiwil   school

jikkah   cigarette

jil&w   a fish--albacore--*Thunnus alalunga*

jilgiwil   thirty

jiliw   three

jiliwbiqiy   three hundred

jiljinew   six

jilkin   send

jiṁ&y   straight, correct, right, honest

jiṁah   beyond, above, more, some--always used with numerals

jiṁeł   together, both

jiṁin qiy   chin

jiṁin ney   heel

jiṁin pay   elbow

jiṁṁah   grandfather

jimagig   fermented coconut toddy, sour toddy

jimattan   half

jimyeṅ   cement, concrete

jimmareq   dawn--period before

jinkadewel   broil--on hot stones

jinniprag   open spathe of coconut tree, stem of coconut bunch from which nuts have fallen jint&b   go barefoot, eat only one food

jipag   help

jipyeł   spell, spelling

jipyij   speech, make a speech

jiqah   sugar

jiqq&y   sand clam--bivalve

jireǵ   nickname for baby girl; adolescent girl--unmarried

jirhak-   to move, push

jiriylaq   slip, slide accidentally

jitawkin   stockings, socks

jiteg   point out something (to someone)

jitweb   stove

jiwen   one, other

jiwibwib   shoot of coconut, pandanus, etc.

jiwij   shoes

jiwijwij   wear shoes

Jiwin   June

jiwinb&ǵ   fishing method--pole at breaker

Jiwjey   Tuesday

jiwjiwir   step on, set foot on

Jiwłahyey   July

jiwtak   to stand up

jiyab   heart of palm

jiyiglij   undershirt

jiyjet   sit down

jjełaq   nothing, nobody, without, destitute of

jjewekwek   always ashamed

jjinew   begin

jjir   slippery

## K

k&b   dig

k&b&w   forever

k&g&y   a plant--*Scaevola frutescens*

k&j   we--(incl.), us--(incl.)

k&j&wtah   supper, eat supper

k&jdat   hate

k&jj&(y&)l   we--three (incl.)

k&jman   we--four (incl.)

k&jrew   we--two (incl.)

k&jw&j   we--more than four (incl.)

k&jyag   we--four (incl.)

k&l   technique, method, way or manner of doing something

K&l&y   place name--island--Rᴴlik--Kili

k&m we or us--more than four (excl.)

k&mj&(y&)l we or us--three people (excl.)

k&mrew we or us--two people (excl.)

k&mw&j we or us--five or more people (excl.)

k&myag we or us--four people (excl.)

k&n for, because, with, concerning

k&nkey because, since, as

k&t&w wind

k&wbah add, cohabit, put together, get together

k&włah coke, cola, soft drink

k&y porpoise

k&y&j case (as of food)

k&y&k cake

k&y&my&m&j remember

k&yin these--around us

k&yin keṁ stick for picking breadfruit

k&yk&b dipper

k&yk&y mature, strong, enough --of goods or needs

k&yr&wr&w be noisy

kab and, too, also, just, finally

kab cup, glass--drinking

kab&wdan dilute, to mix with water

kabb&qb&q clap hands, clapping, applaud

kabiŋ worship, religion

kabijer take by the hand, hold

kabil fishing method--fishing with a torch

kabilegleg amazing, surprising

kaddiyp&np&n lift weights to build up body

kadek intoxicating, drunk, poisonous (fish)

kadikdik slow

kadiw short

kadkad throw, pitch, large stone used as an anchor

kadkad fishing method--use throwing net

kadkad family relationship, position, contents (of a book)

kagir belt

kaha- fuel

kahaj cards--playing, play cards

kahajiriyriy   raise children

kahajliyig   gasoline barrel--empty

kahaṁteh   carpenter, carpentry

kahar   a plant--tree--*Premna corymbosa*

kahar   car

kahk&w   rooster

kahkey   with it, about it

kahn&w&j   very

kahtak   study, learn, to teach

kahwiw   look after a sick person, nurse--a patient

kahwiw   cow

kahwiwbewey   cowboy

ka-   causative prefix

kajikiyah   bump and grind, move hips in dancing

kajin   language

kajiw   mast

kajj&hj&h   nauseating, very ugly, very hateful, mean, despicable

kajjin&k   tired out

kajjireyrey   laugh at, ridicule, mock, deride

kajjit&k   ask, question

kajjiyeṉ   endeavor, try, mock, attempt, imitate

kajjiye-   the location of, the identification of

kajw&r   strong, force, power, strength

kak&lk&l   examine--physically

kak&lk&l   to try to recognize

kakelley   sign, symbol, punctuation, check mark, uniform insignia, miracle, signal, signify

kakijen   gather food

kakilkil   to peel, to skin

kakkij&y   to rest, to resign, vacation, holiday

kakkiṁkiṁ   a plant--grass--*Thuarea involuta*

kaɫ   diaper, loin cloth

kaɫkaɫ   wear a diaper, wear a loin cloth

kaɫɫaɫɫaɫ   to knock

kalan   gallon

kalbiwij   jail, to be thrown in jail, to be in jail

kallib   bury, plant

kallimiɫ   promise, testament, covenant

kallimj&k   to gaze at, to look steadfastly at

kalw&r   to hunt lobster

kaṁ&l&w   party--Marshallese style

kaṁbej   compass

kaṁṁewelwel   to thank

kaṅ   those--particle for things

kaṅey   those--close to you

kan&y   fuel, firewood

kanbej   canvas

kanijnij   swear, curse

kaniw   short

kaniyaqey   sufficient even if it's little--food

kankan   stretch, pull, stand at attention, tug

kanney   to fill

kanniy&k   meat, flesh

kanwed   mend--of nets

kap   roll--of cloth, bolt--of cloth

kapen   captain, officer of high rank

kapewpew   contagious

kapi-   bottom of

kapite-   oil belonging to

kapiyj&y   eat before working

kapiyl&g   western sky, Caroline Islands, Mariana Islands

kapp&q   to look for, search for, hunt for

kapw&r   a shell--clam--giant

kapyel   skillful, clever

kaqqenqen   to put things away, to put things in place

kaqqirey   to destroy, spoil

kar   past tense, conditional--contrary to fact, had

Karewlahyin   Caroline

karjin   kerosene

karkar   cut out copra meat from shell

karp&n   to mend, patch

karwahan   be with, accompany

karwin   scale fish

kat   side--of man or animal

katey   to struggle, to try hard, to apply one's self

Katilik   Catholic

katiw   check the weather, weather lookout, forecast weather

katlaq   allow, permit, to free

katmaney   expect, propose to do

kattar   wait for

kawaj blanket

kawajw&j to use a blanket

kawanpiyip corned beef

kawat steal

kawidpak peel off the end of a coconut shoot

kawiw&y scold, warn, reproach, advise, punish, reprove, admonish

kawiwatahtah dangerous

kawj&k caught on a rock

kawp&y coffee

kay these--close to me

kay torso, figure

kay- ride on a plane, to fly, to spring

kayaj hook, barb

kayal new

kayan its trunk, trunk of (tree), torso of (person)

kayan can--of meat

kayantel candle

kaydik small-waisted

kahyin kind, type

kaylik to go to the ocean side

kayrey mix with water, dilute

kebah copper

kebahathat to smoke

kebayb&y fishing method--fish with a pole

kedaw cloud

kejagjag to play music, musical instrument

kejak make fun, to joke, to kid

kejam door, doorway

kejatdikdik hope

kejatew to take shelter from the rain

kejerray to carry on hips (things)

kejewel ignore

kejeyjey dry under sun, to sun, sunbathe

kejjajet see off on a journey, bid farewell

kejpareq protect, take care of, save

kekkawj&kj&k fishing method--trawling--inside lagoon

kekkerayray to chase women

kelahak put on, assemble, install

kellay to pay

kellah garbage dump

kemanman make good, create

keṁkeṁ  pick breadfruit with a stick

keṁṁhan  make, do, build, fix

keṁṁhahwew  to converse, keep company, conversation

kemalij  brain

kemeḷeyḷey  explain, make clear, disentangle, unsnarl a tangled fish line

kemij  we--(excl.)

kemiyj&(y&)l  you--three persons (excl.)

kemiyman  you--four persons (excl.)

kemiyrew  you--two persons

kemiyw&j  you--five or more people

kemmalm&l  rehearse

kemmayidik  primp, strut, appear sultry

keṅhan  want, like, usually do something

keṅkeṁṁhan  boast, be proud

kennahan  talk, speak, tell, report, testify, declare, reveal, state

kennaw  dish, plate

kenwah  neck

kepewej  prepare

kepeweḷ  surround, include, close-in on, encircle

keppaḷpaḷ  fantastic

kerajraj  whaling

keray  woman, female

kerker  paddling canoe

ketha-  between, boundary line, dividing line

ketka-  plant of

ketlaq  to free, let go, allow

kew  the--plural--non-human

kew  to flee, exodus, run away, escape

kewbah  bamboo

kewebwib  eat fish half broiled but still raw, fish only half broiled

keweḷ  hair

kewerlaq  multiply, increase

kewet  goat

kewkeray  female--animal

kewṁhahan  male

kewnah  corner

kewnah  snitch, sneak away from

kewpay  coat

kewtak  lift, raise

kewwahlaq show, declare, reveal, preach, proclaim

key yes-no question particle, past tense subordinate clause introducer: that

keyegjak bump a sore or wound

keyemyem feast, birthday party

keyhar go from sea side of an island to lagoon side

keyid compare

keyinabbiw a plant--papaya--carica papaya

keykeyel tear, rend

keypahak move closer

kibey excrement, manure, feces

kidiw dog

kij louse

kij&nm&j persevere, patience

kij&rj&r be in a hurry

kijak fellow, guy

kijdik mouse, rat

kijeŋ immoral, immorality, tough--slang--of people, unlawful

kijeŋ desire, brave, bold

kije- food of

kijey hardwood, determination

kijgiyg&y firm, strong, tense

kijiw mast

kijjiye- regarding, in line with, direciton of, location of, identification of

kijyek fire

kik not ripe--fruit, unripe

kik bite, peck

kik&r a shell--clam--small

kil skin

kil&k basket--large

Kilbet Gilbert (Islands)

kilep big, large

kiley recognize, realize

kilhaj mirror, look in a mirror

kilhaj glass

kilhaj class

kilmeyej black

kimhiłak shock

kim&j coconut frond

kimił ointment of leaves and oil

kin&j wound

kin&jn&j wounded

kinhak tattle, complain, betray, accuse, reproach

kiniye-   mat
kipiliyy&y   obedient
kipiliyyah   disobedient
kir   call
kir&y   gray
kirahantew   field--baseball, playground
kirahbabewen   phonograph
Kirijm&j   Christmas
Kirjin   Christian, church member in good standing
kirr&w   gout, rheumatism, arthritis, lame, crippled
kiryij   grease, fat--of meat
kiryin   green
kit&ht&h   very angry, furious, anger
kitah   guitar
kitak   wind from southwest
Kitkew   acronym for Kwajalein Islands Trading Company--KITCO
kittiliy&k   hide-and-seek
Kiwajleyen   place name--atoll --Rälik--Kwajalein
kiwbahak   outrigger
kiwij   cat
kiwim   comb

kiwkiw   carry a person on one's back
kiwmiy   work gang, company, team
kiy   key
kiy&y   beams from canoe to outrigger
kiy&ytak   to bend down--coconut shoots only
kiyaptel   print by hand with manuscript style, capital letters
kiyen   government, law, commandment
kiyew   a plant--*Sida fallax*
kiyew   orange--color
kiyhaj   gasoline
kiyin   now
kiykiy   sleep
kiyl&k   shut
kiyyeh   now
kiyyeh-kiyyeh   immediately, very soon
kk&b   blunt, dull
kk&l   scared, afraid
kk&n   invent, compose
kk&yin   a while ago
kkag   sharp, pointed

kkahal  entice, lead, call or entice animals or children to come

kkal  build

kkan  food, bring food as tribute to chief

kkapit  oil oneself, put on perfume

kkar  suitable, fit, it is fitting, organize

kkar  put in order, arrange

kkat  to plant

kkay  common, usually, very often, repeatedly

kkayaly&l  select, elect, selection, election

kkebahbah  smell of copper

kkebeł  chase

kkeñak  to wear, be surrounded by, to love

kket  strong, great capacity

kkeykahak  pull out, drag, slip out, a drawer

kkiṁkiṁ  fast beating of heart in fear, palpitation

kkiwil  squeeze, hold tight

Ł

ł&g  commit adultery, lust, fornicate

ł&pper  mumps

ł&q&t  pile of trash

ładdik  boy

łag  to crack, open a crack; storm

łaǵ  a fly

łahaṁ  lamp

łahyey  smooth and calm--water

łahyin  line

ła-  prefix to masculine names

łak  to lock

łałłap  old man

łal&m  five

łanten  lantern

łap  big, great, large

łaq  the last, the most recent

łaqa-  after, behind, bottom

łaqin  after

łat  coconut shell, skull

łat-jiṁ  coconut shell--lower half with sharp end

łat-m&j  coconut shell--upper half next to stem with eyes

łattil pakew  a fish--shark pilot--*Echeneis naucrates*

ławł&y  candy

łay  gravel

łayṁeł'an  heritage--land

ɫeǧtak   base, foundation, support, lever, roller for launching canoe, something to protect or lift by putting it under something

ɫehɫeh   weave flowers or shells into a lei

ɫejew   rust

ɫekeṁ   imagine, pretend, make believe, wish for

ɫeṁah   you--to many men in general--not specific

ɫeṁahr&yin   these men

ɫeṁahrew   the men

ɫemṅak   think, thought

ɫet   what man?

ɫeweb   loaf--bread

ɫewen   picket boat, boat with outboard engine

ɫewer(ey)   follow

ɫewrah   place name--islet--main island of Majuro--Laura

ɫewrak   caught, entangled

ɫeyeṅ   he--away from the speaker, that man

ɫeyew   the man

ɫɫahaj   dynamic voice, sonorous

ɫɫahaj   treble, high-pitched sound, piercing sound

L̈

l̈&y   small pool--on reef at low tide or in interior of island

l̈et   canoe mast top

l̈etlaq   faint, disappear

l̈iyit   to slurp, drink noisily

L

l&b   grave, tomb

l&g   up, above, high

l&ggah   riddle

l&k&r   surf-boarding

l&k&y   believe, trust in, depend on

l&l   stuck, hit, hit the mark

l&ɫɫap   old woman

l&ml&m   fold, wrap, packed

l&p   egg

l&qjak   be busy with, be involved, be tied down by a task

l&ql&q   bind, tie on

l&tl&t   stretched tight--of lines, ropes, etc., full--of sails

l&wl&w&rjahkey   take responsibility, urge, make sure

l&yr&w&j   daughter of a queen, high chieftess

l&yw&j   give--to you

laŋ   sky, weather, heaven

lahlah   hen

lahley   look, see, look at, look after, observe, take care of, supervise

laj   cruel, fierce, mean, ferocious

lał   world, on the ground, country (of the world)

lamh&j   to shout, to call

lawbil&j   publicity, in public

lawǰiy   mouth

lawj&t   ocean, sea

lawj&y   stomach

lawjilɢiy   ear

lawlaw   hen

lawmetew   ocean, sea

lawpiden ney   sole--foot

lebah   leper, leprosy, Hansen's disease

leddik   girl

leg   many, much, plenty, full

leg halen   many times, often

lekay   surf-boarding

leklek   a plant--a grass

lełɣaɣ   fright, terror, to be afraid of, fear

lemgewil   fifty

let   what woman?

let   well-sifted, well-cleaned, thoroughly done

letah   letter, mail

lew   tongue

lewmhalew   lagoon

lewwaha-   inside

ley k&t&w   to 'shoot the breeze', soft sell, to proposition, chat

ley-   give, offer

ley-   use, be equipped with, with

leyłemhak   guess, estimate

leyl&ɢ   to lift

leylaq   give away

leyteq   give--to the speaker

lib&w&rw&r   to chase

lib&wb&w   cover

libbiq&y   a shell--cowrie, cowrie shell

li-   prefix to feminine names

lik   behind, in back of, outside, ocean side of

lik   to set--of hens

likahwew   young man

likahyebyeb   top--a toy--of shells or wood

likahyebyeb   a shell--*Conus bandanus*, top--toy, spin

likajik   pistol, revolver

Likiyep   place name--atoll--Ratak--Likiep

likiyyæw   whole, all present, get together, intact

likjab   fall short of, be too late, not reach, less than, owe

likkæw   petticoat, slip

liklik   strain, sift

likten   contraction of: likit bey yen

liṁ   murky water, stirred up, dirty water, fine sand in sea, roiled

liṁahakhak   kite, fly a kite

liṁahræyin   these women

liṁahrew   the woman

limabiqiy   five hundred

lime-   drink (possessive)

limew   interest

liped   baked breadfruit

liqe-   middle of, waist

liqen bæŋ   midnight

liqqiwin   exact, true, right, certain, actual, extremely

lił   calm

liw   scold

liwij   lose

liyæy   this woman

liyew   the woman

liyhaklaq   condemn

liyin   this woman

liyeń   that woman

llæq   tie

llæł   shade

llahdikdik   coolness of a breeze

llew   see

lley   negative reward, it serves someone right

llik   put, leave, lay down, consider, transport, carry in a vehicle or vessel

lliwtæk   pour, overflow, slop out

Ṁ

ṁæd   provisions for a voyage

ṁæj   finished, already

ṁæłæw   cool

ṁæyyar   enter lagoon, go in a pass

ṁad  loiter

ṁad&y  spear

ṁaha-  ahead, before, a place in front of

Ṁahaj  March--the month

ṁahak  money

ṁahan  front, peak

ṁahbiŋ  eat breakfast

Ṁahjeł  place name--Marshall Islands

ṁahṁah  mother, mama

ṁahyey  until, for, toward, against

ṁahyił  mile

ṁahyinah  love song

ṁaj  eel, intestinal worm

ṁaj&y  sneeze

ṁajeł  muscles

ṁajgal  guts, intestines

ṁak&wk&w  to refuse to do something

ṁakitkit  unstable, move

ṁakṁ&k  a plant--arrowroot--*Tacca leontopetaloides*

ṁal  bend toward

ṁałew  lagoon

Ṁandey  Monday

ṁanit  custom, behavior, conduct

ṁaniy  money

ṁał̣ij  to break--as a stick, broken

ṁarey  to marry

ṁarṁar  necklace, to wear a necklace

ṁegay  food, eat

ṁeh  thin--of animals or men

ṁehreh  murder, to kill, murderer, murderous

ṁejawlig&r  lunacy, lunatic

ṁejṅaw  weak, puny

ṁek  tired

ṁekadkad  wander

ṁekaj  fast, speedy

ṁełagł&g  nausea, nauseated

ṁen bid&j  toilet

ṁen jar  church (building)

ṁen jikiwił  school house

ṁen keppewjak  toilet

ṁen takteh  hospital

ṁen wiyah  store, shop

ṁeń  lie, deceive, trick

ṁeṅakṅak  brown, withered, dry

ṁeṅehṅak  happy

ḣeñejñej   itch

Meñewellap   place name--atoll --Ratak--Maloelap

ḣeqtah   before

ḣeḻ   old--of things, rotten, worn out

ḣeray   dry, withered

ḣeraybet   wear wet clothing

ḣettan jidik   soon, almost, in a little bit

ḣewel   truth, that's true, true, right, correct, realistic, real

ḣewetkah   automobile, car, truck

ḣeyiq   goods, provisions, wealth, gifts

ḣeyiyey   rich, wealthy

ḣeylik   leave lagoon, go out a pass

ḣijbar   cut hair, haircut

ḣijḣij   cut

ḣil   act, behavior, manner

ḣilạy   dove

ḣilaḻ   deep

ḣiqḣiq   rub clothes--washing

ḣiḻ   hip

ḣiḻ   ancient chant

ḣiḻiy   owe

ḣirar   reddish color

ḣiwpiy   a movie, to see a movie

ḣiyew   coconut leaf chain used in fishing

ḣuhahan   man, male, wife's brother

ḣuhan   good

ḣuhar   fishing basket

ḣuhewel   to be thanked, generous

## M

m&d   cooled off--of food once hot

m&d&y   young coconut meat

m&g   smell of taste--sour or bitter--as milk or vinegar or rice soup, etc., sour

m&j   dead, numb

m&j   the opening between islets

m&j&nmah   kiss

m&jj&y   the opening between islets

m&jjiyy&y   quick to die

m&jjiyyah   long in dying, slow to die

m&jkiy   sleepy

m&jwahan   a plant--breadfruit variety--seeded

m&y   fort, fortified place, coral weir to trap fish, coral wall

m&yriyah   plumeria

mab   map

mag   coconut beginning to turn brown

magide-   children of a man's sister, nephew, niece

magig   coconut sap--old and sour

magk&w   mango

mahag   pandanus leaf

mahat   empty, no more, all gone

mahrewrew   green

mahwew   bruised

maj   eye, face

maj   sun glasses, diving mask, eye glasses

majet   match

majinmiwir   wake up early in the morning

majił   sleep

majiłlep   sleep soundly, late in awakening

majmaj   to wear glasses

Majr&w   place name--atoll--Ratak--Majuro

mak&y   alone, self

makijkij   often, frequent, common

małeǰ   drown

małim   permitted, allowed, lawful, permission

maletlet   smart, bright

malley   coal, charcoal, coals--of fire

maniy   thin

mar   bush, shrub, boondocks

mar&w   thirsty

mareǰ   can, be able to, ability, power

mareq   dark, darkness

markibeybey   a plant--*Wedelia biflora*

mat   cooked

materter   very angry, furious

mattiyy&y   easy to cook, easy to satisfy with food

mattiyyah   hard to cook, greedy for food

maw   taboo, forbidden, prohibited

mawar   fish bait

may   a plant--general term for breadfruit

May&y   May--the month

mayal   axe, hatchet, adze, iron, steel, metal

mayañ   burn, smart--as medicine on a sore

meh   elastic, stretch

mejaḷ   unsnarl, disentangle

mejanwed   a shell--clam--medium

mejewib   coconut--nearly ripe

mejiyneydey   missionary

mejyin   common cold

meḷah   time between rain showers

meḷaqḷaq   forget

meḷeyḷey   understand, well-defined, well-ordered

men   thing

menewkadiw   perspiration, perspire, sweat

meqañ   a food--pandanus juice cooked and preserved

merah   light--of weight

meram   bright, light

metak   pain, hurt, ache

metew   sea, ocean, navigation, navigate

mew   to heal

mewet   wind-squall

mewij   white

mewir   live, life, existing

mey   that, which, who

Meydiy   personal name--Mary

meyej   mate--ship's

meyej   dark--in color

meygey   although

meyjin   sewing machine

mij&l   thick, thickness

mijak   fear, afraid

miḷ&y   a place name--atoll--Ratak

milik   milk

minit   minute

Miyeykew   acronym for Marshall Islands Import Export Company, MIECO

miyjeḷ   missile

mm&j   keep awake, stay up

mmahan   be at anchor, tie up a vessel

mmakijkij   often

mmeḷew   far apart, wide apart

mmewirwir   lively, living, active

mmin&yn&y   habit, practice, used to, accustomed to, have the habit of, practiced

## Ṅ

ṅah  locative particle

ṅahjiki-  make room for

ṅahkije-  provide food for

ṅahkineye-  provide mat for

ṅahlime-  provide food for

ṅahpite-  provide pillow for

ṅahyey  against

ṅaṁ  mosquito

ṅeq  wet

ṅeq  midrib of a coconut leaf

ṅew  a wave

ṅey  that--close to you

## N

nab&j  outside

nahaj  will be, future tense marker

nahajdik  to feed, nourish

nahan  word

nahgin  almost

nahginm&j  sick, sickness, pregnant

nahnah  bad, wicked, evil

naji-  son, daughter, child, toy, pet, money

najn&j  to keep as a pet, pet

nam  smell, taste

naṁ  lagoon--secondary

Naṁ&w  place name--atoll--Rālik--Namu

Naṁdik  place name--atoll--Rālik--Namorik

naṁnaṁ  to wash bottles

nebar  to praise, admire, recommend, glorify

nehej  nurse

neṁbah  number, figure

nemaym&yi-  appearance

Newbeṁbah  November

ney  leg, foot, wheel, paw

Nibbeǰ  Japan

nignig  baby

niknik  industrious

niqiy  relatives, family

niqniq  clothes, cloth, clothing, dress up

niteł  needle

niwijp&ybah  newspaper

niy  a plant--general term for all varieties of coconut trees and fruits

nn&y  container, fill a container

nnahan   news

## P

pɛdkat   mud

pɛjpɛj   shallow

pɛn   solid, firm, strong, difficult, hard, strict

pɛnawiyyɛy   smart, quick to learn

pɛnawiyyah   stupid, slow to learn

pɛnja-   stopper, protector

pɛq   entangle, disorder, confuse, troubled, messed up

pɛr   coconut--small sprouted, tumor, swelling

pɛt   pillow

pɛtkɛj   biscuit, cracker

pɛtpɛt   use a pillow

pɛybah   paper, card

pɛyij   page

pɛyinabel   pineapple

pad   be somewhere, stay, remain, be left

pahan   band--musical

pahtah   war

pahwew   appearance

pakew   a fish--shark

pakij   long-winded in diving, able to stay under water long

paljej   a food--very ripe breadfruit baked in coconut milk

palɛylɛy   marriage, married

palye-   spouse, wife, husband

pap   coconut frond, midrib of coconut frond

parek   faint

pat   swamp

pawpɛw   bind, tie, bound, coil

pay   arm, hand, wing

payagkel   bracelet, bangle, to wear a bracelet

payak-   bag, sack

payantɛrɛy   cupboard, pantry, food cabinet

payat   ebb tide

payat meñakñak   ebb tide--lowest

paytɛrɛy   battery

penkeh   vinegar

pepah   pepper

peqpeq   cough

peran   loud

pew   lower sail, land--sailing vessel, arrive--sailing vessel pewib  busy

pewtak  torn

peyah  pair

peyeł  bell

peyen  pen

peyet  bed

peypey  council, bargain, plan, authority, decide, confer

peytak  drift eastward

pid  posterior, butt, ass, buttocks

pid&wd&w  soft

pidiyyet  period

pijah  picture, camera, draw a picture

pik&t  coward, one who flees from battle, afraid to

Pikinniy  place name--atoll--Rålik--Bikini

piknik  picnic

pikpik  propeller--of plane or ship, flap, flutter-- as of wings

pil  drop--of liquid

pil&w  blind, trachoma, not see well, inflamed eye

pil&y  play cards for stakes, play poker

piliglig  bleed, to drip

pilyej  plate

pinahnah  a plant--a general term for banana

pinjeł  pencil

pinneyep  coconut oil

pit  Gilbertese, a clan

pitpit  rub--with oil, massage

piwał  coward, dastardly

piyah  beer

piyahnew  piano, play piano

piyaw  chilly, fever and chills

piybah  fever, feverish

piyig  pink

piyik  pig

piyił tiryep  field trip

pp&q  search for, look for, hunt for

ppakij  able to hold breath under water

ppał  astonish, confound, senile, absent-minded

ppeŷ  hoarse

Q

q&ł&yiyahat  nude, shirtless

q&l&y  hungry

qamh    you--plural (excl.)

qamja(ya)l    you--three

qamwaj    you--five or more people

qamyag    you--four people (excl.)

qapaj    trash, garbage

qapajpaj    clean up waste food or trash

qar    frightened, afraid

qayat    octopus

qaylaq    to assemble, assembly, meeting, to meet together

qayqay    to scrape, to scratch

qagqirej    congress

qałiyniy    tiny coconut not fully grown

qałmay    fall prematurely--coconuts

qałqał    wash

qanjin    a food--breadfruit cooked on coals and scraped, to roast breadfruit

qebba-    contents of

qedyak    beard, whiskers

qehar    you--plus particle of past tense (sing.)

qej    you (sing.) progressive

qej    congeal, thicken, solidify, stiffen, freeze, hardening of starch or tallow or lead

qeley    kernel, fruit, seed, nut, testicle

qemjah    head of a governmental organization, magistrate, district administrator, educational administrator, administrator

qemhewel    thank you

qemrew    you--two persons

qeṅ    tight, well-organized

qeṅqeṅ    able to catch many fish

qena-    a catch--fish, crabs, birds

qenewnew    read, talk

qerak    tie, wrap up, bandage

qetin    a plant--*Gossypium barbadense*

qetin    cotton

qey    you--absolute (sing.)

Qijjahyey    place name--Kusaie

qiłab    club, to go drinking at a club

qiḷiḷ    an insect--cockroach

qinaha-    contribution, duty

qiq    cook

qiq gathered together

qiɬeb baseball glove

qiɬebɬeb wear a baseball glove

qirahaghag dry hair (not oily)

qirar small cut

qirqir gargle, brush teeth

qit thick, dense (of shrubbery), crowded--of people, close together

qiwat can--of food, tin can

qqaɫ coconut sennit, cord made from coconut fibre

qqanjinjin smell of roasting breadfruit

qqejarjar holy, sanctified, righteous, pure, spotless, clean

qqin extinguish, go out--of light, put out a fire

qqir&y play game

qqit(qit) often, close together

R̈

ɬag hole, shelter pit--air raid

ɬag platform over the lee side of a canoe--opposite outrigger

ɬebah rubber

ɬebbah horn, trumpet

ɬejak spar--of sail

ɬemhak shine, to light

ɬet kind, type

ɬij wake up

ɬijɬij to break

ɬiṁij slow, delay, tardy, late

ɬiɬ pick--flowers

R

r&k south, southern

r&ṁ to crumble a mound or pile --as of sand

r&ṁ rum

R&wjiyah Russia

r&ybah river

r&yin these--people

r&ytiy&w radio

r&yyahar east

rah branch

rahan day

rahank&y grate--coconuts, grater

rahantak daybreak, dawn

rahlaq slow, easy going

rahr&h clean up an area

Rahtak   place name--eastern chain of the Marshall Islands--Ratak

rahwin   go around, go on a field trip

rahyelep   noon

rahyinyin   today

raj   whale

rajjiyyah   yaws, ulcerated framboesia

rak   south, summer

rañ   those--people

raqej   physique, shape--body, looks

rawal   to return, to rotate, come back

rawalten   come back in order to

ray   these--people

rahyij   rice

rayjet   apart, divided into two parts, partly

Raylik   place name--western chain of Marshall Islands--Rälik

raylik   west

reŋ   to hear

reŋiyyεy   be good of hearing

reŋiyyah   hard of hearing

reŋjakey   listen

regewil   twenty

rehar   they have, they were, past tense 3rd plural

rej   they--progressive

ren   they should

rew   the (human, pl.)

rewej   rose, hibiscus flower

rewejwej   wear a rose or hibiscus flower

rewrew   hang on the line

reyejtak   to assist, ally, agree, to second, concur

reyjah   razor, shave

reyrey   laugh, breaking of waves, smile

reytam   the outrigger side of a canoe

ribiqiy   two hundred

rikakiy   teacher, preacher

rikewreya-   uncle--mother's brother only

Riq   place name--Truk

riq   yaws

rittew   old age, old, adult, mature, of age

riwahliytεk   eight

riwahmayejet  stranger, not familiar

riwahtimjiwen  nine

riwew  two

riwhak-  move (with directionals)

riwiñ  room

riwriwey  slander

riyab  lie

riyig  ring

riyigyig  wear a ring

riyi-  husband, wife, spouse

riylik  on the west side

riyliki-  cross cousin

Riytah  place name--islet--Majuro Atoll--Rita

rrey  wide awake

rreyew  clean

rreyew  clean, pure, sanitary

rran  mark with a pencil, dirty, mar, soil

## T

teltel  collect

teptep  taking gifts to a wedding, party, or funeral

teqteq  scratch in ground for food--chickens only

tereyreyi-  side, edge

tew  disembark, come off of, climb down

tewłak  westward

tewtak  dig up, uproot

tab  obscured, cloudy, unclear weather, fog, dim, haze

tabeł  double

tabił  hesitate, be reluctant to

tah  what, which

tahłah  dollar

tahłaq  eastward

tahtah  superlative particle, most

tahwinyin  why, what is the reason

Tahyijey  Thursday

tahyikeh  tiger

tahyiñañ  mosquito net

tahyiybiwin  typhoon

takin  socks

takinkin  wear socks

takteh  doctor, see a doctor

talbewen  telephone

talleg  climb up

tañtañ  glare, blinded by sunlight

tanij    dance--western style

tariyñahyey    war, fight a battle

tar-    go on a vehicle or sailing canoe

tarrin    about, approximately

taw    a plant--*Saccharum officinarum*--sugar cane

tawal    towel

tawar    pour out, run--water, flow

tawar    boat passage through a reef, canal

tawijin    one thousand

tawɫ&y    doll

tayag    have sex appeal--of males, 'lady-killer', have a way with women

tayag    water container, tank spout

tayap    provide food for family from local sources (not from the store); provide for someone

tebak    cigar, breadfruit bud

tegal    sweet

teghak    porch

tekyak    arrive, come to land, reach destination

teɫahwew    sitting mat

teĺ    hill, mountain

tel    to lead

temak    believe, faith

teñ    a tune

teñ    eel that lives in fresh water--toothless

tenak    dream

tepar    arrive, reach

teprak    accomplish, carry out, succeed, achieve

teqaylik    afterwards, later

teqja-    value

ter    greedy

terak    ceiling

teryej    thread

teryej    straight--in playing poker

tet    stay still

tew    a long time, prolong

tewnahaj    a food--doughnut--with hole

tewtew    hang up

teybeɫ    table, desk

teyegkiy    flashlight, light

teye-    what location? what relation?

teyej    test

tibbaq   stumble, slip

Tijeṁbah   December

tikɛt   ticket

tikjiyneydey   dictionary

tiljɛk   thrifty, careful, painstaking, faithful

tiṁ   be late for and miss--a plane, boat, car, etc.

tiṁtiṁ   to pull and break--string or rope or grass

tipdikdik   small pieces, fragments, crumbs

tipgel   outrigger canoe--for sailing--large

tipjɛk   stumble, slip

tiḷ   end of an islet

tiḷi-   next to, close to, near

tiḷiṁ   play trump--a card game

tiḷin maj   face

tirabeḷ   trouble

tirahyip   to drive--a car

tirak   truck

tiraṁ   drum, barrel

tirewrew   wrap with leaves

tirtir   wrap in basket or leaves

tirwet   cabinet, wardrobe, closet

tiryep   trip

tiw   stomach, gizzard

tiw   a locative, where, there

tiwdek   gizzard, stomach

tiwlɛg   at the upper part

tiwlaq   go down, dive, take a bath

tiwrɛyyahar   eastern part

tiwraḡ   skin-diving, spear fishing

tiwriylik   westward

tiwtiw   bathe, take a bath, wet

tiwwahak   go into the water

tiwyag   northern part

tiy   tea, put tea in

tiybat   teapot, tea kettle, coffee pot

tiyey   lips

tiyin   tin, piece of tin roofing

tiyjeḷ   diesel, diesel oil

tiyṁah   ship, steamer, motor vessel

tiyṁeṅ   ghost, demon

tiypiy   tuberculosis

tt&g   laugh

tt&g dikdik   smile, titter, giggle

tt&r   run

tt&w&n   dirty

ttah   conceive, become pregnant

ttal   leak

ttay   low, lowly, menial

ttay b&r&w   humble

tteŋ   sleep soundly

ttew   fishing method--use fish pole at night

ttewɬak   far

tteyig   fill--with liquid

ttil   burn, light, set fire to, ignite

## W

w&b   chest

-w&j   suffix denoting movement toward the person(s) addressed

w&jk&y   plant--general word for tree

w&jk&y   whiskey

w&jɬay   a sail

w&k   net

w&kjak   overturn, upset, upside down, fall--from erect position, capsize

w&ṁ   hermit crab

w&n   turtle

w&p   a plant--*Barringtonia asiatica*

w&r   lobster

w&rɬaq   asthma

w&rm&j   wash one's face

w&t   rain

w&t&mj&j   all, every

w&tlaq   fall down, drop down-- as from a height

w&w   pale

wab   pier, wharf

wah   canoe, ship, boat, vehicle

wahɬaq   appear, happen, get up --from lying down

wahyiniy   copra

waj   to watch, guard

waj   watch

wajwaj   wear a watch

wanhar   go or come towards the lagoon

wan-   walk toward, go toward

wanl&g   ascend, climb

wanlał  go or come down

wanlik  go or come towards the ocean side of an island, go back

wanmetew  go or come seaward

wanyan&y  go or come ashore--toward land, shoreward

Waqej  August

waqen  organ--musical

wat  puffer fish--*Tetraodon hispidus*

waw&w  circle, zero, mark to show absence

wawaj  horse

way  injection, receive injection, shot

wayar  crawl on belly

wayl&j  to transmit (radio), radio transmitter, to talk on the radio

wayl&l  good marksmanship--spearing

wayt&w  land tract

wayt&w  go westward

wayteq  come

wayw&y&-  form, shape, figure, method of, manner of, how

webin  stove, oven

webrak  full, tight--not used with liquids

wed  coral reef, coral

wedah  able to catch a lot of fish, lucky--in fishing

weg  homesick, longing for

wejak  do

Wejjay  place name--atoll--Ratak--Wotje

wekar  root

Wektewbah  October

wekwek  pick pandanus

wełał&w  weakling, coward

wełaq  tipped over, fallen prostrate, felling of a tree

weńya-  price of, salary of, cost of

Wenjey  Wednesday

wenmahyey  meet, to go and meet

wepiyjah  officer

wepyij  office

weqin bahd&y  stevedore, working party

wera-  number of, quantity

weran  orange--fruit

werwer  pen, fence, enclosure

wet  only, still, just

wetem  entirely, absolutely, very

wetewbahyiy  scooter, motorcycle

Wettew  place name--atoll--Rālik--Wotho

wew  oh, oh my, darn it

weyah  wire

weyeppan  complete, of upright character, perfect, improved, well done

weylaq  go, go away

weytak  go eastward

wib  tender skin of a baby, soft, tender

wid  piece, smallest unit of something

wididdid  tremble, quake, chills

widyakyak  crazy, delirious, insane

wig  complete, whole, total a correct amount

wiggar  beg--for food only

wijlag  place name--atoll--Rālik--Ujelang

wijw&j  a plant--general term for grass--*Vittaria elongata*

wijwij  to pull out, root out

wikey  take, bring, lead--of people or animals

wikw&k  change, turn, translate, interpret

wiliy&w  handsome--men only

Wilkah  place name--islet--Uliga (Majuro Atoll)

willepa-  uncle--mother's brother only

wiṁ  native oven, earth oven

wiṁṁah  kiss

wiṁwiṁ  bake--usually in earth oven

win  reason, purpose, cause; problem--arithmetic

winew  treat--medically, to paint, paint, medicine

winhak  birds flying looking for fish

winteh  window

wiphaj  fireplace, open fireplace for cooking, ashes

wiqleyley  ukulele

wir  swollen gland

wir&k  fishing method--to fish from a canoe

wirhak  to move

wirw&r  cluster, bunch of ripe and drinkable coconuts

wirw&r  murder

wirwir  flame, flash, burning

wit  a plant--general term for flower or any hedge plant

witak   shoot--coconut

witaṁ&y   unhealthy, sick, busy

witał   squall

witeŋ   noodles

wite-   mixture

witiy&j   high

Witr&k   place name--atoll--Ratak--Utirik

wiw   pale

wiw   fish trap

wiw&y   to board, ride, get on

wiwahak   reply, answer, consent

wiwan   kind of, number of

wiwaṅ   grey-haired

wiwareŋ   annoyed or bothered by noise

wiwatah   be afraid of, in danger of

wiweyew   there--far off

wiyah   buy, sell

wiyik   week

wiyik yin lał   next week

wiyin   win, gain

wwan   industrious, hard working

wwar   beg

wwat   ripe--of pandanus

wwir   coryza, to blow one's nose, nasal mucous

wwiy   smell of cooking fish

## Y

y&dj&ŋ   taste--food or drink

y&gjahkey   feel

y&gtahan   suffer

y&j&j   nothing, none, not any

y&k   fish

y&k&jka-   how

y&k&y   blood vessel, vein, artery

y&kyeṅ   a plant--pandanus cultigen--Aur

y&ṁ   house

y&mjak   anchor, tie up to a buoy

y&my&m&j   memory, remember

y&ntak   pick green coconuts from tree

y&q   you--sing. obj.

y&r&m   become, change from one thing to another

y&rj&(y&)l   they--three

y&rw&j   they--more than four

yaryag    they--four

yaw    here it is, take it

yawtahak    wrestling

yay    he, she, it (absolute)

yabiqiy    four hundred

yag    north

yaŋ    sprout, grow

yaŋed    go fishing

yagden    hungry

yagin    escort, lead, show where to go

yagyiginteq    call to come

yahab    no

yaj    weave

yajmiwir    healthy, robust

yakey    with it, about it

yakil    peel

yakilkil - to skin, to peel

yakit    delouse, sort out bad copra

yaktaw    discharge, unload

yal    shave

yaɫ    coconut milk

yalij    repeat, review

yalik    back, last

yaliki-    after, outside, back

yaliklik    ashamed--concerning food

yaliktahtah    very last, final, finally

yalqej    to fold, to bend

yamjay    empty

yanay    islet, island

Yanayweytak    place name--atoll--Rɨlik--Eniwetok

yanbin    body

yanyan    bail out water from canoe or boat

yanyin    this islet

yar    haul canoe or vessel up on shore

yar    lung

yat    name

yat    smell

yat    eyebrow

yatyat    pack, put in container

yawan wet jiwen    flat, level

yawat    striped or spotted (as in ancient tattoo)

yawreŋ    respond to, find out, answer to call

yawreŋ nahan    gather news or information

yawy&w   bind with sennit, lash

yayindeyin   thus, as, so, just as, therefore, likeness

yayinjiwen   different, unlike, otherwise

yayinłaq   more similar to, almost alike

yayinwet   too, also, same

yayinwet jiwen   same, alike, never mind, that's all right

yayiyy&rłaqwet   et cetera

yegewil   forty

yegiyyeṅ   that over there--singled out

yegṅeyṅey   that close to you--singled out

yegyew   this, here it is

yegyin   this thing here between us, thus, that is, that's it, here it is

yekajet   judge, try in court

yekjab   idol

yekl&yjiyah   members of the church

yekpay   change clothes--from good to dirty

yektak   to load

yełaggey   if

yełben   elephant

yełtan pay   workmanship, penmanship

yeman   four

yemłaq   nostalgia, speak fondly of a person or place where one has been, have fond memories of

yeṅ   that

yenjeł   angel

yentah   why? what for?

yephak   near, soon, nearly

Yepjay   place name--islet--on Kwajalein Atoll--Ebeye

Yepreł   April

Yepwen   place name--atoll--Rälik--Ebon

yeqey   well, okay

yełyak   level off, ceremony performed six days after burial--gravel is spread over grave

yerak   spread mats

yerey   canoe part--outrigger platform

yerkay   here they are

yerkiy   where are they--non-humans

yerrew   they--two people

yerriy   where are they--of humans

Yetahwew   sly, trickster--legendary--name of

yetal   go

yetal laḷ   walk, go on foot

yetal yin wet jiwen   steadily, continuously

yetaley   go over, look over, inspect

yetkey   why?

yettew   a long time ago

yetyetal   walk

yew   the--abstract, out of sight, or in the past

yew   line, fishing line

yew yɛkɛy   nylon fish line

yewejjahak   fishing method--at night from a canoe near lagoon shore

yewiy   where--singular?

yewjewjew   fishing method--throw out line from lagoon beach

yewḷepa-   middle of

yewlaḷ   fishing method--bottom fishing in lagoon

yeyiten   similar to, same as, almost

yi'yɛgɛy   here it is (close to me)

yi'yɛg-rɛyyahar   northeast

yi'yɛwɛj   middle of the island

yi'yah   where? how?

Yi'yahab   place name--Yap District

yi'yahat   yard

yi'yakiyiw   baseball, play baseball

yi'yaḷɛw   yellow

yi'yaqey   greet, to love, bid farewell, sympathize

yi'yaraj   a plant--taro--general term--*Cyntosperma chamissonis*

yi'yegɛy   here it is (close to me)

yi'yewe-   on, upon, top, surface

yi'yewḷap   middle

yibij   high tide

yidahak   drink

yidig   sudden, abrupt decision, suddenly, change of plans

yidik   neap tides--period of

yidyid   stinging sensation, sting

yiggay   yes

Yiglen   place name--England

yigrɛk   sprain

yigyig   twirl, to turn--around and around, wind

yi-   come

yij   yeast

yij&k&yin   somewhere here around us

yij&y   here

yijekay   somewhere here around me

yijeĺ   like, have an appetite for

yijeń   there

yijeńey   there by you

yijew   here, where, there

yijewkew   those places

yijewkey   however, nevertheless, but as, maybe

yijin   here

Yijiteh   Easter

yijiw   star

yijjiyeń   yonder, in that place

yik&g   silence, keep silent, quiet

yikeyŧiḿij   slow moving, very slow, tardy--chronically

yikir   change, rearrange

yikiyen   frolic, play, pester, bother, play practical jokes

yil&wm&j   mourn the dead, visit the bereaved, visit home of dead person with gifts

yil&y   string, wire--for stringing fish

yilahrak   fishing method--trolling--outside lagoon

yilam   contraction of yilaq yim

yilan   contraction of yilaq yin

yilaqlawj&y   diarrhea

yilb&k   scared, startled, surprised, shocked

yilew   at, in

yilewwaha-   inside, in

yiljiw   tomorrow

yiljiw yim men   future, days--within the next few

yim   and

yin   to, of

yin   grass skirt

yin&j   fleet of canoes or ships

yin&k   decoration, to decorate, decked out

yin&yn&y   carry on shoulders

yin&ypahtah   worry, anxious, troubled, angered

yin&yyah   giant

yinaɥ   legend, story--folkloristic

yind&yyew   forever

yine-  sisters of a male, female parallel cousins of a male, taboo female relatives of same generation

yineknek  adorn, decorate

yinewj&yik  ignore, drift away from

yiney  seed

yinij  inch

yinik  ink

yinjin  engine, motor

yinjiniyah  engineer

yinnam  then

yinney  yesterday

yinp&l  coconut cloth

yip  awry, askew, crooked

yippa-  with

yiɫij  alarm, excitement

yirekew  here they are--non-humans only

yirey  to fight

yirw&j  chief

yiryir  rub

yit  make fire by rubbing sticks

yit&k  draw water, dig up--water

yit&w  go west

yit&w-yitak  travel, go around, go back and forth

yitakɫaq  go eastward

yitem  come and--contraction of yiteq yim

yiten  come in order to--contraction of yiteq yin

yiteq  come--to me

yiteq-limew  arouse interest

yithak  clash, strike against, collide with, arrive at, bump into

yittit  breast

yiw  spongy meat of sprouted coconut, sprouted coconut

yiw&j  go, come--to you

yiwin  push

yiwṁi-  under, beneath

yiy&y  an animal--centipede

yiyaɫ  road, path, street, way

yiyaɫap  great tidal variation--period of

yiyep  basket

yiyhar  lagoon beach--at the

yiyiṁ  swift, fast

yyaǰed  go fishing frequently

'yiy&h  this--singled out--close to me, here it is

'yiy&k  mixture, mix, stir up

'yiy&t  few, less, several

'yiyah  rainbow

'yiyahy&w  reunion

'yiyeh  year

'yiyen  time

'yiyeñ  that--singled out

'yiyig  yes

FINDER LIST

English-Marshallese

## A

abhor   dikey

ability   mareŋ

be able to   mareŋ

able to catch a lot of fish   wedah

able to hold breath under water   ppakij

able to stay under water long   pakij

about   tarrin

about it   kahkey

above   jiṁah

abrupt decision   yidig

absent-minded   ppaɫ

absolutely   wetem

accident   jeɫɫayan

accompany   karwahan

accomplish   teprak

accuse   kinhak

accustomed to   mmin&yn&y

ache   metak

achieve   teprak

acronym for Kwajalein Islands Trading Company   Kitkew

acronym for Marshall Islands Import Export Company   Miyeykew

act   mil

actual   liqqiwin

add   k&wbah

not add up   jawig

smoking addict   hagirlep

address to   hateryej

address--a letter   hateryej

adjoining   hatartar

admire   nebar

admonish   kawiw&y

adolescent girl--unmarried   jireŋ

adorn   yineknek

adult   rittew

commit adultery   l&g

advise   kawiw&y

367

adze   mayal

afraid   kk&l, q&r, mijak, wwiwetah

be <u>afraid</u> of   le₹ɟaɟ

afraid of ghosts   habinmak&y

afraid to   pik&t

after   laqa-, laqin, yaliki-

after part of canoe when outrigger is on port side   jabidik

afterwards   teqaylik

against   ṁahyey, ṅahyey

of <u>age</u>   rittew

old <u>age</u>   rittew

agree   reyejtak

agree among selves   b&r&w-qiq

ahead   ṁaha-

air   mejatewtew

airplane   ba₹win

alarm   yi₹ij

alight   jeq

alike   yayinwet jiwen

most <u>alike</u>   yayin₹aq

all   w&t&mj&j

all gone   mahat

all present   likiyy&w

that is <u>all</u> right   yayinwet jiwen

allow   kat₹aw, ket₹aq

allowed   malim

ally   reyejtak

almost   ṁettan jidik, nahgin, yeyiten

alone   mak&y

already   ṁ&j

also   barayinwet, kab, yayinwet

although   meygey

amaze   bileg

amazed   le₹ɟaɟ

amazing   kabilegleg

America   Hamedkah, hay&l&gin palley

among   bilji-

anchor   hagkeh, y&mjak

be at <u>anchor</u>   mmahan

and   kab, yim

angel   yenje₹

anger   kit&ht&h

angered   yin&ypahtah

very <u>angry</u>   kit&ht&h

annoyed or bothered by noise   wiwareɟ

another   bar jiwen
answer   wiwahak
answer to call   yawreğ
anxious   yin&ypahtah
any   jabdeywet
anything   jabdeywet
anywhere around here   jekaykay
apart   j&p&l, rayjet
take apart   jaɬjaɬ
wide apart   mmeɬew
appear   jad&y, wahɬaq
appearance   nemaym&yi-, pahwew
have an appetite for   yijeḽ
applaud   kabb&qb&q
apple   habeɬ
apply one's self   katey
approximately   tarrin
April   Yepreɬ
arithmetic   b&nb&n
arm   pay
go around   rahwin
arrange   kkar
arrive   tekyak, tepar

arrive at   yitahak
arrive--sailing vessel   pew
artery   y&k&y
arthritis   kirr&w
as   k&nkey, yayindeyin
ascend   wanl&g
ashamed   jewek
always ashamed   jjewekwek
ashamed--concerning food   yaliklik
ashes   melqaharhar
ask   kajjit&k
askew   yip
assemble   keɬahak, q&ylaq
assembly   q&ylaq
assist   reyejtak
assuming that   bey betah
asthma   w&rɬaq
astonish   ppaɬ
astound   ppaɬ
at   yilew
at the end of   jaben
atoll   hay&l&g
attempt   kajjiyeğ
attracted by bait   hanhan

August   Waqej
Australia   Hawijterełiyah
authority   peypey
automobile   ṁewetkah
keep awake   mm&j
wide awake   rr&y
awry   yip
axe   hilhil

## B

baby   niɲig
back   yalik, yaliki-
in back of   lik
backbone   diylep
bad   nahnah
bag   payak-
bail out water from canoe or boat   yany&n
bait   hanhan
fish bait   mawar
ball   bawał
native ball game   haniydep
ball made from pandanus leaves   haniydep
balloon   biwjenteṁah
make balls   bewbew

bamboo   kewbah, bahyey
band--musical   pahan
bandage   qerak
bangle   payagkeł
barb   kayaj
go barefoot   jint&b
bargain   peypey
barrel   tiraṁ
gasoline barrel--empty   kahajliyig
base   łeɟtak
baseball   yi'yakiyiw
wear a baseball glove   qiłebłeb
basket   yyep
fishing basket   ṁṁhar
hand basket of fine weave   bejaw
basket--large   kil&k
bat--baseball   bettah
take a bath   tiwlaq, tiwtiw
bathe   tiwtiw
battery   payatr&y
fight a battle   tariyṅahyey
be left   pad

be somewhere   pad

lagoon beach--at the   yiyhar

two beams from canoe to out-
    rigger   kiy&y

bear fruit   ley

beard   qedyak

fast beating of heart in fear
    kkiṁkiṁ

beautiful   deyaw

because   bey, k&n, k&nkey

beckon with the hand--downward
    motion   jeyyahał

become   y&r&m

bed   peyet

beer   piyah

before   ṁaha-, meqtah

befriend   jeray

beg   wwar

beg--for food only   wiggar

begin   jjinew

behavior   ṁanit, ṁil

behind   lik, łaqa-

believe   l&k&y, temak

bell   peyeł

belly   j&y

belt   kagir

bench   jeyah

bend   yalqej

bend down--coconut shoots only
    kiy&ytak

bend toward   ṁal

beneath   yiwṁi-

betray   k&ytak, kinhak

between   ketaha-

bewail one's state   haweł

beyond   jiṁah

Bible   Bahyibel

bicycle   bahajkeł

big   kilep, łap

bind   l&ql&q

bind with sennit   yawy&w

bird   bahwew, pawp&w

frigate bird   hak

birthday party   keyemyem

biscuit   p&tk&j

bite   kik

not biting--of fish   jakkik

black   kilmeyej

bladder   b&q

blanket   kawaj

use a blanket   kawajw&j

371

bleed    betektek, piliglig
blessed   jerahaṁṁan
blind    pil&w
blinded by sunlight    taṁtaṁ
blocked    beṅ
blood    betektek, dah
blood vessel    y&k&y
blossom    bb&l
blow one's nose    wwir
blue    biłiw
bluing    biłiw
blunt    kk&b
board    ray
boast    jajjaj, keṅkeṁṁan
boastful    jajjaj
boat    bewej
picket boat    łewen
boat with outboard engine    łewen
body    yanbin
boil    diw
boil pandanus    hayintiyin
bold    kijeǰ
bolt    jikriw
bolt--of cloth    kap

bomb    bahaṁ, baqitaq
bone    diy
book    b&q
boondocks    mar
border--on mats    hapar
both    jiṁeł
bother    yikiyen
bottle    batew
small bottle or jar    bekay
bottle used for collecting coconut sap    j&yib
bottom    łaqa-
bottom of    kapi-
bound    pawp&w
boundary line    ketaha-
wooden bowl    jap&y
box    bawak
boy    ładdik
bracelet    payagkeł
brag (about one's self)    jajjaj
brain    kemalij
branch    rah
brave    kijeǰ
seat of brave emotions    hat

baked breadfruit    liped

breadfruit bud    tebak

break    bilaq, ḷijḷij

breaking of waves    reyrey

breast    yittit

bright    maletlet, meram

bring    wikey

bring food as tribute to chief (western dialect only)    kkan

broil--on hot stones    jinkadewel

broke    jar

broke--money    jar, birwek

broken    jeḷḷayan

broom    birwiṁ

older brother    jeyi-

younger brother    jati-

brother-sister relationship    jᴀṁnajin

brown    birahwin, ṁeṅakṅak

bruised    mahwew

brush    biraj

brush teeth    qirqir

bucket    bakej

build    keṁṁan, kal

build a canoe or boat    jᴀkjᴀk wah

bulldozer    bariw

bullet    jewet

bump a sore or wound    keyegjak

bump and grind    kajikiyah

bump into    yitahak

bunch of ripe and drinkable coconuts    wirwᴀr

burn    bil, mayaṅ, ttil

burning    wirwir

bury    kallib

bus    baj

bush    mar

busy    pewib, witaṁᴀy

be busy with    lᴀqjak

but    hak

but as    yijewkey

butt    pid

butter    betah

butterfly    babbib

buttocks    pid

button    batin

buy    wiyah

by-product of jekarew--coconut sap    jekajeyjey

## C

cabinet   tirwet

food cabinet   payant&r&y

cake   k&y&k

calf of leg   hajhaj

call   kir, lam&j

call or entice animals or children to come near   kkahal

call to come   yagyiginteq

calm   lil̊

camera   pijah

can   mareg̊

can--of food   qiwat

can--of meat   kayan

canal   tawar

candle   kayaṅtel̄

candy   lawl̄&y

coconut candy   hameytemhah

cannot   ban

canoe   wah

paddling canoe   kerker

canoe mast top   l̊et

canoe part   hagtikliy

canoe part--bottom part of canoe   jewij

canoe part--curved piece connecting outrigger to hull   hap&t

canoe part--end of yard-boom   bal̄

canoe part--foot of sail--edge fastened to the boom   hayeykeray

canoe part--outrigger platform   yerey

canoe part--socket for end of boom   diypayakyak

outrigger canoe--for sailing--large   tipgel

canvas   kanbej

great capacity   kket

cape--geographical   b&k&y

capital letters   kiyaptel̄

capsize   w&kjak

captain   kapen

capture   bek, j&bj&b

car   kahar, mhewetkah

card   p&ybah

play cards for stakes   pil&y

cards--playing   kahaj

care for   bek ddew

take care of   kejpareq

careful   tilj&k

Caroline   Karewl̄ahyin

| | | | |
|---|---|---|---|
| Caroline Islands | Kapiyl&g | causative prefix | ka- |
| carpenter | kahaṁteh | cause | win |
| carpentry | kahaṁteh | ceiling | terak |
| carry | halj&k | cement | jimyeṅ |
| carry a child on the hip | jahjah | cent(s) | jayan |
| carry a person on one's back | kiwkiw | centipede | neqanyej, yiy&y |
| | | certain | liqqiwin |
| carry in vehicle or vessel | llik | chain | jeyen |
| | | chair | jeyah |
| carry on hips (things) | kejerray | chalk | jawak |
| carry on shoulders | yin&yn&y | change | wikw&k, yikir |
| carry out | teprak | make change | janij |
| push cart | diyakah | change domicile | j&pj&p |
| case (as of food) | k&y&j | change from one thing to another | y&r&m |
| cat | kiwij | | |
| | | change of plans | yidig |
| able to catch many fish | qeṅqeṅ | ancient chant | ṁił |
| catch many fish--inability to | jaqeṅqeṅ, jewdah | charcoal | malley |
| | | charge on account | hakkawin |
| catch up--in a game | bektak | chart | jahat |
| catch with net or basket | bawir | chase | kkebeł, lib&w&rw&r |
| a catch--of fish | keña- | chase women | kekkerayray |
| Catholic | Katlik | chat idly | ley k&t&w |
| caught | łewrak | cheap | dik weṅya- |
| caught on a hook | kawj&k | check mark | kakełłey |

| | |
|---|---|
| check the weather katiw | sand clam--bivalve jenaw |
| chest w&b | a clan pit |
| chick j&wj&w | clap hands kabb&qb&q |
| chicken bahwew | clapping kabb&qb&q |
| chief yirw&j | clash yitahak |
| high chieftess l&yr&w&j | class kilhaj |
| child hajiriy, naji- | clean qqejarjar |
| raise children kahajiriyriy | clean a fish or chicken j&jj&t |
| children of a man's sister magide- | clean up an area rahr&h |
| chills wididdid | clean up waste food or trash q&p&jp&j |
| chilly piyaw | clear halikkar |
| chin jiṁin giy | clever kapyel |
| chip of green coconut husk used as spoon hawiłakłak | not clever jakapyel |
| chop j&kj&k | climb wanl&g |
| chop down j&wkay | climb down t&w |
| Christian Kirjin | climb up tall&g |
| Christmas Kirijṁ&j | cling to ddap |
| to chum for fish hanhan | clock hawah |
| go to church jar | close to tiłi- |
| church member in good standing kirjin | close together qit, qqit(qit) |
| church (building) ṁen jar | close-in on kepeweł |
| cigar tebak | closet tirwet |
| circle dewilwil | cloth niqniq |

coconut cloth   yinp&l

clothes   niqniq

change clothes--from good to dirty   yekpay

clothing   niqniq

cloud   kedaw

cloudy   tab

club   qiłab

cluster   wirw&r

coal   malley

coals--of fire   malley

coat   kewpay

coconut beginning to turn brown   mag

coconut juice   dannin niy

coconut leaf chain used in fishing   ṁiyew

young coconut meat   m&d&y

tiny coconut not fully grown   qałinniy

coconut sap   jekar&w

coconut sennit   qqał

coconut shell   łat

coconut shell--lower half with sharp end   łat-jiṁ

coconut shell--upper half next to stem with eyes   łat-m&j

coconut syrup--boiled down from sap   jekṁayiy

coconut--nearly ripe   mejewib

coconut--small sprouted   p&r

coffee   kawp&y

cohabit   k&wbah

coil   jalj&l, pawp&w

coke   k&włah

cola   k&włah

common cold   mejyin

collect   hay&y, t&lt&l

collide with   yitahak

comb   kiwiṁ

come   wayteq, yiteq

come and--contraction of yiteq yim : yitem

come back   rawal

come back in order to--contraction of   yiteq yin : yiten

come off of   t&w

come to land   tekyak

come--to me   yiteq

come--to you   yiw&j

commandment   kiyen

common   kkay, makijkij

company   kiwmiy

compare     hanlaq

compass     kaṁbej

complain    haweł

complain of others    kinhak

complete    weyeppan, wig

not complete    jawig

completed   d&yd&y   d&yd&yłaq

compose     kk&n

conceive    ttah

concerning  k&n

concrete    jimyeṅ

concur      reyejtak

condemn     liyahakłaq

conditional--contrary to fact    kar

conduct     ṁanit

confer      peypey

confound    ppał

confuse     p&q

congeal     qej

congress    qagqirej

consent     wiwahak

consider    llik

constipated beṅ

contagious  kapewpew

container   nn&y

water container    tayag

container for liquids--coconut shell    bekay

contents (of a book)    kadkad

contents of    qebba-

continuously    yetal yin wet jiwen

contraction of yilaq yim :  yilam

contraction of yilaq yin :  yilan

contrary to    jekkar

contribution    qiṅaha-

conversation    beybeynahtew, keṁṁahwew

converse    keṁṁahwew

have convulsions    diw

cook    qiq

easy to cook    mattiyy&y

hard to cook    mattiyyah

cooked    mat

cool    ṁ&ł&w

cooled off--of food once hot    m&d

coolness of a breeze    llahdikdik

copper    kebah

copra   wahyiniy

copra pieces--taken out of the shell   jekak

coral   wed

cord made from coconut fibre   qqa&l;

cork   bawar

corned beef   kawanpiyip

corner   jaben

correct   ji&m;&y;

coryza   wiwir

cost of   we&n;ya-

cough   peqpeq

council   peypey

count   b&nb&n;

country   hay&l;&g;

country (of the world)   la&l;

cross cousin   riyliki-

younger cousin (parallel)   jati-

covenant   kalli&m;i&l;

cover   lib&wb&w;

cover with gum   bilbil

covered over   bal

cow   kahwiw

coward   pik&t;, piwa&l;, we&l;a&l;&w;

cowboy   kahwiwbewey

cowrie shell   libbiq&y;

hermit crab   w&m;

crab--general term   bariw

crack   &l;ag

cracker   p&tk;&j;

cramped   hapag

crave cigarettes   hagir

crave fish   bati&l;

crazy   b&yb;&y;, widyakyak

create   ke&m;an&m;han

crippled   kirr&w;

crooked   hank&yk;&y;, yip

crowbar   bahar

crowd   bij, jar

a crowd of   bijin

crowded   hapag

crowded--of people   qit

cruel   laj

crumble a mound or pile--as of sand   r&m;

crumbs   tipdikdik

cry   jag

cuddle   hatbaqej

cup   kab

| | |
|---|---|
| cupboard payant&r&y | the day after tomorrow jekłaj |
| good current hayeṁhan | daybreak rahantak |
| curse kanijnij | days--within the next few yiljiw yim men |
| custom ṁanit | |
| cut biqabeq, j&kj&k, ṁijṁij | dead m&j |
| | near death hahih |
| small cut qirar | debt likjab |
| cut down--trees j&wkay | December Tiyjeṁbah |
| cut hair ṁijbar | decide peypey |
| cut off j&pj&p | deceive ṁeṅ |
| cut off copra meat from shell karkar | decked out yin&k |
| | declare kennahan, kewwahłaq |

## D

| | |
|---|---|
| damage caused by termites or bookworms diyley | decorate yineknek, yin&k |
| | decoration yin&k |
| damaged jeṅṅayan | deep ṁilał |
| dance--western style tanij | defend j&wj&wmar |
| dangerous kawiwatahtah | delay ṅiṁij |
| dark--in color meyej | delirious widyakyak |
| darn it wew | delouse yakit |
| dastardly piwał | demon tiyṁeṅ |
| daughter naji- | dense (of shrubbery) qit |
| daughter of a queen l&yr&w&j | depart biṅlik |
| dawn jewrahantak, rahantak | depend on l&k&y |
| dawn--period before jimmareq | depend on people hatartar |
| day rahan | deride kajjireyrey |

description   kadkad

desire   hank&laha-, hayiqij

desk   teybeł

despicable   kajj&hj&h

destiny   haniylen

destitute of   jjełaq

destroy   kaqqirey

determination   kijey

devote presents to the gods   hajey

diagram   hannag

diaper   kał

wear a diaper   kałkał

diarrhea   yilaqlawj&y

dictionary   tikjiyneydey

quick to die   m&jjiyy&y

slow to die   m&jjiyyah

diesel   tiyjeł

diesel oil   tiyjeł

different   yayinjiwen

difficult   p&n

dig   k&b

dig up   t&wtak

dilute   kab&wdan

dim   tab

diminish   hapdik

dip up--water   yit&k

dipper   k&yk&b

direction of   kijjiye-

dirty   rran, tt&w&n

dirty water   lim̊

disappear   ″letlaq

discharge   yakt&w

disembark   t&w

disentangle   kemełeyłey

dish   kennaw

a dish--baked very ripe breadfruit and coconut milk   pal̈jej

strongly dislike   dikey

dislike to do   habin

disobedient   b&t, kipliyyah

disorder   p&q

dispute   haweł

district   biqen

District Administrator   Qem̊jah

disturbed   habn̊ehn̊eh

dive   tiwlaq

divided into two parts   rayjet

dividing line   ketahadivination    biwbiw

divination method--using knots in pandanus leaf    biwbiw

divination--result of    bey

division of an atoll or islet    biqen

divorce    jɐpɐl

dizzy    haddebewilwil

do    keṁhan, wejak

do one's duty    bek qeṅaha-

doctor    takteh

see a doctor    takteh

dog    kidiw

doll    tawɬɐy

dollar    tahɬah

domesticated    hawiyyɐy

door    hawer, kejam

doorway    kejam

double    tabeɬ

dove    ṁïlɐy

go down    tiwlaq

drag    kkeykahak

hard to drag in water    hatakiyyah

easy to drag in water    hatakiyyɐy

draw a picture    pijah

draw water    yitɐk

a drawer    kkeykahak

dream    teṅak

dress    jewkankan

dress up    niqniq

drift away from    yinewjɐyik

drift eastward    peytak

cedar driftwood    hayik

drink    yidahak

drink (possessive)    lime-, nime-

provide drink for    ṅahlime-

drink noisily    ḻiyit

drinking water    hayɐbɐj

drip    piliqliq

drive--a car    tirayip

drop down--as from a height    wɐtlaq

drop--of liquid    pil

drought    jahwɐtwɐt

drown    maleǧ

drum    hajey, tiraṁ

drunk    kadek

dry    ṁeṅakṅak, ṁeray

dry fish or copra by heat   hatiytiy

dry spell   jahw&tw&t

dry under sun   kejeyjey

duck   badik

dull   kk&b

dullness (of people)   haddiyṁak&wk&w

dumbfounded   beṁ

garbage dump   kellah

dumpling   jayibew

dust   bigal

dusty   bigal

duty   qiṅaha-

dwell   j&q&y

be dying   hahih

long in dying   m&jjiyyah

dynamic voice   ɬahaj

dynamite   baqitag

### E

each   jabdeywet

ear   lawjilgiy

wear earring   diy&d&y

earth   bid&j

east   r&yyahar

Easter   Yijiteh

eastern part   tiwr&yyahar

eastward   tahɬaq

go eastward   yitakɬaq

easy going   rahɬaq

eat   ṁegay

eat before working   kapiyj&y

eat breakfast   ṁahbiŋ

eat fish half broiled but still raw   kewebwib

eat only one food   jint&b

eat supper   k&j&wtah

edge   hapar, hilhil, t&r&yr&yi-

Educational Administrator   Qeṁjah

eel   ṁaj

eel that lives in fresh water--toothless   teṁ

egg   l&p

eight   riwahliyt&k

elastic   meh

elbow   jiṁin pay

elect   kkayaly&l

election   kkayaly&l

electricity   jaɬem

elephant   yeɬben

hard to embarrass
  jajjewekwek

embarrassed   jewek

embrace   hatbaqej, baqej

empty   mahat, yamj&y

encircle   kepeweł

enclosure   werwer

end   jeṁłaq

end of an islet   tił

endeavor   kajjiyeǵ

engine   yinjin

engineer   yinjiniyah

enough   bey

enough--of goods or needs
  k&yk&y

not enough--of counted things
  jawig

entangle   p&q

entangled   łewrak

enter   d&yłaǵ

entice   kkahal

entirely   wetem

be equipped with   ley

error   b&d

escape   kew

escort   yagin

estimate   leyłemṅak

et cetera   yayiy&rłaqwet

Europe   hay&l&gin palley

evening   j&wtah

last evening   jewtah

every   jabdeywet

evil   nahnah

exact   liqqiwin

exaggerate   hagłap

examination day at end of term
  j&ṁnajin

examine--physically   kak&lk&l

exchange   janij

excitement   yiłij

be excommunicated   biǵ

excrement   kibey

existence   mewir

exodus   kew

expel   kakkij&y

experienced   mmin&yn&y

explain   kemełeyłey

extinguish   qqin

extremely   liqqiwin

extricate   harhar

eye   maj

eyebrow    yat

## F

face    maj, tiłin maj

face away from    jełłaq

face to face    jelṁahyey

facing east    jałłetak

faint    ḯetlaq, parek

fairly    jahad

faith    temak

faithful    tiljɛk

fall down    wɛtlaq, biɉ, biɉlaq

fall short of--in length    jɛn

fall--from erect position    wɛkjak

fame    biɉbiɉ

not <u>familiar</u>    riwahmayɛjɛt

family    bij, niqiy

famous    biɉbiɉ

a <u>fan</u>    deyel

fantastic    keppałpał

far    ttewłak

far apart    mmejew

bid <u>farewell</u>    kejjajet, yi'yaqey

fast    ṁekaj, yiyiṁ

break a <u>fast</u>    dahwew

fat--of meat    kiryij

fate    haniylen

father    bahbah

fault    bɛd

fear    lełɉaɉ, mijak

fear of being alone in the dark or at sea    habinmakɛy

feast    keyemyem

February    Papewdey

feces    kibey

feeble    haddimɛj

feed    nahjidik

feel    yɛgjahkey

felling of a tree    wełaq

fellow    kijak

female    keray

female parallel cousins of a male    yine-

taboo <u>female</u> relatives of same generation    yine-

carry <u>female</u> to or from vessel    bekkeray

female--animal    kewkeray

fence    werwer

fender    habaw

fermented coconut toddy
   jimagig

ferocious   laj

fever   bil, piybah

fever and chills   piyaw

feverish   piybah

few   j&jj&w, jet, 'yiy&t

field trip   piyił tiryep

go on a field trip ship--
   Marshalls   rahwin

field--baseball   kirahaṅtew

fierce   laj

fifty   leṁgewil

fight   yirey

figure   kay, neṁbah, wayw&y&-

fill   kanney

fill a container   nn&y

fill--with liquid   tteyig

filled up   b&w&ł

final   yaliktahtah

finally   kab, yaliktahtah

hard to find   hałakiyyah

easy to find   hałakiyy&y

find out   yawreǧ

finger   haddiy

middle finger   haddiy yewłap

fingernail   hakkiy, hakkiyin pay

finish   jeṁłaq

finished   ṁ&j

entirely finished   d&yd&yłaq

fire   kijyek

fireplace   wiphaj

open fireplace for cooking
   wiphaj

firewood   kan&y

firm   kijgiyg&y, p&n

fish   y&k

fish only half broiled
   kewebwib

fish pole   bay

a fish--Albacore--*Thunnus
   Alalunga*   jil&w

raw fish--edible dish   jahajmiy

a fish--flying fishes--family
   *Exocoetidae*   jewjew

a fish--red snapper--*Lutjanus
   Vaigiensis*   jahap

a fish--salmon   jaṁeṅ

fish--scarcity   jayikey

a fish--scorpion fish   n&w

a fish--shark   pakew

a fish--shark pilot--*Echeneis Naucrates*   łattil pakew

puffer fish--*Tetraodon Hispicus*   wat

a fish--tuna--*Neothunus Macropterus*   beybey

go fishing   yaǧed

fo fishing frequently   yyaǧed

fishing line   yew

fishing method   hałeyłey

fishing method--at night from a canoe near lagoon shore   yewejjahak

fishing method--bottom fishing in lagoon   yewlał

fishing method--fish with a pole   kebaybæy

fishing method--fishing with a torch   kabil

fishing method--pole at breakers   jiwinbæǧ

fishing method--throw out line from lagoon beach   yewjewjew

fishing method--to fish from a canoe   wiræk

fishing method--trawling--inside lagoon   kekkawjækjæk

fishing method--trawling--outside lagoon   yilahrak

fishing method--use fish pole at night with either lure or bait   ttew

fishing method--use throwing net   kadkad

fishing method--using long net at day time along reef ridge   jabiq

fit   kkar

fit tightly   bab

it is fitting   kkar

poorly fitting   bewełweł

five   łalæm

five hundred   limabiqiy

fix   keiłuhan

flag   bełyak

flame   wirwir

flap   pikpik

flash   wirwir

flashlight   teyegkiy

flat   yawan wet jiwen

flat--music   benah

flat--music or voice   biłyat

flee   kew

one who flees from battle   pikæt

fleet of canoes or ships   yinæj

flesh   kanniyæk

flirting   habjey

flock   bijin

a flock of birds flying over
  a school of fish    winhak

flow    tawar

hibiscus flower    rewej

flutter--as of wings    pikpik

a fly    laŋ

fly    kay-

fly a kite    liṁahakhak

birds flying looking for fish
  winhak

fog    tab

fold    l&ml&m, yalqej

fold arms in front    beqpay

follow    ɫewer(ey)

follow trail or track    hanek

followers    dewen

have fond memories of    yemɫaq

speak fondly of a person or
  place where one has been
  yemɫaq

food    kkan, ṁegay

first food after fast    dahwew

provide food for    ṅahkije-

provide food for someone    tayap

food of    kije-

a food--breadfruit cooked on
  coals and scraped    qanjin

a food--breadfruit soup
  jeqqeb yin may

a food--doughnut--with hole
  tewnahaj

a food--dried overripe breadfruit    jayanqin

a food--pandanus chip    jekahkah

a food--pandanus juice cooked
  and preserved    meqaṅ

a food--preserved breadfruit
  biyr&w

a food--very ripe breadfruit
  baked in coconut milk
  paḷjej

foolish    b&yb&y

foot    ney

set foot on    jiwjiwir

for    bey, k&n, ṁahyey

forbid    bebrahyey

forbidden    maw

force    kajw&r

forecast weather    katiw

forehead    daṁ

forever    k&b&w, yind&yyew

forget    meɫaqlaq

fork    jibwin

form    wayw&y&-

fornicate    l&g

fort  m&y

fortified place  m&y

fortunate  jerahaṁhan

fortune teller  biwbiw

forty  yegewil

forward part of canoe when outrigger is on port side  jabłap

foundation  leɉtak

four  yeman

four hundred  yabiqiy

fowl  bahwew

fragments  tipdikdik

France  Birahnij

free  katłaq

freeze  qej

frequent  makijkij

fresh water  mamet

Friday  Bełahyidey, Berahyidey

friend  jeray

fright  lełɉaɉ

frightened  q&r

frolic  yikiyen

from  jan

coconut frond  kim&j

front  ṁahan

fruit  qeley

fry  birahyey

fuel  kaha-, kan&y

full  b&w&ł, bab, leg, webrak

full--of sails  l&tl&t

make fun  kejak

furious  kit&ht&h

near future  yiljiw yim men

future tense marker  nahaj

G

gain  wiyin

gall bladder  hat

gallon  kałan

game  qqir&y

work gang  kiwmiy

garbage  q&p&j

gargle  qirqir

gasoline  kiyhaj

gather food  kakijen

gather news or information  yawreɉ nahan

gathered together  qiq

gaze at  kallimj&k

generous  ṁḣewel

389

get   bek

get on   wiw&y

get out   diw&j

get together   k&wbah

get up--from lying down   wah&laq

ghost   tiyṁeń

giant   yin&yyah

giddy   haddebewilwil, b&yb&y

gifts   ṁeyiq

taking gifts to a wedding or funeral or party   t&pt&p

giggle   tt&g dikdik

Gilbert (Islands)   Kilbet

Gilbertese   pit

girl   leddik

give   ley-

give away   ley&laq

give away without remuneration   hajey

give up   bahaj

give--to the speaker   leyteq

give--to you   l&yw&j

gizzard   tiw, tiwdek

swollen gland   wir

glare   taṁtaṁ

glass   ki&haj

broken glass   batew

glass-drinking   kab

eye glasses   maj

sun glasses   maj

wear glasses   majmaj

glorify   nebar

glorious   hayib&w&jw&j

baseball glove   qi&eb

go   jeblahak, weylaq, yetal, yiw&j

go and meet   wenṁahyey

go around   yit&w-yitak

go away   weylaq

go away for a change of scene   jaṁb&w

go back and forth   yit&w-yitak

go backward   wanlik

go drinking at a club   qi&ab

go eastward   weytak

go from sea side of an island to lagoon side   keyhar

go in a pass   ṁ&yyahar

go into the water   tiwwahak

go on a vehicle or sailing canoe   tar-

| | |
|---|---|
| go on foot    yetal la⁀ł | no good    j&tteqja- |
| go or come ashore--toward land    wanyan&y | goods    ṁeyiq |
| | gout    kirr&w |
| go or come down    wanla⁀ł | government    kiyen |
| go or come out of water or fire    hat&w | grandchild    jiɓi- |
| go or come seaward    wanmetew | grandchildren    jiɓi- |
| go or come towards the lagoon    wanhar | grandfather    jiṁṁah |
| | grandmother    bihbih, jiɓi- |
| go or come towards the ocean side of an island    wanlik | grapple with    gijlaq |
| go out    diw&j | grate--coconuts    rahank&y |
| go out a pass    ṁeylik | grater    rahank&y |
| go out--of light    qqin | grave    l&b |
| go over    yetaley | gravel    dekay, ⁀łay |
| go to the ocean side    kaylik | gravy    jal&yl&y |
| go toward    wan- | gray    kir&y |
| go west    yit&w | grease    kiryij |
| go westward    wayt&w | great    ⁀łap |
| goat    kewet | greedy    ter |
| god    hanij | greedy--for food    mattiyyah |
| gone    jak&w | green    kiryin, mahrewrew |
| gone forth    mewet | greet    yi'yaqey |
| gonorrhea    jeplej | grey-haired    wiwaṅ |
| good    ṁṁan | grip    dapd&p |
| make good    keṁanṁan | ground    bid&j |

391

on the ground   laɫ

group   bijin

any group of people--as a class   jar

grow   ddek, yaǥ

grow smaller   j&n

guard   bilijmayań

guess   leyɫemńak

guitar   kitah

chewing gum   bil

gummy   bilbil

gums   gad

gun   biw

guts   ṁajgal

guy   kijak

## H

habit   mmin&yn&y

have the habit of   mmin&yn&y

had   kar

hair   keweɫ

dry hair (not oily)   qirahaghag

haircut   ṁijbar

half   jimattan

half-caste   hapkahaj

halted   bahaj

hammer   harṅah

hand   pay

handicraft   hamiyṁeńew

made handicraft   hamiyṁeńew

handsome--men only   wiliy&w

hang on the line   rewrew

hang up   tewtew

Hansen's disease   lebah

happen   wahɫaq

happy   biǥ-b&r&w, ṁeńehńeh

harass   hapag

hard   p&n

hardening of starch or tallow or lead   qej

hardwood   kijey

harmful substances   bahyijin

harvest time for arrowroot   hagenyag

hat   hat

wear a hat   hathat

hatchet   hilhil, mayal

hate   hakk&jdat, dikey, k&jdat

haul canoe or vessel up on shore   yar

| | |
|---|---|
| have a way with women tayag | her han |
| haze tab | here yij&y, yijew, yijin |
| he y&y | right here jewijew |
| he--away from the speaker łeyeń | here it is y&w, yegyew, yegyin |
| head bar | here it is (close to me) yi'y&g&y, yi'yeg&y |
| lineage head hałap | here they are yerkay |
| head of j&yban | here they are--non-humans only yirkew |
| head of a governmental organization qeṁjah | heritage--land łayarwan |
| heal mew | hers han |
| healthy yajmiwir | hesitate tabił |
| hear reǰ | hew j&kj&k |
| hard of hearing reǰiyyah | hide-and-seek kittiliy&k |
| good hearing regiyy&y | high l&g, witiy&j |
| heart baṁ, b&r&w | high-pitched sound yełłahaj |
| heart of palm jiyab | hike jaṁb&w |
| heartburn bilm&ly&g | hill bat, teł |
| heat rash b&q hayidik | hinder bebrahyey |
| heaven hay&l&ginlag, lag | hip mił |
| heavy ddew | move hips in dancing kajikiyah |
| heel jiṁin ney | his han |
| help jipag | history beybeynahtew |
| hem in hapag | hit l&l |
| hen lahlah, lawlaw | hit the mark l&l |

hoarse ppeǧ
hold dapd&p, j&bj&b
hold out--as a baby for
    another to take    jahkey
hold tight    kkiwil
hold up or catch with both
    hands    bawir
hole    łag
holiday    kakkij&y
holy    qqejarjar
homely    dak&lk&l
homesick    weg
honest    jiṁ&y
hook    kayaj
hope    kejatdikdik
horse    wawaj
hospital    hawijpitel, men
    takteh
hot    bil
hour    hawah
house    y&ṁ
small house on canoe    bakt&k
how    wayw&y&-, y&k&jka-,
    yi'yah
how many    jetey
however    bethab, yijewkey

hug    baqej
human being    harm&j
humble    ttay b&r&w
hundred    jibiqiy
one hundred    jibiqiy
hundred of    biqiy
hungry    haghagey, q&l&y
hunt for    kapp&q, p&q
hurray    wirr&w
be in a hurry    kij&rj&r
hurry up    menłaq
hurt    metak
husband    palye-, riyi-
coconut husk    beyaw
husk--coconuts    dd&b
hymn    halin jar

# I

I--absolute    gah
ice cream    hay&j qiryiṁ
identification of    kijjiye-,
    kajjiye-
idol    yekjab
if    gey, yełaggey
ignite    ttil
ignorant    jahj&yłaqjeṅ

| | | | | |
|---|---|---|---|---|
| ignore | kejewel, yinewj&yik | | an insect--cockroach | qiḷiḷ |
| serious illness | dawlel | | inside | lewwaha-, yilewwaha- |
| imagine | ḷekeṁ | | uniform insignia | kakeḷḷey |
| imitate | hanek, kajjiyeg̊ | | inspect | yetaley |
| immediately | kiyyeh-kiyyeh | | install | keḷhak |
| immoral | kijeg̊ | | musical instrument | kejagjag |
| immorality | kijeg̊ | | insufficient | jabey |
| impossible | ban | | intact | likiyy&w |
| improper | jekkar | | intercede | j&wj&wmar |
| improved | weyeppan | | interest | limew |
| in | yilew, yilewwaha- | | arose interest | yiteq-limew |
| in danger of | wiwetah | | interpret | wikw&k |
| inch | yinij | | intestinal worm | ṁaj |
| include | kepeweḷ | | intestines | ṁajgal |
| increase | kewerḷaq | | intoxicating | kadek |
| industrious | niknik | | invent | kk&n |
| inflamed eye | pil&w | | be involved | l&qjak |
| information | meḷeyḷey | | iron | hayen |
| injection | way | | iron | ṁayal |
| give an injection | way | | island | hay&l&g, yan&y |
| receive injection | way | | islet | yan&y |
| ink | yinik | | this islet | yanyin |
| innocent | jahj&yḷaqjeṅ | | small islets of an atoll | hayetaw |
| insane | widyakyak | | | |

| | | | | |
|---|---|---|---|---|
| it | y&y | | kiss | m&j&nmah, wiṁṁhah |
| itch | ṁeṅejṅej | | KITCO | Kitkew |
| | **J** | | kite | liṁahakhak |
| jail | kalbiwij | | knee | biq&y |
| to be in jail | kalbiwij | | knife | diy |
| Japan | Nibbeǰ | | long knife | jayj&y |
| jar | batew | | knife--small | bakbek |
| get a job | jawab | | knock | kałłałał |
| joke | kejak | | knoll | bat |
| judge | yekajet | | knot of hair--women | biwj&k |
| July | Jiwłahyey | | knot--in wood | b&k&y |
| June | Jiwin | | know | jełay |
| just | bajj&k, d&y, kab | | not know | gak |
| just as | yayindeyin | | Kwajalein | Kiwajleyen |
| | **K** | | | **L** |
| keep as a pet | najn&j | | lack | hayiqij |
| keep company | keṁṁawew | | lady killer | tayag |
| kernel | qeley | | lagoon | lewṁałew |
| kerosene | karjin | | lagoon--secondary | naṁ |
| tea kettle | tiybat | | lame | kirr&w |
| key | kiy | | lamp | łahaṁ |
| kid | kejak | | land | hay&l&g, jiki- |
| kill | ṁehreh | | to land | jeq |
| kind | jewij, kahyin, łet | | land of the white man | hay&l&gin palley |
| kind of | wiwan | | | |

land--sailing vessel   pew
language   kajin
lantern   lanten
large   kilep, ḷap
lash   yawy&w
last   yalik
the last   ḷaq
very last   yaliktahtah
late   haḷew, bat, ṛiṁij
be too late   likjab
be late for and miss--a plane   tiṁ
late in awakening   majiḷlep
later   teqaylik
laugh   reyrey, tt&g
laugh at   kajjireyrey
launch forth   billaq
law   kiyen
lawful   malim
lay down   llik
lazy   jewwan
lead   kkahal, yagin
to lead   tel
lead--of people or animals   wikey

leaf   b&l&k
pandanus leaf   mahag
leak   ttal
not leak   jettal
lean   hatrak
lean back   hatartar
lean upon   hatartar
learn   kahtak
leave   llik
leave it   dewer
leave lagoon   ṁeylik
left   hanbijban
left half of human body   hanmiyig
left hand   hanbijban, hanmiyig
left over   bey
leg   ney
legend   yinaǵ
leper   lebah
leprosy   lebah
less   'yiy&t
less than   likjab
less than half full   jakapen
less (quantity)   hapdik

| | | | |
|---|---|---|---|
| lessen | hapdik | in line with | kijjiye- |
| let go | ketłaq | lineage | bij |
| lethargic | haddim&j | lips | tiyey |
| letter | letah | liquid | dan |
| level | yawan wet jiwen | strong liquor | dannin kadek |
| level off | yełyak | listen | redjakey |
| lever | ledtak | little | dik |
| lick | daṁd&ṁ | a little | bajj&k |
| lie | ṁeṅ, riyab | in a little bit | ṁettan jidik |
| lie down | bahbiw | a little more | bar jidik |
| life | mewir | live | mewir |
| lift | bawir, kewtak | live somewhere | j&q&y |
| to lift | leyl&g | liver | haj |
| lift weights to build up body | kaddiyp&np&n | to load | yektak |
| | | loaf--bread | łeweb |
| light | ṁeram, teyegkiy ttil | lobster | w&r |
| to light | łemhak | to hunt lobsters | kalw&r |
| light--of weight | merah | what location | teye- |
| light--weight | bełał | location of | kijjiye- |
| lightning | jałem | a locative | tiw |
| like | keṅhan | locative particle | ṅah |
| likeness | yayindeyin | to lock | łak |
| likewise | barayinwet | loin cloth | kał |
| line | lahyin, yew | wear a loin cloth | kałkał |

| | | | | |
|---|---|---|---|---|
| loiter | ṁad | | to love | kkeñak, yi'yaqey |
| a long time | tew | | love song | ṁahyinah |
| lonely | jeraṁel | | secret lover | batin |
| long | hayeteq | | low | ttay |
| long time ago | yettew | | low salary | dik weñya- |
| long-winded in diving | pakij | | lower sail | pew |
| longing for | weg | | lower the head | badik |
| look | jiwjal- | | lucky | jerahaṁhan |
| look after | lahley | | lucky--in fishing | wedah |
| look after a sick person | kahwiw | | lumber | haɫhaɫ |
| look at | halw&j, lahley | | lunacy | ṁejawliger |
| look for | pp&q | | lunatic | ṁejawliger |
| look in a mirror | kilhaj | | lung | yar |
| look over | yetaley | | lure | hanhan |
| look steadfastly at | kallimj&k | | lust | l&g |
| looks | jjed | | lustful--males only | b&w&ɫ |

M

| | |
|---|---|
| loose | beweɫweɫ |
| loosen | jaɫjaɫ | 
| lose | liwij |
| lost | jak&w |
| be lost | jebayb&y |
| loud | peran |
| louse | kij |

| | |
|---|---|
| machete | jayj&y |
| sewing machine | meyjin |
| magistrate | jewenjew, qeṁjah |
| mail | letah |
| make | keṁhan |
| make believe | ɫekeṁ |
| make clear | kemeɫeyɫey |

399

make fire by rubbing sticks yit
make sennit qqaɬ
male kewṁahan, ṁuhahan
mallet made from clam shell dɛkɛynin
man ṁuhahan
old man ɬaɬɬap
that man ɬeyeñ
the man ɬeyew
what man ɬet
young man likahwew
mango magkɛw
manner ṁil
manner of waywɛyɛ-
manure kibey
many leg
many times leg halen
map mab
mar rran
March--the month Mahaj
Mariana Islands Kapiylɛg
mark to show absent wawɛw
mark with pencil rran
good marksmanship--spearing waylɛl

marriage palɛylɛy
married palɛylɛy
to marry ṁarey
marvelous hayibɛwɛjwɛj
diving mask maj
massage pitpit
mast kajiw, kijiw
mat jakiy
provide mat for ñahkineye-
mat of kiniye-
mat woven from coconut frond jeyinahyey
floor mat--coarse jɛpkaw
match majet
ill-matched jekkar
mate--ship's meyej
mattress biteǰ, mayteryej
mature kɛykɛy, rittew
May--the month Mayɛy
maybe bɛlɛn
mean kajjɛhjɛh
measles bɛq hayidik
meat kanniyɛk
meat course jalɛylɛy

spongy meat of sprouted
    coconut    yiw

medicine    winew

meet    jalṁahyey

meet together    q&ylaq

meeting    q&ylaq

melodious    ɫɫahaj

members of the church
    yekel&yjiyah

memory    y&my&m&j

the men    ɫeṁahrew

these men    ɫeṁahr&yin

mend    karp&n

mend--of nets    kanwed

menial    ttay

menstruation    betektek

messed up    p&q

metal    mayal

method    k&l

method of    wayw&y&-

middle    yi'yewɫap

middle of    liqe-, yewɫepa-

middle of many things    bilji-

middle of the island
    yi'y&w&j

midnight    ɫiqen b&ɡ̊

midrib of a coconut leaf    ṅeq

midrib of coconut frond    pap

MIECO    Miyeykew

mile    ṁahyiɫ

milk    ṁilik

coconut milk    yaɫ

mine    hah&h

minute    minit

miracle    kakeɫɫey

mirror    kilhaj

miscellaneous    jabdeywet

mischievous    b&t, dewyebyeb

missile    miyjeɫ

missile--for throwing only    b&w

missing    jak&w

missionary    mejiyneydey

mistake    b&d

mix    'yiy&k

mix with water    kab&wdan

mixture    wite-, 'yiy&k

mock    kajjireyrey, kajjiyeɡ̊

Monday    Mandey

money    jayan, ṁahak, ṁaniy

month    hallɛg

next month    hallɛg yin laɫ

moon    hallɛg

more than    jiṁah

desire more--of a delicious food    jaṁjań

morning    jibbɛɉ

mosquito    jaqjeq, ńaṁ

most    tahtah

mother    ṁahṁah

motor    yinjin

motor cycle    wetewbahyiy

mound    bat

mountain    teɫ̈

mourn    birɛwṁɛj

mourn the dead    yilɛwmɛj

mouse    kijdik

mouth    lawɉiy

move    ṁakitkit

to move    jirhak-, wirhak

move (with directionals)    riwhak-

move away    jɛpjɛp

move closer    keypahak

move something closer by using a stick    hadɛbdɛb

a movie    ṁiwpiy

much    leg

nasal mucuous    wiwir

mud    pɛdkat

multiply    yineylep

mumps    ɫɛppɛr

murder    ṁehreh, wirwɛr

murderer    ṁehreh

murderous    ṁehreh

murky water    liṁ

muscle    ṁajeɫ

music    hal

must    hayiqij

my    hahɛh

N

nail    diylah

name    yat

narrow    hayiqij

naughty    hahɛh

nausea    ṁeɫagɫɛg

nauseating    kajjɛhjɛh

navel    bije-

navigate    metew

navigation    metew

| | | | |
|---|---|---|---|
| neap tides--period of | yidik | last night | b&g̃ |
| near | tiłi-, yephak | nine | riwahtimjiwen |
| nearly | yephak | no | jahab, yahab |
| neck | kenwah | no more | j&j, mahat |
| necklace | ṁarṁar | of no use | j&tteqjan |
| need | hayiqij | nobody | jjełaq |
| needle | niteł | noise | hayinikiye- |
| negative future tense | ban | be noisy | k&yr&wr&w |
| nephew | magide- | none | y&j&y |
| nervous | habṅehṅeh | noodles | witeg̃ |
| net | w&k | noon | rahyelep |
| mosquito net | tahyiṅaṁ | north | yag |
| never | jahgin | northeast | yi'y&g-r&yyahar |
| will never | jamin | northern part | tiwyag |
| never mind | jekdawan | nose | bawtiy |
| never will do | ban | nostalgia | yemłaq |
| nevertheless | bethab | not | jab |
| new | kayal | not any | y&j&j |
| news | nnahan | not enough | jabey |
| newspaper | niwijp&ybah | not have the ability to | ban |
| next to | tiłi- | not know | jahj&y |
| nickname for baby girl | jireg̃ | not matter | jekdawan |
| niece | magide- | not yet | jahgin |
| night | b&g̃ | will not--determination or simple future | jamin |

notches cut in a tree for
   climbing   jekayiyej

nothing   y&j&j, jje£aq

nourish   nahjidik

nourishing   h&n

November   Newbeṁbah

now   jah, kiyin, kiyyeh

nude   q&£&yiyahat

numb   m&j

number   neṁbah

number of   wera-, wiwan

numerous   pahtah

nurse   nehej

nurse--a patient   kahwiw

nut   qeley

nylon fish line   yew y&k&y

O

oar   jebey

obedient   kipiliyy&y

obscured   tab

observe   lah£ey

obstructed   beñ

occasion   halen

ocean   lawj&t, lawmetew,
   metew

ocean side of   lik

October   Wektewbah

octopus   q&y&t

odor   biyi-

of   yin

off-key--voice   benah

offer   jahkey, ley-

church offering   jahbahwet

office   wepyij

officer   wepiyjah

officer of high rank   kapen

often   qqit(qit), leg halen,
   makijkij

very often   kkay

oh   wew

coconut oil   pinneyep

oil belonging to   kapite-

oil oneself   kkapit

ointment of leaves and oil
   kimi£

okay   yeqey

old   rittew

old man--term of respect   ha£ap

old--of things   ṁe£

on   yi'yeweone   jiwen

one who has taken care of
    another's child   jemanji-

onion   haniyen

only   wet

only--indicating relative un-
    importance of verbal activ-
    ity   bajj&k

open a crack   ɬag

the opening between islets
    m&j, m&jj&y

operate   biqabeq

have an opinion   bahab

or   hak

orange--color   kiyew

orange--fruit   weran

orate   wayjepadik

organ--musical   waqen

organize   kkar

other   bar jet, jiwen

each other   dewen

others   bar jet

a few others   jet

otherwise   yayinjiwen

ought to have   kar

our--dual incl.   harrew

our--exclusive   ham

ours   ham, harrew

outline   hannag

outrigger   kiwbahak

outrigger side of a canoe
    reytam

outside   lik, nab&j, yaliki-

oven   webin

earth oven   wiṁ

native oven   wiṁ

overflow   lliwt&k

overturn   w&kjak

owe   likjab, miɬiy

## P

pack   yaty&t

packed   l&ml&m

paddle   haheṅheṅ, jebey

page   halen, p&yij

pain   metak

painstaking   tilj&k

paint   winew

pair   peyah

not paired off   jawig

palate--of mouth   gat

pale   w&w, wiw

palpitation   kkiṁkiṁ

's pandanus   daha-

panties (women's)   jakk&lk&l

pantry   payant&r&y

paper   p&ybah

parent-child relationship   j&ṁnajin

participate   bek qeṅaha-

partly   rayjet

party--Marshallese style   kaṁł&w

pass--in card games   bahaj

boat passage through a reef   tawar

passenger   bahjinjeyyah

go as a passenger   bahjinjeyyah

past tense   kar

past tense marker   har

past tense subordinate clause introducer: that   key

past tense 3rd pl.   rehar

patch   karp&n

path   yiyał

patience   kij&nm&j

pattern   hanek

pause   b&jrak

paw   ney

pay   kełłay

peaceful   hay&n&ṁṁan

peak   ṁahan

peck   kik

peel   yakil

to peel   yakilkil

peel off the end of a coconut shoot   kawidpak

pen   peyen

pencil   pinjeł

penmanship   yełtan pay

people   harm&j

pepper   pepah

perfect   weyeppan

put on perfume   kkapit

perfume--imported only   bekaygaj

perhaps   b&l&n

period   pidiyyet

permission   malim

permit   katłaq

permitted   malim

persevere   kij&nm&j

not <u>persevering</u>   janiknik

person   harm&j

person or thing that causes trouble or bad luck   Jewnah

personal name--Mary   Meydiy

perspiration   menewkadiw

perspire   menewkadiw

pester   yikiyen

pet   najn&j, naji-

petticoat   likk&w

phonograph   kirahbabewen

physique   raqej

piano   piyahnew

play <u>piano</u>   piyahnew

pick breadfruit with a stick   keṁkeṁ

pick green coconuts from tree   y&ntak

pick out   kkayaly&l

pick out--food from teeth--splinters   harhar

pick pandanus   wekwek

pick--flowers   ḷiḷ

picnic   piknik

picture   hannag, pijah

piece   ṁetta-, wid

pier   wab

pierce with husking stick or spear   dd&b

piercing sound   yeḷḷahaj

pig   piyik

pile up   paniq

pill   batin

pillow   p&t

use a <u>pillow</u>   p&tp&t

provide <u>pillow</u> for   ṅahpite-

pineapple   p&yinabeḷ

pink   piyig

pipe--plumbing   bahyib

pipe--smoking   bahyid

pistol   likajik

pitch   kadkad

place   jiki-

in that <u>place</u>   yijjiyeṅ

a <u>place</u> in front of   ṁaha-

place name--atoll or island--Rḧlik
  --Ailinginae   Hay&l&ginhayey
  --Ailinglapalap   Hay&l&gḷap-ḷap
  --Bikini   Pikinniy
  --Ebon   Yepwen
  --Eniwetok   Yan&yweytak
  --Jabwot   Jebat
  --Jaluit   Jalw&j

--Kili      K&l&y
--Kwajalein   Kiwajleyen
--Lae    Ḷahyey
--Lib    Yellep
--Namorik    Naṁdik
--Namu    Naṁ&w
--Rongelap    Reğḷap
--Rongerik    Reğdik
--Wotho    Wettew
--Ujae    Wijahyey
--Ujelang    Wijlag

place name--atoll or island--
    Ratak
--Ailuk    Hay&l&q
--Arno    Harṅew
--Aur    Hawir
--Bikar    Pikhar
--Erikub    Yadqip
--Jemo    Jamaw
--Knox    Ṅahdikdik
--Likiep    Likiyep
--Majuro    Majr&w
--Maloelap    Meneweḷḷap
--Mejit    Majy&j
--Mili    Mil&y
--Taka    Tekay
--Taongi    Beqhak
--Wotje    Wejjay
--Utirik    Witr&k

place name--miscellaneous
--China    Jeyinah
--Eastern Chain of the
    Marshalls    Rahtak
--Ebeye    Yepjay
--England    Yiglen
--Germany    Jamney
--Japan    Jephan
--Kusaie    Qijjahyey
--Laura    Lewrah
--Palau    Belahwiw
--Ponape    B&w&np&y
--Rita    Riytah
--Samoa    Jahṁiwwah
--Western Chain of the
    Marshalls    Raylik

--Uliga    Wilkah
--Yap    Yi'yahab

plan    hannag

plank    haḷhaḷ

plant    kallib

to plant    kkat

plant of    ketka-

a plant
--a general term for banana
    pinahnah
--a grass    leklek
--arrowroot    ṁakṁ&k
--banana varieties (Takeuchi)
    hay&l&g-k&yin, jeyinah,
    mil&y
--*Barringtonia asiatica*    w&p
--breadfruit variety--
    seeded    m&jwahan
--general term for all vari-
    eties of coconut trees and
    fruit    niy
--general term for flower of
    any hedge plant    wit
--general term for grass--
    *Vittaria elongata*    wijw&j
--general term for the bread-
    fruit    may
--general term for tree
    w&jk&y
--*Gomphrena globosa*
    habḷajtiyig
--*Gossypium barbadense*
    qetin
--grass--*Thuarea involuta*
    kakkiṁkiṁ
--pandanus cultigen--Aur
    y&kyeṅ
--pandanus cultigen--Eniwetok
    haniydep
--pandanus--a general name
    for any pandanus plant
    beb

--papaya--*Carica papaya*
  keyinabbiw
--*Pemphis acidula* k&g&y
--*Plumeria acuminata*
  m&yriyah
--*Saccharum officinarum*
  taw
--*Sida fallax* kiyew
--*Wedelia biflora*
  markibeybey
--*Ximenia americana*
  kayl&kl&k

plastic  biłajtiyik

plate  kennaw

platform over the lee side of a canoe--opposite side of the outrigger side  łag

play  qqir&y

seldom play  jaqqir&yr&y

play baseball  yi'yakiyiw

play cards  kahaj

play ground  kirahańtew

play music  kejagjag

play music on radio or phonograph  jag

play practical jokes  yikiyen

play volleyball  bahł&ybawał

plentiful  hałakiyy&y

plenty  leg

plumeria  m&yriyah

pocket  bejaw

point  jaben

point out something (to someone)  jiteg

pointed  kkag

poison  bahyijin

poisonous (fish)  kadek

play poker  pil&y

police  bilijmayań

polio  bewłiyew

small pool--on reef at low tide or in interior of island  l&y

poor  jerańel

porch  teghak

porpoise  k&y

port tack  jabłap

position  kadkad

possessive for earrings and other things worn on ear  kiye-

posterior  pid

coffee pot  tiybat

iron pot  hayinbat

pound  bawin, degdeg

pour  lliwt&k

pour out  tawar

poverty  jerańel

| | |
|---|---|
| powder | bawitah |
| power | kajw&r |
| chicken pox | b&q hayidik |
| practice | mmin&yn&y |
| practiced | mmin&yn&y |
| praise | nebar |
| pray | jar |
| preach | kewwahłaq |
| preacher | rikakiy |
| precious | haw&r&k |
| prefix to feminine names | li- |
| prefix to masculine names | ła- |
| pregnant | berawr&w, nahginm&j |
| become pregnant | ttah |
| prepare | kepewej |
| prepared | pewjak |
| president | bireyjeten |
| pretend | łekem |
| pretty | hayib&w&jw&j |
| pretty (of woman) | deyaw |
| prevent | bebrahyey |
| price of | weńya- |
| prickly heat | b&q hayidik |
| priest | bahtah |
| primp | kemmayidik |
| half prince--royal father but commoner mother | bidak |
| print by hand with manuscript style | kiyapteł |
| probably | b&l&n |
| problem--arithmetic | win |
| proclaim | kewwahłaq |
| prodigal | jerwahan |
| prohibited | maw |
| prolong | tew |
| promise | kallimił |
| propeller--of plane or ship | pikpik |
| property | jiki- |
| propose to do | katmaney |
| proposition | ley k&t&w |
| fallen prostrate | wełaq |
| protect | kejpareq |
| protect from rain or spray at sea with mat | beqtak |
| protector | p&nja- |
| Protestant--religion | Birewtiyjen |
| proud | biŋ-b&r&w |

be proud   keṅ

proverb   mał&jj&ǰ

a proverb   'bbiddikdik mareǧreǰ'

provide food for family from local sources (not from the store)   tayap

provisions   ṁeyiq

provoke to a quarrel   hirej

in public   lawbil&j

publicity   lawbil&j

pull   hatak, kankan

pull and break--string or rope or grass   tiṁtiṁ

pull out   kkeykahak, wijwij

pulse   baṁ

pump   baṁ

punch--beverage   ban

punctuation   kakełłey

punish   kawiw&y

puny   ṁejṅaw

pure   qqejarjar, rr&y&w

purpose   win

push   jirhak-

put   dewer, llik

put alongside   hapar

put down   llik

put in container   yaty&t

put in order   kkar

put out a fire   qqin

put things away   kaqqeṅqeṅ

put things in place   kaqqeṅqeṅ

put together   k&wbah

Q

quake   wididdid

quantity   wera-

question   kajjit&k

yes-no question particle   key

quick to learn   p&nawiyy&y

quiet   yik&g

R

radio   r&ytiy&w

radio transmitter   wayl&j

rain   w&t

rain water   hay&b&j

rainbow   'yiyah

seldom rains   jahw&tw&t

not rainy   jahw&tw&t

raise   kewtak

| | | | |
|---|---|---|---|
| rat | kijdik | regarding | kijjiye- |
| rather | jahad | rehearse | kemhalm&l |
| raw | ham&j | related to each other | j&nq&n |
| razor | reyjah | what relation | teye- |
| reach | tepar | relation between two brothers-in-law who are married to two sisters | jemanji- |
| not reach | likjab | | |
| reach destination | tekyak | family relationship | kadkad |
| read | qenewnew | relatives | niqiy |
| ready | d&yd&y | relay race | did&y |
| realistic | mewel | religion | kabig |
| realize | kiley | reluctant to | tabit |
| rearrange | yikir | remain | pad |
| reason | win | remainder | bey |
| receive | bek | remember | k&y&my&m&j, y&my&m&j |
| the most recent | łaq | remnants | birar |
| recognize | kiley | rend | keykeyel |
| not recognize | jakiley | repeat | yalij |
| recommend | nebar | repeatedly | kkay |
| red | birehreh | reply | wiwahak |
| reddish color | mirar | report | kennahan |
| coral reef | wed | reproach | kawiw&y, kinhak |
| reflection | hannag | reprove | kawiw&y |
| refuse | habin | resign | kakkij&y |
| refuse to do something | mak&wk&w | resist | dapd&p |

respond to   yawreŋ

take responsibility
  l&wl&w&rjahkey

assume responsibility for
  bek yeddew

rest   kakkij&y

rest on   hatartar

resurrection   jerkakp&j&y

return   jebłahak, rawal

reunion   'yiyayy&w

reveal   kennahan, kewwahłaq

review   yalij

review day program   j&ṁnajin

revolver   likajik

negative reward--to receive
  one's   lley

rheumatism   kirr&w

rice   rahyij

rich   jeban, ṁeyiyyey

riddle   l&ggah

ride   wiw&y

ride on a plane   kay-

roof ridge   berwaj

ridicule   kajjireyrey

right   hanbijmareŋ, jiṁ&y,
  liqqiwin, ṁewel

right hand   hanbijmareŋ

right here   jewijew

righteous   qqejarjar

rim   hapar

ring   riyig

wear a ring   riyigyig

not ripe--fruit   kik

ripe--of pandanus   wwat

ripped   jar

rise from the dead   jib

river   r&ybah

road   yiyał

roast breadfruit   qanjin

robust   yajmiwir

rock   bar, dekay

rolled   liṁ

roll   dapilpil

roll back and forth   jabilbil

roll up--as dried pandanus
  leaves   jalj&l

roll--of cloth   kap

roller for launching canoe
  łeŋtak

room   riwiṁ

make room for   ṅahjikirooster   kahk&w

root   wekar

root out   wijwij

rose   rewej

wear a rose or hibiscus flower   rewejwej

rotate   haddebewilwil

rotten   ṁeḷ

round   dewilwil

row   haheṅheṅ

rows of houses   halen

rub   yiryir

rub clothes--washing   ṁiqṁiq

rub--with oil (medical treatment)   pitpit

rubber   ḷebah

rudder   jebey, jebeybey

rum   r&ṁ

run   tt&r

run away   kew

run--of engines   jaw

run--water   tawar

Russia   R&wjiyah

rust   ḷejew

## S

the Sabbath   Jabet

sack   payak-

sadness   bir&wṁ&j

sail   w&jḷay

sail away on a voyage   jeplahak

sail out to sea   biǵlik

go sailing   jerakr&k

sailor   jeyḷah

salary of   weṅya-

salt   jawaḷ

same   yayinwet, yayinwet jiwen

the same   barayinwet

same as   yeyiten

sampan   jempahan

sanctified   qqejarjar

sand   beq

fine sand in sea   liṁ

sanitary   rr&y&w

sap   bil

coconut sap--old and sour   magig

sardines   jahtiyin

satisfied   jiw-b&r&w

not satisfied   jaṁjaṁ

hard to satisfy with food
    mattiyyah

easy to satisfy with food
    mattiyy&y

Saturday   Jadeydey

sauce   jal&yl&y

save   kejpareq

saw   jidpan

say   bah

say in vain   bah pahtah

scale fish   karwin

scales   bawin

scarce   hałakiyyah

not scare easily   jawiwatah

scared   kk&l

school   jikiwił

school house   ṁen jikiwił

school of fish   bijin

scold   kawiw&y, liw

scooter   wetbahyiy

scrape   q&yq&y

to scratch   q&yq&y, rahqitak

scratch in ground for food--
    chickens only   t&qt&q

screw   jikriw

scrub   biraj

scrub--using wet cloths
    jewkiyig

sea   lawj&t, lawmetew

search for   kapp&q, pp&q

seat of emotions   b&r&w

to second   reyejtak

second base   jeken

second--of time   jeken

section of some atolls--windward
    --usually northeast   hayetaw

see   lahley, llew

see a movie   ṁiwpiy

see off on a journey   kejjajet

not see well   pil&w

see-saw   habentawin

seed   qeley, yiney

seize   j&bj&b

seldom   j&yjah

select   kkayaly&l

selection   kkayaly&l

self   mak&y

sell   wiyah

send   jilkin

senile   ppał

separate   j&p&l
September   Jepteṁbah
it serves someone right   lley
set fire to   ttil
to set--of hens   lik
seven   jijilimjiwen
several   jet, 'yiy&t
severe   p&n
have sex appeal--of males   tayag
shade   ll&ł
shadow   hannag
shallow   p&jp&j
shape   hannag, wayw&y&-
shape--body   raqej
sharp   kkag
sharpen   j&mj&m
shave   reyjah, yal
she   y&y
sheet of paper   halen
a shell--clam--giant   kapw&r
a shell--clam--medium   mejanwed
a shell--clam--medium large   dimwij
a shell--clam--small   kik&r
a shell--*Conus bandanus*   likayebyeb
a shell--clam--large   haded
a shell--top   jiddiwil
white shell--used in head leis   haliw
a shell--cowrie   libbiq&y
take shelter from the rain   kejatew
shelter pit--air raid   rað
shelter with mat at sea   beqtak
shine   łemhak
ship   tiyṁah, wah
to ship water   dewij
shirt   jehet
wear a shirt   jehethet
shirtless   q&ł&yiyhat
shock   kiṁhiłak
electric shock   jałem
shocked   yilib&k
shoes   jiwij
wear shoes   jiwijwij
shoot   biw
shoot of coconut   jiwibwib

| | |
|---|---|
| shoot the breeze  ley k&t&w | sign  kake‡‡ey |
| shoot--coconut  witak | signal  kake‡‡ey |
| shop  men wiyah | signify  kake‡‡ey |
| short  kadiw, kaniw | silence  yik&g |
| fall short of  likjab | keep silent  yik&g |
| shorten  j&pj&p | silhouette  hannag |
| shot  way | silly  b&yb&y, jahj&y‡aqjeñ |
| shoulder  hayeray | silver  j&lbah |
| shout  lañ&j | similar to  yeyiten |
| shovel  jabe‡ | more similar to  yayin‡aq |
| show  kewwah‡aq | sin  b&d, jerawiywiy |
| show where to go  yagin | since  jan, k&nkey |
| shrink  j&n | sing  hal |
| shrub  mar | siren  jayidiyig |
| shut  kiyl&k | older sister  jeyi- |
| shy  jewek | younger sister  jati- |
| older sibling  jeyi- | sisters of a male  yine- |
| younger sibling  jati- | sit down  jiyet |
| sick  nahginm&j, witañ&y | six  jiljinew |
| sickly--chronic  haddim&j | skillful  kapyel |
| sickness  nahginm&j | not skillful  jakapyel |
| side  hilhil, t&r&yr&yi- | skin  skin |
| side--of man or animal  kat | to skin  kakilkil, yakilkil |
| sift  liklik | tender skin of a baby  wib |

skin-diving tiwraṅ
grass skirt yin
skull łat
sky lag
slander riwriwey
slap degdeg
sleep kiykiy, majił
sleep soundly majiłlep, tteṅ
sleepy m&jkiy
slide accidentally jiriylaq
slip jiriylaq, likk&w, tibbaq, tipj&k,
slip out kkeykahak
slippery jjir
slop out lliwt&k
slow bat, kadikdik, rahłaq, łiṁij
very slow yikeyłiṁij
slow moving yikeyłiṁij
slow to learn p&nawiyyah
sluggishness haddiyṁak&wk&w
to slurp łiyit
sly Yetahwew
small dik
small pieces tipdikdik

smart maletlet p&nawiyy&y
smart--as medicine on a sore mayaṅ
smear birar
smell biyi-, nam, yat
smell of clothing or mats under sun bbidetdet
smell of cooking fish wwiy
smell of copper kkebahbah
smell of fish--lingering on hands or body or utensils jegaw
smell of roasting breadfruit bbiyr&wr&w
smell of smoke on breath or body or clothing bbahyidyid
smell or taste--sour or bitter-- as milk or vinegar or rice soup m&g
smell--fragrant gaj
smile tt&g dikdik
smile (show the white of the teeth) reyrey
smoke hatiytiy, bahathat
to smoke kebahathat
smooth and calm--water łahyey
sneak away from kewnah
sneeze ṁaj&y
snitch kewnah

| | | | |
|---|---|---|---|
| so | yayindeyin | love song | halin ṁahyinah |
| so that | bey | sonorous | łłahaj |
| soak | jewjew | soon | ṁettan jidik, yephak |
| soap | jeweb | very soon | kiyyeh-kiyyeh |
| socks | jitawkin | sorrow | bir&wṁ&j |
| wear socks | takinkin | sorry | bir&wṁ&j |
| soft | pid&wd&w | sort out bad copra | yakit |
| soft drink | k&włah | her (soul) | han |
| soft sell | ley k&t&w | his (soul) | han |
| soil | bid&j | my (soul) | hah&h |
| sole--foot | lawpiden ney | our (soul) | ham |
| solid | p&n | your (soul) | haṁ |
| solidify | qej | our (souls) | harrew |

some--always used with numerals  jiṁah

your (souls)   hamiy

sound   hayinikiye-

something that is put under something to protect or lift  łeÿtak

soup of soft rice or breadfruit  jeqqep

| | | | |
|---|---|---|---|
| somewhat | jahad | sour | m&g |

somewhere here around me  yijekay

| | | | |
|---|---|---|---|
| | | south | r&k, rak |

somewhere here around us  yij&k&yin

| | | | |
|---|---|---|---|
| | | southern | r&k |
| son | naji- | spank | degdeg |
| steering song | halin ṁił | spar--of sail | łejak |

| | | | |
|---|---|---|---|
| song | hal | | |

open spathe of coconut tree  jinniprag

speady   ṁekaj

| | | | |
|---|---|---|---|
| speak | kennahan | sprouted coconut | yiw |
| spear | ṁad&y | spy | kejjahad |
| to spear | d&bd&b | squall | witaḷ |
| spear fishing | tiwraǵ | squeeze | kkiwil |
| speech | jipyij | stains | birar |
| make a speech | jipyij | stammer | hallew |
| spell | hanijnij | stand at attention | kankan |
| spelling | jipyeł | stand still | b&jrak |
| spend | haman | stand up | jiwtak |
| giant spider | kiribl&y | star | yijiw |
| spin | likayebyeb | starboard tack | jabdik |
| spine | diylep | stare at | kallimj&k |
| spirit | j&t&b | start a fire | j&nj&n |
| splendid | hayib&w&jw&j | startled | yilb&k |
| split | jar | state | kennahan |
| split open | bełgak | status | kadkad |
| spoil | kaqqirey | stay | pad |
| spoon | jibwin | stay up | mm&j |
| spouse | palye- | steadily | yetal yin wet jiwen |
| spout | tayag | steal | kawat |
| sprain | yigr&k | steam | bahathat |
| spread mats | yerak | steamer | tiyṁah |
| to spring | kay- | steel | mayal |
| sprout | yaǵ | steer | jebeybey |

step on   jiwjiwir

stevedore   weqin bahd&y

stick   ha⅃ha⅃

sharp stick for husking coconuts   d&w&n

stick for picking breadfruit   k&yin-keṁ

stick to   ddap

sticky   ddap

stiffen   qej

stiffness--of a corpse   haje⅃kay

still   jah, wet

stay still   tet

sting   yidyid

stinging sensation   yidyid

stir   haw&j&k

stir up   'yiy&k

stirred up   lim

stockings   jitawkin

stomach   j&y, lawj&y, tiw, tiwdek

stone   dekay

large stone used as an anchor   kadkad

stop   bebrahyey

stop--in the sense of stay   pad

stopper   bawar, p&nja-

store   ṁen wiyah

storm   ggat

story   beybeynahtew

story of a house   pew

story--folkloristic   yina𝑔

stove   jitweb, webin

straight   jiṁ&y

straight--in playing poker   teryej

strain   liklik

stranger   riwahmay&j&t

stray   jebayb&y

street   yiya⅃

strength   kajw&r

stretch   kankan

stretched   hay&r

stretched tight--of lines   l&tl&t

stretchy   meh

strict   p&n

strike against   yithak

string   yil&y

striped or spotted (as in ancient tattoo)   yawat

strong   kajw&r, k&yk&y,
    kijgiyg&y, kket, p&n

strong--physically   diyp&n

to struggle   katey

strut   kemmayidik

stuck   l&l

study   kahtak

stumble   tibbaq, tipj&k

stump   dapd&p

stupid   p&nawiyyah

stymied   beñ

subjects   dewen

substance   h&n

subtract   bek

succeed   teprak

sudden   yidig

suddenly   yidig

suffer   y&gtahan

sufficient   bey

sufficient even it it's little
    --food   kaniyaqey

sugar   jiqah

suitable   kkar

appear sultry   kemmayidik

summer   jeṁar, rak

summer vacation   jeṁar

sun   ha⁺

to sun   kejeyjey

sunbathe   kejeyjey

Sunday   Jabet

sunshine   det

superlative particle   tahtah

supervise   lahley

supper   k&j&wtah

well supplied with food and
    property   jeban

support   ⁺eǰtak

suppose   bahab

make sure   l&wl&w&rjahkey

high surf   biǰñew

surf-boarding   l&k&r, lekay

surface   yi'yewe-

surprise   bileg

surprised   yilb&k

surprising   kabilegleg

surrender   bahaj

surround   kepewe⁺

be surrounded by   kkeñak

swamp   pat

swear   kanijnij

| | |
|---|---|
| sweat | menewkadiw |
| sweet | tegal |
| sweetheart | batin |
| swell | bbaq |
| to swell | bbej |
| swelling | p&r |
| swift | yiyiṁ |
| swim | haheh |
| swollen | bbaq, bbej |
| sword | jayj&y |
| symbol | kakełley |
| sympathize | yi'yaqey |
| syphilis | jeplej |

## T

| | |
|---|---|
| table | teybeł |
| tablet--medicine | batin |
| taboo | maw |
| taboo relationship | j&ṁnajin |
| take | bek, wikey |
| take by the hand | kabijer |
| take care of | lahley |
| take downwards | bekłałłaq |
| take it | y&w |
| take part in | bek qeñaha- |
| take sides | jep |
| take upwards | bekłegłaq |
| taken aback | bahaj |
| talk | beybeynahtew |
| talk harshly | bireğ |
| talk on the radio | wayl&j |
| tall | hayeteq |
| tame | hawiyy&y |
| tank | tayag |
| tardy--chronically | yikeyłiṁij |
| taro patch | b&l |
| tarry | łiṁij |
| taste | nam |
| taste--food or drink | y&dj&ğ |
| not tasty--of fish | jawwiy |
| tattle | kinhak |
| tea | tiy |
| teach | kahtak |
| teacher | rikakiy |
| team | kiwmiy |
| teapot | tiybat |
| tear | keykeyel |
| tears | dannin keṁjahałhał |
| technique | k&l |

teeter    habentawin
telephone    talbewen
tell    jireǧ
temperature    bil
ten    jegewil
tender    wib
tense    hat&ybar, kijgiyg&y
terror    leɫǧaǧ
test    teyej
testament    kalliṁiɫ
testicle    qeley
testify    kennahan
than    jan
to thank    kaṁḥewelwel
thank you    qeṁḥewel
to be thanked    ṁḥewel
that    bey, mey, yeṅ
that close to you--singled out    yegṅeyṅey
that is    yegyin
that over there--singled out    yegiyyeṅ
that--close to you    ṅey
that--singled out    'yiyeṅ
that's it    yegyin

thatch    haj
the--abstract    yew
the--people (pl.)    rew
the--plural--non-human    kew
theirs    hay&r
theirs (five or more persons)    hay&rw&j
theirs (four persons)    hay&ryag
theirs (two persons)    hay&rrew
theirs (three persons)    hay&rj&(y&)l
then    yinnam
there    tiw, yijeṅ, yijew
there--far off    wiweyew
therefore    yayind&yin
these--around us    k&yin
these--close to me    kay
these--people    ray, r&yin
they have    rehar
they should    ren
they were    rehar
they--four    y&ryag
they--more than four    y&rw&j
they--progressive    rej
they--two people    renrew, yerrew

| | |
|---|---|
| thick qit, mij&l | thrifty tilj&k |
| thicken qej | thirsty mar&w |
| thickness mij&l | throat b&r&w |
| thin hayinig, maniy | not thoroughly done jalet |
| thin--of animals or men ṁeh | throw jew-, kadkad |
| thing men | to be thrown in jail kalbiwij |
| think bahab, ɫemṁak | thumb haddiy lep |
| thirty jilgiwil | Thursday Tahyijey |
| this yegyew | thus yayind&yin |
| this thing here between us yegyin | ticket tik&t |
| this--singled out--close to me 'yiy&h | great tidal variations--period of yiyaɫap |
| | tide bekay |
| thorn in a pandanus leaf ṁakiɫ | ebb tide payat |
| thoroughly done let | high tide yibij |
| those places yijekewkew | ebb tide--lowest payat ṁeṅakṅak |
| those--close to you kaṅey | tie qerak, ll&q, pawp&w |
| those--particle for things kaṅ | tie a knot--string or rope biwbiw |
| those--people raṅ | tie on l&ql&q |
| thought ɫemṁak | tie up a vessel mmahan |
| one thousand tawijin | tie up to a buoy y&mjak |
| thread teryej | be tied down by a task l&qjak |
| three jiliw | tiger tahyikeh |
| three hundred jiliwbiqiy | tight hay&r, dim, qeṅ |

tight--not used with liquids
    webrak
time    halen, 'yiyen
time between rain showers
    mełah
times    halen
tin    tiyin
tin can    qiwat
piece of tin roofing    tiyin
tipped over    wełaq
seldom tire    jakkijayjay
tired    ṫhek
tired out    kajjinak
titter    ttag dikdik
to    gan, yin
today    rahyinyin
sour toddy    jimagig
toe    haddiy
big toe    haddiy lep
toenail    hakkiy, hakkiyin ney
together    jiṁeł
toilet    ṁen bidaj, ṁen keppewjak
tomb    lab
tomorrow    yiljiw

tongue    lew
tongue-tied    hallew
tonight    biŋniyin
too    kab, yayinwet
tooth    giy
tooth of a comb    tahał
top    yi'yewe-
at the top of    jayban
top--a toy--of shells or wood
    likahyebyeb
torn    pewtak
torn off    jar
tornado    hayirey
torso    kay
torso of (person)    kayan
total a correct amount    wig
touch    wiggir
tough--slang--of people    kijeŋ
tow    hatak
toward    ṁahyey
movement toward the person(s)
    addressed    -waj
towel    tawal
toy    naji-
trace    hanek

| | | | |
|---|---|---|---|
| traces | birar | that's true | ṁewel |
| trachoma | pilɜw | Truk | Riq |
| trade | janij | play trump--a card game | tiṗiṁ |
| translate | wikwɜk | trumpet | ṗebbah |
| transmit (radio) | waylɜj | its trunk | kayan |
| trap | wiw | trunk of (tree) | kayan |
| trash | qɜpɜj | trust in | lɜkɜy |
| pile of trash | łɜqɜt | truth | ṁewel |
| travel | yitɜw-yitak | try | kajjiyeǰ |
| travel on a vacation | jaṁbɜw | try hard | katey |
| treat--medically | winew | try in court | yekajet |
| treble | yełłahaj | try to reach | jibadek |
| tremble | wididdid | try to recognize | kakɜlkɜl |
| tribe | bij | wooden tub | japɜy |
| trick | ṁeṅ | tuberculosis | tiypiy |
| trickster--legendary--name of | Yetahwew | Tuesday | Jiwjey |
| small tridachnus | haded | tug | kankan |
| trip | tiryep | tumor | pɜr |
| trouble | hayiriwarew | tune | teṅ |
| troubled | yinɜypahtah | turn | halen |
| trousers | jedawijij | easy to turn | jahłiyyɜy |
| truck | ṁewetkah, tirak | hard to turn | jahłiyyah |
| true | liqqiwin | to turn--around and around | yigyig |

turtle  w&n
twenty  regewil
twins  bew
twirl  yigyig
twist around  kepewel
twist the hair into a knot  biwj&k
two  riwew
two hundred  ribiqiy
type  kahyin, ℓet
typhoon  tahyiybiwin

## U

ugly  dak&lk&l
ukulele  wiqleyley
skin ulcers  dekay
unable  ban
unacquainted  jajiny&t
unbecoming  jekkar
uncle on the mother's side  halap
uncle--father's brother  jema-
uncle--mother's brother only  rikewreya-, willepa-
unclear weather  tab
uncomfortable  habṅehṅeh

uncooked  ham&j
under  yiwṁi-
underpants--men's  jeṁṁetah
undershirt  jiyiglij
understand  meleyley
understandable  halikkar
stay underwater long--inability to  japakij
undomesticated  hawiyyah
unhealthy  witaṁ&y
smallest unit of something  wid
form a united group  b&r&w-qiq
unlawful desire  kijeǧ
unlike  yayinjiwen
unload  yakt&w
unprofitable  j&tteqjan
unripe  biℓ, kik
unripe coconut  wib
unskillfull  jekapyel
unsnarl  jaljal, mejal
unsnarl a tangled fishline  kemeleyley
unstable  ṁakitkit
unsuitable  jekkar

| | |
|---|---|
| until | ṁahyey |
| unwind | jałjał |
| up | lɛg |
| upon | yi'yewe- |
| at the upper part | tiwlɛg |
| of upright character | weyeppan |
| uproot | tɛwtak |
| upset | habṅehṅeh, wɛkjak |
| upside down | wɛjkar |
| urge | lɛwlɛwɛrjahkey |
| us--(incl.) | kɛj |
| use | haman, ley |
| used to | mminɛynɛy |
| usually | kkay |
| usually do something | keṅhan |

### V

| | |
|---|---|
| vacation | kakkijɛy |
| vain | habjey |
| valuable | hawɛrɛk |
| value | teqja- |
| of no value | jɛtteqja- |
| vehicle | wah |
| vein | yɛkɛy |
| venereal disease | jeplej |
| very | kahnɛwɛj |
| very hateful | kajjɛhjɛh |
| very ugly | kajjɛhjɛh |
| motor vessel | tiyṁah |
| vigorous | pegpeg |
| vinegar | penkeh |
| lose virginity | biğ |
| visit home of the dead person with gifts | yilɛwmɛj |
| visit the bereaved | yilɛwmɛj |
| vitamin | hɛn |
| voice | hayinikiye- |
| volleyball | bahłɛybawał |

### W

| | |
|---|---|
| waist | liqe- |
| small-waisted | kaydik |
| wait for | kattar |
| wake up | łij |
| wake up early in the morning | majinmiwir |
| wake--ship or fish--foam | biqaharhar |
| walk | yetal lał, yetyetal |
| walk fast and vigorously | jełjeł |
| walk slowly | hajadik |

429

| | | | |
|---|---|---|---|
| walk toward | wan- | breaking waves | biɉñew |
| coral wall | m&y | way | yiya⅃ |
| wander | jebayb&y, ṁekadkad | way or manner of doing something | k&l |
| want | keñhan | we or us--five or more people (excl.) | k&mw&j |
| want more | jaṁjaṁ | we or us--four people (excl.) | k&myag |
| war | pahtah | we or us--more than four (excl.) | k&m |
| wardrobe | tirwet | we or us--three people (excl.) | k&ṁj&(y&)l |
| warn | kawiw&y | we or us--two people (excl.) | k&mrew |
| wash | qalq&⅃ | we--(incl.) | k&j |
| wash bottles | naṁnaṁ | we--four (incl.) | k&jman, k&jyag |
| wash hands | haṁin | we--more than four (incl.) | k&jw&j |
| wash one's face | w&rm&j | we--three (incl.) | k&jj&(y&)l |
| waste | jerwahan | we--two (incl.) | jeñrew |
| watch | waj | weak | ban, ṁejñaw |
| to watch | waj | weak feeling--usually from hunger | haje⅃kay |
| wear a watch | wajwaj | weakling | we⅃a⅃&w |
| water | dan | wealth | jerahaṁhan, ṁeyiq |
| drinking water | dannin yidahak | wealthy | ṁeyiyyey |
| rain water | dannin hay&b&j | to wear | kkeñak |
| salt water | dannin lawj&t | wear a bracelet | payagke⅃ |
| well water | dannin la⅃ | | |
| water for washing hands | haṁin | | |
| water-tight | jettal | | |
| wave | ñew | | |

| | | | | |
|---|---|---|---|---|
| wear a necklace | ṁarṁar | | western sky | kapiyḷag |
| wear the hair loose on one's back--women | halyak | | westward | tawḷak, tiwriylik |
| wear wet clothing | ṁeraybet | | wet | ṅeq, tiwtiw |
| weather | lag | | whale | raj |
| weather lookout | katiw | | whaling | kerajraj |
| weave | yaj | | wharf | wab |
| weave flowers or shells into a lei | ḷehḷeh | | what | tah |
| Wednesday | Wenjey | | what for | yentah |
| week | wiyik | | what is the reason | tahwinyin |
| next <u>week</u> | wiyik yin laḷ | | whatever | jabdeywet |
| weight | bawin | | wheel | ney |
| coral <u>weir</u> to trap fish | may | | when | gayat, gey |
| well | hayabaj, yeqey | | where | tiw, yijew, yi'yah |
| well done | weyeppan | | where are they--non-humans | yerkiy |
| well-cleaned | let | | where are they--of humans | yerriy |
| not <u>well-cleaned</u> | jalet | | where--singular | yewiy |
| well-defined | meḷeyḷey | | whet | jamjam |
| well-informed | jeḷay | | which | mey, tah |
| well-ordered | meḷeyḷey | | a <u>while</u> ago | kkayin |
| well-organized | qeṅ | | whirl | haddebewilwil |
| well-sifted | let | | whiskers | qedyak |
| west | raylik | | whiskey | wajkay |
| on the <u>west</u> side | riylik | | whistle | hajweywey |

whistling--long continued
hajweywey

white mewij

who mey

whole likiyy&w, wig

why tahwinyin, yentah,
yetkey

wicked nahnah

wide depakpak

wife palye-, riyi-

wife's brother ṁṁahan

wild hawiyyah

will hank&laha-

will be nahaj

win wiyin

wind k&t&w, yigyig

wind from southwest kitak

window winteh

windy season hagenyag

wing pay

wintertime hagenyag

wire weyah

wire--for stringing fish
yil&y

wish for łekeṁ

with k&n, ley, yippa-

be with karwahan

with it kahkey, yahkey

withered ṁeṅakṅak, ṁeray

without jjełaq

wizardism biwbiw

woman keray

old woman l&łłap

that woman liyeṅ

the woman liyew

this woman liy&y, liyin

what woman let

the women liṁahrew

these women liṁahr&yin

wonder bileg

wood hałhał

word nahan

work jerbal

work on a job jawab

working party weqin bahd&y

workmanship yełtan pay

world lał

worn out ṁer̈

worry yin&ypahtah

worship    kabiŋ

worthless    jɛtteqja-

wound    kinɛj

wounded    kinɛjnɛj

wrap    lɛmlɛm

wrap in basket or leaves    tirtir

wrap up    qerak

wrap with leaves    tirewrew

wrestling    yɛwtahak

write    jɛyjɛy

wrong    bɛd

## Y

yard    yi'yahat

yaws    dekay, rajjiyyah, riq

yaws--ulcerated type    bakkey

year    yiyyeh

yeast    yij

yellow    yi'yałɛw

yes    hayɛt, yiggay, 'yiyig

yesterday    yinney

yonder    yijjiyeṅ

you (sg.) progressive    qej

you--absolute (sing.)    qey

you--five or more people    qɛṁwɛj, kemiywɛj

you--four people (excl.)    qɛṁyag, kemiyman

you--plural (excl.)    qɛṁ

you--plus particle of past tense (sing.)    qehar

you--(sing.)    yɛq

you--three persons (excl.)    kemiyjɛ(yɛ)l, qɛṁjɛ(yɛ)l

you--to many men in general--not specific    łeṁah

you--two persons    kemiyrew, qeṁrew

young    dik

your    haṁ, hamiy, hamiyjɛ(yɛ)l, hamiyrew, hamiywɛj, hamiyyag

yours (four persons)    hamiyyag

your (three or more persons)    hamiyjɛ(yɛ)l, hamiywɛj

yours (two persons)    hamiyrew

yours--plural    hamiy

yours--singular    haṁ

## Z

zero    wawɛw

zorie(s)    jewdiy

INDEX

Address: 153, 159

Adjective-like words: 131-134; singular-plural in dimensional words: 143-148

Affirmative: hay&t 11

Become: y&r&m 234-235

Canoe parts: 313

Causative: 111-112, 199-201, 303-304, 309-310

Classroom procedures: xxii-xxiv

Clothing: 33-37

Coconut: 155-158

Colors: ref. 198, 209-214

Comparative and superlative: 74, 124, 193, 212

Compounds: 205, 296-297

Conditional: gey 12, 153, 154, 163, 210, 211, 239-243, 250, 292-293

Conjunctions: yem 192, 195, 213-214; kab 191-194, 212, 233; yim 242-243

Construct particle yin: 23-25, 27, 73, 171-174, 211-212, 240-241, 257-258, 303

Contractions: yilan 25, 220-221, 293-294; yiten 25; rawalten 34; ri + yan&y + demonstratives 159; ri- + rittew 159; yin vs. -in 171-172

Contrary to fact: kar 82, 93, 96, 154, 222, 239-243, 292-293

Culture: taboos xiii; names 48, 82; the human head 125; intimacy 159

Days of the week: ref. 53

Demonstratives: 39, 48, 72, ref. 76; sentence demonstratives 82, ref. 87; personal demonstratives 82, ref. 87-88; locative demonstratives 83, ref. 88-89; with yime- > me- 97; 104, 134-136; jab 233-235; 294-297

Dialects: xii-xiii, 28-30; naji- 22; 87; lime- 122; kahkey-yahkey 243-244; yeyitah-yebaj y&t 259; har-kar 292; jahaih 297

Dialogues: where are you going 3; where is Timŭj going 10; do you have a pencil 15; are you two coming 23; where are you coming from 33; what is your name 43; what time is it 55; whose pencil is that 67; can you build houses 77; MelaĦ, sing 90; is the food cooked 103; how are you 118; I have a headache 129; what kind of work do you do 141; hello folks 152; can

435

you play an instrument 162; where is your older brother 170; who fixed your hair 178; may I use your watch 188; do you have any sardines 188-189; do you have any books to read 199; let's go to the meeting 199-200; what flag is that 209; what are you doing Sunday morning 209-210; is Tom married 218; Obed, where are you going 218-219; there's a party tomorrow 219; what do you have in your hand 230; is there a barber shop around here 230-231; where were you yesterday 238; did you have alcohol in these islands 238-239; I'm thirsty 248; do you have any cold coke 248; I'm thinking of working this summer 256; Lina, have you finished cleaning that room 256-257; my back hurts 257; Herman really loves animals 264; I have a dog 264; I'm hungry 274; is the food at the school good 274-275; do you have a spear 290; let's go fishing 302; did you catch anything 302-303

Directionals: 25-28, 39, 130, 232, 266-270, 279-285, 306-307, 310

Distributive: flora and fauna 202-205; colors 212-214; actions 250-252, 291-292

Double consonant stems: 26-28

Earlier stages of the language: 19-20, 38, 60; *yiṁe 96

Exhortations with qehar 240, 243, 258

Exist: wer 15, 68, 71, 118, 129; yewer...-n 165, 190-191, 219-221, 232, 249-250, 275

Finish ṁ&j: 142, 171, 212-213, 234, 258, 303-304

Fishing methods: 291

Formative law-: 123

Frequency: 166, 260

Future: nahaj 10, 240; nahaj vs. ban 23-24; mettan jidik 152; 257-258, 302

Give: ṅah 277-279

Gone: mahat 104, 191; mewet 48, 152; jak&w 48

Imperative (jussive): 90-96, 163, 213, 223, 240, 293-294

Intensifiers: liqqiwin 120; kahn&w&j 120; jjeɬaq wet...-n 120; mak&y 120, 179, 182, 193, 294; nahgin (as understatement) 180-182; baj 241

Intonation: xxii, 181-182, 304, 308-309

Just: kab 191; baj 241, 256, 304, 308

Kin: 69-71, 170-171, 218-227, 308-309

Like keṅhan: 93-94, 96, 163, 191, 223, 232, 305

Loan words: 20, 38, 60

Locative: yiy 24; locative

demonstratives 83, ref. 88-89, near yitiłi- 130; location of kajjiye- 194; direction tiw 306-307, 310

Maps: Marshall Islands x; Majuro Atoll 284

Months of the year: ref. 53-54

More than (quantities) jimah, yim men: 308

Names: 48-49, 82, 232, 277-278; personal name prefixes 88-89, 283-285, 305

Negative: jab 10-12, jahab 12; answers to negative questions 13-14; ban 23-24; jahj&y 79; ja- 163-166, 259-260, 292; jjahgin 220, 258

Numerals: ref. 53; ordinals 112

Occupations: with ri- 141-142

On (yi')yewen, rahan: 231-232

Origins yin yi'yah: 211

Other: 173

Past: har 77, 82; kar 82, 183-184, 238-240

Possessives: 15-20, ref. 22; yippa- 29-30; 39, 47-48, 73; yiłłe- 96-97; 118-120; used to embed clauses 132-134; 165-166, 190, 193-195, 265-266, 307

Prepositions: gan 3-4; jan 33; 74, 243-244

Progressive: 5

Prose selections: the Marshalls 61-62; the people 83-84; entertaining 98; the Ten Commandments 98-100; importing food 112-113; public health 126; native medicine 137-138; schools 149-150; coconut 159-160; drums 167; custard jayanqin 174-175; legends 184-185; wakes 195-196; Marshall Islands Congress 206; Congress of Micronesia 214-215; field trips 227-228; coconut oil 236; toddy 244-245; starch 252-253; divination 253; wells 261-262; animals 271; outer-island schools 271; radio 286-288; preserving fish 298-299; preserved breadfruit 311

Proverbs: haste makes waste 31; don't bite the hand 40; two birds 50; kindness 66; losing 84; he who hesitates 100; share with love 113; men fool 126; our mother 138; blood 150; don't sleep 159; small but mighty 168; woman 175; one who has too much 185; a penny saved 196; persevere 206; the tide never ceases 216; small but mighty 228; Jaluit 237; stomachs 245; walking, eating 253-254; each man 254; he that hears 262; don't drift away 272; canoes 288; the early bird 288; Likiep 311-312.

Questions: yes-no key 11, 73-74; is there 13-14, 72, 118, 129; when gayat 25-26, 275; where yi'yah 3, how many jetey 43, 174; who wen 67, 178; which -t(ah) 181, 194-195; yes-no (fut. with -n) 92, 96; yes-no (contrary to fact with -n kar)

93; what kind ƚet 93, 130-131, 141, 165; like keńhan 103; alternative 133; where yewiy 68-70, 142; do what y&t 173; why tahwinyin 180; why (nahgin with rising intonation) 182; who else yat 183; what tah 231, 249; what relation teyen, teyek 224-226; yewiy kadkadin 226-227; what's the matter yeyitah, yebaj y&t 259, 277, 304; why jahańh 297; in what direction, exactly where tiw yi'yah 306-307

Reduplication: 38-39, 204

Reflexives: katey 147

Relative: mey 165-167

Relatives: when (fut.) gey 57-59, 79-80; when (past) key 58-59, 73-74, 79-80

Same, similar, different: 121, 124, 234-235

Self: makey 120, 131, 178-179, 183, 191, 294

Sickness: 119-120, 127-129

So that: bey...-n 96, 121-122; 124, 293-294

Song: Yij yi'yaqey laq... 74

Sound drills: b-p 60-61; d-r 125; double consonants 148-149; &-e 30; &w-ew 39-40; i-&-e 50; q 137; ł-1 97; long vowels 112; Ĭ 136; ńh-m 4-6; ńhńh (double consonant stems) 74; ń-n 83; g 4-5; ɉ 136-137; ƚ 136; t-j 83

Sounds: xiii-xxi, 20

Sounds--specific pointers: a vs. aha 14; m > ńh 20; ł > 1 30; i... e > & 123; ...n > nn- 124; j > t 195

Straightway jah: 152, 154, 248, 303

Subject prefixes: ref. 8-9, 104

Then when lak: 213-214

Tides, waves, and water: 292, 294

Times: 44-45, ref. 53-54, 55-60, ref. 63-66, 103, 171, 307

Tractable: -iyy&y vs. -iyyah 164-167

Transitive: 39, 104-111, ref. 114-117, 135-136, 148, 195, 243-244

Understatement nahgin: 180-182

Until now d&y, yelaq: 220, 227

Use ley: 201

Used to: k&n 163-165; k&yin 241, 243

Useful expressions: xxiv

Verb phrases: 13-14

Wishes: yi'yaqey bey...n kar 222; yen kar 240

With: yippa- 25-27, 30, 306; yi'yaha- 183-184

Word order: 13-14, 19, 39

www.ingramcontent.com/pod-product-compliance
Lightning Source LLC
Chambersburg PA
CBHW031306150426
43191CB00005B/93